Selling: A Behavioral Science Approach

Selling:

A Behavioral Science Approach

Joseph W. Thompson, Ph.D.

Professor, Graduate School of Business Administration
Michigan State University

McGraw-Hill Book Company

New York   St. Louis   San Francisco
Toronto   London   Sydney

SELLING

a behavioral science approach

Library of Congress Catalog Card Number 65–28511

64375

1 2 3 4 5 6 7 8 9 0 M P 7 3 2 1 0 6 9 8 7 6

PREFACE

This book is what the title states: the analysis of and the application of the behavioral sciences (psychology, education, educational psychology, and social psychology) in selling. Further, it draws heavily from the disciplines of communication, economics, marketing, and management for concepts, ideas, and principles that are basic to the selling function as it exists today. This form of knowledge is crucial to selling success. To illustrate, reflect for just a moment on the fact that some authorities have estimated that man has gained more new knowledge in the past twenty-five years than he has in the entire civilization of man and that knowledge in some fields is doubling every ten years. Think of the incredible technological and social change in which we are presently involved. In brief, we are faced with an explosion of knowledge. Each potential buyer of a salesman's product or service cannot be expected to know the technical aspects of that product or proposal and how it can best be used by his firm. This tells the salesman that he must function as an educator. He has to communicate. He has to be a problem solver. He has to get feedback, and, in fact, because it is in the vortex of human life in which a salesman works, he must understand much about the behavioral sciences as they relate to the individual.

This book is based on experience and research. Over a span of ten years, it involved 29 companies and 167 salesmen. It included traveling with salesmen, making joint calls on hundreds of customers and potential customers, as well as conducting for the companies manpower development programs designed to equip their salesmen not only to understand the behavioral sciences but to use the behavioral sciences in their selling efforts.

This book, since it is based on the behavior sciences and is reinforced with extensive "marketplace" research, is structured to accomplish five major but related objectives:

1 To provide for the practicing salesman, whether he is selling an intangible or a tangible product, a general theory of selling that will establish a backdrop against which he can better evaluate the effectiveness or ineffectiveness of his sales effort. It should be made clear that it will take thinking, time, and effort to comprehend the material in this book. Most salesmen want to understand the "why" of the sales process. They want to elevate selling to the professional level it so rightly merits. Thus, this book is directed to that kind of salesman: a salesman who is intelligent, who is mature, who is creative, and who has a desire to do.

2 To provide for the marketing student an accurate picture of what personal selling is and the kinds of excellence needed to succeed in this challenging field. Further it is anticipated that the student, through a study of this book, can better comprehend the role of selling within the broad concept of marketing.

3 To provide for marketing management and sales management some solution as to why the 80-20 principle of marketing is in operation. This principle states in part that 80 percent of a firm's products or services are sold by 20 percent of its salesmen, or, conversely, 20 percent of the salesmen sell 80 percent of the firm's output in goods or services.

This suggests excellence by a few and mediocrity by most. Why? One reason is misdirected marketing effort. Many firms do not have the best product mix, distribution mix, promotional mix, or human-resource mix. The focal point of this book is the development of human resources, and two solutions to the 80-20 principle of marketing as it relates to human resources are given in this book. First, the salesman functions as a market manager of his territory. Second is the traditional maxim in selling: Like sells to like. Jim sells to Jim, Jack to Jack, and, in brief, the salesman sells in those situations where it is easiest for him to sell. But the salesman today must completely cultivate his markets and sell to all potential users. Few business firms today can afford to have a limited basis for market development in a given territory. All possible accounts in a sales territory must be developed by the salesman. Thus the salesman in the new world of selling must have a problem-solving approach to the needs of the potential buyer or customer of the salesman's product or services, and he must have a coping behavior that will permit him to adjust to the personal, status, or emotional needs of individual buyers or customers This aspect of selling should not be minimized. A salesman may have product knowledge and he may be able to solve problems for the potential customer, but it is the customer who makes the final decision to buy or not to buy. Frequently he makes this decision, at least partially, on the basis of his feelings.

It is in this way, through a two-dimensional problem-solving approach, that the salesman truly differentiates his company's product or services. And in the new world of selling, it *is* the salesman who differentiates his company's products or services. Through this process of differentiation the salesman can have a profound effect on the 80-20 principle of marketing as it operates in his particular company.

4 To provide in one book not only a general theory of personal selling and the establishment of a salesman's role as a market manager of his territory, but to provide two special chapters on some aspects of manpower development and how manpower development can be accomplished with the conference-dialogue approach to sales training. Since most of the strategies and tactics of selling are illustrated, explained, and demonstrated with dialogues, most firms can apply this book to their sales training programs.

5 To provide some programmed learning. In several sections of this book dialogues are used as a basis for programmed learning. The various tactics and strategies being illustrated in the dialogues are numbered for ease of analysis.

Special thanks are extended to Mrs. Merrilyn Vaughn for her editing

Preface

and typing of the manuscript and to Professor William L. Ziegler of Seton Hall University for his review of the book and for his helpful suggestions. Special thanks are also extended to the many salesmen and executives who made numerous suggestions and, in fact, provided the author with the framework for the book. For without the interest of such executives as Paul N. Stanton, Vice-president of Marketing of Pratt & Whitney; National Machinery Sales Manager, Wally Tefft; National Manager, Cutting Tools, George Crittenden; Alfred Johnson, Vice-president of Pratt & Whitney; and Frank McGurkin, Director of Training, this book would not have been written.

Special thanks are due to Lloyd Banks of Blue Cross for his very helpful suggestions, William Evans, Vice-president of Marketing, Carborundum Company, and Donald Masson and Arnold Green of Carborundum for their helpful suggestions in developing materials for Carborundum which in turn are incorporated in this book.

Joseph W. Thompson

CONTENTS

Preface   v

1 THE NEW WORLD OF SELLING   1

Introduction   1
The Old Image and Selling as a Career   2
Salesmanship in Transition   6

2 PROBLEM-SOLVING SITUATIONS   23

Cases
  1 *Industrial Selling*   23
  The Salesman as a Manager   25
  The Market Manager and the Sales Manager   27

  2 *International Minerals and Chemicals*   29
  3 *Standard Block and Supply Company*   31
  4 *Marble Office Furniture Manufacturing Company*   32
  5 *Manufacturers' Representative Calling on Dealers,
  Architects, and Contractors*   34

3 PLANNING AND MANAGING SALES EFFORT   38

Theory of Management Programming   43
Management Programming—Territory Analysis   49
Company Controls   52

4 CHANGING PATTERNS OF PERCEPTION   57

Introduction   57
Perception   58

5 NEEDS AND THE MOTIVATIONAL CYCLE   70

Needs   72
Feedback   78
Identifying Motives, Needs, or Wants   80
Incentives as Motivation   84

Contents

6 ROLE   91

Self-image and Role   91
Role Perception, Role Expectation, and Role Enactment   92
Number of Roles   94
Acting and Role Playing   96
Tension Binding   101
Empathy and Sympathy   102

7 THE SALESMAN AS AN EDUCATOR   107

Introduction   107
General Educational Psychology   108
Dialogue Illustration—Application of the Laws of Education   112
Summation   114
Organization or Grouping   117

8 THE ROLE OF MATURITY, CONFLICT, AND   120
EGOCENTRISM IN SELLING

Maturity   120
Mechanisms of Adjustment   124
Egocentrism   128
Conflict   131

9 SIX APPROACHES TO SELLING   136

Introduction   136
Simple Stimulus-Response Selling   139
Formulized Selling   142
Needs-satisfaction Approach to Selling   145
Mood Selling   148
Barrier Theory of Selling   149
Depth Selling   151

10 THE WHY AND HOW OF COMMUNICATION   156

Salesmen View Their Sales Talk   157
A Communication Model   158
Some Aspects of Communicating with the Executive   177

Contents

11 THE ART OF LISTENING EFFECTIVELY   183

What Is Your Communication Score?   183
Interest in What Your Prospect Has to Say   184
Reaction to Peculiarities of the Fellow Communicator   187
Faking of Attention   188
Stepping on Sentences   190
Equalizing Speech Listening Speeds   191
Failure to Get the Facts   193
Emotional Deaf Spots   194

12 THE CONTACT   part one   198

Introduction   198
Set, Readiness, and Empathy   200
An Overall View of the Contact Stage   204
Contact General Strategy   205
Ways of Making an Initial Contact   206
Ten Variables of Any Contact   213
Dialogue Cases Illustrating the Ten Variables of
    the Contact Stage   216

Cases
   1 *Cultural Growth of the Family through Dining Out*   216
   2 *Office Furniture Salesman*   218
   3 *Industrial Distributor Salesman of the Emerson*
     Supply Company   219

The Techniques Approach and the Removal of Sales Tension   220

13 THE CONTACT   part two   225

The Four Quarters and the Ten Variables of the Contact Stage   225

Cases
   1 *Franklin Machine Shop*   232
   2 *Lobby Case—Contact Stage*   235
   3 *James Wentworth, Distributor Salesman*   235

14 DISCUSSION THAT MOTIVATES   part one   237

Introduction   237
General Educational Psychology   238
Telling, Explaining, or Lecturing   238

Discussion   239
Showing or Demonstration   239
Performance   242
The Art of Questioning—The Common Denominator of
Education and Selling   243
Evaluation by Observation   249
Use of Indirect Questioning   254

15   DISCUSSION THAT MOTIVATES   part two   **259**

Dramatization of the Sales Process   259
Attention   260
Isolation, Novelty, and Incongruity   266
Showmanship through Action Words   269
Painting the Prospect into the Picture   270
How to Handle the Interrupted Interview   272

16   SOLUTIONS TO PROSPECT DOUBTS   part one   **279**

Introduction   279
A Guideline for Handling Objections   281
Tactics for Handling Objections   286
Price   291
Handling the Price Situation   292

17   SOLUTIONS TO PROSPECT DOUBTS   part two   **299**

Knowing the Prospect   299
Prospect Characteristics and Tactics to Use   300

18   COMPLETING NEGOTIATIONS: STRATEGIES   **308**
AND TACTICS

Introduction   308
Trial Closes   309
Eight Basic Closing Techniques   312
Prospect Characteristics and Closing Tactics   318

19   A MANPOWER DEVELOPMENT PROGRAM   **321**

Introduction   321
Characteristics of the Developmental Approach   322

Contents

20 THE CONFERENCE: A CASE-DIALOGUE APPROACH   339
   TO MANPOWER DEVELOPMENT

   The Conference Defined   339
   The Conference Leader   341
   The Conference in Action   342

21 GROUP SELLING OR COMMUNICATION IN   352
   THE GROUP

   Introduction   352
   Planning for the Group Sale   353
   Intent or Role of the Participant   363

   Bibliography   369

   Index   373

the new
world of
selling

1

INTRODUCTION

At sometime or another, most people have seen a movie or television program where the king of the country had died. Throughout the streets the town crier proclaimed, "The King Is Dead—Long Live the King." This pronouncement may be appropriately used for selling today. It can be said, "The Salesman Is Dead—Long Live the Salesman."

The cry "The King Is Dead—Long Live the King" wasn't made in disrespect, but rather it symbolized the end of one era and the beginning of another.

This is true of selling. Historically speaking, selling has carved deeply its position of importance in the development of the United States to a great industrial power. In fact, looking at other nations' industrial progress, it becomes apparent that aggressive selling was and is one of the distinguishing characteristics of this nation's economy; nevertheless, the old has passed and the new is here.

In this decade, personal selling is identified with a company representative who is a market manager in his territory, who sells within a keenly competitive business structure, and who uses highly sophisticated motivational tools, combined with a problem-solving approach to business. In this new world of selling, competition between salesmen is razor-sharp. Functioning in a highly competitive marketplace and using motivational tools skillfully are, however, relative terms. Looking back, there can be seen such periods in the development of our country as the colonial days, the transportation revolution, the Industrial Revolution, and the formation of trusts by big business. It would be crass to suggest that, in the past, fierce competition between firms and their salesmen didn't exist. It did. What is more in some ways, some of the great salesmen of years gone by, such as John H. Paterson of National Cash Register fame, Charles Goodyear of the rubber industry, Robert S. Bookings of the furniture field, and yes, even Diamond Jim Brady might be emulated today. More on Diamond Jim later.

The point being made is this: Today in science, some principles of years gone by have been modified considerably. Knowledge is ever chang-

Selling: A Behavioral Science Approach

ing, and in the same way a vast body of knowledge relating to the social sciences (psychology, sociology, education, anthropology, etc.), marketing, and management is available to the salesman today which wasn't available in the past. Technology, business, industry, communications, and a host of other factors affecting our social and economic life are changing substantially as well. Perhaps the impact of many of these changes can be seen in the dramatic statement made in the Decade of Incentive. It states: "Assuming only that there will be no recurrence of war, the decade promises a giant step toward a goal sought by nations since earliest times: the eradication of material want."[1]

Thus today on almost every front, we are entering a new period in this nation's life—the space age. It affects both business and science. In the past quarter of a century there has been an explosive increase in the amount, the kinds, and the complexity of knowledge. In fact, knowledge, some authorities say, is doubling every twenty years. In science some of the older principles have been modified considerably. This doesn't mean that scientists who thought the world was flat lacked ability or didn't make a contribution to science. Not at all. Many brilliant men thought the world was flat. Yet as knowledge increased, it was found that the earth was round, and now in the space age it has been discovered that the earth is somewhat pear-shaped. Like the scientist who thought the world was flat, the salesman of yesterday was a product of his times. The salesman of the past has been libeled in about every way possible from accusations involving his moral posture to statements that he was a fast-talking, story-telling extrovert who cared little about his customers. He sold when he could. He sold what, where, and when he could, and then left the scene of the crime. There may be some truth to the charges; there may well have been salesmen whom these stories describe accurately. Nevertheless, the salesman of yesterday was a product of his times. He was part of the development of this country from the settlement of the East to the winning of the West. He was part of the great Industrial Revolution with all of its rugged individualism. He mirrored the society of his times, and he worked with the accepted sales strategies and tactics of that time.

THE OLD IMAGE AND SELLING AS A CAREER

One question confronting the man contemplating selling as a career or the man who has taken selling as a career is the carry-over of the old image of selling. Unfortunately this image carry-over appears justified. Selling has been slow to change. Too many companies and too many salesmen are still operating within the old world of selling. In fact, many nationally known speakers performing at conventions or company sales rallies still put on a road show of enthusiasm, jokes, songs, and talk about broad generalities in selling. They appear to know little about the new world of selling.

These men who are still perpetuating the old world of selling are still with us, but they are, to paraphrase the title of E. B. Weiss' controversial

[1] *A Marketing Profile of "The Big Sixties,"* McCann-Erickson, Inc., New York, 1960, p. 1.

book, "the vanishing American salesmen."[2] These vanishing salesmen are being replaced by highly professional, competent, intelligent men who possess mature personalities and who exemplify the best in the world of business. Any man can be proud to be associated with selling, that is, any man who understands, and who can function in the new world of selling and all that this concept implies. It is easy for the academician who still sees selling in its old image to criticize it, but it would be difficult for the academician or any other man to criticize selling as it exists in the new world of selling.

As the new world of selling evolves and becomes understood and practiced by the majority of salesmen, the field of selling will achieve status not only in the eyes of the salesman but also in the eyes of the perceiver— the buyer and the public in general. Thus salesmanship may become one of the most sought-after occupations by the college graduate. Right now the field of selling offers a challenge to the most perceptive student. It offers an opportunity for the student who has a desire to do, to achieve, to demonstrate ability. It gives a chance to perform useful and rewarding work and to earn a high level of income. It only lacks status. This will come.

Specifications for Selling

In this new world of selling, two areas of knowledge—"situation management"[3] and "selling in its broader dimensions"[4]—bulk large. Situation management borrows heavily from psychology, educational psychology, social psychology, education, and communication for its body of knowledge. Situation management stresses that every contact the salesman has with prospective customers (individuals) involves different human problems or situations.[5] In brief, there is no one sales situation and no one way to sell. One salesman's strategy and tactics can be quite different from another's and yet may be extremely successful. Extroverts, introverts, and ambiverts all sell effectively; but each, to obtain his greatest effectiveness in the new world of selling, must understand the principles of psychology, education, and communication that form the backbone of persuasion or personal selling or managing human situations. Each must understand not only how to sell but also the "why" behind the concepts, principles, and ideas utilized to communicate and motivate. The why will provide the fundamental knowledge needed to develop an individualized or personalized approach to selling.

[2] E. B. Weiss, *The Vanishing Salesman*, McGraw-Hill Book Company, New York, 1962.

[3] A term used by John McCarthy of General Electric in his five-volume Psychology of Selling Series. This series was published in New York by the General Electric Company, but the publishing date is unknown to this writer.

[4] Taken from the title of the book by Taylor W. Meloan and John M. Rathwell, *Selling: Its Broader Dimensions*, The Macmillan Company, New York, 1960.

[5] Frequently in this book the term *individual* or *respondent* is used in place of such terms as *prospect*, *customer*, or *client*. It is more descriptive of the salesman's role in selling. He communicates with many individuals who are not buyers or customers in the traditional sense. Further, the terms *respondent* and *individual* suggest two-way communication with emphasis on the needs of the individual.

Selling: A Behavioral Science Approach

Success in selling is like success in writing. There are fairly well-accepted methods of writing, yet styles may differ considerably. Some writers are known for their individualistic style, as is Ernest Hemingway. Hemingway used accepted principles of grammatical construction. His acclaimed individualistic style evolved from his mix of the various components of grammar. In the same way, a highly individualistic style in selling evolves from the mix of techniques, concepts, ideas, and principles that the salesman utilizes to manage various human situations. He adjusts the mix so that he can cope with each different situation. He communicates. He persuades. He sells. He manages situations. And don't forget that this process takes keen self-analysis. It is the salesman who adjusts to the personal, social, or emotional needs of the other individual.

In the new world of selling, however, more is demanded. Managing situations refers to the average two to three hours per day each salesman has face-to-face contact with another individual or individuals. It may be, depending on the situation, a prospect, a client, a customer, a contact who affects the ultimate sales of the salesman's product or service, for example, doctors in the drug field; architects in the building, construction, and equipment fields; engineers in the industrial field; or it may be a group of individuals such as a board of directors or a buying group. But what about the other six or eight hours in each salesman's day? Here the salesman is involved with selling in its broader dimensions. He must think in terms of marketing potential, distribution channels, the market-power structure, the marketing mix, management, and finally he must be able to differentiate his product or service through a problem-solving approach.

It must be understood that when a salesman is selling his product or service to another firm, two sets of problems are involved. One is the buyer's or decision maker's personal, social, or emotional mix of needs, and the other is the needs of the firm with respect to the salesman's product or services. This represents two sets of needs, but frequently they are inextricably bound together. And it is the individual who makes the decision to buy. Thus the salesman develops a coping behavior or a form of human problem solving as well as a problem-solving approach to the firm or user's business situation.

This demands much of the salesman. At first glance, the preceding specifications for selling may appear to be almost beyond what the salesman could do or may want to do. Surprisingly enough, however, many salesmen not only understand the concepts involved in the specifications above but also function effectively day in and day out as problem-solving marketing men. Frequently such men are company quota busters.

These quota busters represent the 20 percent of the twenty-eighty principle of marketing. This principle states, in part, that more than 80 percent of the total sales of products and services in this country is produced by less than 20 percent of the salesmen. Some companies have reported that less than 10 percent of their salesmen produce more than 80 percent of the company's sales. The fact of the twenty-eighty principle of marketing may be due to misdirected marketing effort by management. But, in part, the

The New World of Selling

principle is true because of the excellence by a few salesmen and the mediocrity by most.

Types of Sales Effort

It should be made abundantly clear that specifications for selling will vary with the sales task confronting the salesman. Knowledge needed for situation management and selling in its broader dimensions will vary considerably.

If a scalar spectrum could be designed showing types of salesmen and sales jobs, it would have a multitude of colors and shadings. The diffracting would depend on the eyes of the beholder. Thus definitions and descriptions of various types of salesmen vary considerably among sales authorities. Beckman segments selling into low-level or service selling (wherein the buyer was previously determined to buy) and high-level or creative selling (wherein demand is aroused).[6] Stanton and Buskirk classify salesmen with two interactive variables: (1) for whom the man is working and (2) to whom he is selling.[7]

Other authors are more specific. Russell and Beach break salesmen's work into five categories: a manufacturer's salesman, the wholesaler's salesman, the retail salesman, the specialty salesman, and the sales engineer.[8] Kirkpatrick's classification of sales types or sales jobs according to the purposes of buyer, types of buyer, characteristics of salesmen, skill and training of salesmen, type of product or services, employer type, and compensation method for salesmen mathematically identifies thousands of sales jobs.

As Kirkpatrick says, "It is well to remember that, despite all this variety, the selling function is built around a single pattern—that there is a common core found in practically all forms of selling."[9] This common core is in two sharply delineated areas of knowledge: the knowledge needed to understand selling in its broader dimensions and the knowledge related to situation management.

It must be pointed out that the degree of knowledge and skill required will vary substantially according to the sales task. This will be clearly seen if the reader compares these five sales situations: (1) the door-to-door salesman for vacuum cleaners; (2) the route salesman for a nationally known product whose job is largely one of stocking, goodwill, etc.; (3) a manufacturer's salesman who has three states as his territory and who sells direct to retailers; (4) an industrial manufacturer's salesman who sells highly complex industrial equipment to other manufacturers and who not only selects industrial distributors to represent his company but is also

---

[6] Theodore N. Beckman and William R. Davidson, *Marketing*, 7th ed., The Ronald Press Company, New York, 1962, p. 448.

[7] William J. Stanton and Richard H. Buskirk, *Management of the Sales Force*, Richard D. Irwin, Inc., Homewood, Ill., 1959, p. 117.

[8] Frederic A. Russell, Frank H. Beach, and Richard H. Buskirk, *Textbook of Salesmanship*, 7th ed., McGraw-Hill Book Company, New York, 1963, p. 39.

[9] Charles Atkinson Kirkpatrick, *Salesmanship: Helping Prospects Buy*, 3d ed., South-Western Publishing Company, Cincinnati, 1961, p. 21.

required to train the industrial salesman as well; and (5) the life insurance salesman. The door-to-door salesman for vacuum cleaners, like the life insurance salesman, may be required to be highly skilled in motivating people, but he needs relatively little knowledge concerning selling in its broader dimensions. Each of the sales situations may call for substantially different forms of market knowledge as well as substantially different levels of sales sophistication.

In order to present a clearer picture of the new world of selling, a panoramic view of selling in its broader dimensions follows.[10] Salesmanship in transition, the concept of a differentiated product, problem solving, market potential, the market mix, and time management are all components of this picture. Time management is especially crucial in most forms of selling today and it is therefore the subject matter of Chapter 3.

SALESMANSHIP IN TRANSITION

The Early Years

Looking back, the United States is seen as young in years, but in growth it is seen as one of the wonders of the world. It has been and is a dynamic economy. Starting with 1800, it was a country with a population of approximately 5,300,000. At this time little manufacturing existed; waterways, dirt roads, horses, and wagons were used for the transportation of manufactured goods. Travel, transportation, and communications were painfully slow. It was estimated by Wright in his colorful *Hawkers and Walkers in Early America*[11] that in 1800 a rider on horseback with a light load could cover only ten miles a day. Travel was largely restricted to the East. The center of population in 1800 was eighteen miles west of Baltimore, Maryland. Shortly this peaceful countryside economy was to become an economic power. In 1831 the first railroad emerged. It was rough by modern standards. It boasted a few miles of track, a wood-burning iron horse, but with the coming of the railroad, westward expansion began with vigor. The next sixty to seventy years saw transcontinental transportation systems emerge, great business and industrial empires built, and in fact a change from an agrarian to an industrial economy.

In 1831, the year of the first railroad, the population in the United States was but 13 million; by 1840 it jumped to slightly over 17 million. In this decade 3,000 miles of railroad were built. The next decade produced 6,000 more miles of railroad, and soon the total population reached 23 million.

Most of this dynamic expansion had taken place east of the Mississippi

---

[10] For an excellent and fast moving discussion of a development of sales and sales management thought, see Robert Bartels, *A Development of Marketing Thought*, Richard D. Irwin, Inc., Homewood, Ill., 1962, chap. 6. For an interesting and thoroughly researched account of how salesmen were harassed by restrictive and hostile licensing laws, see Stanley S. Hollander, "Nineteenth Century Anti-drummer Legislation," *Business History Review*, vol. 38, no. 4, Harvard University Graduate School of Business Administration, Winter, 1964.

[11] Richard Wright, *Hawkers and Walkers in Early America*, J. B. Lippincott, Philadelphia, 1927, p. 26.

The New World of Selling

River. It wasn't until 1859 that a railroad spanned the Mississippi. At about this time the nation was thrown into Civil War. Expansion ground to a halt. In four years the war was over. Again the nation turned to forging a great industrial power. The first transcontinental railroad came in 1869 with the hammering home of the "golden spike" in Promontory, Utah, that symbolized the joining of the Central Pacific and Union Pacific Railroads. During this period, from 1860 to 1890, the nation was in the grip of an industrial revolution.

After 1890 and until 1940, the nation grew at a slower pace. Again, in the 1960s, another industrial and social revolution developed—one that is developing such highly technical equipment man will reach the moon, and one that, according to some researchers, promises a giant step toward a goal sought by nations since earliest times: the eradication of material want. Salesmanship will be just as important in this revolution as it was during the colonial days, and the transportation and the industrial revolutions of the nineteenth century. Above, the emphasis is on the transportation and industrial revolutions, for it was transportation that produced the modern-day traveling salesman. First, it was the peddler. Men who, like the Yankee Peddler, took products from seaport towns and small manufacturing centers to frontier towns and backwoods areas. Pots, pans, and other necessities were moved by pack, by horse, and finally horse and wagon as roads were extended and improved. Peddlers sold directly to the consumer—the frontier family. In one form or another, the peddler existed from the earliest colonial days throughout the period of Western settlement. He became decreasingly important as stores became available to frontier families. The peddler sold to retailers and frontier towns as well as to consumers. However, he primarily sold directly to consumers since the prevailing buying custom of the retailer during this period was to visit a "wholesale" city about twice a year to select merchandise. Telling this story, A. H. Saxton wrote:

> The buyers would come to New York in great droves twice a year to replenish their stocks, and this was the drummer's great opportunity. A country merchant would want dry goods, boots and shoes, hardware, drugs, groceries, etc. An agreement or compact would be formed between, say, half a dozen jobbing firms, all representing distinctly different lines. A suite of rooms would be rented and fitted up in comfortable shape, with ample accommodations for eating, drinking and smoking . . . and drummers from different houses in the compact would watch the hotel registers for their prey. A dry goods drummer, for instance, would light on a man and introduce him to the drummers in all the lines of trade represented in the compact. He would be wined, dined, smoked, theatred, etc., and most carefully kept in tow until all the houses in the arrangement had a crack at him, with the result that nine times out of ten he would purchase all of his supplies from the houses represented in the association and the only real competition was one association of merchants working against another association of like character.[12]

[12] A. H. Saxton, "Jobbing Trade 50 Years Ago," *Iron Age*, Chilton Company—Book Division, Philadelphia, Pa., p. 149, Jan. 4, 1906.

Selling: A Behavioral Science Approach

New York originally was the only wholesale center. But as the West opened, wholesale centers were created in Buffalo, Cincinnati, Cleveland, and Chicago. New York lost its monopoly position; thus drummers were sent to the retailers' hometown to drum up or get business.

The newer wholesale centers followed suit. The result was that by 1900 traveling men were spanning the nation. A rapid increase in traveling men for the post-Civil War period is vividly shown by census data. Just prior to the Civil War, only 1,000 salesmen were on the road. By 1870 the figure is given as 7,260; it jumped to 28,800 by 1880 and advanced to 92,919 by 1900.[13]

An interesting account giving both the exciting and the difficult side of the traveling man's life is told by Gerald Carson in *The Old Country Store*. Writing of the enviable life, he gave this glowing account:

> Every shipping clerk or stock boy in a jobber's warehouse hoped that he might some day put aside the broom, the brush, and blacking pit, say good-bye to marking cases, and go on the road, telling yarns that were escapes from Joe Miller's joke book, or cribbed from John R. Walsh's Chicago Jokes and Anecdotes for Railroad Travelers and Fun Lovers, and blowing up his samples to the trade. His chances were good if he was young, energetic, and had a winning personality. When the head of a firm decided that a lad might hatch out as a drummer, he gave him a few weeks' training in prices, the line of merchandise, and mentioned a few maxims. Never let the prospect sense that you are in a hurry to make the next train. Never "sass" the customer. Smile when the dealer says "I've already bought your line." Always have your samples in good order. Expenses? Keep them down; there is too much money spent by young men on cigars. Don't sell merchandise you can't deliver. Don't throw dirt at the competition. Never admit trade is dull. Watch your credits. Keep in touch with the home office.

> What a glorious prospect, to drop one's postcards and circulars into the mail!! "Will be calling on you with a full fall line on such-and-such date." He would see the country, make new friends, be practically his own boss, with control of a large personal trade, and command a handsome salary. To a country boy hanging around the little store at a four corners, the drummer was a gay bird of passage, his home where his hat hung, a hero to be compared favorably with the engineer on the fast freight. His confident bearing and city ways made the counter-sitters, man and boy, seem like wild creatures who had ventured briefly out of the brush. There was an ineffably worldly grace about his gesture as he proffered his pasteboard on a first call: "My name and connection, sir." He smoked good cigars—no drumheads or stogies for him—and certainly knew his way around. He knew how to undress in a Pullman berth, and called the porter "George." He ate dollar dinners, knew how to order a meal from a bill of fare, and could handle a complicated layout of knives and forks without turning a hair.[14]

---

[13] Hollander, *op. cit.*, p. 5. In reference to these data, Stanley C. Hollander states that, "The census figures probably seriously understated the total number of commercial travelers." His statement is strongly supported by data gathered from a number of sources.

[14] Gerald Carson, *The Old Country Store*, Oxford University Press, Fair Lawn, N.J., p. 164.

The New World of Selling

The story giving the other side of the coin makes the handsome salary of the traveling man seem less attractive. As the story goes,

It took courage, unquenchable optimism, and a sound stomach to stand the life of the road in the wooden coach days. The early bird call in the hotels came between four and six in the morning. All day the drummer hustled sample cases. He met each situation as it came up; the man who always tried to get an extra discount, the merchant who thought that when he sent in an order, the house should get out the hand organ and declare a champagne celebration. He had his own nominee for Meanest Man in the World; the retailer who liked to abuse a commercial traveler in his own store.

At noon the salesman grabbed a hasty sandwich and before he ate again he made a long evening's ride to the next town large enough to have a water tank and a hotel.[15]

The showmanship of the sales character described in the above colorful account, who would ". . . wave his Havana with the bright band still on it, and feel himself the leading character in a satisfying drama," was considered perhaps even during the "great age for the drummer" as gauche. But he was a product of the times. He made a major contribution to his country. Don't apologize for selling. The record speaks for itself. Nevertheless, all too frequently, speakers, writers, professors, and others have a tendency to take a point out of context or happenings from another period of history to support their theory or viewpoint.

The author remembers well a professor of United States economic history whose avowed intention was, as he stated it, "to take marketing, advertising, selling, and business in general to task." Businessmen in general and the "robber barons" were cut from the same cloth. During one lecture in which salesmanship was described as an economic waste, he held up an article in *Fortune* titled "The Greatest Capital-Goods Salesman of Them All." That day, Diamond Jim Brady was his target. To students of this course, Diamond Jim will be remembered as a salesman who "indulged prodigiously in venery, victuals, and vestments." He will be known as an exhibitionist who wore up to $250,000 in diamonds at one time and who became "the freest-spending, best-known sport on Broadway where theater spotlights turned on him down in the front row, where he sparkled like a Christmas tree." He will be known for "Babylonian style parties, imperial expense-account entertaining, and his friendship with Lillian Russell." These students will not know him as the man who did much to advance the United States railroad industry. He will not be known as the man who introduced the pressed steel car or as the man who "accelerated the railroads' adoption of the all-steel freight car, the technological innovation of the day."[16] They will not know that Jim's skill as a capital-goods salesman was based on more solid ground; that

Jim was a keen and accurate observer with an eye for the tiny details. His reports were a marvel of completeness. They covered the past, present,

---

[15] *Ibid.,* pp. 171–172.
[16] *Fortune,* p. 114, October, 1954.

Selling: A Behavioral Science Approach

and future needs of each particular rail system. Moore (his boss) reading them in New York, was able to size up the situation just as well as if he had been in the field.

Such a passion for detail was unusual in those days. Jim's interest in scientific analysis of sales markets really belonged to a following generation. There was no precedent for it. Nor was there precedent for private notebooks he kept for his own edification. The scribbled memoranda in these covered everything from case histories of railroad workers and their families to the exact amount of equipment in use in every division. In the years to follow, these greatly amplified records were to form the largest part of his stock in trade.[17]

To the same professor, another American salesman of record, Brookings, was ridiculed as a "fiddler." Yes, he played a fiddle, but Dr. Stanley Hollander, in his extremely interesting *Sales Devices Throughout the Ages,* describes the story in this way.

Robert S. Brookings always carried a fiddle with him when, around 1870, he started by selling furniture and hardware, throughout the West, to accumulate the fortune that ultimately created Washington University and the Brookings Institution. *As an eagerly awaited guest of his customer,* the local storekeeper in each settlement, he amused the family at night with music and card tricks.[18]

If you must, apologize for Diamond Jim and for selling in general, but only in the sense as *Fortune* states: "He mirrored and exaggerated some of the engaging and unpleasant national traits of a time when virtue and wickedness alike, in this energetic, democratic republic, were simpleminded and excessive."[19] But no one has to apologize for the sales function performed by Brady and others. As *Fortune* says, he was the greatest capital-goods salesman of them all and, as any economist knows, capital goods is one of the most effective ways to expand the nation's gross national product.

One of the greatest testimonials to selling as a career and its professional status is given by an article in *Fortune.* The backgrounds of 900 major business executives were analyzed to determine the job type or department in which a man was employed immediately before he was elevated to the top position. According to the study, 25 percent of these 900 major business executives held a sales position before they moved to the top job, whereas 16 percent came from finance, 16 percent came from general management, 23 percent came from production operations, 11 percent came from engineering and research, and 8 percent came from law.[20]

Another testimonial to its importance is the sales function given by two of the nation's leading authorities in marketing. Beckman and Davidson say:[21]

---

[17] Parker Morell, *Diamond Jim*, Garden City Books, New York, 1935, p. 30.

[18] Stanley Hollander, *Sales Devices Throughout the Ages*, Joshua Meier Co., Inc., New York, 1953, p. 20. (Italics supplied.)

[19] *Fortune*, p. 113, October, 1954.

[20] *Fortune*, November, 1952. Figures do not add to 100 because of rounding.

[21] Theodore N. Beckman, Harold H. Maynard, and William R. Davidson, *Principles of Marketing*, 6th ed., The Ronald Press Company, New York, 1957, p. 429.

The New World of Selling

Personal selling activity is a natural and inevitable characteristic of a private enterprise economy in which buyers may purchase from alternative sources without compulsion. In a democratic system with a large number of complementary and competitive productive agencies, the work of the salesman is essential in consummating the exchange of goods between retailers and ultimate consumers, wholesalers, and retailers, manufacturers, farmers, and wholesale organizations. It is inconceivable that we could enjoy the benefits of large-scale mass production without the work of the salesman who is the informative link between the various parties engaged in the exchange of goods in our specialized economic system.

A later and more specific comment concerning the effectiveness of salesmen is given by Dr. Auston Smith, president of the Pharmaceutical Manufacturer's Association. Smith stated that in a large sample ". . . 87 percent of physicians rated the detail man as 'competent to very competent' in their jobs."[22]

Hundreds and even perhaps thousands of quotes could be given attesting to the importance of selling and to the effectiveness of salesmen. On the other hand, an increasing number of critics suggest that the salesman has, in many instances, become the weak link in the marketing process. Some of this criticism, as previously implied, stems from mounting evidence that many salesmen have not made the needed transition from the old to the new. In many cases, the transition needed is one of degree.

The New Salesman

Although the salesman of yesteryear has disappeared, the functions he performed have lived on. Varying with the company, the product, and the customer, the traveling salesman of yesterday, just as the traveling salesman of today, sold by samples, pictures, or models, negotiated problems, sold his company, collected accounts, met competition, gave information, received information, and solved problems. And just as the performance difference between the educator, the minister, the doctor, and the lawyer of yesterday and today is one of degree, so is the difference between the salesman of yesterday and the salesman of today.

One difference between the salesman's task of yesterday and today is that today's salesman faces stiffer competition. In many product lines, probably until after World War I, a seller's market existed. Furthermore, products and services were more widely differentiated. Today the competitive gap has narrowed. What is product uniqueness[23] by one company today appears to be almost commonplace tomorrow.

Competition and the differentiated product   Not uncommon today is a sales call on the East coast and on the West coast on a single day by one salesman. Comparing the painful ten miles per day the salesman traveled 160 years ago, or to the horse and buggy travel of fifty years ago, transportation today is almost instantaneous. This mobility combined with idea

---

[22] *United States Congress Hearing on Administrative Prices*, 2d Sess., part 19, pp. 107–109.
[23] As used in the text above, any form of monopolistic competition can be considered as part of the market adjustment mechanism.

creativity gives the salesman an indispensable role in the competitive market adjustment system. As world traveler Abrams, president of the Abrams Aerial Survey Corporation, relates:

> Salesmen today are pollinizers. They are like bees. They can move back and forth across the nation in a day. Or within their territories, they move from company to company, firm to firm, store to store, taking ideas, adjusting them, changing them, modifying them to fit into their situations.

They must, Abrams adds, not only develop new ideas and move them horizontally, but they must move ideas vertically back to their own companies.

Add to this company research and the many communication devices today such as television, scientific journals, the trade press, industry and scientific inventions, and it is easy to understand how quickly competitive adjustment can take place today. It is easy to understand how new products or modified products seem to merge overnight.

The constant and oftentimes rapid market and product adjustment points out that although a company may have an initial monopolistic or even monopoly position in the marketplace, competition plus communication may substantially shorten the first company's monopolistic position.

A case in point is the Norge Company. It developed a coin-operated laundry facility called "Norge village." Norge had a monopoly; it was the only company on the market with a coin-operated dry-cleaning unit. Its dry-cleaning machines were of a sixty-minute cycle type, that is, it took sixty minutes for a load of dry cleaning to be cleaned. Norge sold its dry-cleaning and laundry machines to distributors. Distributors had territories assigned to them. Compensation programs varied among distributors, but frequently salesmen were paid commissions of about 5 to 7 percent of sales. Some companies combined salaries plus commission forms of payment. Buyers or investors in Norge villages needed land, buildings, and equipment; therefore the total investment in many cases exceeded $100,000.

Norge village was the first on the market and Norge had perhaps a year's lead on other manufacturers, but communications and competition affected this monopoly position. One aggressive company advertised a thirty-minute cycle, coin-operated dry-cleaning machine in the *Wall Street Journal*. The company invited inquiries from prospective investors.

At that time, according to Norge salesmen, this competing company was not in a position to ship or service its machines or to do both. Norge salesmen reported that although they could give prospective Norge investors a glowing account of customer satisfaction with the quality of Norge dry cleaning, show them a large market potential, and present income-cost data which painted an excellent profit picture, some buyers or prospective investors postponed their decisions to invest. They wanted to see the thirty-minute cycle machine. In theory an investor would need only have half as many thirty-minute cycle machines to process a given volume of business as he would sixty-minute cycle machines. It is apparent that today the salesman cannot depend on a differentiated product to sell itself, but rather the salesman has an extremely functional role in making the product differentiated. It is the combination or mix of product and salesman that is differentiated.

The differentiated product To *differentiate*, as defined by Webster, is to "make unlike; develop specialized differences in." "To make unlike" is the keystone to differentiation. Today most products are basically similar or are relatively undifferentiated. However, the salesman has the ability to differentiate or make his product unlike others; he therefore holds a position of pivotal importance in the marketing system today.

This seemingly paradoxical statement is a marketing fact if the salesman and the salesman's effort are considered as part of the product package. It is the salesman who contacts prospective buyers, who discusses the merits of his product, who solves prospects' problems, who has personality, and who adjusts to the status needs of the buyer. Are there not far greater shades of differences among salesman as to personality, ability to communicate, ability to solve problems, eagerness to get a sale, enthusiasm, appearance, and mental ability, than there are among products? In today's competitive situation, it is the salesman who makes his product unlike other products. Whether the products are substantially the same (minor product differentiation) or whether major product differentiation exists, for example, substantial differences in product design, price, durability, long life, and product productivity, the salesman capitalizes on these differentiations as they relate to the prospect's use of the particular product.

To clarify this concept, further analysis of differentiation as it relates to economic theory and how a salesman may differentiate the product through his ability to solve prospect problems follow.

Largely through advertising and promotion, some products are presold, for example, foods sold in supermarkets. In these cases, the salesman's function is not as vital to differentiation as in the preceding discussion. Products which are highly advertised and promoted are drawn or pulled through the marketing channels. In brief, the urge to buy a specific product is established in the customer's mind. Customers expect to find these products on the shelves. In such situations, the salesman's function may be to discuss with management the merits of handling a new product in the retail outlets, but the discussion would be of minor impact on management's decision to handle the product. This would be the situation especially in the case of a large manufacturer selling a frequently purchased, commonly used household item. In fact, at times, the power structure is with the salesman and his firm. And management of, say, a supermarket, must stock the item if it wants to stay in the competitive race. General Mills in the marketing of its flour Wondra illustrates this situation.

"On All the Shelves at Once" was the title of an article in *Business Week* (October 5, 1963) which told how General Mills ". . . had performed a rare and complex maneuver: It had put a new consumer product on sale in every market in the country—attaining, for all practical purposes, simultaneous national distribution." Wondra is differentiated. It is flour, granular in form that overcame the homemaker's chief objection to flour,

Selling: A Behavioral Science Approach

that is ". . . it won't stick to your fingers, and it pours like salt—even a fumble-fingered husband can make gravy without lumps." Advertising copy was to pound home the theme that Wondra was "the first truly new form of flour in 4,000 years. . . ." According to *Business Week,* "The story had the components of a cloak-and-dagger thriller; the dedicated scientists in the secret laboratory; the few 'cleared' people; the guarded rooms, elaborate camouflage—and frustration when victory was within grasp."

Since Wondra was highly secret, marketing's task was made complex. It couldn't run any tests to gauge consumer acceptance or check the impact of advertising form. Thus ". . . 98% of the acceptance testing of Wondra was done in the company's Betty Crocker kitchens. The remainder in the kitchens of a few highly trusted General Mills' employees. . . ." Even so, marketing developed a program to attain simultaneous national distribution—a tremendous feat in itself.

Now, what was the salesman's role as part of the marketing team? *Business Week* reports that within three days after the 700 members of General Mills Grocery Product sales organization were told about Wondra ". . . they had called on everyone of approximately 3,000 flour buyers in the country, for both chain stores and wholesale grocery houses—as well as some retailers who didn't buy direct from General Mills, but who do have a pretty good idea of what the consumer likes." F. C. Blodgett, product manager for flour marketing in the grocery products division, says, "The responses from these accounts, ordinarily a hard-nosed bunch, was amazing."

These salesmen performed an important function, but the sales situation was not difficult. It was the case of a salesman selling a General Mills packaged program (the company's national advertising and promotional program), selling a highly differentiated product manufactured by a company which was already getting 31 percent of the total flour market without Wondra, and selling for a company with $524 million in annual sales. The power structure was with the salesman.

Other cases showing how a salesman may differentiate a product will follow, but first an analysis of economic theory to understand more of the why behind the concept of differentiation.

Economic theory and differentiation   In many instances, differentiation is basic to the business or corporate success story and its struggle with competition. The author cannot overstate the importance of this concept to the salesman specifically and to marketing in general.

A discussion of competition and differentiation go hand in hand. Utilizing Figure 1, several forms of competition can be discussed.

Besides pure competition, administered price, and monopoly, economists discuss other forms of competition such as monoposony and oligopoly. In each competitive case the economist makes a number of assumptions relative to each form of competition. This discussion will be restricted to pure competition, administered price, and monopoly. It will include assumptions economists associate with each form of competition.

Pure competition exists where there are numerous buyers and sellers, where the products are substantially the same, and where no one buyer or

The New World of Selling

seller has control over price, and usually where there is an organized market exchange or auction existing.

The farmer's situation is an example of pure competition. He produces corn, wheat, etc., which he sells at market price. He can't sell above market price since no one would buy; he doesn't sell below market price because he can sell his total output at market price. The key point is that he has no còntrol over price. He can't color his product. He can't brand his product. His personality or personal ability cannot be used to affect the sale of his product. In brief, there are no ways in which he can affect the sale of his product. He sells his product at market price less the costs of getting it to market. Obviously, in contrast to the farmer, the business firm attempts to develop its business so that it is substantially away from position X toward position M or even point Y.

Pure Competition	Administered Price	Monopoly
X————————————	— M ————————————	— Y

Figure 1 Competition

At the other extreme, monopoly exists. The monopolist has complete control over price. His product is unique. There are no close substitutes. If only one firm manufactured cars, the company would enjoy a monopoly position and the consumer, if he did not want to buy the car at the established price, would have to use substitute forms of transportation. A monopoly price does not necessarily mean a high price. Other things being equal, the monopolist may sell at a price which will yield the greatest profit. Thus a monopolist may establish a price that would be lower than under a competitive situation. Examples of pure monopoly are rare in our economy, but we do have companies which enjoy patent privileges or technological know-how and thereby produce a highly differentiated product.

General Mills' Wondra was discussed previously as a differentiated product. Wondra, as a differentiated product, brings the company a major plus. "For at least some time," *Business Week* editors note, "it will be a unique product, selling for a premium price. And as ordinary flour is always subject to extreme price pressure, General Mills is in the happy position of being able to push a product that, just because it is unique, can't be put under price attack."

In between the two extremes—pure competition and monopoly—lies the area of imperfect competition, also called monopolistic competition or the area of administered price. As noted economist Paul A. Samuelson puts it: "Most of modern life falls around the heading of monopolistic competition: for example, barber shops, radio and electrical industry, steel, automobiles, retail stores, etc."[24] Here elements of monopoly and elements of competition exist side by side. Any feature that distinguishes one company's product or the firm itself from another product or another firm gives the differentiated firm an element of monopoly. On the other hand,

[24] Paul A. Samuelson, *Economics*, McGraw-Hill Book Company, New York, 1961, p. 496.

elements of competition exist side by side to the extent that each product or firm is similar to others and, therefore, can be substituted one for the other. This is clearly seen with General Mills' Wondra. Prior to the introduction of Wondra, General Mills Gold Medal Flour was the largest selling flour in the market place. The very name Gold Medal differentiated General Mills' flour from other manufacturer's flour, but obviously competitors provided close substitutes. Now, with the introduction of Wondra, General Mills has a flour that is more differentiated than its Gold Medal brand. Thus General Mills has moved from point M in Figure 1 toward point Y, a monopoly position. How far it has moved is a moot question, but in any event General Mills now has greater flexibility in establishing price than it had prior to the introduction of Wondra.

Just like General Mills, each firm attempts to differentiate its product through branding, making product changes, establishing liberal guarantees, or establishing a reputation of "always taking care of customer complaints and making liberal adjustments," or doing a host of other functions so that it can be claimed "our products are different." To the extent a firm has, in the mind of the buyer, a unique product or service, the more opportunity the firm has to sell its product at a specific price.

It follows that the more unique a company's product, service, etc., is, the more the company has moved in the direction of monopoly with all the benefits that accrue to the monopolist. The more common a firm's product is, the more the firm has moved in the direction of pure competition, and consequently the less administrative control it has over price or success in selling against competition.

Another element of differentiation which hasn't been discussed is personality. Every salesman has encountered competing salesmen with such sales personalities that customers apparently want to buy from them. This is especially true in fields where products are similar and are selling for comparable prices. In fact, the salesman well liked may have such an outstanding personality that, even though a competing salesman may have a better product, the salesman well liked still keeps the prospect's business. The prospect, buyer, customer, etc., regard the well-liked salesman and his product more favorably than they regard other salesmen's products and personalities. The buyer looks at the salesman and product as a package and obviously gives personality great weight.

Let us assume, however, that a company's product has many cost-saving features that product X does not have. Would the customer still buy from salesman X? Probably not, since most businessmen are inclined to make decisions on the basis of the benefits to be derived from the product, provided that they have the necessary information on which to base a decision. Nevertheless, there are cases where the product differences would have to be almost drastic before a personality salesman would be dropped. Fortunately such cases are in the minority, but personality cannot be disregarded as a type of product differentiation. Nevertheless, all too frequently, personality is used as a crutch in selling. And it is sometimes said, and with considerable truth, that the less the company or salesman has to offer, the more inclined the company and especially the salesman are to resort to personality and price as a sales tool.

The salesman's function—problem solving? The salesman can be a unique, influential force in differentiating his company's products. But in the new world of selling he will go one step beyond the normal selling procedure. He will be a problem solver.

Problem solving includes, but is not restricted to, "benefitizing" or interpreting the qualities of the product in terms of what it will do for the buyer.[25] In situations where feasible, it includes the concept of going one step beyond or solving customer problems which may or may not be directly related to the salesman's product.

In the first part of this chapter, salesmanship was divided into two major areas—situation management and selling in its broader dimensions. Situation management referred to communication; the face-to-face or salesman-to-prospect situation generally thought of as the normal selling procedure. Selling in its broader dimensions was set forth as the subject matter of this chapter. Situation management and selling in its broader dimensions are dual functions of the salesman, each complementing the other for, after all, the salesman persuades in the process of problem solving. Nevertheless, for purposes of this analysis, problem solving is considered part of selling in its broader dimensions.

As defined by Webster, a problem is "an unsettled matter demanding solution or discussion, and requiring considerable thought or skill for its proper solution or discussion."[26]

Unsettled problems needing solutions and decisions exist in every sales situation.[27] Solving these problems demands thinking ability.

Thinking Thinking is an ability which involves examining the problem, identifying the specific problems, segmenting the problem into manageable parts, suggesting possible solutions, testing those suggested solutions, and evaluating the results. The results of this thinking process must be communicated to the other individual. In selling, after the salesman has exposed the problem and identified the possible solutions, the other individual must make a decision. Thus a salesman must not only develop skills in problem solving, but he must understand the mechanics of the decision-making process.

Problem solving in transition Many experienced salesmen will exclaim, "Why I have been doing just that for years—that's the way I sell." Of course, they have! It can be safely assumed that successful salesmen have intuitively been assisting customers or prospects in solving unsettled problems for centuries. Yet, it was not until recently that what many salesmen have been doing intuitively for years has found its way into sales literature. Until about 1920–1925 neither early professional writing nor company

---

[25] See Purpose and Product Knowledge in Chap. 10 for a discussion of the concept of benefitizing and how this form of product knowledge is communicated to the prospect.

[26] *Webster's Third New International Dictionary*, 1961, p. 1807.

[27] See Chaps. 12 and 13 for a more complete discussion of problem solving and decision making.

Selling: A Behavioral Science Approach

materials on salesmanship contained specific reference to prospect needs and problem solving. Several of the earliest publications are mentioned by Hollander. His research shows that

> In 1862, the Home Life Insurance Company of New York issued an imposing 275-page "Agents Manual." In 1870, Philip Sayles' "Practical Aids for Assurance Agents" appeared. John H. Patterson, founder of the National Cash Register Company, distributed his first manual, the "Primer" to his men in 1887. In 1903 a magazine, *Salesmanship,* was devoted entirely to techniques of selling. Schools of salesmanship were taught in 1903.[28]

One of the earliest books on salesmanship, *Salesmanship and Sales Management,* was produced in 1917 by the Alexander Hamilton Institute. This book implied a problem-solving approach to selling, but such an approach was never formally declared. Statements such as "the you-attitude" or "the talk to the jobber should . . . picture him selling the commodity offered to his customers" are found in one paragraph of the text, but this advice wasn't given with the thought of problem solving. It was given to make the salesman understand the definition of salesmanship, that is, ". . . taking the prospect's viewpoint and then swinging him around to ours."[29]

For the next thirty years, books and articles generally remained within the perimeters established in this and earlier works. There were several exceptions, however. Significantly outstanding among these earlier writers was psychologist E. K. Strong, who not only presented a well-integrated work on selling but also recognized his chief predecessors and his contemporaries for their contributions as well. He stated that in 1898, "E. St. Elmo Lewis formulated the slogan to attract attention, maintain interest, create desire. . . ."[30] Later, he added the fourth term, "get action."

Strong gives credit to Sheldon for adding the concept of satisfaction to Lewis' approach. The next major contribution was Eastman, who in 1916 organized his material under the headings of preapproach, approach, solicitation, objections, and closing.

Strong briefly discussed the approaches of the writers mentioned above as "theories of selling."[31] He identified attention, interest, desire, action, satisfaction, or mental states as the first theory. The second approach he identified as a theory was "situation-response" or "appeals-wants." His third theory viewed man as a "dynamic being" and whether man buys or not depends very largely upon the internal factors within him which are summed up in the word *wants.* Strong also recognizes Charters, who ". . . pictures the prospect having a need to be satisfied or a problem to be solved."[32]

---

[28] Hollander, *op. cit.*

[29] *Salesmanship and Sales Management,* Alexander Hamilton Institute, 1917, p. 67.

[30] E. K. Strong, *Psychology of Selling and Advertising,* McGraw-Hill Book Company, New York, 1925, p. 349.

[31] *Ibid.,* p. 348.

[32] *Ibid.,* p. 357.

The New World of Selling

Strong referred to the contributions of the writers above and others as sounding ". . . a new note in selling literature." Strong's book was written in 1925, yet it did not revolutionize sales literature. Perhaps this was to be expected. Referring to a number of his contemporary writers, he stated, "These writers outline what is to be done and how to do it. Whatever theory they have is practically excluded from their works."[33] And most textbooks of salesmanship even today use major headings of preapproach, approach, demonstration, meeting objections, and closing the sale, and combine the steps of selling with the mental stages.

Occasionally emphasis on prospect's needs and problem solving, especially by psychologists, appeared in some articles, but the breakthrough apparently came in 1947 when Dr. Edward C. Bursk developed what appears to be the first full-scale analysis of the problem-solving approach to appear in a management magazine. He wrote about a ". . . customer problem-solving approach . . ."[34] in which the buyer was encouraged to talk about his problems. This approach is centered around the customer's wants, his needs, how a product could fill these needs and ultimately leave the customer emotionally satisfied.

After Bursk's article, low-pressure selling got off to a fast start. It was enthusiastically hailed and widely accepted in the business community. Ten years later, Bursk, in a thought-provoking article, indicates his dissatisfaction with the use of the low-pressure approach.

He asks management,

> What has happened to selling? Have sales managers been so lulled by the coziness of the sellers' market which has existed since World War II that they have forgotten what it means to sell? Is it possible low-pressure selling, which became so fashionable ten years ago, has turned into no-pressure selling? Do salesmen themselves like to be nothing but glorified order takers? Will company management rue the day when they began to rely so heavily on service, price, and advertising to move their product?[35]

In 1956 Bursk's pointed questions were not without cause. Sales effort appeared to be in a slump. Perhaps it was more a transient period—the lull before the storm. Perhaps management was assessing the value of, or attempting to adjust to the problem-solving, low-pressure approach to selling, because today the low-pressure, problem-solving approach is indeed being practiced by energetic-thinking-ahead management. Salesmen are practicing it on every side. Leading salesmanship books, articles, and speakers are now emphasizing this new approach. Two exponents of this theory are Cash and Crissy, who use the needs-satisfaction approach as a central theme in their excellent monograph, "A Point of View for Salesmen."[36] Their emphasis is on the needs of the individual. Cash and Crissy

---

[33] *Ibid.*, p. 353.
[34] "Low Pressured Selling: Is It a Forgotten Art?" *Sales Management*, p. 50, Apr. 15, 1947.
[35] Edward C. Bursk, "Thinking Ahead," *Harvard Business Review*, p. 25, September–October, 1956.
[36] Harold C. Cash and Dr. W. J. E. Crissy, *A Point of View for Salesmen*, Personnel Development, Inc., New York, 1958, vol. 1.

Selling: A Behavioral Science Approach

have developed a series of eight pocket-size monographs that cover the field of personal selling.

Nevertheless, this new world of selling has neither been accepted on all sides nor understood. "The Salesman Isn't Dead—He's Different," a timely article by Carl Rieser, describes the problem well. Rieser relates that,

There is no more abused figure in American life than the salesman. One group of critics scorn him for certain qualities that another group sneers at him for losing. To many novelists, playwrights, sociologists, college students, and many others, he is aggressively forcing on people goods that they don't want. He is the drummer, with a dubious set of social values— Willy Loman in the Arthur Miller play. The second group of critics, which includes the Secretary of Commerce and many business executives all over the U.S., charges the salesman with lacking good, old-fashioned, hard-hitting salesmanship. He was spoiled by the postwar days when competition was easy. If only he would get up off his duff, and get out and *sell*, the goods would move and business would be in fine shape.

Both sets of critics are swatting at a target that doesn't matter much any more. The plain fact is that, as one Boston sales executive recently said, "The old drummer type of salesman has gone by the board." Nor are his talents especially needed in today's economy. To be sure, there are plenty of aggressive, hard-hitting salesmen still around, and there will always be a place for their brand of selling. But this kind of man is no longer the archetype.

From bits and pieces of evidence in all sectors of U.S. business, it is now possible to discern the emergence of a new dominant type, a man with a softer touch and greater breadth, a new kind of man to do a new—much more significant—kind of job. Whereas the old-time salesman devoted himself primarily to pushing a product, or a line of products, the new-era salesman is involved with the whole distribution pipeline, beginning with the tailoring of products to the customer's desire and extending through their promotion and advertising to final delivery to the ultimate consumer.

The salesman has been cast in his new role by "the marketing concept," a term that originated at General Electric around 1950 and has gained wide attention recently. It means essentially that companies are orienting their organization and effort toward the market, toward the ever changing needs of the customer, and the ever shifting calculations of their own production costs and opportunities. The emphasis is less concentrated on the isolated point-of-sale; it is spread forward, into the buyer's operations, and backward into the seller's operations. The profound consequences of this trend have been suggested by Orm Henning, Marketing Manager of industrial products of Texas Instruments:

One should remind oneself that selling is only part of marketing—particularly in the scientific-industrial world. Marketing is communicating back to your factory your individual customer's needs and particular problems. When you realize and practice this, you open an entirely new vista in the area of sales. You cannot afford to sell a product, a static product—not in our business.

And what's true today in the electronics business—and many others—is going to be true of more and more businesses tomorrow.

The New World of Selling

The great change in selling affects practically all industries and all kinds of goods, whether they are what the marketing profession calls "pull-through" or "push-through" products.[37]

In short, the salesman today is a customer-oriented, problem-solving, needs-satisfaction salesman. He differentiates his product and services.

Summary

The old-time salesman—the story-telling, hard-living, back-slapping salesman of playwright Arthur Miller—is dead. He has been replaced by a company representative who is a market manager of his territory, who sells within a keenly competitive business structure, who functions as an educator, and who is intelligent and mature. He is also a problem solver always aware of the business needs of the buyer or firm and always sensitive to the emotional needs of those with whom he is conducting business. This changing character of the salesman's role came to light in the early fifties, gathered momentum in the late fifties, and by the sixties was well-accepted by the business community.

As a market manager, the salesman has become increasingly responsible for planning and managing his sales effort. functioning as a market analyst in his territory, acting as the eyes and ears of his company in his territory, and representing his company on the highest ethical plane.

As a problem solver, he must understand his customer's business needs. He must know how his product can best service the needs of his customers or prospects. He must differentiate his product and service in competition with other products and the services of other salesmen. The salesman, however, is increasingly acting as a consultant to his customers, especially the smaller firm. Depending on the salesman, the product, and the customer's situation, salesmen may be required to give assistance in one or more areas such as cost control, sales promotion and advertising, stock control, training of a sales force, training of employees to use equipment, production methods, quality control, design and layout of equipment, etc. This type of systems selling is especially important today in the electronics and computer fields. More and more salesmen are required to sell to a group of men representing various interests within the purchasing company. He also is called upon to function as one member of a group of experts from his company who survey the needs of a potential user company and present a solutions program to a group of men representing the surveyed firm.

This is the new world of selling.

[37] Carl Rieser, "The Salesman Isn't Dead—He's Different," *Fortune*, pp. 124–125, November, 1962.

Selling: A Behavioral Science Approach

Chapter 1   DISCUSSION QUESTIONS

1   What do you think are the basic differences between the salesman of the the early years from 1800 to 1920?

2   Is the field of selling vulnerable to negative comments from members of other professions?

3   How would you explain to others that selling needs highly competent men? Should you explain?

4   Describe several different types of sales jobs. Could one man be successful in all forms of selling? Why? Why not?

5   Select three products—one from the industrial field, one from the intangible field (for example, insurance or stocks and bonds) and one consumer-household item—and describe how the company attempts to differentiate its product or services. How would the salesman differentiate the three products?

6   Are salesmen differentiated in the mind of the potential buyer? How? Can the ways in which the salesman is differentiated be cultivated through training?

7   Discuss the relationship between economic theory and the concept of the differentiated product.

8   What is the broad interpretation given to problem solving in this chapter?

problem-solving
situations

2

Each of the following five cases presents a slightly different focus on the problem-solving aspect of selling. The fields represented are industrial selling of machine tools, cutting tools, and gauges; chemicals; commercial building; wholesale office furniture; and manufacturer's representative calling on dealers, architects, and contractors.

After Case 1, "Industrial Selling," and before Case 2, "International Minerals and Chemicals," some newer concepts of the salesman as a market manager and the roles of the vice-president of marketing and sales manager are identified. That material is a logical extension of Case 1, but the reader may wish to utilize it as basic material for analyzing Cases 2, 3, 4, and 5.

CASE 1 *Industrial Selling*

This case partially represents a major manufacturer of machine tools, cutting tools, and measuring systems sales strategy in 1965. This company, through its vice-president of marketing and its national product managers, executed a program which was designed to equip its salesmen to be absolute market managers of their territories as well as problem-solving salesmen now, and in the future—the seventies.

The background for the program is told by the vice-president of marketing in these words:

> During the fall of 1963, our market research department reported that 1964 held promise of being an exceptional year for machine tools, cutting tools and measuring systems. Further, articles, government forecasters and others also gave optimistic business reports for 1964. In view of these forecasts I met with my product managers and discussed our needs in terms of these general optimistic reports for 1964. We wanted to decide in 1963 what we had to do in 1964 to best capitalize on market opportunities in 1964 and 1965, as well as looking ahead to the seventies.
>
> We knew we had a long and a good product line. But we knew too that our competition had good lines as well. Thus, as an output of these meetings in the fall of 1963, our most profitable course of action appeared to be a

Selling: A Behavioral Science Approach

sales manpower development program. We wanted a sales force that could significantly differentiate our product line from our competitors. This meant we needed a sales force that could sell in depth, a sales force that could manage their territories as markets and above all be problem solvers always aware of the business needs of the users of our products.

To obtain the knowledge and skills needed to implement these roles each salesman participated in a twenty-six-day manpower development program, spaced over a ten-month period, covering in depth such subjects as marketing, market potential, planning and managing sales effort, sales psychology, sales training, and conference leadership. Through this program, the salesmen were equipped to enact a number of roles basic to implementing the company's marketing program. The roles are:

1. Each salesman is trained to sell before and to a group of potential buyers. Salesmen are trained and equipped to survey the production needs of a particular user company and design a solutions program utilizing the salesman's company's machine tools, cutting tools, or measuring systems according to the needs of the user company.

2. Each salesman is trained to sell as a member of a team. In this dimension of the company program, sales engineers survey a user or a potential user company's production needs and they, in turn, as a team present a solution proposal to a group of men who represent various areas in the surveyed company. As in role 1, frequently represented in these group meetings are decision makers from finance, production, shop foremen, or other men in the organization with knowledge concerning the application of the product being investigated.

3. Each salesman is trained to function as a conference leader. Essentially the conference approach is used by the company in its own regional sales meetings and by the salesmen in their meetings with their distributors whenever they have to convey information to distributors about market opportunities, product changes, or any other information that is of value to the distributor.

4. Each salesman is exposed to the educational theory and given the role training (practice) needed to equip him to take an extensive sales manpower development program to his distributors. However, the salesman is supported in his training efforts by a manpower expert from the company as well as being provided with unique educational tools to assist in conducting his distributor-training program. The conference method is used extensively by the salesmen in conducting their distributor-training programs.

5. Each salesman receives training in problem solving and the decision-making process and how to employ these concepts to assist the prospect in making the best decisions for his company.

6. Each salesman is required to understand the market research concept. Thus each salesman is responsible, at least in part, for determining the potential in his territory. In the final analysis management establishes the dollar or unit volume expected from a territory, but it is done in cooperation with the salesman.

7. Each salesman receives training in the importance of being a communication source. He is to function as the eyes and ears of the company in

the marketplace. He obtains market feedback from customers and from the market in general. He transfers this information to the company.

And as the vice-president of marketing comments:

> The roles of our salesmen are demanding specifications for any salesman. Obviously some of our men cannot function effectively in all roles. If a man is weak in one role, we try to give him training in that area and/or support his efforts in the field, or we de-emphasize that aspect of his job. There is one role, however, in which we accept no compromise. It is a role that is becoming increasingly important in many companies throughout the United States. That is the role of the salesman as a manager of a territory.

THE SALESMAN AS A MANAGER

In terms of selling in its broader dimensions, the salesman is viewed as a manager of a sales area, territory, or marketplace. He, like management in general, is involved in a process of planning, forecasting, establishing a program, fixing a schedule, utilizing the entire company organization to achieve his goals and solve customer problems, and finally coordinating all activities to achieve customer satisfaction. (In more general terms, the salesman plans, organizes, executes, and evaluates his activities.) More specifically within the scope of the above functions of management, the salesman engages in a management approach to territory screening, account classification, developing a sales call pattern, planning production according to geographical areas, budgeting sales expense, and time analysis. (How the salesman functions within these areas is discussed in Chapter 3.)

Companies are increasingly realizing that the job of the salesman has strategic and innovistic dimensions. The many editorials and articles in business publications related to problem solving and selling makes this clear. They identify the salesman's role as one of the singularly important aspects of the company's business life. The salesman is a problem solver for customers. He serves the customer and without the customer (and this is too frequently forgotten by the business executive) there is no reason for the existence of the company. And too frequently executives forget that the salesman can be a powerful link between the firm and the market area. Management must remember that the customer holds veto power over the company. The salesman is the one who interacts with the customer. And it is through the activities of the salesman that customer problems are identified, solved, and in this way the salesmen's company objectives are attained.

Thus this distinction between the older idea of salesman and the newer idea of the salesman as a manager of a market area is an important one. It is not just a distinction of concepts or terms. It is a difference between viewing the salesman as a pusher of a product or viewing him as a member of a market management team.[1]

---

[1] Among the first to advance this concept in a text were William Lazer and Eugene J. Kelley, *Managerial Marketing: Perspectives and Viewpoints*, Richard D. Irwin, Inc., Homewood, Ill., 1962, pp. 378–384.

Selling: A Behavioral Science Approach

This new concept affects the way the salesman perceives his own job. Principles of psychology, educational psychology, and motivation tell us that under the market area management concept the creative powers of the field sales force are more likely to be brought to bear in achieving company goals.

Further, the market area management concept can bring about a fundamental change in the character of the sales manager's job. This new viewpoint of the salesman as a market manager is not easy for some sales managers to accept. They see it as diluting their own effort and weakening their position in the company. Viewing salesmen as market managers, however, does not deemphasize the importance of sales management. Instead it raises sales management to a higher strategic position in the company. Under this new concept he spends more time in planning and the control of the sales force. For instance, one industrial firm which enjoys national distribution uses the conference method in regional meetings to discuss all phases of the salesman's role as a market manager; thus very little of the sales manager or the sales supervisor's time is spent in man-to-man work in the field. Not only does this approach save the sales manager's time, but the conference method eliminates possible friction that can exist in a person-to-person supervisory basis in the field, permits the salesman to be recognized before the group for his accomplishments, and enables each salesman to participate as a thinking, problem-solving member of the market management team. This last idea is not always understood. Thus, from a company's advertising program an example follows to illustrate one segment of the salesman's role in a company that is developing an integrated marketing team.

Each salesman has an opportunity to contribute sales ideas to the format and copy content for sales and advertising brochures via the conference method to the director of advertising. These brochures announce new products, new uses of old products, and pertinent general information to manufacturers. As a result of ideas from the sales force, some of these brochures are designed so that the manufacturers' salesmen plus distributor salesmen can use them as mailing pieces, or as introductory material during the contact stage, or as visual tools in their discussions with potential customers. For instance, an attractively designed brochure for measuring equipment was titled *Solutions*. Approximately ten solutions to problems that a specific measuring system could solve were colorfully set forth on the cover of the brochure. There was a slot provided so that the salesman could insert a card, and there was another slot so that the salesman could write in facts pertinent to the potential user's plant, problems, or solutions. If a salesman had adequate advance information about the potential buyer situation, he could jot down a few ideas specifically related to the buyer's situation and mail the brochure to the prospect and later follow up with a personal customer contact. Also, as indicated above, the salesman can use this space for writing down ideas during an actual interview with the potential user of the product.

One industrial salesman uses the above-mentioned brochures (as a mailing piece) in a unique way. He writes, in the space provided, a note such as "Mr. Jones, I understand your company has an XYZ piece of equipment. If that is the case, the attached card from Machinery Trading Corporation may be of interest. MTC indicates such equipment as yours is bringing high prices in the used-equipment market at this time. Used-equipment prices plus the new 7 percent tax credit for new-equipment purchases plus the new depreciation allowances suggests that this could be an excellent time to replace older equipment with new equipment. Within a few days I will call your office for an appointment, and I would appreciate an opportunity to discuss your equipment with you." (Signed respectfully yours.)

This creative salesman is cultivating potential customers through his knowledge of used equipment, new equipment, tax and depreciation advantages, and in general, his problem-solving ability. But in this case, it is specifically identified that this company uses its sales force for generating new sales ideas as part of its program to develop an integrated marketing and personal selling program.

THE MARKET MANAGER AND THE SALES MANAGER

A brief description of the job of the vice-presidential market manager and sales manager plus an example showing some aspects of the role of the salesman as a market manager of a territory will show the validity of the above reasoning.

Just ten years ago the marketing function was commonly viewed as those efforts related to getting the product from the manufacturer to the consumer. Today in the modern-market-oriented corporation the market manager holds a vice-presidential position and is in the business of creating markets. And if the philosophy is accepted that the business firm is in the business of satisfying customers' needs at a profit, then it is clear that many company's activities come under the market manager's domain.

According to the committee on definitions of the American Marketing Association, marketing management is,

> . . . the planning, direction and control of the entire marketing activity of a firm or division of a firm, including the formulation of marketing objectives, policies, programs, and strategy, and commonly embracing product development, organizing and staffing to carry out plans, supervising marketing operations, and controlling marketing performance.

Stanton and Buskirk state more concretely, "Market management included all activities connected with the administration of the following four major areas which typically constitute marketing in an organization."[2]

1. Product Policies. The marketing manager is generally responsible for final decision making regarding all aspects of product planning and development. This task includes decisions concerning what products shall

---

[2] William J. Stanton and Richard H. Buskirk, *Management of the Sales Force,* Richard D. Irwin, Inc., Homewood, Ill., 1959, p. 12. See also the 1964 edition for a further discussion of the topics above.

Selling: A Behavioral Science Approach

be made or purchased for sale, the length and variety of the product lines, and the color, styling, branding, and packaging of each product.

2. Pricing Policies. It is the job of the marketing manager ultimately to approve all pricing policies. This includes the determination of the original or list price as well as policies regarding discount schedules, prepayment of freight, fair trade, price lining, and price guarantees and allowances.

3. Channels-of-distribution Policies. The marketing department has to analyze the market to determine its quantitative and qualitative nature and location. Next, it is the responsibility of the marketing executives to determine what channels and how many middlemen are needed to reach the market.

4. Promotional Policies. The two major areas of marketing activities included in promotion are personal selling and advertising. One is personal, the other impersonal; one is generally aimed at specific customers, the other is used to reach an impersonal mass of customers. But both are forms of selling and thus are fundamental to the marketing effort.

The older role of sales management is that of managing the personal selling efforts of the sales force. The Committee on Definitions states sales management is "the planning, direction, and *control of the personal selling activities* of a business unit, including recruiting, selecting, training, equipping, assigning, routing, supervising, paying and motivating as these tasks apply to the personal sales force."[3] The use of italics in the preceding definition is the author's. It serves to score the difference between the older and the newer concept of sales management. Admittedly the difference is one of degree, but if the salesman is viewed as the market manager of his territory, then the sales manager, of necessity, must be more involved in the planning and directing of total sales effort. This new added responsibility is, of course, in addition to his previously mentioned duties.

These descriptions of the marketing manager and the sales manager's role tell what they do. In the following example the interaction of the market manager, the sales manager, and the salesman's job is seen. This company, a nationally known manufacturer of sterling silver tableware, visualizes market management (vice-president of marketing), sales management, and the salesman as a vertically and horizontally integrated marketing team. Management, confronted in 1964 with a booming economy but almost static sales in sterling silver tableware, implemented a decision to investigate the possibility of manufacturing stainless steel tableware, a product which apparently was enjoying greatly increased consumer acceptance.

The market manager, through his sales managers and the sales force, researched the marketplace to discover what types, patterns, and price range of stainless steel tableware were being purchased as well as who were purchasing and where. Based on this research, market management

[3] Charles J. Dirksen et al., *Readings in Marketing*, Richard D. Irwin, Inc., Homewood, Ill., 1963, p. 65.

Problem-solving Situations

in cooperation with production designed and produced a number of possible patterns of stainless steel tableware. Market management then in cooperation with sales management had the new patterns of stainless steel tableware market tested by the sales force. Results of these tests were reported to sales management. Reports were then made by sales management to market management. A decision was then made by the market manager in cooperation with finance and production (obviously the president made the final decision, however) to produce an extensive line of stainless steel tableware in a specific price range. Market management directed the advertising department to prepare an advertising and sales promotional program. Meanwhile each salesman selected in his territory retail outlets for the sale of the company's new line. Finally market management meshed the activities of the advertising department, sales management, and the sales force into one smoothly functioning selling team.

A major point being made in the case above is this: Sales management in this company still retained many of its functions of recruiting, selecting, compensating, etc., but the more the company utilized its sales force as market managers of a territory, the more the sales manager's role was involved with controlling and directing the market activities of the sales organization rather than supervising, stimulating, and motivation. Psychological fact suggests that when the salesman is viewed as a manager, less personal or sales-management-to-salesman supervision, stimulation, and motivation is needed.

The company above is largely decentralized. It pushed decisions down to the salesman as a manager of his territory. But this company, through a continuous manpower development program, equips its salesmen to function as market managers of their territories.

CASE 2   *International Minerals and Chemicals*

This excellent case of product differentiation through marketing and sales effort is provided by Harvard's Levitt.[4]

Levitt reminds management, and it could equally apply to the salesman, that there comes a time in the life of every company when it must do what is right. To Levitt, doing what is right means management has to become market-minded. It has to differentiate its product through marketing. Management's responsibility is to implement a problem-solving program and then utilize its sales force to carry out the program.

Management must become more market-minded because, according to Levitt, basic products and brands are getting more and more alike; prices in general and even under the table prices are getting more alike; and technical services are getting more alike, even though there are still distinct differences

[4] Theodore Levitt, "Marketing R & D for Marketing Innovation," *Chemical and Engineering News*, vol. 39, no. 42, p. 30, Oct. 16, 1961.

Selling: A Behavioral Science Approach

between competing companies. At the same time customers are growing more sophisticated, purchasing agents are getting more knowledgeable, companies are using their own laboratories to test purchased items, and even the housewife is getting more sophisticated. She buys more and more from private-brand items primarily because she feels confident enough to be able to do so without the reassurance of the big, well-known brand.

Levitt uses the fertilizer field as an example of how, through market innovation, International Minerals and Chemicals differentiated its products. The case is described as follows:

> There are numerous small fertilizer manufacturers who usually serve an area of 15 to 20 counties from single plants. They buy their ingredients in bulk from a handful of competing suppliers and generally mix and package them in small gravity-feed factories. The prices charged by the competing raw material suppliers are identical and their credit, delivery, and technical services are about alike. The best way for one supplier to differentiate himself from his competing competitors is to be quicker in grabbing the lunch tab or in giving the Christmas turkey. But this type of a sales effort never produces any really big payoffs. The reason is that it doesn't give the customer any solid reason to prefer one supplier over the other. To get an edge on the others, a company needs better marketing; it must offer the customer a superior bundle of value of satisfactions. This is exactly what IMC did and as a result greatly outpaced the other raw material suppliers.
>
> IMC began by asking this question, "What are the real needs and problems of the small fertilizer companies—not just technical problems associated with using our materials, but any kind of problem?" Careful studies showed IMC that their customers' major problems were estimating demand by counties, training and supervising salesmen, dealer relations, freight routing, breakage and insurance, and advertising and promotion. When it got this information, IMC organized a small consulting service within its own company to help customers with these problems and it prepared a "how-to" manual for customer use. It carefully trained its salesmen to promote and use the service and the manual. The result was a sales boom.

The pure essence of this case to the marketing executive, to the economist, and to the problem-solving salesman is told by Levitt in these words:

> What is important to understand about this successful sales-building program was that it effectively changed IMC's product. Instead of just selling its generic line of potash, phosphate, and superphosphates, plus the usual technical services, IMC offered a cluster of customer-getting value satisfactions, of which the generic products were only a small part. Indeed, it can be argued that they were not even the most important part. The important part is that which effectively differentiated IMC from its competitors and raised sales—namely, the management services with which it surrounded the generic products.[5]

It must be pointed out that Professor Levitt did not present this case to illustrate the effectiveness of selling. On the contrary, he writes: "This shows how crucial marketing is to the success of a firm. But not selling. Selling is

[5] *Ibid.*, p. 32.

Problem-solving Situations

merely concerned with the tricks and tactics of separating the unwary consumer from his loose change."[6] What is needed, Levitt claims, is "marketing— the careful and systematic process of discovering, arousing, creating, and delivering solid value satisfactions to the customer. Selling tries to convince the customer to want and buy what you have. Marketing tries to supply what he wants."[7]

Levitt would find supporters for his views because for too many companies and for too many salesmen his charges that "selling is merely concerned with the tricks and tactics of separating the unwary consumer from his loose change" and that "selling tries to convince the customer to want and buy what you have" are true. But in this new world of selling Professor Levitt's salesmen are dead. Levitt is, as Rieser would say, "swatting at a target that doesn't matter much anymore." For as Rieser comments in his aforementioned hard-hitting article, "The old-time drummer has been replaced by a new kind of salesman. He doesn't sell the product; he sells service. He knows the customer's business almost as well as his own. He is a trouble shooter, marketing expert, executive, all in one."[8]

The next situation illustrates how Rieser's salesman functions with a small company.

CASE 3   *Standard Block and Supply Company*

This company has sixty-plus employees. It has a large plant producing cement blocks used in commercial and home construction. The company handles a complete line of building supplies except lumber. Its plant, fleet of trucks and related equipment, is kept up to date. The company operates in an excellent market since industrial construction and home building are especially heavy. Its sales force calls directly on construction contractors. And although there is no significant difference between cement blocks produced by competing manufacturers (they all must meet specifications established by the state), Standard's price per block is more than competition. This was the crux of a problem voiced by a number of salesmen at one of the weekly sales meetings. These salesmen wanted a price cut—to meet competition.

Management analyzed its sales effort, market potential, the market price, and company policies. The decision was then made—no price cut. Instead it was decided to further differentiate Standard's services in the marketplace. Activities of three salesmen provided the key to this solution. These salesmen had gone beyond a normal sales procedure and had become problem solvers. They were consultants to contractors. The company initiated a program to equip each man in its sales force to duplicate the activities of its three high producers.

One major problem of the construction contractor is to program his work production schedule to obtain maximum productivity from his working force.

---

[6] *Ibid.*, p. 32.
[7] *Ibid.*, p. 33.
[8] Rieser, *op. cit.*, p. 125.

Selling: A Behavioral Science Approach

Many times he has several construction jobs working at once. Having materials available in the right amount, in the right place, and at the right time is a basic concern of construction contractors.

This is the problem Standard's three top salesmen solved. Being in close contact with contractors, they knew in many cases when individual contractors had jobs, but in addition they investigated their territories, and at the first sign of a "cold excavation" (one which they didn't know about) they contacted the contractor. (Frequently starts for buildings, etc., were being done by small contractors or non-customers.)

These salesmen talked service, procedures, cost, specifications, time schedule, etc. They became experts in blueprint reading. They read the blueprints with the contractor. They scheduled the material and the amount needed, where needed, and when needed. They managed. They checked on the jobs frequently to determine progress. They consulted with the contractors. And in many cases contractors, especially smaller ones, leaned heavily on these salesmen to bring about a smooth-running production system.

These salesmen went one step beyond the normal selling procedure and entered the new world of selling. These salesmen differentiated Standard and its products through sales, service, and problem-solving ability.

One additional comment is in order. If management had cut price, competition would have probably cut price as well. The result: All companies would have been in the same relative market position but at a lower-price level.

CASE 4 *Marble Office Furniture Manufacturing Company*

Office furniture manufacturers produce desks and chairs of every type for use in industry, business, education, and the professional man's office. These products vary greatly in price, quality, design, and materials. A few manufacturing firms operate small companies producing small amounts of cut-rate desks and chairs sold in regional markets. Thus, like most businesses, the office furniture field is one with severe competitive problems.

The Marble Office Furniture Manufacturing Company insulated itself from price competition and differentiated itself by specializing in high-priced, quality office furniture. Its sales force contacts dealers throughout the United States, but most of the sales effort is concentrated in large cities or metropolitan markets. Recently the company began designing, manufacturing, and equipping executive offices with custom made, ultradeluxe office furnishings. Some of these offices have electronically operated paneling, doors, etc. This line of custom-made office furniture is distributed through its dealers. These dealers represent small businesses, having in many cases as few as two or three salesmen who handle both retail sales in the store and outside sales. Many times the owner-manager makes outside calls in addition to his duties as office manager, business manager, sales manager, and inside or floor sales duties.

Management of the Marble Office Furniture Manufacturing Company was satisfied with the quality and performance of its sales force. They believed that their sales force emerged favorably when compared with other office furniture salesmen. But as is often the case, one man, Dan Fields, began doing some-

Problem-solving Situations

thing special in his territory and as a result had become the company's top producer. What Dan Fields was doing was discussed during the National Office Furniture Association Annual Convention.

The vice-president of marketing, Ralph Godee (who was also general sales manager) was planning to ask Dan Fields to be the sales manager for Marble's new deluxe office furniture line. In this new capacity, Dan Fields would work directly with the company's four regional sales managers. The conversation between Dan Fields and Ralph Godee took place in the company's convention suite and proceeded along these lines.

VP Dan, I especially wanted to thank you for the great job you are doing and also to tell you some good news concerning our new deluxe line.

DAN Thanks for the kind words, Ralph.

VP Here is what we have in mind. We want you to become our sales manager directly responsible for the new line. What do you think?

DAN I like the idea of sales manager and I appreciate the confidence, but why me?

VP You, because you have not only been doing the best sales job and are well liked by your dealers, but I have heard some good things from dealers and Frank (Frank is the regional sales manager) about your dealer-training program. Dan, I don't know as much about your training program as I would like to know. How are you handling it?

DAN I am not sure it's a training program. I would think that it is more of a developmental type of effort. I use the NOFA sales manual. It provides the basic material for a dialogue-conference approach to manpower development. It has all the dialogue methods in it as well as a description of the conference method. Dealer salesmen seem to like it because they can participate and solve their sales problems.

VP That's just it, Dan. And how would you like to do this job with all our salesmen?

DAN I don't think you need me for that. Most of the more experienced men or the regional managers can do it, I think.

VP Well, I want to talk more with you on salary and other plans, but I want you for that job.

The author left the room but later, during the convention, the vice-president related the end result of the conversation. It seems that Dan did not want the sales manager job. He had a well-cultivated territory which was going better and better. His present salary, combined with his commissions, was much higher than he would make on the new job. If the new line was a success, Dan's income would be much higher than it was now. But Dan didn't want to risk it. He gave the vice-president an alternative suggestion of staying with his territory and doing some developmental work on the new line. The vice-president took the matter under consideration.

How Dan differentiated his product by going one step beyond is clear in the above dialogue. His dealer sales training program was a success. He not only stocked the dealers with desks and related equipment but also gave them additional assistance in selling to the ultimate consumer. He helped keep the marketing pipeline clear.

Selling: A Behavioral Science Approach

CASE 5 *Manufacturers' Representative Calling on Dealers, Architects, and Contractors*

As a fellow salesman, what would you have replied to this salesman who with almost utter dejection asked, "What do you say to a customer after you have been calling on him ten or eleven years?" This is a question a salesman asked the author.

The place was Pittsburgh, Pennsylvania. The time—1963. The company—The Ronson Manufacturing Company, a large manufacturer of building materials as well as a substantial distributor for such products as Anderson windows, Ready-Hung doors, etc. Its salesmen were assigned territories, were well paid on a salary-commission basis, given liberal car allowances and expense accounts, and were asked to call on dealers, contractors, and architects.

The author was traveling with various company salesmen as an observer in preparation to conduct a three-day sales seminar with the company salesmen. It was after a joint call (that is a call in which the author participated as an observer) that salesman John Blank raised the question above. It caught the author by surprise. No salesman had asked this question before. But perhaps it is one most salesmen selling to dealers or other middlemen have asked themselves in some way sometime or other.

After a moment's thought, the author replied, "John, that is a tough question and perhaps one that only you can answer. You know the field, the business, and your customers. I don't."

At that moment John interjected, with intense emotion, "That's a poor answer. You know, you are *supposed* to be the expert."

"Not an expert, John," said the author. "All I try to do is relate to salesmen ways in which I have observed other salesmen handle sales problems. Take for instance the one you have stated. This isn't a how-to-do-it answer to your question, but there is a way to attack the question you have raised. One of the solutions to dealer-salesmen success stories lies with the problem-solving approach. Ask yourself this question: 'What can I do as a salesman to help my customer in his business specifically as it relates to my products?' "

"Well, what does that mean?" John inquired.

"Think about this, 'What did I do to help my dealer in his efforts to sell my products?' as we listen to the recording of your conversation from your last call." (The author carried a small recorder which could be concealed, equipped with a speaker for playback.)

The following is the dialogue of John's call. Jack Hines is the dealer, Liz is a sister, and Frank is an employee. The dealer involved is fairly successful. The dealership also has a cashier, bookkeeper, a delivery man, and three men who double as outside and inside salesmen.

JOHN   Hello, Jack. Hi, Frank. Hi, Liz. Great day, isn't it?

DEALER   Sure is. Should be great for hunting. Think I'll put a sign on the door—Gone Hunting.

LIZ   Don't believe him. He would never leave us here alone. He would be afraid we would ruin the business.

JOHN   (*laughing slightly*) I don't believe that, but I am ready to talk business anyhow.

Problem-solving Situations

DEALER   No business, John. I think we are pretty well set on everything. What do you think, Jack?
JACK   Can't think of anything.
JOHN   Jack, I want you to meet Professor Joe Thompson. He is doing some research in our business.
DEALER   Hello. Nice to meet you. What have you been finding out that I can use? What am I supposed to do about these cash-and-carry, self-service lumber yards around here? They are wrecking business. It's all price nowadays.
PROF   I wish I could tell you, but the reason I am doing research is to find out what you think.
DEALER   Well, I don't know either, so I guess that is the story of my business.
JOHN   You said that you were pretty well fixed. You have plenty of doors and windows. What about aluminum windows? Are you pretty well stocked there?
DEALER   Yes, I'll see you in about two weeks.
JOHN   OK. Two weeks.

That was the end of the sales call, but the dialogue between the author and the salesman continues.

PROF   That is the call, John. Now do you think you had a problem-solving approach?
JOHN   No, but what am I supposed to do? What do you mean anyhow? I am not sure I know.
PROF   It is being constantly aware of ways in which you can satisfy the needs or solve problems of your customers. To be more specific, "How can you help him in running his business as it relates to selling your products?"
JOHN   I still don't see what I am supposed to do. Tell him how to run his business?
PROF   We have a three-day sales clinic ahead of us. Would you ask that question again at the end of the program, John?

In two days the three-day seminar began. At the end of the three days, a dinner was scheduled. It was one of three dinners scheduled to introduce Ready-Hung doors to contractors, dealers, architects. About sixty to seventy guests attended the dinner. The Ready-Hung Door Company described its product as "a door and frame trim, both sides ready to install in any rough opening. It is a precision-made, prepackaged door with precision manufacturing, and a second-rate man can install it so that every door will open and close perfectly."

After the dinner the company unveiled its Ready-Hung door. It was a great show. It was well staged. Ready-Hung doors were erected at various spots around the display areas. The company's sales executives took turns explaining the merits of the new Ready-Hung door. They had large charts showing in great detail the costs of Ready-Hung doors as compared to traditionally built doors.

Costs were pretty important to these dealers, contractors, and architects. The sales executives reasoned that if these men could be shown that cost structures were less with the Ready-Hung doors they would use the doors in their building work.

Selling: A Behavioral Science Approach

The reasoning was good, but one important factor was left out. Not many of the men present had the same perception of costs. Further, situations were substantially different. For instance, some contractors built custom homes, that is, one home at a time. Others built three or four at a time and offered them for sale; other contractors built large numbers of homes at a time. Some of the men present were involved in large, low-priced subdivisions; others in high-priced suburban areas; some contractors had friends, relatives, or reciprocal agreements with other contractors.

Costs are important, but in this situation there was no rush to buy Ready-Hung doors. Were there other, even perhaps, more important considerations? Let's see how salesman John Blank handled his research in an effort to develop a problem-solving approach.

After dinner small groups of contractors gathered around various displays of Ready-Hung doors and other products. John approached one group of three contractors who were inspecting a Ready-Hung door. (The Ready-Hung doors were in frames and operated just as if they were installed in a home.)

JOHN "What do you think of them?"

CONTRACTORS Good. (*The answers appeared to be in the affirmative.*)

JOHN How do the cost data seem to you?

CONTRACTOR 1 You never know about that.

CONTRACTOR 2 Okay, I guess. (*Contractor 3 was noncommittal.*)

JOHN Each of you has built homes for resale. From your experience what is one of the first things that your prospective customers look at?

CONTRACTORS Let me see. (*A number of points were mentioned by the contractors. But doors, windows, closets, etc., were all suggested as things both men and women looked at and tested.*)

JOHN Then am I right in assuming that to some degree your customers judge, judge what you have behind the walls by how easily the doors, windows, and closets open and close?

CONTRACTOR 1 Hadn't thought of that, but by gosh, they do.

JOHN You men are all top contractors, so you don't have to answer this question; but it is something to think about. Have you ever had a door, window, or closet that wouldn't work, that was poorly hung, that rattled and jammed, etc.?

CONTRACTORS (*with some laughter*) Oh, that has never happened to me. That should happen to me.

JOHN Do you think that these Ready-Hung doors, remembering, of course, that each works perfectly, that they come in the type of wood that you want and can be installed quickly, and the fact that they are always perfectly mitered, would help you *sell* your homes?

ONE CONTRACTOR You know, I have had some problems getting the kind of finishing work I want done and seasoned wood isn't easy to come by either.

ANOTHER CONTRACTOR John, it might just do that—help sell my houses.

A little later, John looked at the author and said, "What do you think of that, Prof?"

He merely replied, "I wish every salesman here could have listened to that discussion."

Problem-solving Situations

John then remarked: "I know now what to say to my dealers. Here is an idea I have. What do you think of it? Each of our salesmen can spend a certain amount of his expense money working with dealers in any way he wants. And tomorrow I am going to develop a series of joint ads and start presenting them to my dealers. I want to sell out our line of old display doors and windows and get in new ones. Why, some of our dealers have had that old stuff around for years! They can't make money that way. What do you think of the idea? Do I have the problem-solving approach?"

Rather than give my answer here, the reader, as a fellow salesman, may answer the question. What would your reply be?

Chapter 2   DISCUSSION QUESTIONS

1   Do you think it is possible for one salesman to enact and function in all the roles described in Case 1?

2   What is meant by the idea that the salesman is part of an integrated marketing team?

3   If the salesman is considered a market manager of his territory, then what becomes of the role of the sales manager?

4   In the International Minerals and Chemicals case, is the salesman a problem solver in the narrow sense of problem solving or in the broader sense of problem solving as developed in Chapter 1?

5   Do you agree with Professor Levitt's description of selling? Why? Why not?

6   Take the role of the salesman and select any product you wish and describe how you would develop a broad problem solving approach to selling that product.

7   What can happen if one company lowers the price of its products? Will that company get increased business?

8   Do you note any difference between the salesman who sells on the basis of price and the salesman who sells on the basis of problem solving?

9   Assume you are a manufacturer's salesman stocking dealers with office equipment of various types. Would you be more successful in the eyes of your company if you stocked all of your dealers to the hilt or if you helped your dealers keep the marketing pipeline clear? Would there be a difference in the short run and in the long run? How could you as a salesman help the dealer keep his stock moving to the potential user?

10 Discuss John Blank's problem-solving approach as discussed in Case 5.

11 Discuss the statement made in Case 5 that problem solving is "being constantly aware of ways in which you could satisfy the needs or solve problems of your customers." To be more specific: How can you help him in running his business as it relates to selling your products? Does the salesman really tell the user how to run his business? If so, in what way?

planning and managing sales effort

3

Tommy Armor, the veteran golf pro, tells us in his book, *A Round of Golf,* to use our brains and not our brawn.[1] He reminds us that planning or thinking through every shot will permit us to play a scientific game—to reduce strokes, to reduce tension, to reduce errors—with the end result being that we play up to our potential and enjoy playing the game. He suggests that it will be more fun for others to play with us when we play a planned game.

If you are a golfer, you will appreciate Armor's planning strategy which calls for each golfer to look down the fairway and to program each hole. He implores each golfer to analyze each hole for distance, hazards, traps, doglegs, and wind and then to select the proper club after the above factors have been weighed and considered. You are now ready to select your hoped-for position down the fairway. Relax and hit the ball. Results will be great!

This is his consistent plea for planning. Armor tells of golf pros who have failed to plan each stroke and as a result lost tournaments. This is the exception, for seldom does a top professional golfer just start around the course with vigor. Not at all. A professional must plan his efforts. He must think his way around the course. In the same way, sales effort must be planned effort. And regardless of ability, a salesman cannot effectively sell by the seat of his pants. Today in this new world of selling, the salesman is a manager. He manages his time, his sales effort, his markets, his customers; in brief, he duplicates at the territorial-level, top-management's management effort.[2] In most cases, whenever you see a truly effective salesman in operation, you see a planner: a man who thinks ahead, who knows what he is going to do, why he is going to do it, when he is going to do it, where he is going to do it, and how he is going to do it.

A salesman once asked the author, "From your experience how would you select the best planner you have been in contact with and describe his activities?" Before answering this question, I thought a moment. There

---

[1] Tommy Armor, *A Round of Golf,* Simon and Schuster, Inc., New York, 1959.
[2] For further analysis of the salesman's role as a manager, see Chap. 2.

was no spontaneous answer on my part, for many salesmen I knew were thinkers and doers. Images of men in various sales situations began to flow through my mind almost like the spinning wheels on the old-fashioned gum drop machines and coming, sometimes, to a surprising halt. In this case, the man that came to my mind was indeed a surprise. I tried to reject his image. I tried to think of another salesman, a million-dollar producer of life insurance, or a top industrial salesman, or some other more glamorous sales activity, but here he was, my choice, still in my mind and not an impressive choice, I thought. He was a coffee route salesman. More than this, however, was the fact the man selected was under six feet tall, not good-looking, not young, not well groomed, nor a college graduate. He was, in fact, just the opposite of the usual picture of the successful salesman.

My choice was about five feet five inches tall, about fifty to fifty-five. He talked about his aches and pains; the clothes he wore left a great deal to be desired. He had a common, down-to-earth personality. He was a humble man and people liked him. And he was, as I have stated, a planner.

What did he do that made him stand out in my mind? My impression of him as a planner came as a result of my bouncing around for an entire afternoon sitting on a jump seat in the front of his truck and following him in and out of fourteen assorted restaurants, institutions, and clubs.

You may say at this point, "Sure, it's easy for a route man to be well routed. He has a territory, a given number of restaurants, clubs, and institutions to sell to, and he is an order taker besides. He arranges the frequency of his calls according to his customers' needs." This is all true except that this man was not an order taker and that he had an ability to manage his time beyond what is expected of the average route salesman or any salesman for that matter.

Here is the story as I recall it from my notes. At around one o'clock in the afternoon I drove up to his home and introduced myself. Before long he was busily going over his supplies, checking his records, and at the same time enthusiastically telling me about his company and how much he enjoyed his work. Soon we were leaving his home and on our way to his first stop. En route, in answer to my question, "What have you got planned for this afternoon?" he replied, "Well, I've got fourteen stops to make, plan to try for Allied Sales in six of those stops, and make one cold call." That afternoon he did exactly what he said he was going to do. A record was kept of each account. He knew each customer's business needs and they knew him. They knew him as a cheerful, confident, nervous, bustling figure who would enter the restaurant door carrying an armful of coffee bags and greeting the manager-owner with a "Hello, Mr. Banks." Or if Diane, the waitress, happened to be close by, he would inquire, "How's your boy? Doing OK now?" Or as he was filling the coffee bins with assorted-size coffee bags, he might turn to another waitress, "You girls are selling a lot of coffee—bet the boss likes that," or make some similar remark, never stopping, appearing to be on the move, perhaps nervously as he inspects the equipment, asking questions like, "Everything OK, Diane?" "Coffee taste good?"

Selling: A Behavioral Science Approach

For customers where allied items could be sold he was always ready with prepackaged french fries, mustard, peppers, olives, pickles, and relishes, and especially ready to check the prospects' stock, tell them of their needs, mention special deals, new items, or anything else that would benefit his customers.

On his preplanned cold calls, his targets were small independent restaurant operators. Our joint call resulted in no sale, but Paul explained, "You've got to work on them in this business—it's tough competition. Coffee is coffee and service is the difference." His call on one of the prospects follows. His contact was like his service approach to restaurants—direct, a little forced, a little terse, perhaps too much so:

S: *Salesman*
R: *Respondent*

S   Hello, I'm Paul Blintz of National Coffee, and I'm here to see if you can use our coffee and services.

R   No, sure can't.

S   Why not? It's good coffee and I will give you real good service.

R   Pretty satisfied. I've got good coffee and service now.

S   Sure, but did you ever have your equipment break down and lose coffee sales?

R   Oh, I guess it has happened.

S   Well, if it does, you can call me any time even at night. You can call me when you run out of coffee and I'll deliver some to you. That's the kind of service I'm talking about.

R   What's your price?

S   The same as Ideal. That's your coffee company, isn't it?

R   Yes, but everything is OK.

S   How about me looking at your equipment for leaks? Or perhaps you need a new glass; it might be stained or something. There is no charge. I'm just glad to do it.

R   No, I'm OK. Our regular man takes care of it pretty well.

After the conversation Paul related that his idea was to get in and service the equipment to show the prospect that he meant business with respect to service. Eventually he hoped he could work his way into the account, but, as he mentioned, it takes time in most cases. He also stated that he didn't make initial calls on institutional prospects classified as A prospects. He left that to the district manager. He explained that he couldn't handle the big accounts because "I don't look like much and some of those big deals run from $20,000 to $25,000 a year. That's a lot of coffee for a peddler like me to sell, so I have an agreement with the district manager. If he establishes the big accounts, I'll give them lots of service and keep our accounts once we get them."

Mentally I had to agree that Paul wasn't what I would call a salesman who could enact a number of roles, but he had a want "to do" and persistence. And above all, he was a planner. Later I was to find that Paul was the company's top salesman, largely because he kept his customers once he got them. He sold the most coffee and consistently sold the largest volume of allied items. In fact, he had established a company record that netted him $460 one month over and above his salary and his commission from coffee sales.

Without question, Paul's greatest asset was time management and always thinking in terms of what was best for his customers. This coffee route salesman gives every salesman a good example of planning, thinking ahead, keeping records, and establishing a time schedule.

What is an example of poor planning? It could be stated that poor planning is just the opposite of good planning, and let the above example suffice, but it doesn't dramatically illustrate the situation as does the following story.

This case involves a salesman in a field where his fellow salesmen were making up to $70,000 in one year. The salesman was selling Norge dry cleaning and laundry villages. Call him Jack Ferris. After a sales meeting, Jack asked the writer to make a few calls with him. He stated he had been in the field for close to three months and had yet to make a sale. This was serious. Jack Ferris was on a straight commission and paid his own expenses. He did, however, receive some expense money from a district manager in the form of a draw which was not covered in the company policy. Therefore, other than covering his modest expenses, he had little or no income. After a few minutes of conversation with Jack, it was apparent he had great drive and wanted desperately to make a sale, but it was also apparent that he was a very disorganized individual. Jack's idea of covering his territory and planning his sales effort was to go to a town or city in his territory, place an ad in the paper telling about investment opportunities in Norge dry cleaning and laundry villages, and then wait at the local Elks for calls. With great pride he told about the miles he put on his car when covering his territory. He would arrive in the town, put an ad in the paper, and depart at noon the following day if he didn't receive a lead from the ad placed the day before. It was on to the next town or city with the same almost tragic comedy of errors. A short time after, Jack was replaced by the company. He had failed.[3]

It may be safely assumed that Jack Ferris could not manage his sales activities. He was like the proverbial ship at sea without a rudder. He did not know where he was going or why he was going. Contrast Jack Ferris to a salesman that J. O. Vance, management consultant for McKinsey and Company, tells about. This salesman allocated his calls on the basis of customer groups and subgroups within his territory. He made estimates of his firm's share of market by product line and classified customer potentials on the same basis. He kept careful records for purposes of sales control including records of competitive activity and of sales expense in relation to volume. Vance's salesman understood principles of management and put them into practice. This salesman was doing what Sidney Weil, president of the American Safety Razor Corporation, wants salesmen to do: "Every salesman should look upon himself as a sales manager in his

---

[3] If management makes extensive job analysis, determines the type of man they want, and establishes a program of selection, training, compensation, motivation, supervision, stimulation, etc., to verify and develop their choice, few salesmen would fail.

Selling: A Behavioral Science Approach

territory duplicating at this level all things that make for successful sales management at the top of the organization."[4]

As every salesman knows, this is easy to suggest but difficult to do. Yet to some degree it is expected by many companies. J. O. Vance states that "a survey of more than 100 companies showed that a majority of them permit the salesman to cover the territory as he sees fit."[5] This policy is based on the reasonable premise that sales management knows less than the salesman about his market conditions in his territory, buying habits of customers, distance between accounts, and facilities for travel. Since the salesman is closer to his territory and more familiar with it, he is considered better able to plan thorough coverage. On the other hand, Vance emphasizes that ". . . even though your firm may leave you comparatively free to make intra-territorial decisions, it wants you to operate systematically and expects you to classify customers on the basis of sales potential and devise a call pattern that will result in balanced coverage."[6] This freedom that Vance speaks about does, however, vary considerably among firms. Some firms control closely the salesman's territory coverage. There are firms that schedule time so closely that a salesman is expected to call on a particular customer and in a given area at a certain time.

Generally the salesman has more control over his sales activities if he represents a small firm, is a manufacturer's agent, is introducing a new product for which the market is undeveloped, or is selling intangibles like investments or insurance. Frequently the salesman who is an independent agent or dealer is the freest of all. He is able to sell according to his own desires and judgments. It must be understood that the freedom given to the salesman to manage his own sales effort and his time within his territory varies with each company.

Nevertheless, regardless of the type of selling involved, "every salesman should look upon himself as a sales manager in his territory duplicating at this level all things that make for successful sales management at the top of the organization." He should understand a theory of management programming and put this theory into effect in his territory according to his company's needs, his needs, and the needs of the customers in his territory.

An emphatic testimonial telling what this approach can mean to the salesman and to the company is given by a nationally known industrial concern. This company's market success story was told in a recent article in *Steel*. This company, after only one year of training its salesmen to be market managers, found that:

1. Its share of the market on several product lines had more than doubled.

2. Several territories traditionally in the under $100,000 category were elevated to the $1 million-plus level.

3. Sales costs fell 16 percent.[7]

[4] Sidney Weil, "Good Old Fashioned Selling: What Is It?" *Sales Management*, pp. 24–25, Dec. 15, 1963.

[5] J. O. Vance, "The New Salesman," *Sales Management*, pp. 139–143, Dec. 15, 1963.

[6] *Ibid.*, p. 27.

[7] *Steel*, Penton Publishing Company, Cleveland, Feb. 1, 1965, p. 33.

Planning and Managing Sales Effort

One of the most interesting developments concerning this program is the fact that "four of seven winners of top sales awards presented a few weeks ago by a machine tool builder were 'novices.' None of the four has been selling machine tools more than eighteen months. How did they succeed almost overnight in this complex business? The answer has two parts, a new approach to marketing and sales training combined with a solid line of new products."[8]

THEORY OF MANAGEMENT PROGRAMMING

Management at almost all levels, in most organizations, is involved in planning, forecasting, establishing a program, fixing a schedule, utilizing the entire organization to achieve goals, and finally coordinating all activities to achieve customer satisfaction.

Planning

Planning is largely mental. It may be thought of as a process of thinking through before doing. Planning involves thinking through the general procedure to be followed in order that the work to be done will be done with the greatest certainty of economy of time. Planning is a process of the salesman asking himself what is to be accomplished? In planning, the salesman identifies the situation and the problem he wants to get at.

For instance, one group of industrial salesmen are advised to ask, and determine answers to, such questions as: Where are the best markets for our products? How do I get prospects? How do I use presently established accounts or users of our products in my work to obtain prospects? What kind of sales talk am I going to use in general? Will I change my sales talk for various situations and prospects? What do I have to know about the technical aspects of our products? How do I go about using this knowledge with the various prospects?

This same company advises its salesmen that in the process of planning, the salesman should be concerned with establishing standards of personal time control plus criteria that will indicate to the salesman whether excellent, mediocre, or poor performance has been achieved in developing his territory.

In this process of thinking through or planning, each salesman is automatically involved in the development of goals or objectives; in forecasting; in establishing programs, procedures, schedules; in coordinating and building an organization.

Above all, sales planning must be in terms of company policy and company plans which will establish the most advantageous course for the salesman and the company with respect to sales in the salesman's territory. For instance, one manufacturer's policy is to establish the strongest posible distributor organization. Thus the salesman, in managing his time and sales effort within his territory, should be directly concerned with engaging in activities that will carry out his policy. Another company requires that

---

[8] *Ibid.*

investors have a minimum of 15 percent down payment on equipment they purchase. Thus the salesman in planning his work should never think in terms of submarginal customers unless it is cleared through the home office. In most firms there is company policy with respect to working with other departments within the organization. In the salesman's planning and thinking through, these policies must never knowingly be ignored or circumvented.

This is not idle talk. Speaking on this point, it is asked in the *Norge Dry Cleaning and Laundry Village Sales Manual* why a company establishes a minimum as a down payment or margin of safety with respect to purchases. The answer is, "It is established to assist the salesman and the prospect. The simple fact is that when you the salesman establish a village in a productive market area, and this village is sold to a 'going concern,' financially, you have the best advertising source that you can possibly have—a satisfied customer with a money-making installation." This same manual advises its salesmen as follows: "You are a professional salesman. The customer looks to you for professional counsel and advice. Even though ethics tell you never to violate this confidence or trust, good business sense also tells you that one poor sale can cost you many sales, thus, cost you thousands of dollars."[9] This same manual also notes that

> Company policy states that no salesman will be allowed to rebate part of his commission to a customer. If it is done, the ramifications are obvious regarding future sales. To be sure, the investment group, the individual, the manufacturer, the business firm, or the executive who may be a possible customer will not respect the salesman who tenders such an offer. And surely such an act on the part of the salesman would not be the reason why a good prospect would invest in a village. He invests in a village to make money. A partial rebate of a salesman's commission is certainly minor when the total investment and future revenues are concerned.[10]

The discussion above illustrates what is meant by planning within company policy and operational procedures.

It becomes apparent that in the process of planning, the salesman establishes goals and objectives. Actually it is difficult to determine where planning ends and where establishing goals or objectives begins. It is difficult to identify a particular activity the salesman is undertaking as associated with just one phase of management. The salesman will find that on many occasions his activities will embrace a number of management functions just as when he plans he also sets goals and objectives. For instance, when the salesman establishes that he wants to talk to two new prospects each day, he is planning, but he also has established a goal.

Forecasting

To forecast means to estimate or to calculate in advance what will happen in a specified future period of time. A company forecasts not only

[9] Joseph W. Thompson, *Norge Dry Cleaning and Laundry Village Sales Manual*, Rich Machinery Company, Grand Rapids, Mich., 1962, pp. 12–13.

[10] *Ibid.*, p. 23.

what it expects future sales to be, but it allocates its market expectations according to political divisions, such as states, counties, etc.

A salesman forecasts when he plans in terms of the order of the development of his territory. One company sales manual advises:

> Look ahead in terms of six months or more. Compare less populated with more heavily populated sections in your territory as to which are the most productive sales areas at this time. Compare small towns to cities as to their marketing potential at the present time in contrast to six months or a year from now. You may decide that rural areas, small towns, etc., follow activities of the major population areas by as much as six months or a year. Therefore, you may decide to concentrate on the "easy" market, and then as these markets are developed, you may move into the more difficult markets.[11]

The Pratt & Whitney sales training manual tells its salesmen,

> You are forecasting when you determine when, where and how you are going to develop your territory. This calls for decision making. You have to make a choice and facts are the raw materials of decision making. Get the facts first and then decide what, when, where and how you are going to develop your markets within your territory. Logically your thinking will be adjusted from time to time as different situations emerge.[12]

In order to get facts, the salesman, either by himself or with the aid of his firm, will have to develop a composite inventory or, in other words, make a value analysis of his territory. Such an analysis will tell the salesman who are his best, average, and poorest accounts now and what he can expect in the future from these accounts. Such a value analysis or inventory will include potential prospect accounts and will rate them as to the best potential, average potential, and poorest potential now and in the future.

In the new world of selling more and more companies are cooperatively working with their salesmen to determine the market potential that exists in a salesman's territory. This change is especially true in the industrial field. The market potential for a particular product comes from the salesman and his analysis of his territory. Obviously the company must examine this analysis and compare it with various indices that it uses to determine market potential in given areas.

In cases where the salesman's estimate is too high or too low, the reasons for this must be determined and communicated by the company to the salesman.

A Program

Through planning, forecasting, and developing a customer and prospect inventory for his territory, the salesman has the raw materials from which to develop a program. A program is a sequence of activities structured to implement policies and accomplish objectives. If a salesman were

[11] *Ibid.*, p. 10.
[12] Joseph W. Thompson and William Lazer, *Pratt & Whitney Manpower Development Program*, Pratt & Whitney Corp., Inc., Hartford, Conn., 1964, Chap. 12, p. 3.

to state that he planned to sell as much of his product as he possibly could in his territory and to make as much money as he possibly could, he would, in a sense, be establishing a goal or an objective. Nevertheless, a goal should be more specific, more tangible, and not just a good resolution with no limits. Suppose instead that the salesman states he plans to locate one new prospect each day, or assume that he is a manufacturer's salesman and plans to have three product-knowledge sales meetings each year with each distributor of his company's products. He would then be establishing goals, since his objectives are specific, tangible, and obtainable.

The salesman now has a goal. To establish a program, he must determine the activities he will perform to accomplish this goal. In brief, what must he do to locate one new prospect each day? The salesman is now concerned with procedures. Procedures tell the manner in which the job is to be done. In planning, the salesman is more concerned with establishing what is to be done. Procedures tell how it is to be done. Whenever a goal is established and the work needed to accomplish that goal is to be carried out in a uniform way, the salesman must prepare procedures telling how it is to be done.

Procedures are analogous to specifications. Specifications are to the purchasing function in industry what sales procedures are to the salesman. As an illustration, part of the salesman's program in selling is to call on potential customers and get information from them. The procedural aspect is how to call on prospects and obtain information. In the contact stage he elicits information from prospects by asking verification and permissive questions. These are procedures. This same analogy applies to market planning. The salesman plans to analyze and classify his accounts and prospective accounts according to potential. The procedures will tell him how to do it.

It appears to be more difficult for salesmen to follow procedures than to plan. Apparently salesmen by nature are planners. They look ahead. But many times in the rush to sell they neglect procedures. They want to make mileage, that is, cover distance, get to the market areas, try to see a prospect, and close a sale. The salesman's drive and thirst to sell are basic to sales success, but in many cases the salesman's thirst is never slaked because procedures were neglected along the way. Attention to detail is vital in any planning process and procedures are the detail of a plan.

Scheduling

Scheduling is a process of establishing a time sequence for the work to be done. In the planning stage, time is rubber time—it can be stretched or contracted as a salesman thinks through what is to be done. Scheduling is another matter. This is hard time. Scheduling is the activity that puts a program into effect on time.

Scheduling, the order of scheduling, and the timing of scheduling should be highly flexible and should be adapted to each man's territory, his background and needs, but it is imperative that a schedule be established and followed.

Planning and Managing Sales Effort

Flexibility can be built into a schedule in many ways. For instance, one salesman with part of the state of Illinois as his territory classified all of his accounts according to potential. He then divided his accounts geographically. He also developed a list of potential users of his products. He knew he could make, on the average, eight calls per day. He followed a 75–25 formula which meant he planned his day to make six calls per day on regular customers and two cold calls per day on potential users. He found that whenever he was diverted from his schedule because of travel conditions, special needs of customers, or any one of fifty other reasons, he used his cold call time as a buffer. This gave him considerable flexibility in his scheduling. He also made a rule that if a particular situation arose in his territory that demanded his complete time for a day or even a week, he merely dropped all calls planned for the week and took care of the urgent business at hand and made no attempt to cover the accounts scheduled.

Perhaps the most important general rule for the salesman to have in mind is this: Plan the day so that if some calls do not materialize, have cold calls, service calls, goodwill calls, or paper work that needs to be done as alternative uses of time. This policy is just as important for the salesman selling intangibles as it is for the salesman who has a territory to manage.

The following schedule illustration taken from a company sales manual is an example of how one salesman scheduled one phase of his overall market program so that it carried out company policy.

Company policy stated the salesmen were to select locations for coin-operated Norge dry cleaning and laundry villages. This site development included the establishment of an adequate building to house a village.

These salesmen selected sites according to market potential. They had adequate market data furnished by their company with which they could analyze each site. The management job of the salesman was to select a site, determine its market potential, construct a complete portfolio for each site prior to contacting a prospect.

TABLE 1 Schedule for Site Development

Area	Possible sites selected	Number to be selected	Final market evaluation	Cost-layout and design	Completed portfolio
Cleveland	April 15	6	April 15, 17, 19, 21, 23, 26	April, etc.	April, etc.
Round Lake	June 10	3	July 10, 12, 14		
Fosterville	July 20	1	July 25		

Organization

In managing his territory, each salesman must have a high regard for the role of the total organization of the parent company. Every company has an organization, be it formal or informal. Organization refers to the structure created in order to define responsibility, to delegate authority, and to establish and clarify relationships among company personnel. Organizations many times grow like Topsy; nevertheless, the organizational structure is formed as a result of identifying and grouping similar forms of activities associated with carrying out the purpose of the company. And organizational experts tell us there is no one best organization and that organizational needs vary with the type of business, the financial resources, the human resources, the size, the products, and the markets. One organization may successfully employ a decentralized structure, whereas another may be highly successful with a centralized form of organization.

A highly decentralized sales organization exists in the company that has a philosophy of pushing the decision mechanism down—to the salesman. A company that wants its salesmen to manage a territory and permits its salesmen to establish their own procedures is following the principle of decentralization. A company that has a highly centralized organization specifically identifies how, why, where, and what the salesman is to do.

Not only must a salesman be alert to utilizing each segment of the parent organizational structure that might assist him, but he also must be aware that he individually can establish an organization to aid him in carrying out his sales effort.

Most organizations have staff positions. A staff position is normally occupied by an individual who gives specialized assistance to a company over a short period. He is not a permanent employee of the company and usually works on a consulting basis. He is not a policy determiner but rather makes recommendations. For instance, a frequent staff position found in many organizations is in the area of manpower development in sales and marketing. Many times the salesman, by going through the proper channels, can utilize staff men for assistance in their sales job.

In the same way, any source of help that the salesman can use in the field other than from his own parent organization may be looked upon as part of his organization designed to assist him in achieving his sales goal. Any individual who can help the salesman in any work he wants done with dealers, or distributor organization, development of accounts, getting leads, investigating a customer's financial position, or getting advice related to his sales program may be considered as part of a salesman's organization. For instance, Norge salesmen were instructed to build a solid organization of realtors who could assist them in discovering site locations and in the development of those sites. They were told, too, to be alert to individuals who could assist them in investigating local ordinances against, for instance, commercial establishments in various areas and construction problems. These salesmen were told to regard these men as part of the organization they were building in their territory.

Another dimension to building an organization is described by Vreeland in his excellent article, "Customers: A Neglected Sales Force."[13] Vreeland makes the point that a satisfied customer can be an important asset to the firm and to the salesman. He explains that customers are will-

[13] Richard C. Vreeland, "Customers: A Neglected Sales Force," *Small Marketeers Aids*, no. 83, pp. 1–2, September, 1962.

Planning and Managing Sales Effort

ing to be part of the salesman's auxiliary sales force for several reasons. First, they often want to justify their own purchases. And when they convince someone else to buy the same item, their judgment is reaffirmed.

Second, people like to share their discovery. Most customers like to pass on the benefits they have gained from trading at a certain store or from using a certain product.

Third, people enjoy a chance to help others. They feel that they are helping their friends when they tell them about their experiences—good and bad—they have had in shopping.

Fourth, some customers like to impress other people with their judgment. Passing along the results of their shrewd shopping gives these customers a chance to display their ability.

Fifth, almost everyone feels a need to boast now and then. Some people do it by bragging a little about the good buy they got.

MANAGEMENT PROGRAMMING—TERRITORY ANALYSIS

From the preceding discussion of planning and managing sales effort, it is clear that in this new world of selling one of the salesman's most profitable activities is to think and act in terms of the order of development of the territory assigned to him. It is his market. He must determine, identify, and manage the market opportunities existing therein. He must determine who are his customers and potential customers. Why? Where are they? When are they customers or potential customers? How can they be cultivated? A discussion of territory screening, account classification, sales call patterns, production requirements, production planning, budgeting sales expense, and time analysis will give the salesman *one possible way* to attack the problem. The statement "one possible way" is emphasized because it is recommended that the salesman understand the principles of management explained in the previous section of this chapter and develop his own ideas on how to best manage his territory.

Territory Screening

Territory screening gives the salesman an overall view of his market. In the process of territory screening, an alphabetical card listing of all accounts split between current and prospective is compiled by the salesman. For some salesmen it may take six months to a year to alphabetize their market, and further, it must be recognized that such a process is a continuous one. Business is in a constant state of flux. A business firm may substantially expand or curtail its operations, production, or sales in any one given year. Moreover, the number of business firms that fail each year and the number of new firms started each year run into the thousands.

It is recommended that the salesman use two sets of 4- by 6-inch or 3- by 5-inch file cards. One file is for prospective accounts and the other for present accounts. The salesman begins to compile a list of all his present accounts by examining his records, by memory, and by referring to company records. This last point is especially important, since every year

Selling: A Behavioral Science Approach

there is a significant turnover of salesmen in territories and between companies.

Prospective accounts can be compiled by observation and from the various directories that are available. Business associations and trade associations, as well as many trade publications, list business firms related to a particular line of business. But probably the best way of all is simply for the salesman to explore his own territory, ask questions, and make cold calls. For instance, Pratt & Whitney salesmen state that every manufacturing firm that drills or cuts metal is a potential prospect for Pratt & Whitney products and services. Blue Cross–Blue Shield salesmen state that each business having more than six employees is a first-rate prospect for Blue Cross–Blue Shield health care program. It may come as quite a shock to management and to the reader that less than 10 percent of a sample of more than 140 salesmen had inadequate records concerning present accounts and prospective accounts in their territories. It cannot be too strongly emphasized that through proper record keeping by the salesman and company, the sales and marketing effectiveness of the average salesman can be greatly increased.

Account Classification

Account classification involves assigning an A, B, C, or D rating to the accounts compiled through the process of territory screening. This rating is applied to both current and prospective accounts. The letter designation given to a particular account may be arrived at by the amount of business currently received or projected as available from an account.

Salesmen in different lines of endeavor will obviously expect business from prospective and potential accounts according to the prospect's or customer's needs for the salesman's product and services and the price of those products and services. A coffee route salesman will assign substantially less dollar volume of business to each account than will, for example, the stainless steel silverware manufacturer salesman selling direct to large department stores or gift shops. A class A account for some types of businesses may involve several hundred thousand dollars, whereas in others a class A account may involve $5,000 per year.

Sales-Call Pattern

With the completion of step two—account classification—the salesman has determined the value in sales revenue of each actual account and its potential, and the potential of each prospective account as well. He is now ready to establish a sales-call pattern. But before he can do this, he must determine how many effective calls he can make in each day. How many calls a day should the manufacturer's salesmen, the engineering salesmen, the wholesaler salesmen, the intangible salesmen, or the distributor salesmen average per day? If a salesman can make eight effective calls per day or forty effective calls per week, he will make 1,900 calls in a forty-eight-week year. Taking, as an example, the figure eight calls per day or forty calls per week, the salesman can develop the frequency of the sales-call

Planning and Managing Sales Effort

pattern. For instance, a distributor salesman may plan one call every four weeks or twelve calls per year on the most fertile accounts, and on the other extreme one call every eight weeks or six calls per year on the least fertile accounts.

Production Planning

Production planning is concerned with the systematic coverage of a salesman's territory to obtain maximum market penetration in each section of his territory.

Whether the salesman has a number of states, part of a state, or a city, his territory can be divided into sections on a geographical basis. Each section of each territory can be examined with respect to the number of A, B, C, and D accounts. A sales-call program can then be developed that will enable each salesman to lay out a specific four-week-call program by writing his eight customers a day into a production or spread sheet.

If possible, each section should be squared with accounts in such a way that each day each salesman can call on six active accounts and two prospective accounts. This arrangement is based on a call division formula of 75 percent of the time spent on active accounts and 25 percent of the time spent on potential accounts.

Budgeting Sales Expense

Budgeting sales expense means allocating expenditures in terms of account classification. Many companies give each salesman an expense budget that may be used for dinners, lunches, entertainment, golf fees, and meeting rooms. Again, the practice varies considerably among firms and the type of selling involved. Assume, however, that a salesman has an entertainment budget of $1,200 for the year. He may budget $100 per month and then allocate this sum according to customer potential. He may of course spend more on accounts that he wants to cultivate rather than invest his entertainment budget on the most profitable accounts. There is no set or best procedure.

The purpose of budgeting sales expense is to give the salesman the control he needs to invest his entertainment budget so that he best cultivates his market and judiciously allocates entertainment among the various customer classifications.

Time Analysis

Time analysis is a story of men versus time. If there is any one shortcoming salesmen have in general, it is in all probability, the matter of time and the lack of systematic attention to it. One of the purposes of the previous analysis is to enable the salesman to utilize his time to best advantage. But in addition, a company may assist its salesmen in other ways. For instance, a company may:

1. Enlist the cooperation of its customers by asking them how often they feel they should be called on by the company salesman.

Selling: A Behavioral Science Approach

2. Have each salesman capitalize on service calls to customers in his territory.

3. Make sure the salesman has a second possibility or alternate call scheduled for a particular time in the event that an appointment is canceled.

4. Simplify the paper work so that the salesman can work harder in meeting his daily call requirements.

COMPANY CONTROLS

Companies control their sales forces in many ways. Compensation programs, quotas, contests, training, supervision, and reports can all be regarded as control devices. But in this discussion the term *control* is restricted to management guidance. Some companies keep tight control over their sales force; others do not. More often than not, however, management does not provide the necessary management guidance for its sales force. Having a decentralized organization does not absolve management from its basic responsibility to provide each salesman with the knowledge, training, guidance, and assistance needed by him to realize the full potential of his time and ability. The ideal is a company which maintains enough control over the salesman's activity to assist each salesman individually when necessary, but not so much control that the creative efforts of the salesman are contained.

J. M. Wilson, formerly vice-president of sales, National Cash Register Company, a company that has been repeatedly recognized as one of the founders of the science of salesmanship, is preeminently qualified to speak on all phases of selling. The purpose of company control, he tells us, is to assist the salesman to do his job and to help him manage his time. He effectively illustrates what it means to the salesman in dollars and cents when time is wasted. He states, "We have attempted, through the use of activity records, to learn just what a salesman does for what he earns. We have learned that he spends about three hours per day in the presence of prospects. Just three hours per day when he is face-to-face with a man who can buy or recommend the purchase of our equipment."[14]

Wilson reasons that with twenty days per month (allowing for vacations, holidays, etc.) as a work month, a salesman spends sixty hours per month selling. The remainder of the month is "getting ready" time. Thus the salesman spends 720 hours per year in the presence of prospects. If the salesman earns $10,000 per year, Wilson tells us, each salesman's hour is worth $14 to him. If he takes an hour from the selling time for a haircut, it had better be a good haircut, for it would cost him $14 in addition to the price of the haircut. If he takes a half hour from his selling time for a cup of coffee before going into his territory, it is a $7 cup of coffee. This is the value of time to a salesman.

Wilson writes that in many lines of business where a real creative selling job must be done, the salesman who makes five good calls—not just

[14] John M. Wilson, *Open the Mind and Close the Sale: The Key to Success in Selling!* McGraw-Hill Book Company, New York, 1953.

Planning and Managing Sales Effort

to visit, but five calls where he can begin the development of a selling plan—has done a good creative day's work. Five calls a day will be 100 creative calls a month, or 1,200 calls in a year. This same salesman who earns $10,000 can place a value of about $8 per call on his efforts. If he can make his calls more effective or if he can make more calls by better planning, he will definitely increase his earnings. Wilson simply offers these analogies as proof that "time is a salesman's most valuable asset."[15]

Quantitative Records

To assist the salesman in his efforts to capitalize on his time, National Cash Register requires its salesmen to maintain certain quantitative records. It should be understood that many companies require records of this type, but again this process varies considerably among companies. National Cash Register Company salesmen maintain the following records:[16]

1. Daily plan card
2. Reports of calls made
3. Weekly summary
4. Monthly summary report and a prospect file

Daily plan card The daily plan card gives the National Cash Register salesmen an overall well-balanced plan for the day's sales activities. It identifies who the salesman is contacting and the purpose of the call (new call, re-call, survey, demonstration, etc.), and it should, Wilson states, give the approximate time the salesman plans to make the call.

Report of call Each salesman is required to complete a report of call for each prospect contacted. This report of call tells management how many prospects have been contacted by the salesman, whether or not there was a tendency to work certain businesses and exclude others, and it tells how much of the selling plan was covered.

Summary of selling activity Each week each salesman recaps his daily activity. It tells branch management what has been done in the past week. National Cash Register finds the report useful for it ". . . is a true indication of what can be expected from the territory in the weeks to come, and it gives management this information in time to take corrective action."

Monthly report This report is compiled by the branch manager. It is a recap of each salesman's weekly summary report, which in turn is forwarded to the divisional offices. This report ". . . eliminates a great deal of the detail found in weekly summary report (which is of interest to the branch manager) and shows only the fundamental activity and sales record of each salesman in the branch." Thus the total monthly activity of each salesman is quickly determined by the divisional offices. And with this information ". . . each supervisor knows exactly where each salesman is weak and plans his work with a particular salesman accordingly. Notice that each report is built from the preceding. The supervisor or instructor can take any salesman's monthly activity and trace it right back to the original records—the daily plan cards."

[15] *Ibid.*, p. 224.
[16] *Ibid.*, p. 226–230.

Prospect file Wilson presents a candid and an effective case why the salesman should maintain adequate prospect files. A salesman's prospect file is in effect a statement of condition in his territory. In every selling field that requires good, creative selling, a salesman justifies his territory operation not only by the number of sales but also by the number of prospects he has in the various stages of his selling plan. Hundreds of hours of selling time have gone into the development of these prospects. Surveys may have been made or propositions may have been submitted in some instances, while other prospects may have been in the office for demonstrations, but the sale has not been closed for one reason or another. It has taken considerable time, effort, and money to develop each of these prospects to a certain point. Why shouldn't this valuable information be recorded somewhere? If there is a change of salesman in a territory, why should the new salesman start from scratch? Shouldn't he learn what has gone on before with each prospect and start his selling effort from that point? Each salesman owes it to himself, to his supervisor, and to his company to record each step of his selling where it is available for all to see. The proper place for this information is in a prospect file.

Any salesman of experience, as he looks back on his career in selling, can recall an infinite number of situations where recorded information regarding the total sales situation would have been helpful to him. Thus, perhaps as a rule of the thumb, it may be stated that every salesman should maintain his records in such a way that another salesman could enter his territory tomorrow and, with a few hours spent pouring over records, have a good view of the condition of the territory he has inherited.

Qualitative Records

A certain company, a medium-size manufacturer of chemicals, has a unique purpose for its record keeping. It selects capable men mainly on the basis of intelligence and the "want to do" their job, and then it begins a process of continuous training. To assist the salesman in doing his job, the company compiles the usual statistical information on each salesman's calls and his productivity in his territory. But more than this, each salesman, for one specific week out of each month, is required to furnish a qualitative evaluation of each call he makes in that week.[17] The company wants to keep its salesmen free of what it refers to as "torturous reports" and give him as much time as possible for face-to-face contact with prospects. To accomplish this, the company provides each salesman with a battery-operated recorder, so that the salesman can dictate an evaluation of each call immediately after each call. These records are sent to the main office, typed, and a copy is sent to the district sales manager and one to the salesman. In giving his oral report, the salesman follows a uniform report form. He is asked to reply briefly to these questions:

---

[17] The company's sales force is divided into four groups. Thus during the course of each month the entire sales force submits qualitative reports. In this way the home office can handle the work load and, at the same time, three or four salesmen can be serviced by one piece of recording equipment in the field.

Planning and Managing Sales Effort

1. What is the potential of this account? *a.* ——— *b.* ——— *c.* ———
d. ———
2. What was the specific purpose of this call?
3. Whom did you talk to? For how long? About what?
4. Did you discuss any particular problem or situation of the prospect? If so, what specifically?
5. Considering the purpose of your call, what did you accomplish?
6. Have you any suggestions at this time regarding your next call?

Such reports can be of considerable importance to the district manager and to the salesman. Since the district manager or supervisor's job is to assist the salesman to perform his sales functions, he must have a continuous record in order to evaluate effectively the salesman's work and then develop a plan to assist the salesman if necessary. Reports, for instance, may show that Jim Budding is making most of his calls on the most profitable accounts and not devoting any time to cold calls or customers in the D classifications. It may show that Budding never requests the opportunity to make a survey, or perhaps he doesn't make a second call on the same prospect. Another report may show that Frank Lodge is apparently avoiding discussing a customer's or prospect's problems.

These qualitative reports were especially effective in that they were designed to reinforce in the mind of each salesman the type of sales effort that was expected of him on each call.

Summary

In the last decade the salesman has emerged as a market manager of a territory. Thus he is to manage his time, his sales effort, his markets, and his customers. He, like management in general, needs to understand the theory of and to employ management principles; that is, he must plan, forecast, establish procedures, establish a program, fix a schedule, and build an organization in his territory.

Planning is a process of thinking through what is to be done. It is largely mental and has no time commitment. Goals or objectives are established in the planning stage.

Forecasting is concerned with market potential. It is the process of looking ahead to determine the market potential of a territory in a specified future period of time. It involves getting the facts concerning the most profitable areas for market development or the order of development of accounts according to their potential.

A program is a sequence of activities structured to implement policies and accomplish objectives or goals. Procedures tell specifically how the sequence of activities is to be done.

Scheduling is a process of establishing a specific time sequence for the work to be done. It is hard time in contrast to planning which involves rubber time.

Organization at the territorial level means making provisions for ways in which segments of the parent organization, other business firms, other individuals, and customers themselves can assist in making the salesman's territory an effective market unit of the parent company.

In territory analysis the salesman puts into operation the principles or theory of management. One possible way to do this is for the salesman to classify his accounts, develop a sales-call pattern, develop a production plan, budget his sales expense, and thoroughly analyze how he is utilizing his time.

Although the salesman is a market manager of his territory, the parent company maintains control in varying degrees. Controls are maintained in the broader sense by all activities of sales management. But in addition, specific controls are maintained by many companies by requiring both quantitative and qualitative reports.

Chapter 3   CASE AND QUESTIONS

MARKETING AND IN-PLANT TELEVISION SYSTEM

Your company has just produced a new product—a television monitoring system. At the simplest level, a television screen is placed in the lobby of a plant and connected to, for example, a purchasing agent's office. Thus it can be used by, say, the purchasing agent to screen salesmen and others in the lobby. On its most elaborate level, it could be a television system connecting all departments within the plant.

Your company has held a series of technical product meetings in its plant. You have attended these. You know all about the technical application of the product. Your company has equipped you with a complete sales portfolio.

Your company reminds you that you are the market manager of your territory, and it expects you to cultivate and develop your territory with respect to this new product. The company does not want you to get involved in advertising and other promotional efforts. These are being done by the company on a national scale. Initially you are to market the product only on the basis of its use as a screening device such as the purchasing-agent-to-salesman situation.

QUESTIONS ABOUT CASE

From the perspective of being a market manager of your territory:

1 What are the first five things that you would do in order to establish a market plan? Identify them in order of importance.
2 What is the relationship between the market plan you organized for question 1 and the principles of management discussed in this chapter?
3 Discuss your plan in terms of the four general management concepts: (a) planning, (b) organization, (c) execution, and (d) evaluation.

changing
patterns of
perception

4

INTRODUCTION

In Chapter 3 the salesman's role was seen as twofold, embodying (1) the act of communication and (2) the concept of understanding selling in its broader dimensions. The communication segment of the salesman's role refers to the two to three hours per day in which he is in face-to-face contact with the prospect, customer, or individuals involved in the sales situation. Selling in its broader dimension refers to the other five or six hours in the salesman's day. It involves all those support functions which enable the salesman to make the best use of his time and sales effort.

The purpose of this chapter and following chapters about the be havioral sciences is to discuss a number of concepts, ideas, laws, and principles from such disciplines as psychology, sociology, anthropology, and education in terms of their relationship to the communication or person-to-person segment of the salesman's day.

Frequently it is difficult to identify specifically a particular concept, idea, or principle as stemming solely from one discipline. Today there are many branches of each discipline. Moreover, each branch contributes to the main discipline's stream of knowledge. For instance, educational psychologist Blair states, "Since the turn of the century, educational psychology has probably contributed as much to general psychology as it has had occasion to borrow."[1]

In addition to this, leading interdisciplinary marketing exponents Kelley and Lazer project a word of caution:

Psychologists, sociologists, anthropologists, and other social and behavioral sciences are not necessarily any more unified in the concepts they hold in their disciplines than are marketers. Complete agreement does not exist among these scientists as to the most promising lines of development for particular aspects of their subject matter areas . . . as a result, the attempt to integrate numerous and often conflicting explanations of behavioral sci-

[1] Glen M. Blair, R. Stewart Jones, and Ray H. Simpson, *Educational Psychology*, The Macmillan Company, New York, 1962, p. 4.

Selling: A Behavioral Science Approach

entists into a practicable solution can become a highly perplexing experience.[2]

This word of caution is especially meaningful to sales practitioners. Sales situations deal, by and large, with the interaction of two individuals. Therefore the area of most promising help from the behavioral sciences is limited to those sections of the sciences dealing with the individual in contrast to the group or society. And in the behavioral sciences, especially in psychology, it is in the analysis of the individual where several schools having what is sometimes conflicting theory exist. This is understandable.

In the field of marketing, for instance, it is relatively easy to use the term *social classes* or *income groups* in forecasting sales for a firm enjoying national distribution. It is relatively easy to state that since the state of California has 9.3 percent of the United States total population, 11.3 percent of the United States total disposable income, and 10.9 percent of retail sales, the firm selling certain types of consumer goods should obtain approximately 10 percent of its sales in California.[3] But it is more difficult to say which ten individuals out of one hundred will buy the firm's product. This difficulty is compounded if an attempt is made to state why or what motivated the individual to buy the particular product. In fact, if a Freudian, Pavlovian, and a social psychologist were asked to state, from a motivational concept, why a woman might purchase yellow sheets, three related but different viewpoints may be given. The first may think in terms of sex motivation; the second, in terms of learning experience or feelings; and the social psychologist, in terms of status needs.

It is apparent that the study of the individual holds great promise of giving the salesman a rationale for the many problems he faces in his person-to-person communication. On the other hand, owing to the very complexity of the individual and the several schools of thought which exist, the study of the individual poses many problems. Nevertheless, once the underbrush is cleared away through selective analysis, the differences in the various approaches to studying the individual are all manageable and the behavioral sciences will offer much to selling. Moreover, the field of selling provides a profitable field of research for the behavioral scientists and selling will, like educational psychology, contribute as much to the behavioral sciences as it will have occasion to borrow.

PERCEPTION

Perception is a complex subject. Krech and Crutchfield speak of "the many worlds of different perceivers." They write:

Our worlds are . . . to a considerable degree, one world, and this makes human communication possible. Were we not to believe that another person's world is basically similar to our own, we would not feel that we could communicate with him. We live in Hotel Universe, each of us permanently locked in his own private room, tapping out messages on walls to neigh-

[2] Eugene J. Kelley and William Lazer, *Managerial Marketing: Perspectives and Viewpoints*, Richard D. Irwin, Inc., Homewood, Ill., 1958, p. 597.

[3] "Survey of Buying Power," *Sales Management*, New York, 1965.

Changing Patterns of Perception

boring rooms in the belief that though we can never really visit the other rooms, they are furnished very much like our own. Yet, to extend the metaphor, we come to realize that the rooms are not precisely alike. The rooms of the blind are dark; those of the deaf are silent; and that occupied by a neighbor, who belongs to the "other" political party, or church, or nationality, is equipped with viewing or hearing devices that somehow permit him to see or hear things that we have never seen or heard.[4]

These eminent psychologists are saying that our worlds are very much alike, but *there are differences* which are often difficult to comprehend.

Salesmen are not concerned with the extremes in the world of other people, such as the schizophrenic, or the dark world of the blind, or the world of the habitual drunkard, or the world of the mentally retarded. He is concerned with different worlds and with the behavior characteristics that might identify the other individual's world. In brief, the salesman must indeed be involved with understanding the rationale for the differences among the many worlds of his different perceivers—his prospects and customers. And this interest will give him insights into the world he perceives. And if anyone needs these insights, the salesman does. There is an old truism in selling which states that "the salesman must perceive and adjust—not the other person. He doesn't have to."

People become aware or conscious of objects or other data through their sense of vision, hearing, smell, taste, and touch. These sense organs respond or react to energy changes, or stimuli in the external environment. And although each individual has the same sense organs, each may respond differently to the same stimuli. Why? The answer is simple. Each individual has a different world. Each individual has a unique makeup. Age, maturity, intelligence, color, religion, experiences, cultural background, abilities, values, motives, traits, and, in short, all factors of life interact to cause each person to perceive any given stimulus or situation as he does. Speaking more broadly, an individual's needs, wants, desires, and drives, his knowledge and his emotional state all affect his perceptual sensitivity to objects, acts, or situations and his *interpretation* of these stimuli.

It is now clear why books have been written about perception. It is clear, too, why the salesman is concerned with perception, for it is in this vortex of human life in which the salesman works. Every skilled salesman knows that the words *profit, margin, economy, leadership, effectiveness, volume, guarantee,* or a thousand other words all mean, at least to some degree, something different to each customer. This is true of all situations. To illustrate, quickly interpret the statement, "He drew a gun." From where do you think he drew the gun? Certainly, various individuals would make different statements or have different thoughts on the matter. There may be such answers as from a hip holster, from an inside holster, from his coat pocket, from a back pocket, or even from the end of a cane. The point is that watchers of westerns would perhaps answer differently from a detective. Also, would not some individuals consciously or unconsciously

⁴ David Krech and Richard S. Crutchfield, *Elements of Psychology*, Alfred A. Knopf, Inc., New York, 1961, p. 35.

reflect for a moment on the type of gun or its caliber? Or, if the perceiver were an artist, may he not think in terms of drawing or sketching a picture of a gun? In brief, individuals would perceive the situation "he drew a gun" differently, just as words are perceived differently in the world of business.

This example also illustrates that ranges in perceptional differences, while at times great, frequently fall into manageable dimensions.

How sharply the salesman can, as an instrument of understanding and communication, calibrate these qualitative differences in perception is a true index of a salesman's ability to sell in depth. This book is, at least in a number of chapters, dedicated to presenting ideas, concepts, principles, and relationship so that the salesman will better understand what he is measuring, why he is measuring or identifying, how he is measuring, and finally, how he can quantify the relationships of various factors dealing with the individual.

Perception and Set

As a rule-of-thumb definition, perception refers to the act of perceiving or awareness, whereas set affects *what* will be perceived and *how* it will be perceived. Set is, in general, the readiness of the individual to make a particular response.

There are many determinants of set. An individual's prior experiences, his needs, his values, his emotions, and his attitude all interact to effect his readiness to act or think in a given way. Thus each individual brings to any given situation various readinesses and expectations that substantially affect his interpretation of and his reaction to stimuli, or as Krech and Crutchfield comment, "The perceiver's state as he encounters any given stimulus-pattern is never completely 'neutral.' In a word, he is set to perceive something more or less specific."[5]

This statement applies equally well to the three most commonly accepted forms of set: motor set, mental set, and perceptual set. In all three forms the key word is *predisposed,* that is, ready to react in a specific way upon perceiving certain stimuli. Motor set is the readiness of the individual's muscles to respond to stimuli, like the baseball player running at the crack of the bat. A mental set is an individual's readiness for a particular thought process. And perceptual set is the readiness of an individual for a particular organization of stimuli; for instance, after hearing the word *salt,* many people are ready to hear the word *pepper.*

Normally salesmen are not too concerned with motor set. It matters little to the salesman that the prospect may accompany his statement "I don't know" with head scratching or rubbing his hand around his chin and assuming a thoughtful pose. He may, however, be concerned with individuals who habitually turn away and look out windows or exhibit some other motor set or habit while the salesman is talking. Methods by which the salesman may effect these sets are discussed under the section Determinants of Attention.

[5] *Ibid.,* p. 96.

Changing Patterns of Perception

In contrast to motor sets all salesmen are concerned with the customer's or prospect's mental and perceptual set. For all practical purposes mental and perceptual set may be discussed simply as set.

At first glance it may be thought that a salesman need not be concerned with an individual's set, but this isn't the case. It is true that a salesman is not expected to change the *basic* experiences, values, or emotions of an individual. These are given. He operates within the given framework. But what is important is that a skilled salesman be able to effect whether or not a particular set will be brought into play at a given moment. Don't forget that set refers to the readiness of the individual to respond in a certain way.

It is a commonly accepted psychological principle that set may be produced by immediately preceding experiences, by long-established practices or the very frequency with which the stimulus pattern has previously been perceived. For instance, the more familiar a word the greater will be the individual's set toward its perception.

Each man perceives his own name or the name of his wife, the ornithologist the facts of bird life, and the geologist the facts of rock formations.

This simple rule tells the salesman to communicate in language that the other individual understands. In the case of a detail salesman communicating with a doctor, he should talk in the medical terms that the doctor expects. In the case of the sales engineer selling to highly competent technicians, he should discuss his product and proposal in the technician's language, that is, in terms the prospect expects or is set to hear. But in general there is a tendency among salesmen to be too technical and use terms that the other individual does not fully comprehend. In any event, from the principle that "the more familiar a word, the greater will be the individual's set towards its perception," a rule pertaining to selling can be established: "Whenever a salesman describes his proposal or product in terms that the other individual is not ready or set to hear, the salesman may arouse the emotions of frustration." Don't forget that the case is rare where the other individual will stop the salesman and indicate that he does not understand. He will frequently permit the salesman to continue talking, but the main result is negative communication.

In the same way, thinking is often guided by set. As Morgan states, "Practice in solving problems one way tends to set us to solve a new problem in the same way providing the new problem situation contains stimuli similar to those in the practiced problems."[6] In brief, the individual develops a habit or set in responding to certain stimuli in a specific way. These sets bias the thinker at the start of a problem. They start him on a certain track. Depending on the set established, it may be a help or it may be a block in the problem-solving process.

These concepts of set explain in part why some individuals or prospects react as they do to salesmen. Over the years prospects or customers have developed a set toward salesmen. The appearance of a salesman initiates a problem. Too many salesmen have used canned sales talks. Too many salesmen have been self-oriented and not customer-

[6] Clifford T. Morgan, *Introduction to Psychology*, McGraw-Hill Book Company, 1956, p. 150.

Selling: A Behavioral Science Approach

oriented. Too many salesmen have used tired, worn phrases, such as, "I'll only take a few minutes of your time," "You can tell me to leave any time you wish," "I'm not trying to make a sale," "There will be no sale today," or "I just want your advice or opinion," etc. Thus the prospect has a specific set toward a certain problem—the salesman. Enter salesman A, Mr. Average. He uses the canned sales talk, he uses a salesman-oriented sales "pitch" and he, of course, strikes out. It wasn't meaningful.

Enter salesman B, Mr. Selling in Depth. He has planned his sales program. He is a problem solver. He understands the prospect's situation. He determines his needs and the prospect becomes receptive. He develops a favorable set. Why did this take place? Why the change? Research shows that, depending on the relative strength of the original set in comparison to the induced set, a set aroused at the moment can overcome a set derived from frequency of prior experience.

Why this happens and how the salesman can redirect the prospect's or customer's set is explained by psychologists in terms of structure of stimulus pattern, compromise, and redirection of set.

Stimulus-Response

Of all the concepts, principles, ideas, or terms associated with the behavioral sciences, stimulus and response apparently are utilized most in other disciplines. They are used to explain theory in advertising, drama, art, spoken communication, written communication, and many others, as well as in sales literature. The concept of stimulus response is easily understood and readily applied to practical situations in these fields.

A stimulus, as defined by Boring[7] is ". . . any change in external energy that gives rise to such an excitation of the nervous system as to arouse a response. A stimulus cannot exist without a response because it is defined as producing a response . . . in this sense a conscious event must be regarded as a response." Morgan[8] defines it similarly, but he emphasizes that a stimulus is ". . . any energy or energy change in the physical environment that excites a sense organ."

To the salesman, both definitions mean that in face-to-face contact with an individual, a stimulus is any factor such as tone of voice, a word, phrase, movement, visual, or the appearance of the salesman that produces an effect on the senses of sight, hearing, smell, taste, and touch.

A response is the end result of a stimulus. However, when the stimulus is complex or has special meaning to the receiver, it is often called a situation. And when the responses to the stimuli are complex, psychologist Boring suggests that it is ". . . better to call them behavior."[9] Nevertheless, behavior has the same relation to a situation that a response has to a stimulus.

[7] Edwin G. Boring, Herbert S. Langfeld, and Harry P. Weld, *Foundations of Psychology*, John Wiley & Sons, Inc., New York, 1948, p. 16.

[8] Morgan, *op. cit.*, p. 644.

[9] Boring, Langfeld, and Weld, *op. cit.*, p. 60.

Changing Patterns of Perception

Salesman are interested in both the simple stimulus-response patterns, those responses to stimuli that occur with little or no hesitation, and the more complex stimuli situation which involves more sophisticated levels of behavior.

A simple stimulus-response pattern is illustrated by the housewife shopping in the local supermarket who travels up and down the aisles selecting items with relatively little reflection or hesitation. This, of course, is not true of all housewives. Some come to the supermarket equipped with detailed purchase notes, and some consider objectively the relative value of each purchase. Thus what may be a simple stimulus-response pattern in the case of one individual may be something considerably more complex to another.

Although responses to the same stimuli vary among individuals, the typical route salesman (for example, selling coffee and related items to an established customer) is involved in relatively simple stimulus-response situations.

He regularly calls on the restaurant, hospital, or other institutional user and checks the number of coffee bags in stock, makes out an order for the number of bags needed to bring the stock to the required level, and submits the order to the appropriate person for signature. This salesman, of course, still should be personable, cheerful, exact, efficient, on time, and always cooperative in handling customer complaints, but he is involved in relatively simple stimulus-response patterns.

A number of companies involved in route selling, comparable to the above situation, recognize the difference between tending to the established customer and developing new accounts. These companies employ district sales managers who, in addition to managing the route sales force, have the responsibility of opening up new accounts. Since a new account, say, a large hospital, may generate up to $20,000 in coffee orders each year, a relatively more complex sales situation exists, that is, a more complex decision-making process is required of the purchaser.

This last example sets the stage for today's salesmen. They are, by and large, concerned with behavior patterns associated with the problem-solving, decision-making process—a hesitation-choice pattern of behavior. Therefore, as the stimulus-object,[10] the salesman develops a sales strategy knowing that in most sales situations a period of hesitation precedes choice.

Structure of Stimulus Pattern, Compromise, and Redirection of Set

Having in mind that a sales message may be viewed as having a stimulus pattern or a series of stimulus patterns, it is readily discerned that a stimulus pattern also involves a dimension of strength of structure. A

---

[10] "A stimulus-object, like colored paper that we see or a sweet substance that is tasted, is often called a stimulus, but it is more correct to call it a stimulus-object, since it determines a change of energy but is not the change . . . when the pistol shot makes you jump, the pistol is a stimulus-object, the sound in the air is the stimulus . . ." (*Ibid.*, p. 16.)

strongly structured sales message or stimulus pattern has intensity, clarity, simplicity, meaningfulness, and is subject to strong grouping factors. A weakly structured sales message or stimulus pattern is found when the stimuli are at threshold level or barely perceptible, unclear, complex, irrelevant, and are not subject to strong grouping components.[11]

Thus, as a general rule, a salesman employing a weakly structured stimulus pattern will have less positive effect on the individual's set than will the salesman employing stimulus patterns developed around the dimension involving strength of structure. Looking at it from a reverse position, an established set will have a greater effect on a weak stimulus-pattern structure than it will have on the strong stimulus-pattern structure. To the salesman this discussion indicates the prospect or customer will be more readily effected when the salesman uses a strongly structured stimulus pattern. This change may be effected by a compromise or by a redirection of set.

When a prospect or customer is confronted with a strong stimulus pattern, a compromise may resolve the conflict between the prospect's set and the salesman's strongly structured sales message or a redirection of set may result. These two concepts—compromise and redirection—are clearly illustrated in the experiment by psychologists Bruner and Postman.[12]

In their experiment these psychologists exposed playing cards to participants and then asked them to name the card. Some of the playing cards were regular cards, others had been specifically manufactured with reverse colors of the various symbols. For example, a black four of hearts and a red four of spades and a black six of hearts and a red six of spades. When briefly exposed, the participants identified the cards according to their expectations or set. The red four of spades was identified as the red four of hearts, and the black six of hearts as the black six of spades. In longer exposures *compromise* resolved the conflict. The red six of hearts was identified as a purplish six of spades. This illustrates a compromise between the expected color (black) and the actual stimuli (red). As would be expected, however, some participants immediately recognized the irregularities of some cards and eventually everyone in this experiment was able to do so after exposure time was lengthened or repeated or both. At the same time, with recognition of the irregularity in the cards the abnormal features of the cards became accentuated. The individual was not "set" to see the irregular cards. This concentration on the irregular cards had in turn the effect of *redirecting* the prior set of the participants.

Referring to this experiment, Krech and Crutchfield say, "When a strongly structured stimulus-pattern is markedly dissonant with the prevailing set, the effect may be an accentuation of the discrepant aspect of the stimulus-pattern. The person becomes clearly aware of the discrepancy and pays special attention to it."[13]

---

[11] Krech and Crutchfield, *op. cit.*, p. 100.

[12] J. S. Bruner and L. J. Postman, "On the Perception of Incongruity: A Paradigm," *J. Personnel*, vol. 18, pp. 206–223, 1949.

[13] Krech and Crutchfield, *op. cit.*, p. 102.

Changing Patterns of Perception

"As a consequence," these psychologists say, "there is often a rejection of a prior set. The expectation involved in the set is so sharply challenged by 'the hard facts' of stimulus reality that the set now proves powerless to bring about the 'required' organization, but in its turn is forced by the stimulus 'facts' to take a new direction."[14]

Now for the major task of showing how compromise can take place in a sales situation and of showing how the salesman can redirect the prospect's set. This will be accomplished in three stages. First, a simplified explanation and an illustration of expectancy will be given. This will be followed by a sales situation in which the potential buyer has a normal set. Then a more complex sales situation, one in which the potential buyer has an emotionally charged set will be analyzed.

To repeat, expectancy is the expectation of the individual that there is something else coming or something else is to happen in a given situation or that something is expected of him. Expectancy is one of the forces which enables a set *aroused* at the moment to overcome a *prior* set. Morgan states, "Of the various factors that determine attention and thus perception, expectancy is probably the most important. . . ."[15] This is simply illustrated by a geologist and an ornithologist walking through the woods. The geologist will observe the type of rocks, rock structure, features of the terrain, etc., while the ornithologist will observe the type, number, and variety of birds. If you were to ask the geologist about the birds he saw, he would not be very specific, and of course if you were to ask the ornithologist about the rock strata, he would be apt to reply that he did not notice any particular rock formations. Both the ornithologist and geologist have firm habits or sets concerning what they will perceive as they walk through the woods. But as was stated above, a set that is aroused at the moment can overcome a set derived from frequency of prior experiences. And a set can be aroused at the moment by the use of *instructions*. If, prior to the walk in the woods, the ornithologist was instructed to observe rock formations and the geologist, bird life, and the instructions were heeded, both would have changed sets. Thus the set aroused by instructions reflects the expectation of what will come next. Through instruction the individual becomes set to perceive birds or rocks or vice versa.

In the same way, salesmen can redirect a set of the prospect or customer by using the concept of expectancy. How can he do this? By interrogating the prospect or customer in such a way that the individual more readily will see a viewpoint because he realizes the salesman in a sense expects analysis of a specific point. This is highly comparable to giving instructions. The following situation illustrates this. You are the salesman.

You are selling carrier (trucking) service to a manufacturer of frozen orange juice, who habitually ships by train to central markets. He believes the best policy for his company is to ship in carload lots to central markets and store in these markets until the juice is needed. You, being a

---

[14] *Ibid.,* p. 102.
[15] Morgan, *op. cit.,* p. 165.

salesman for an interstate trucking company, firmly believe in the great value of rapid point-to-point delivery and the merchandising flexibility that such a service offers, plus the fact that trucking can offer a hedge against the risk of price reduction should another firm dump its orange juice in a specific market where one manufacturer has a large quantity of juice stored.

During your sales interview with the manufacturer, your discussion brings about an analysis of the company's marketing philosophy. For instance, is it good to have a large supply of juice in a central market when the company stands the risk of a price decline should that locality become a dumping spot for other producers? Would it be better to retain the major supply of juice in outlying lower-cost storage facilities rather than in higher-cost central market facilities and use rapid point-to-point trucking services to move juice to market areas as needed? Is the company concerned with shifting population, storage facilities in the central market, terminal facilities, congestion of truck traffic, or the month-by-month changes in availability of storage facilities? These are just a few of the marketing problems that might be important to the producer of frozen orange juice.

In the case mentioned, the salesman has utilized the psychologists' concept of expectation to temper the manufacturer's set toward habitual systems of marketing. He has induced, through questioning, a momentary set which could overcome the set derived from frequency of prior experiences. The new set caused the prospect to expect a broader, deeper, a more penetrating analysis of his prior marketing situation. Thus the salesman made use of the psychologists' concept of expectation to open the manufacturer's mind to a discussion of the service the salesman was selling.

In this situation the prospect's set was acquired from experience. This manufacturer was not emotionally involved in the change. Frequently, however, salesmen have the problem of changing the set of an individual who is emotionally involved in a situation. Again you are asked to take the role of salesman.

Assume you sell freight shipping by truck. Your prospect is the manufacturer. He is the president of his company. The company owns a fleet of trucks. His business is seasonal in nature; thus seldom does the company utilize the fleet to capacity. Also, in extremely heavy shipping periods he must ship by public carriers. He is an ego-oriented individual and professes to be a great believer in rugged individualism.

In twenty years he has built his company from a small two-man shop in 1945 to a large successful manufacturing firm in 1965. His fleet of trucks are always well maintained and frequently receive a new coat of golden paint. He is proud of his fleet of trucks. They serve as a constant reminder of his business enterprise. Frequently he points out his trucks to friends when the occasion arises either on the highway or in the city. Your job as the salesman is to convince this manufacturer to eliminate his fleet of trucks and depend solely on your company's shipping service. You have accumulated a mass of data showing that this would be a feasible move, and the weight of the evidence definitely suggests that it would be a logical move for the company.

It can be safely assumed that this manufacturer has maximum rigidity in the set—retaining his fleet of trucks. His pride, his prestige, his feeling of importance, etc., are reflected in the truck image. The importance of these trucks dominate his thinking. Thus if at the outset of a sales call you suggest eliminating the company's fleet of trucks, you will have established maximal dissonance of set and, in a word, emotional conflict.

Conversely, if a salesman representing a truck painting service were making a call to inform this man of his company's painting service, there would be a consonance of set and structure. The set of the individual would favor the stimulus pattern of painting the trucks. He is ego-involved with them, and therefore the salesman's message is well received. It fits into the readiness of the executive to perceive. No major emotional adjustments are required.

Returning to the more difficult situation of "retiring" the manufacturer's fleet, what shall be done?

You, as the salesman, must have a strongly structured facts, sales message, or stimulus pattern. But you must first establish empathy and mutual compatibility. You must expect to make several calls in order to accomplish your mission. You must be alert to the role of compromise. You must be prepared to accept compromise and offer compromise. Suggest the gradual readjustment of the prospect's situation, say, so many trucks replaced now, so many next year, etc. Finally you must be prepared to offer a substitute to replace the lost status symbols, power, management controls, etc., with which the prospect is involved. You may offer the substitute in the course of your discussion with the prospect. You may indirectly and subtly get across the concept that "the forward thinking, intelligent executive is ever flexible and always ready to make change if that change will benefit the company." You must build up the prospect's ego at the same time you destroy the object of his status needs.

Summary

The behavioral science chapters are devoted to discussing numerous concepts, ideas, laws, and principles from such disciplines as psychology, sociology, anthropology, and education in terms of their relationship in the communication or person-to-person segment of the salesman's day. Nevertheless, many of these concepts relate to the problem-solving, planning, and managing part of the salesman's day as well.

Behavioral scientists are not unified in their definitions or employment of specific concepts, ideas, or principles from their disciplines. This is especially true of psychology. This is understandable. Psychology deals with the individual. And like marketing it is relatively easy to employ concepts or ideas when speaking of aggregates, but employing these con-

Selling: A Behavioral Science Approach

cepts in microanalysis is considerably more difficult. Assume a company has determined that 10 percent of its market potential exists in California. If the index is properly correlated with the company's product, the company will be fairly accurate in its prediction. But it will be more difficult for the company to determine which ten Californians out of a hundred will buy its product and increasingly more difficult to determine why those ten individuals purchased the product.

Perception, set, the structure of stimulus pattern, compromise, redirection of set, stimulus and response, the motivational cycle, needs, identifying motives, needs or wants, and maturity are all interrelated concepts.

Perception deals with the awarenes of the perceiving process. Set is concerned with the readiness of an individual to make a specific response to the perceived stimulus. The salesman must understand that individuals may perceive the same product, problem, or situation differently. How they perceive it, at least to some degree, is conditioned by the individual's entire life cycle.

At times the salesman may be required to change an individual's set. After thoroughly comprehending the individual's understanding of the problem or situation, the salesman may, through the structure of the stimulus pattern, reach a compromise, or he may redirect the set of the individual. In general, a salesman employing a weakly structured stimulus pattern will have less positive effect on the individual's set than will the salesman employing stimulus patterns with the dimension of strength of structure.

Expectancy, or what the individual expects to occur, is a strong determinant of set. The salesman may, through the judicious use of statements and questions, capitalize on the concept of expectancy to change or adjust an individual's set concerning a specific problem or situation. It's possible for the salesman to redirect set even when the individual is emotionally involved with that set.

The concepts of stimulus and response are two of the most widely used terms in other disciplines. They are frequently used in advertising, drama, art, spoken communication, written communication, as well as in sales literature. A stimulus is any verbal or nonverbal act that is perceived by the prospect. What the prospect perceives determines his response. The salesman judiciously employs certain stimuli to produce desired responses.

Chapter 4 DISCUSSION QUESTIONS

1 Discuss the statement, "The area of the most promising help from the behavioral sciences is limited to those sections of the sciences dealing with the individual in contrast to those behavioral sciences dealing with the group or society in general." Do you agree with this statement? Why?

Changing Patterns of Perception

Why not? Would the statement have the same validity if this were an advertising or marketing book?

2   A salesman has just attended a two-week seminar in which his company has educated the salesman concerning the technological advances both in his product and in its application to a potential customer's use of that product. The salesman, in turn, is required to educate his potential users. Do you see the relationship between the concept of perception and the salesman's role as an educator?

3   Why may a prospect or customer have a negative set regarding salesmen, a particular product, or company? Could the set be positive? Why?

4   Does the concept of set have any implications for a salesman concerning how he words his sales message?

5   Does the analogy as discussed in this chapter of the geologist and the ornithologist and how their sets were changed by a mere question have a useful implication in selling?

6   Is it possible for a salesman to redirect a prospect's or customer's negative set? How? Select some situation from your everyday life in which a friend of yours exhibited a negative set and explain how you may have redirected that set. Do the same thing for a product.

7   Would a discussion of a customer's problem and the feeding of new information into the customer's thought process have any implications as to how a salesman can change a prospect's or customer's set?

8   Describe any case from your experience of a businessman who had an emotional set concerning a product, salesman, or company, and explain why that individual may have that set and how he may have obtained it.

needs and the
motivational
cycle

5

Motivation is ". . . behavior that is instigated by needs within the individual and is directed toward goals that can satisfy these needs."[1] This definition establishes the broad framework for the seven major dimensions of motivation as illustrated in Figure 2.

1. *Need:* A lack of something, a deficit condition, a disequilibrium. (In general, the terms *needs, wants, desires,* and *motives* may be used interchangeably.)

2. *Unconscious tension buildup:* An unconscious or conscious physical tension buildup as the result of a need.

3. *Force:* The drive or impetus provided by a felt need or motive.

4. *Behavior activities:* The actions, both mental and physical, that are brought into play in the process of satisfying a need or motive.

5. *Goal:* The object or incentive at which behavior activities are directed.

6. *Satisfaction:* The attainment of a goal.

7. *Tension reduction:* The equilibrium attained when a need or motive is satisfied.

Psychologists are not in complete unanimity on how the motivational cycle operates. There are various viewpoints with respect to how tension buildup functions and the use of the term *deficit conditions* as applied to needs, motives, and desires. It is generally agreed, however, that the concepts of need, behavior activity, goal, and satisfaction are closely interrelated and that the motivational cycle begins with a felt need, want, desire, or motive. This in turn causes an unconscious or conscious physical tension buildup. The need is goal-directed and now has a drive, force, or impetus associated with it. This brings into play certain behavior activities designed to reach a specific goal and satisfaction in the need. Upon attaining the goal, satisfaction results and it is accompanied by a tension reduction.

A few illustrations will indicate how the motivational cycle operates.

[1] Clifford T. Morgan, *Introduction to Psychology,* McGraw-Hill Book Company, New York, 1956, p. 46.

Needs and the Motivational Cycle

If an individual's need is thirst, his goal is water; if his need is hunger, his goal is food; if his need is sexual, his goal is sexual satisfaction, perhaps marriage; if his need is security regarding his executive position in his company, his goal will be to make his area of responsibility the most profitable or well run in the company.

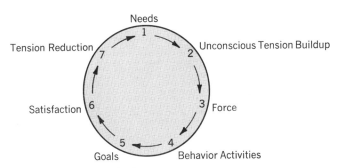

Figure 2 Motivational Cycle

Needs are frequently classified as physiological and social needs. Physiological needs are those internal conditions that cause or stimulate bodily activity. This includes such drives as the drive for sex, hunger, and thirst. Social needs are frequently subdivided into affiliative needs and social needs or status needs. Affiliative needs identify the desire for people to be with people. The need of individuals to feel superior, important, to receive recognition, and to dominate are a few of the many needs called social or status needs.

Achieving the goal of obtaining water or food may involve simple behavior activities, such as walking to a fountain or going to a restaurant. Obtaining the goals of sexual satisfaction, security, approval, mastery, affection, prestige, or numerous other goals may involve relatively complex behavior activities.

The complexity of the behavior activities will depend on the degree of thwarting involved. Thwarting is implied in the attainment of all needs. The individual has a need, say, for prestige. He sets about a course of action leading to the satisfaction of that need, but an obstacle blocks his course of action. This leads to various and usually more intensive behavior activities until a solution to the problem is found. This adjustment process takes place for both physiological and social needs.

This broadly is the motivational-cycle theory. It will assist the salesman to see his relationship to a prospect's needs and how the prospect is motivated. From a selling perspective, two sets of needs are involved in all sales situations. First, there is the firm's need or the businessman's need for the salesman's product or service and the individual's (the decision maker or buyer) social needs, or affiliative and status needs. (In general, the salesman is not concerned with the basic physiological needs of the individual.) Many times the salesman assists the prospect, buyer,

Selling: A Behavioral Science Approach

or customer to identify his business needs (need awareness) and then proceeds to show how his product or services will fulfill that need. But the salesman takes the individual's social needs as given. He does not help the prospect to identify these needs. He does, however, attempt to identify certain predominant prospect traits, for example, dominance, and he evolves a coping behavior to work with that individual. And he does, when possible, bring out certain facts about his product or services that would help satisfy a prospect's need: e.g., the need for money gain or profit or for security.

These two sets of needs are, in most sales situations, inextricably bound together. But the closer the buyer is to utilizing the product, the more involved he will be with how the product will satisfy his status needs. For example, the individual who has a strong need for importance may be strongly motivated to buy a Cadillac convertible to satisfy that need, or the businessman who purchases his own office equipment may be closely involved with his status emotions when it comes to deciding on steel versus wood office furniture. But the further the individual is removed from the actual use or consumption of the product, the less involved he is with how the product will directly satisfy his needs, for instance, the purchasing agent who is making a decision to purchase office furniture for an entire office force. In cases where the buyer or decision maker is removed from the actual use of the product, the salesman is more concerned with the decision-making and problem-solving aspects of the sale. And the salesman is probably more involved with appealing to the buyer's status needs, such as recognition, the need to dominate, or the need to feel superior through his actions and speech. This coping aspect of a salesman's role is important in all person-to-person sales situations. The point being made here is that it is one of degree. This viewpoint will become clearer as the reader analyzes the following discussion of needs. But it is a true truism that in today's world of selling the salesman doesn't motivate; he facilitates. The prospect is self-propelled through his needs. It is a process of use-need awareness, plus coping behavior, plus need fulfillment equals prospect satisfaction. For ease of memory, this can be summarized as:

$$UNA + CB + NF = PS$$

NEEDS

To review, needs may be classified as physiological and social. Felt needs or basic wants, such as food, water, and sex, are physiological, whereas, other felt needs are products of our social life.[2] Social needs, which are often called psychological needs, are classified as affiliative needs and status needs. Affiliative needs and togetherness go hand in hand. For the most part we are a gregarious people. We spend most of our wak-

---

[2] *Felt* is used here to establish the point that the need is at the awareness level. It is understood that at times a salesman must take the prospect through a process of need awareness and need fulfillment, but from this point on, the word *felt* will be understood. Further, needs, wants, motives, drives, and desires will be used interchangeably.

73

ing hours with other individuals—our neighbors, club members, close friends, family, parents, and so on. Our modern society throws people together in transportation, eating, working, play, and entertainment, but most of us seek the company of others even though there is no pressure to do so. Affiliative needs are strong needs and are characteristic of most people. From infancy on, we have learned in the course of our social life to depend on others.

Status needs are fairly distinct from affiliative needs. Whereas affiliative needs may be helpful to the salesman and ones which require little or no analysis, status needs, at least from an analysis standpoint, may be difficult to cope with. Yet, if properly appealed to, they can be powerful forces aiding the salesman. Status needs refer to the need of an individual to obtain a status equal to, or better than, the status of others. These needs are sometimes called egoistic, since they refer to one individual's needs in relationship to others and imply at the expense of others.

On every hand the fulfillment or the satisfaction of status needs, if this is possible, is seen. Observe the seating arrangement at the formal luncheon, or observe the military, or observe the type of accessories such as carpeting, etc., in the businessman's or professor's or dean's or president's office. These are everyday life illustrations of the rank concept. Other examples of status needs are prestige, mastery, power, security, recognition, and desire for social approval. Cars, homes, lodges, dress, clubs, and hundreds of other indicators may be signs of status or what the sociologists call status symbols.

That status needs are powerful motivational forces is pointed out by psychologist Hattwick. He tells us in his excellent and fast-reading book, *The New Psychology of Selling,* that individuals have eight basic wants in life, but that one ". . . leads all the rest in importance. One of them, day after day, stands out as probably the most potent of all in selling. That basic want is the customer's desire to be . . . *superior.*" He tells us that "if you understand this basic want better; if you constantly recognize a customer's want to feel important, to feel needed, to be superior; and if you strive to satisfy this want in an honest and straightforward way in making sales calls, you can't fail to make greater sales."[3]

But there are, of course, a number of roadblocks or problems the salesman must solve before he can effectively utilize appeals to needs. He must understand that the motivational force of various needs varies greatly among individuals, and he must understand that the intensity of the motivation is sometimes difficult to appraise. Further, not all needs lead to motivation. A need may not be perceived, a need may be perceived incorrectly, and a need may be perceived, and even though the disequilibrium may be substantial, no action will result.

For instance, an individual may be hungry and not perceive it, or a businessman may need a whole new business machine system and not perceive it. Normally these inactivities on the part of the individual occur when he is involved in other situations or activities that take a higher

[3] Melvin S. Hattwick, *The New Psychology of Selling,* McGraw-Hill Book Company, New York, 1960, p. 92.

74

Selling: A Behavioral Science Approach

order of priority than do the disturbances. On the other hand, a businessman may not perceive the need for new production equipment because he
is firmly entrenched in his old method and does not see the need for a
new system. Obviously, in such a case, the salesman must make the businessman aware of the need and then proceed from that point.

The second case is where the individual may perceive incorrectly. A
businessman or retailer may see larger margins as a problem leading to
profits, but he may not perceive correctly that new lines, more aggressive
marketing, and lower margins might be the solution to his problem.

A final case is where the individual perceives the need and does not
act. In many such cases, the individual sees the disruption or disequilibrium cause as part of a larger pattern of events, which will eventually
resolve themselves or reduce their disruptive force, so the individual does
not become involved. The business executive may see the need for many
personnel changes in his organization but does not act because of social
pressure or because gradual retirement will resolve the problem.

Much of the material presented above should give rise in the salesman's mind to the question, "Just how can he discover an individual's
true needs when in many situations the problem is obviously complex?"

The fact is there is no one way to identify an individual's needs, nor
is there an easy way. Ways to identify and get at the needs of the individual are discussed in the sections of this book dealing with "Source
Credibility" and "Evaluation by Observation." Here it will be worthwhile
to look at three steps or stages in the process of relating product benefits
to the potential buyer's needs as well as how the individual can adjust his
own behavior patterns to cope with the prospect's needs. Each of these
stages calls for successively greater sensitivity, perception, and maturity
on the part of the salesman. In the first stage the salesman builds a general sales talk that will appeal to the needs or wants of people. In this
process *no* attempt is made to identify a specific individual's needs. Instead, it is a process in which the salesman discusses his product benefits
in such a way that they appeal to the *general* basic needs of people. And
as Hattwick states, ". . . when you use one or more of the basic wants as
your basic appeals in selling, you automatically attract quick and immediate attention and greater interest in your sales presentation."[4]

And the salesman can do this. This is especially true for the salesman
selling products directly to the consumer such as cars, insurance, home
appliances, television, and related products. Here the salesman thinks in
terms of such basic needs as comfort, security, fear, safety, new experiences, affiliation, sex, love, economy, health, and the need or desire for
longer life.

The second stage is a continuation of the first. In this stage the salesman designs a plan that will enable him to use more consistently various
appeals in his product to strike the prospect's needs or wants. He need
merely take ten cards, or whatever number he desires, and head each card
with a basic or more general need as well as more complex social needs.
In addition to the list given in the first stage the following social needs

[4] *Ibid.*, p. 93.

Needs and the Motivational Cycle

may be included: the need for social approval, pride, importance, power, superiority, recognition, and infavoidance. He then lists on a sheet of paper the various qualities or benefits of his product, or, in other words, what the various features of his product can do for or mean to the prospect. The salesman will discover that he can transfer most of his listed product qualities or benefits to the various cards. Frequently each product quality or benefit will be transferred to several of the needs cards. In short, one product benefit may appeal simultaneously to several needs. The insurance salesman knows, although he sells an intangible, that the quality of his product to provide income to a family, in the event of the death of the family provider, appeals to the prospect's need for the welfare of loved ones. But he also knows that this product benefit could appeal, in many instances, to the prospect's need for social approval, pride, self-esteem, or the desire to feel important in the eyes of his family. In the same way, a 400-horsepower sports car may appeal to a man's need, want, or desire for power, importance, adventure, sex, or imitation, or a combination of these wants. (This is a good time to remind the salesman that the individual may want, for example, a 400-horsepower convertible because it appeals to the needs mentioned, but the individual may not buy because of a strong need for infavoidance. We'll return to this idea below.)

After this list is compiled, the salesman has an accurate list of the product qualities or benefits that will appeal to various needs, motives, desires, or wants of prospective customers. This list of benefits now becomes a source of talking points. It forms the core of the salesman's sales message. The salesman, of course, never mentions the prospect's needs, wants, motives, or desires. Instead, he knows that the stimuli in the form of talking points will directly appeal to the prospect's needs and thereby motivate.

Most experienced salesmen know that the sales knowledge the salesman gains from a product-benefits-and-needs-analysis approach must not be utilized to form a canned sales talk. The salesman knows he must interact with the customer. He must get feedback from the customer. And he must adjust his sales message in terms of that feedback to best satisfy the needs of the potential buyer. A cue to this process was given in the previous paragraph. It was mentioned that an individual may want a 400-horsepower convertible sports car, but because he had a strong need for infavoidance (to avoid failure, shame, humiliation, ridicule) he may not buy. Yet in many situations a salesman who is perceptual may receive verbal and nonverbal cues from the prospect which permit him to detect the prospect's need for infavoidance and adjust the sales message to help the prospect rationalize the purchase.

The first two stages were concerned primarily with the needs of the individual with respect to the use or the consumption of a product or service. The third stage is a continuation of the second stage, but the analysis concerns the salesman rather than the product. In this analysis the question is, "What qualities or behavior activities does the salesman exhibit that will appeal to the prospect or customer's needs?" It is a process of "benefitizing the salesman." On the one hand, the emphasis here is on such status or ego needs as the prospect's desire to feel important, to feel superior, the need to feel secure against the loss of status, the need of affiliation, the need for recognition for his accomplishments, etc., and on the other, the qualities and behavior activities (everything the salesman does plus his verbal communication pattern) of the salesman that appeal to these needs.

In a nutshell, the author is stating that not only do the benefits of the product, or what the product will do for the prospect, motivate, but the inherent qualities and the behavior activities of the salesman enhance the appeals various product benefits may have. What is more, he is stating that certain specific qualities and behavior activities of the salesman appeal to the above needs of the prospect in precisely the same way product benefits do. Thus the salesman could utilize the ten cards above and list various status needs of the individual, and in turn, under each status need list the behavior activities that would appeal to these needs.[5]

A purchase of a large industrial numeric control Tape-O-Matic drill may be, on paper, a good investment for a firm, but the buyer cannot detach himself from his own personal feelings. He cannot make what is frequently referred to as a rational decision. "It is impossible," Simon writes, "for the behavior of a single, isolated individual to reach any high degree of rationality. The number of alternatives he must explore is so great, the information he would need to evaluate them so vast, that even an approximation to objective rationality is hard to conceive."[6]

Assume that a buyer has purchased a $15,000 Tape-O-Matic drill for his company. On the one hand, it would be impossible to segment accurately the advantages to the corporation in buying a new Tape-O-Matic from the feelings of the buyer—that he would get or receive recognition or attention for his purchase, or that it would make him feel important, or appeal to his need for power, etc. On the other hand, it would be equally impossible to segment accurately the salesman's behavior activities that appeal to these needs of the buyer from the reasons why the buyer bought.

And it is entirely possible that the last factor, the salesman's behavior activities that appeal to the needs of the buyer, is the most important aspect of the sale. Thus, each salesman must appraise, identify, or assess his own personality, his adjustment to life, and temper his evaluation of the respondent's behavior patterns in view of his own perceptional and emotional framework. By knowing himself, an individual may gain insights into the behavior patterns of others.

Accordingly the reader may wish to analyze the following list of needs and think through what behavior activities on his part would possibly satisfy various needs and what behavior activities on his part would be

---

[5] At this point the reader may profitably turn to ten prospect characteristics or trait analysis chart given in Chap. 15 for both an analysis of what may be some predominant needs of individuals as well as for an analysis of coping behavior that may enable the salesman to work more effectively with certain individuals.

[6] Herbert A. Simon, *Administrative Behavior*, The Macmillan Company, New York, 1961, p. 79.

Needs and the Motivational Cycle

thwarting to the prospect's need. Concerning this list Berelson and Steiner state, ". . . various writers have constructed lists of motives ranging from very short and highly general lists to more specific ones containing as many as fifty or sixty social motives."[7] One classical scheme reduced social motives to four basic wishes—for security, recognition, response from others, and new experience (Thomas, 1923). On the other hand, one of the classifications[8] underlying much current research lists twenty-eight social (psychogenic) needs, as follows:

Need acquisition (acquisitive attitude). To gain possessions and property. To grasp, snatch, or steal things. To bargain or gamble. To work for money or goods.

Need conservance (conserving attitude). To collect, repair, clean, and preserve things. To protect against damage.

Need order (orderly attitude). To arrange, organize, put away objects. To be tidy and clean. To be scrupulously precise.

Need retention (retentive attitude). To retain possession of things. To refuse to give or lend. To hoard. To be frugal, economical, and miserly.

Need construction (constructive attitude). To organize and build.

Need superiority (ambitious attitude). This has been broken up into two needs: the need achievement (will to power over things, people, and ideas) and the need recognition (efforts to gain approval and high social status).

Need achievement (achievant attitude). To overcome obstacles, to exercise power, to strive to do something difficult as well and as quickly as possible. (This is an elementary ego need which alone may prompt any action or be fused with any other need.)

Need recognition (self-forwarding attitude). To excite praise and commendation. To demand respect. To boast and exhibit one's accomplishments. To seek distinction, social prestige, honors, or high office.

Need exhibition (exhibitionistic attitude). To attract attention to one's person. To excite, amuse, stir, shock, thrill others. Self-dramatization.

Need inviolacy (inviolate attitude). This includes desires and attempts to prevent a depreciation of self-respect, to preserve one's good name, to be immune from criticism, to maintain psychological "distance." It is based on pride and personal sensitiveness.

Need infavoidance (infavoidant attitude). To avoid failure, shame, humiliation, ridicule. To refrain from attempting to do something that is beyond one's powers. To conceal a disfigurement.

Need defendance (defensive attitude). To defend oneself against blame or belittlement. To justify one's actions. To offer extenuations, explanations, and excuses. To resist probing.

Need counteraction (counteractive attitude). Proudly to overcome defeat by restriving and retaliating. To select the hardest tasks. To defend one's honor in action.

---

[7] Bernard Berelson and Gary A. Steiner, *Human Behavior: An Inventory of Scientific Findings*, Harcourt, Brace & World, Inc., New York, 1964, pp. 256–258.

[8] Henry A. Murray (ed.), *Explorations in Personality: A Clinical Experimental Study of Fifty Men of College Age*, Oxford University Press, Fair Lawn, N.J., 1938, pp. 35, 257–258.

Selling: A Behavioral Science Approach

Need dominance (dominative attitude). To influence or control others. To persuade, prohibit, dictate. To lead and direct. To restrain. To organize the behaviour of a group.

Need deference (deferent attitude). To admire and willingly follow a superior. To cooperate with a leader. To serve gladly.

Need similance (suggestible attitude). To emphasize. To imitate or emulate. To identify one's self with others. To agree and believe.

Need autonomy (autonomous attitude). To resist influence or coercion. To defy an authority or seek freedom in a new place. To strive for independence.

Need contrarience (contrarient attitude). To act differently from others. To be unique. To take the opposite side. To hold unconventional views.

Need aggression (aggressive attitude). To assault or injure. To murder. To belittle, harm, blame, accuse, or maliciously ridicule a person. To punish severely. Sadism.

Need abasement (abasive attitude). To surrender. To comply and accept punishment. To apologize, confess, atone. Self-depreciation. Masochism.

Need blamavoidance (blamavoidance attitude). To avoid blame, ostracism, or punishment by inhibiting a social or unconventional impulses. To be well behaved and obey the law.

Need affiliation (affiliative attitude). To form friendships and associations. To greet, join, and live with others. To cooperate and converse sociably with others. To love. To join groups.

Need rejection (rejective attitude). To snub, ignore, or exclude. To remain aloof and indifferent. To be discriminating.

Need nurturance (nuturant attitude). To nourish, aid, or protect the helpless. To express sympathy. To "mother" a child.

Need succorance (succorant attitude). To seek aid, protection, or sympathy. To cry for help. To plead for mercy. To adhere to an affectionate nurturant parent. To be dependent.

Need play (playful attitude). To relax, amuse one's self, seek diversion and entertainment. To have fun, to play games. To laugh, joke, and be merry. To avoid serious tension.

Need cognizance (inquiring attitude). To explore (moving and touching). To ask questions. To satisfy curiosity. To look, listen, inspect. To read and seek knowledge.

Need exposition (expositive attitude). To point and demonstrate. To relate facts. To give information, explain, interpret, lecture.

FEEDBACK

In one basic psychology textbook, feedback is described as a general term ". . . referring to the process whereby action initiated by a subject provides further source of stimulation. Thus, the *consequences* of action become apparent to the performer and influence his succeeding acts."[9]

[9] Calvin P. Stone (ed.), *Comparative Psychology*, Prentice-Hall, Inc., Englewood Cliffs, N.J., 1955, p. 450.

Needs and the Motivational Cycle

If it were possible to select any one attribute that is most important to sales success, mastery of this concept, intellectually and in practice would be considered by many as a key tool. Without the ability, the willingness, and the sensitivity to determine the consequences of one's acts and words we might be social or sales duds. Each of us has seen individuals who monopolize conversation, whose table manners leave something to be desired, who just can't seem to understand that the other individual wants to terminate the discussion, or for that matter, a hundred other examples of poor manners by individuals. In most cases it would be correct if it were stated that such an individual does not know how to interpret feedback. He doesn't perceive or can't evaluate cues or a combination of both. He is short in one area where sensitivity counts—evaluation. This includes evaluation of one's self as well as the other individual. One psychologist states in writing of characteristics of the self: "Indeed, one of man's unique distinctions, setting him off most sharply from other animals, may just be his extraordinary capacity to look at himself."[10]

In discussing feedback almost every word used by Krech and Crutchfield underscores its dimensions as a sales attribute.

> Feedback not only makes the learning of a skill possible; it is also essential for the performance itself. The execution of a skilled performance is a continuous process of behavior in which each step is governed by what went before, what will happen next, and the final goal aimed at. This is another way of saying, of course, that a skill always has a temporal organization involving a flexible sequence of acts. For such a continuously changing pattern of adjustments and readjustments, moment-by-moment feedback of information is absolutely essential. Without it, most skilled performances would be impossible.[11]

The presence of feedback in every interview is something we can be sure of, but we cannot be sure that we are always sensitive to it. The prospect's facial expression, the tone of his voice, his general demeanor, or all of these variables combined are needed to guide us as to whether or not the feedback is mild, intense, passive, or aggressive.[12]

These statements suggest that the perceptual salesman sensitive to feedback will have the ability in many ways to perceive his total self. Further, it implies that the salesman should be able to anticipate what prospect feelings will result from each act, or acts, or words, or series of words that he employs. Further, he will perceive how the self will perceive the prospect's responses if the prospect acts as he expects. Further, he will perceive how the self will act if the prospect does not act as expected. Obviously such perception is perhaps an unobtainable goal. It perhaps demands an impossible degree of maturity, intelligence, and sensitivity. Nevertheless, it does give us insights into the complex characteristics of the salesman's role.

[10] Krech and Crutchfield, *op. cit.*, p. 202.
[11] *Ibid.*
[12] Joseph W. Thompson, *Blue Cross–Blue Shield Manpower Development Program Book*, Blue Cross–Blue Shield, Indianapolis, Ind., 1963, chap. 6.

Selling: A Behavioral Science Approach

IDENTIFYING MOTIVES, NEEDS, OR WANTS

It was indicated previously that the motivational cycle begins with felt needs, which take the form of behavior activities that are goal-directed. Attainment of the goal means satisfaction and, thus, equilibrium. Krech and Crutchfield tell us that there are two ways of identifying motives and that each presents special difficulties. One way of doing this is ". . . to study his behavior and infer his needs and desires from the systematic character of the behavior, and his goals from the effects that his behavior brings about. The other way is to ask the person to tell us what his needs, desires, and goals are."[13]

This is where the knowledge, sensitivity, intelligence, perception, character, maturity, etc., of the observer comes into play. For instance, it is not difficult to identify the neophyte playing a musical instrument alongside the accomplished musician; but the finer the shadings of differences, the greater the difficulty of identification. A knowledgeable, sensitive person in the field of music, however, would discern slight quality differences easily. This same analogy is applicable to social situations, and social situations are comparable to sales situations. It is relatively easy to discern poor table manners, or the activities of the extreme ego-oriented individual. The more obvious is the behavior pattern of the individual, the easier it is to discern or to identify. The more subtle the changing behavioral pattern, the more difficult it is to discern. And from our everyday experience we know that the more sensitive each individual is to happenings in social situations (interaction between individuals and between the individual and the group), the more sensitive he will be to cues or behavior activities of the other individual.

Before proceeding further, however, it must be established that it is impossible to infer motives from behavior if we attempt to account for or record the full activities of anyone's activities in a single period of time. It is pointed out that ". . . every muscle twitch, every grunt, every job, and blood pressure—would constitute a mountain of data, unmanageable for analysis."[14] Further, it should be kept in mind that there is not necessarily a motive for every bit of behavior. "This eyewink, this snuffle, this tapping of the finger, this laughter is certainly caused, but it may not be a pattern of goal-directed action in the service of a need or desire; . . . it may merely be . . . a reflex response to a simple stimulus or a rote habit."[15]

The solution is to look instead for organized sequence of behavior. *Sequence of behavior* refers to taking one episode beginning with the individual in one psychological situation and continuing this analysis. The episode may be short or long, simple or complex. It may be complete or incomplete. A sales call is an episode. The sales call may be short or long, simple or complex. A sales call may be complete or incomplete or what is more usual, especially in business or industrial sales situations involving large expenditures, the sales call develops into a series of customer contacts and hopefully each call builds on the previous contacts.

[13] Krech and Crutchfield, *op. cit.*, p. 272.
[14] *Ibid.*
[15] *Ibid.*, p. 276.

Needs and the Motivational Cycle

The following episode illustrates some of the problems involved in analysis by observation.

> Mr. Anyman remarks enthusiastically to his wife about the charms of the woman they met the evening before. After his departure for work, Mrs. Anyman gets dressed, runs for the train to town, and searches for and buys a new spring hat. When her husband returns from work, he tells her how well she is looking, kisses her tenderly, and Mrs. Anyman's episode ends.[16]

It might be assumed that the change in the above situation, as it occurred from the beginning to the end of the episode, is that Mr. Anyman was at first perceived by Mrs. Anyman as admiring another woman and at the end is admiring her. Thus it could be inferred from the episode above that Mrs. Anyman's motive was to retain her husband's attention and to satisfy her need for being admired. But this analysis could be wrong. Mrs. Anyman may have motives for punishing her husband for his unfaithfulness by charging an expensive hat, or she may simply have been gratifying her desire to enjoy wearing a hat, or it may have been a combination of all these factors.

This case illustrates the difficulty of determining ". . . what motive or motives the behavior episode reflects merely from observing the effects produced by the behavior."[17]

Each day each salesman is confronted with a series of episodes or situations that he must analyze. What would you, as a salesman, infer in the way of the prospect's motivation, and what would you do if you were confronted with the following situations? You have an appointment; you call on a business executive; you introduce yourself, complete the amenities, and begin your sales talk. The business executive turns his swivel chair so that his back is to you. As you are talking, he is looking out the window. What does this behavior imply? Is the man insecure? Is he just obnoxious? Does this behavior activity make him feel important or superior? Is it a habit? Is he actually listening to the salesman?

Or what would you infer from the behavior activity of a purchasing agent in Chicago who, with one grand sweep of his hand, pushed a salesman's portfolio from his desk onto the floor?

In either situation the salesman cannot safely draw conclusions with respect to the prospect's needs. The episodes are too brief; the facts are not known. On the other hand, what would you infer from the behavior of a woman purchasing officer who kept you standing at her desk for twenty minutes while two chairs close to her desk remained stacked with boxes, paper, etc.? You are therefore forced to stand and give your sales talk. You begin. You barely mention your company, and she stops you and states, "I'm not interested in your company. All I want to know is the price. If you give me coffee for two cents a pound less than I am now paying for it, I will give you the business."

[16] *Ibid.*, p. 371.
[17] *Ibid.*, p. 372.

Selling: A Behavioral Science Approach

Would it be helpful to you if you observed that there were two other occupied desks in the same office, and that this purchasing officer made several long-distance calls, which she referred to as important, while you stood at her desk? Would it have been helpful if you had heard the many *I's* in her conversation? Would it have been helpful if you noticed she was very dogmatic in her phone conversations and apparently had problems with other suppliers? Would it help in your analysis if you had noticed the many status symbols hanging on the wall in the form of certificates and awards presented to this woman? You note also that some would be considered relatively minor in importance, such as a large certificate of thanks for appearing in a play by a local club.

Apparently she had a strong desire to feel superior, to be important, and to receive recognition. But this analysis may not be correct. Before making a final decision, a second and supplementary method of discovering a particular individual's needs must be put into play.

This method is to infer motives from verbal reports, that is, to "... ask the person what needs and desires he is experiencing, or goals he is seeking. This would seem to be the most obvious method and the one least fraught with error. Yet, it too presents serious difficulties."[18]

One of the clear difficulties is that of communication. The observer cannot be sure that the individual is giving a reliable report of what he is experiencing or has experienced. He may be in an extremely complex situation with multiple motivational determinants and not aware of his complex feelings, or he may simply lie, being unwilling to expose his motives to outsiders. A more basic difficulty is that even if he faithfully reports his motives as he perceives them, it may be found that his report of motives does not correspond with what is revealed in his behavior as analyzed by the outside observer.

From the sales outlook the idea of inferring motives from verbal reports must be modified. Few salesmen would be crass enough to ask the prospect directly, "What are your motives?" Salesmen do, however, like the educator, guidance counselor, market motivational researcher, psychologist, and many other professionals, infer from verbal reports. They subtly interrogate a prospect or customer throughout the sale. Salesmen use verification and permissive questions in the contact stage. They use questions to complete negotiations. Further, like the psychologist, he combines information received from the verbal reports and from his observations, but he does not arrive at a conclusion based on one or two answers or on one or two behavior activities. Instead, he is interested in prospect behavior activities throughout the total sales interview.

Not for a moment is the author attempting to make psychological interviewers out of salesmen, or to infer, even remotely that salesmen are psychologists. The salesman is not interested in abnormal behavior nor is he, in any sense of the word, attempting to determine why or what caused an individual to be as he is. He is interested only in the psychology of everyday life in the business community. But it is interesting to see the parallel between the psychologist interview, as psychologist Schaffer describes it, and the sales interview. The purpose, the situation, and the

[18] *Ibid.*, p. 275.

Needs and the Motivational Cycle

"actors" are different, of course, but the tactics used are very similar. Psychologist Schaffer writes that the direct psychological interview with the patient is the most significant of all procedures used in case study.[19]

The aim of the diagnostic interview, Schaffer tells us, ". . . is to get the subject to reveal the significant facts about his personality and his adjustments."[20] This is hindered by a number of factors which psychologists refer to as resistances. These resistances range from "lack of confidence in the interviewer," "feelings of shame and social disapproval with which the subject regards the behavior being investigated," or what is a more difficult resistance to overcome—"the lack of insight."[21]

In view of these resistances, what must the psychologist do? He must, Schaffer advises,

> . . . establish rapport with the subject, which serves to weaken his various resistances. Rapport implies a condition of confidence, trust, and friendship and the creation of positive emotional response on the part of the subject toward the examiner. This consideration is of such paramount importance that the first interview or several interviews may be spent solely in establishing rapport. All procedures of a well-conducted interview should assist rapport, but at the outset some special devices are often used.[22]

The following is a discussion about these special devices as Schaffer relates it.

> The interviewer should know something in advance about the characteristics of his subject, and may begin his interview by asking him about matters in which he is interested or proficient. The interviewer should show he is interested in and knows about the things that the subject values. This will give him the status of a collaborator. A species of "identification" assist in beginning an interview, which may be accomplished by referring to friends and experiences that the interviewer and subject have in common. A little flattery or humor is not out of place to get the subject into a suitable mood.[23]

Schaffer also tells of the personal characteristics of the interviewer that are important. Both in the process of establishing rapport and in the subsequent procedures. He writes that

> The interviewer must be a well adjusted person himself, in order to avoid making personal, emotional reactions to various aspects of a subject's experiences. The interviewer should not give obvious praise or condemnation of the conduct of his patient, nor show surprise or disgust at any disclosure. The interviewer must secure the respect of the subject without overawing him. He must be friendly, cordial and genuinely interested in the individual and his problems.[24]

[19] Laurance F. Schaffer, *The Psychology of Adjustment*, The Riverside Press, Cambridge, Mass., 1936.
[20] *Ibid.,* p. 456.
[21] *Ibid.,* p. 45.
[22] *Ibid.*
[23] *Ibid.*
[24] *Ibid.,* p. 458.

Selling: A Behavioral Science Approach

The interviewer should also encourage the subject to tell his story. This

> . . . approach adds to rapport, for having told his story, the subject feels that the interviewer is an insider and has less resistance to direct questions than if these had been asked at the outset. In listening to the subject's story, the interviewer is alert to catch any significant indications that are not revealed by the story's obvious content. He writes too that, "Topics of which the subject seems to rationalize or defend his own conduct too warmly indicates sore spots in his adjustive attitude and warrant further investigation."[25]

The end result is that after the subject's confidence has been gained securely, the interviewer can begin a direct questioning procedure.

Schaffer reminds us that ". . . only the most general characteristics of the interview have been described. This is an unavoidable circumstance, for the procedure must be adapted to the patient and to his problems. And, of all clinical procedures, the interview is the one whose value depends most on flexibility."[26]

As described in this book, the salesman plans (gets both personal and impersonal information about the prospect and his firm) prior to the initial contact. During the contact stage, he uses verification and permissive questions; he uses a problem-centered, customer-oriented approach. This approach permits the prospect to tell the salesman about his situation and his business problems. This approach elicits feedback, both verbal and nonverbal. This customer-oriented, problem-solving approach is designed to appeal to the need of the individual to be recognized, the need of the individual to feel that something is being done, the need of the individual to participate, the need of the individual for an intellectual approach to a problem, and, above all, it is designed to assist the salesman to discover whether or not he is on the right track in his sales interview and shift if he isn't. The salesman can do this because he can evaluate both verbal and nonverbal prospect feedback and thus evolve a coping behavior according to the needs of the individual. In brief, it is highly flexible.

INCENTIVES AS MOTIVATION

Motivation, as discussed previously, is concerned with the fundamentals of the behavior system. In that discussion considerable emphasis is given to basic or primary needs and secondary or learned needs. Needs or motives are discussed from a deficit or need reduction viewpoint. They are linked to the concept of homeostasis. In this section motivation is linked to incentives. And, although the incentive approach to motivation is similar to the needs approach, emphasis is somewhat different and should be of special interest to the salesman and sales manager.

Frequently incentives are used to control the behavior activities of people. The salesman with the customer, the executive with the executive,

---

[25] *Ibid.*, p. 458.
[26] *Ibid.*, pp. 458–459.

the mother with the child, the educator with the student, and, in fact, in about every possible situation incentives such as praise, punishment, money, participation, competition, and cooperation are used to motivate.

Praise

Most people like to receive praise, and most people want to avoid punishment. This belief has made praise and punishment two of the most manipulated incentives in our society and in business today. These concepts are mentioned in most books in psychology, education, communication, selling, human relations, sociology, letter writing, and speech.

Overall, from the sales standpoint, praise is more productive than punishment. In each instance that a salesman acknowledges another individual's *positive* attributes, his ideas, his thinking, his performance, even his manners, or taste in clothes, etc., he is using the concept of praise as an incentive.

He is giving credit. Praise will fail with some and succeed with others. Its success depends on the performance level of the salesman and the emotional, mental, and social makeup of the other individual. In any event, in most situations, praise or credit should be used subtly.

Here are a few phrases that suggest the use of the praise concept:
1. I hadn't thought of that.
2. That is a new idea.
3. Your question poses a situation that I hadn't thought about. It will take some reflection.
4. Your offices are getting bigger and bigger (assuming, of course, that the individual had been promoted).
5. That's a good start.
6. I wish I had thought of that.
7. That report was well done, Jim.

Praise is an extremely flexible sales tool. A salesman may capitalize on a negative situation through the concept of praise. Assume that the customer, on the salesman's last call, complained about some element of service. Salesman on his next call: "Your comments regarding shipping delays was like throwing a rock in a pool of water. A lot has happened. And you know, I think everyone appreciates your comments. Our shipping department is more on its toes than ever, and some of our executives in manufacturing are following through on orders. Thank you again for your comments, Mr. Jones. This will give us an opportunity to do a better job for you and other customers as well."

Punishment

This is a negative incentive or motivational device. In sales literature it is often referred to as appealing to the motive of fear. For instance, the customer or prospect will not want to lose the benefits to be gained via the salesman's product or proposal. It is assumed that the prospect may be motivated through the fear of losing the advantages claimed and will,

Selling: A Behavioral Science Approach

therefore, be more apt to buy. A direct approach to motivation through fear is seen in the sales situation of retailer Mr. Middlesize, who has an opportunity to stock a particular product or line that the salesman is representing. And, of course, if he doesn't stock it, there is the possibility that another retailer, especially one in direct competition, will end up with the product.

Another way, and a unique way, of getting at the fear motive is by way of the informative function. This may be quite effective in redirecting the individual's behavior. Take an illustration from the classroom. A low grade on an exam paper is punishment, yet it is an informative function. It informs the student of what he has done or hasn't done. Thus if he wants to avoid this situation, it may well energize his behavior.

Let us carry this same analogy over into selling and, more specifically, into the preceding case of retailer Mr. Middlesize. If in the past this retailer has missed opportunities to handle new or other products that have moved well for other retailers, there is a good possibility a slight reminder or stimuli will energize his behavior.

Every salesman knows, however, at least intuitively, that the effectiveness of the informative function will depend considerably on the retail power structure (the relative success of one store or firm to market its product or services in competition with others and the importance of the manufacturer's product to the success or profit picture of the retailer) as well as a great deal on the individual's psychological makeup.

Participation

Participation or involving others mentally or physically in what is to be done motivates the individual to carry out the ideas of work involved. It is an incentive. Most people who are "brought in" on something are more receptive or open-minded to the ideas or activities involved. Participation appeals to the status needs and affiliative needs which are solidly ingrained in most people's psychological makeup.

Without active student participation education would operate at what degree of effectiveness—20 percent or 25 percent of potential? Thus educators use questions, meaningful problems, programed instruction, visuals, written work, etc., to obtain interest and effective student participation. And the idea of participation and how to get it is just as important in selling as it is in education. Therefore the salesman uses the tools and techniques of the educator; the process is the same.

Here is another illustration stressing the importance of participation as an incentive. It is far removed from selling—or is it? During World War II an attempt was made to change food habits so that meat would be used more efficiently during the shortage.[27] A skilled nutritionist lectured on and discussed with one group of women the nutritional value of heart, brains, kidneys, etc., and ways of preparing them. A follow-up investigation showed that only 3 percent of the group had tried these foods. In

[27] Robert Mills Gagne, *Psychology of Human Performance*, Holt, Rinehart and Winston, Inc., New York, 1959, pp. 78–79.

another group, a discussion leader who knew little about nutrition got the women to discuss the problem themselves. The time spent and the problems discussed were the same as those of the lecture, but the individuals participated in the goals and the decisions of the group. A follow-up study of this group showed that 32 percent of the women had tried the previously shunned foods.

The idea of participation as an incentive is achieving more and more support in industry and especially in the sales field. Salesmen are involved in establishing goals for almost everything they do, from setting their quotas and the management of their territory to structuring the company's sales training programs.

Competition and Cooperation

In our society, competition and cooperation are important motivational forms. Both stem from the needs of the individual and they are closely related concepts. But the framework within which the salesman uses each will differ considerably.

In America we may be so competitive that we may have lost sight of the concept of cooperation as a motivational tool. Businessmen are in competition with other business firms. They handle competing products. They are competing for the same markets; they are competing for employees; and they establish competitive situations throughout their organization. This is especially noticeable in the sales area where sales contests and other incentive programs are utilized frequently. This is not to de-emphasize the importance of competition as a motivational tool, but the fact remains that in competition someone must lose. The winner gains status and satisfies his needs, and the loser may be frustrated. He loses status and can't satisfy a need.

In selling, the salesman frequently appeals to the individual's sense of competition. It is an effective selling tool. He knows that most individuals want to succeed in competition with other individuals, with executives, with other departments or between departments, or in any other of a multitude of competitive situations which exist within firms and between firms. The emphasis here, in contrast to the fear motive, is how a sales proposal or idea will help the customer or prospect win, how it will help him succeed.

We forget sometimes that needs vary greatly among individuals. Some people are motivated in competitive roles and others are best motivated through cooperative roles. For instance, one writer emphasizes that a major number of the retailers like their position as it is (*status quo*).[28] He doesn't want to get big. He wants to stay where he is. If what this writer states is correct, then those retailers may be best motivated by using cooperation as a motivational force. Yet most manufacturers regard the retailers' position as competitive. "It is common practice for manufacturers to force acceptance with a heavy barrage of consumer advertising,

[28] Charles J. Dirksen et al., *Readings in Marketing*, Richard D. Irwin, Inc., Homewood, Ill., 1963, p. 145.

Selling: A Behavioral Science Approach

introductory high-markup offers, free merchandise, cooperative advertising schemes, and the like."[29] This emphasizes the competitive aspects of business. On the other hand, the manufacturer and of course the salesman have a built-in system in which cooperation as a motivational force can be utilized. Turning to McVey again, he tells us this: "Wholesalers and retailers, as well as agent middlemen, enjoy an excellent position from which to make keen judgments of a product's probable success within local markets."[30] This suggests that both the manufacturer and the salesman can utilize the retailer in a cooperative way by getting his reactions to product offerings and his analysis of the marketplace in general.

The motivational power of cooperation in distributing a product rather in competition could be a powerful motivating force in dealing with the retailer who visualizes his role as a buyer for his customers and regards himself as a social and business force in the community and as one who likes the *status quo* of his position. From a sales standpoint, which would be more effective with this retailer, a discussion of how he will be more successful, etc., if he handles X product or a discussion appealing to the cooperative role?

Summary

The motivational cycle is determined by an individual's needs. Needs are physiological and social. Physiological needs are those internal conditions that cause or stimulate body activity. They include such drives as sex, hunger, and thirst. Social needs are those needs of the individual to be with people, the need to feel superior, the need to have recognition and to dominate. Some psychologists list sixty to seventy social needs, some merely three or four.

Needs bring about an unconscious tension buildup which becomes a force resulting in behavior activities that are goal-directed. When the individual's behavior activities enable him to achieve that goal, satisfaction and tension reduction result. This is considered a point of equilibrium. In theory equilibrium may be obtained, but equilibrium with respect to social needs seldom may be obtained. The emotional needs of the individual should be regarded as being in a constant state of movement.

Every salesman will be more successful in selling if he can identify the motives, needs, or wants of the individual and develop a coping behavior to adjust to these needs or wants. The salesman determines the individual's needs by observation and by discussion.

Feedback is the process that tells the salesman whether or not he is on the right track. If it were possible to select any one attribute that is most important to sales success, mastery of this concept, intellectually and in practice, would be considered by many as a key tool. For without the ability to get feedback and evaluate feedback, the individual cannot

[29] *Ibid.*
[30] *Ibid.*, p. 148.

judge the correctness or incorrectness of his actions. The sales situation between prospect and salesman is such a continuously changing pattern of adjustments and readjustment, moment-by-moment feedback is absolutely essential. The salesman must acquire the skill and the knowledge needed to elicit feedback and interpret that feedback, both verbal and nonverbal forms.

The salesman should regard the problem of the firm as signifying one set of needs, and the social needs of the individual should be regarded as another set of needs. Thus the salesman is engaged in a problem-solving and decision-making approach for the need of the firm. He develops a coping behavior to adjust to the needs of the individual. The distinction between the two sets of needs is less important when the individual consumes the product being sold, for example, a car, and more important when the decision maker is far removed from the direct use or consumption of the product.

The sales manager, from a viewpoint of how to best motivate the sales force, and the salesman, from the perspective of how to best motivate his prospects, can learn much from identifying various incentives as a basis for motivation. The incentive approach to motivation is similar to the needs approach, but the emphasis is different. The salesman or sales manager can use such incentives as praise, punishment, participation, and cooperation as methods of motivating.

Chapter 5 DISCUSSION QUESTIONS

1 Describe the process that identifies the motivational cycle.

2 Assume an individual has a felt need for food: he is hungry. What behavior activities might that individual enact in order to satisfy that need? Could you identify those behavior activities if you watched the hungry individual enact them?

3 Take any five social or emotional needs described in this chapter and discuss the behavior activities the individual may enact in order to satisfy those needs. Is it always possible to tell from the individual's behavior activities what his needs are? What cautions would you advise the salesman to exercise in associating behavior activities with needs?

4 Does satisfaction of an emotional need, for example, recognition, mean equilibrium, or is the concept of equilibrium just a theoretical guideline? Why? Why not?

5 What is the difference between a firm's needs and the individual's needs? Are they related in any way?

6 Compare the relationship of a firm's needs and the individual's needs in these two situations: (*a*) the buyer is purchasing an expensive wood office furniture set for his personal office. He is a lawyer. (*b*) A purchasing agent is purchasing 100 desks to be used by various men throughout the firm he represents.

7 Select any product you wish and discuss a salesman's sales effort in terms of the selling formula UNA + CB + NF = PS.

8 Discuss the author's statement: "Not only do the benefits of the product

Selling: A Behavioral Science Approach

or what the product will do for the prospect motivate, but the inherent qualities and the behavior activities of the salesman enhance the appeals various products may have. What is more, certain specific qualities in behavior activities of the salesman appeal to the needs of the prospect in precisely the same way product benefits do." Take a stand and criticize the author's statement. Take a stand and support the author's statement.

9   What is meant by feedback? Why is it important in selling? Is the feedback the salesman obtains that identifies whether or not he is on a problem-solving path the same as the feedback he obtains from the individual concerning that individual's needs?

10   Is there any difference between the concept of incentive as motivating factors and needs as motivating factors? In what way are they related? Are there any ways in which they might be related?

11   Select any five products you wish and discuss how the salesman could use the following incentives as effective tools of motivation in his sales approach: (*a*) praise, (*b*) punishment, (*c*) participation, (*d*) competition, (*e*) cooperation.

role

6

SELF-IMAGE AND ROLE

A shorthand description of self-image is simply "how you view your-self or your attitude, evaluation, or feelings about yourself." Most of us, in some way or the other, have engaged in forms of self-analysis. Popular magazines devise many varieties of self-analysis tests. Qualities or traits such as friendly, snobbish, dogmatic, emotional control, impulsiveness, dominance, egotism, will power, initiative, resourcefulness, criticizing others, accepting responsibility, making decisions, open-mindedness, giving credit to others, patience, poise, etc., are listed, and the participant is told to check off those qualities or traits that he associates with himself in relation to a given situation. The same theme is followed by using mul-tiple choice or true-or-false questions. The individual is scored; he, of course, scores himself, and the score indicates the degree to which he has obtained the goal of the test.

Others may have followed the widely known Ben Franklin route of compiling a list of virtues, as Franklin called them, in which the indi-vidual thinks he needs improvement, and then conscientiously works at each virtue in a prescribed manner for a prescribed period of time.

Some may have engaged in a more sophisticated form of self-analysis by participating in a professionally supervised test, testing device, or ex-periment that was designed to get at the "self-concept." A report of such a test is presented in the *Handbook of Social Psychology*,[1] which tells of an experiment conducted by Sarbin and Rosenberg. These psychologists conducted three experiments. In the first, the self-conceptions of diagnosed neurotics and normal controls were compared. The second experiment compared the self-conception of men and women students, and the third compared the self-conception of three religious groups. Only the findings of the first experiment will be quoted here. This experiment showed that "at least 70 percent of the neurotic group checked the following qualities: anxious, changeable, confused, cooperative, dissatisfied, emotional, gentle, imaginative." On the other hand, "at least 70 percent of the controls checked these qualities: curious, dependable, fair-minded, friendly, in-telligent, sincere, sociable, tolerant." These tests may be appropriately designated as a measure, at least in part, of his self, since the self is a ". . . cognitive organization of attitudes and habits. . . ."[2] Valid tests of

[1] Gardner Lindzey (ed.), *Handbook of Social Psychology*, Addison-Wesley Publishing Com-pany, Inc., Reading, Mass., 1954, p. 244.

[2] *Ibid.*, p. 251.

Selling: A Behavioral Science Approach

this type give cues as to the participant's self-image or self-concept. They tell the participant how he views himself.

Self and role are interdependent concepts. They are not identical, however. Self is what the person *is*. Role is what the person *is to do* or *to be*. Role behavior or role enactment is the doing or the action of the individual with reference to a given status, position, or role. When the social psychologist is interested in the self, he regards the person as an organization of qualities. When he studies roles, he regards the person as an organization of acts.[3]

For the salesman there are hopefully written specifications or requirements for his job or position. His duties are described in terms of what he is expected to do. These specifications enumerate the obligations and establish the activities of a salesman. He may be required to call on six established accounts and two potential customers each day, attempt to discuss their needs, determine ways to satisfy those needs, solve problems, be a goodwill ambassador, and be friendly, considerate, understanding, good-natured, analytical, enthusiastic, etc.

This is his role. How he performs his role is described in terms of role behavior or role enactment. His sales manager will perceive the salesman's role (role perception) and have expectations (role expectations) as to what the salesman should do and be.

ROLE PERCEPTION, ROLE EXPECTATION, AND ROLE ENACTMENT

A shorthand definition of role perception is "how you see others." "The building blocks of role perception," as Sarbin so aptly puts it, "are the overt acts of others." These acts ". . . may be defined as everything the other does. This includes his gross skeletal movements, his verbal behavior, what he wears, his facial expressions, his posture, his gait, his accent and intonation, his adornments, visible emblems and tattoo marks, etc."[4]

This is what the viewer sees and hears. He perceives and reacts to the stimuli according to all the factors which determine perception—his education, his emotions, his experiences, etc.

Role expectation or role expectancy is what the viewer expects of the doer or actor or individual in a role. It is what is anticipated. The viewer (the other) expects the individual who, for example, is in a social role to exhibit certain actions and qualities.

A mother's role is to provide food for the children. This is an action. She is expected to be warm, sympathetic, and understanding. These are qualities associated with the role.

A salesman's role is a social role. It calls for a person-to-person meeting. He, for example, is supposed to contact new accounts. Certain dialogues and behavior activities will evolve. These are actions associated with the role. The salesman, in carrying out these activities, should exhibit certain qualities such as enthusiasm, poise, confidence. These actions and

[3] *Ibid.,* p. 244.
[4] *Ibid.,* p. 230.

Role

qualities, for example, will be what the sales manager may expect in terms of the salesman's role. Thus the salesman's actions and qualities validate or invalidate the expectations of the viewer—the sales manager or customer.

This relationship of role, role perception, role expectation, and role enactment can be further clarified by looking at the role of a policeman. A uniform, a gun, and silver badge are symbols of the policeman's role. He wears the uniform and silver badge as part of his role as policeman. In addition to the actions of wearing a uniform, walking a beat, or directing traffic, the officer is expected to have certain qualities. He may be thought of as honest, considerate, dogmatic, or when it comes to the law in a particular instance, protector of children and older citizens, etc. Upon seeing a policeman in uniform, the viewer immediately has certain expectations both as to the functions he performs and qualities exhibited. And the policeman in turn will validate or invalidate these expectations by the way he enacts his role.

It follows that in general it can be expected that the burglar and an elderly lady will each perceive the role of a policeman in different ways. It follows also that the policeman, if he knew the role of the viewer, would react to each differently. Nevertheless, regardless of an individual's self-conception, he may objectively analyze the ways in which a policeman views his job. A burglar may think of the policeman as one who disrupts his "trade" and, in fact, dislike policemen, yet he may be able to evaluate objectively that wearers of police uniforms regard themselves as upholders of the peace, protectors of the innocent, destroyers of vice, crime, etc.

Now for the obvious point with respect to salesmanship. It is the author's opinion that the perceptual salesman can, by perceiving the role of other individuals as the individual sees himself, substantially enhance his chances of influencing the other. Sarbin states that "perceiving the position of the other, then, becomes a matter of attention to and organizing cues."[5] There are, in fact, many types of cues available to the salesman which will facilitate his analysis of a situation. To explore this concept further, the scene will shift to the office of an executive. It is true the executive may view his role in many different ways. He may regard his role as one of policy formation and decision making or he may regard his position as the one who really controls company destiny. He may have many self-images of himself. He may regard himself as:

Important	Successful
Sharp	Ruthless
Independent	Cautious
Aggressive	Dominant
Powerful	Sophisticated
Moral	Capable
Experienced	Imaginative

Each executive is different. Each may regard his position or role as different. Each may have several different self-images. Nevertheless, the

[5] *Ibid.*, p. 230.

Selling: A Behavioral Science Approach

salesman may obtain guidelines to understanding the individual through such cues as the executive's behavior activities, his speech, his comments, obvious status symbols such as lodge, rings, office furniture, plaques, and awards hanging in office.

Evidence supports the statement that most people pass judgment concerning others. At times each individual views the behavior activities of others and responds and evaluates. Surely each individual reading this material has, at some time or another or in some form or another, viewed the behavior activities of another person consciously or unconsciously and thought of the other individual in terms of self-satisfied, impatient, casual, angry, shy, surprised, disinterested, resigned, suspicious, undecided, modest, ashamed, or in terms of the numerous traits of others that affect us.

How we view others is, according to Randall Harrison, exceedingly important. "Interestingly enough," Harrison states, "it has been estimated that in face-to-face communication no more than 35 percent of the social meaning is carried in a verbal message."[6] In brief, decisions you make based on nonverbal cues are important. For example, if you find differences in power, trustworthiness, and competence in two people you see, you have made some important decisions. Harrison tells us, "Research indicates that these may be some of the key dimensions of source credit-ability, which in turn is believed to be a vital element of persuasiveness. In short, whether you are persuaded or not may rest on non-verbal cues."[7]

The author is not implying that a salesman can analyze why an individual acts in a certain way, but he is stating that a salesman can and should obtain cues and thereby adjust his role in terms of the needs of the other individual. This means that the salesman must be both perceptive and flexible; he must enact a number of roles; he must have a high threshold of tension binding, and he must be an empathic person.

NUMBER OF ROLES

As expressed earlier, role enactment is the overt performance of a role. It is a verbal and nonverbal expression of a given position. It was recognized that the salesman performed many functions or activities and exhibited a number of accepted qualities in enacting his role. The concept that the individual or the salesman performs a number of roles is subject to observation and report. Anthropologists have followed a given subject for a representative number of days and recorded all instances of role behavior and also rated the intensity with which the individual enacted various roles.[8] Another form of getting at the number of roles played, as well as the intensity level at which the individual performs a role, is in observing small group settings such as a conference-discussion group.

Both settings, the "follow and observe" and the "conference-discussion" group, have been used extensively by this author. Over a ten-year period he has made joint calls on prospects, customers, etc., with more

[6] Randall Harrison, *op. cit.*, p. 161.
[7] *Ibid.*, p. 161.
[8] Lindzey, *op. cit.*, p. 232.

than 140 salesmen representing twenty-seven different companies. Many of these joint calls were tape-recorded on a midget tape and later transcribed. During the two-year term, 1962–1964, he observed for approximately 360 hours a total of more than 120 salesmen and sales managers in man-to-man selling roles.[9]

In sales situations and in discussion groups certain roles characteristically arise.[10]

In sales situations the behavior pattern or actions of the salesman can be described as (1) information giver, talker; (2) information getter, listener; (3) negative, afraid; (4) meek, apologetic; (5) brash, overly positive, overpowering; (6) mature, poised, friendly, positive; (7) joker, glad-hander, overly friendly, overenthusiastic; (8) impulsive; (9) neutral, friendly; (10) goodwill, order taker.

The roles of prospects can be described as (1) hostile, recalcitrant, or stubbornly defiant; (2) ego-involved, superior ego, or Mr. Big; (3) joker or glad-hander, nothing serious; (4) silent; (5) skeptical, suspicious; (6) slow, methodical; (7) mature, poised thoughtful executive; (8) Mr. Average; (9) impulsive; (10) overly cautious.

The behavior patterns or actions of the individuals in discussion groups can be described as (1) information giver, (2) information seeker, (3) coordinator, (4) evaluator-critic, (5) follower, (6) aggressor, (7) dominator, (8) playboy, (9) sympathy seeker, (10 self-defender.

From the author's research, each participant—the salesman and the prospect in person-to-person sales situations as well as participants in discussion groups—usually plays a limited number or roles, and each role is played with perhaps the same degree of organismic involvement or intensity of enactment. On the other hand, a skilled conference leader may vary his role from being a dogmatic and accusative individual to that of being a conciliatory force. He will also display a greater range in intensity enactment in his roles than will the salesman. Why? Because a conference leader is trained to play a number of roles and to exhibit a range in the intensity enactment of each role. This is how he perceives his role and attempts to enact it accordingly.

Furthermore, and this is vitally important, one of the major reasons for this is that the conference leader is given *accepted* tools to use, such as overhead and direct questions, etc., and he is concerned with skills, knowledge, and attitudes that will permit him to judge the correctness or incorrectness of his efforts. He understands the "why" of what he is doing. He knows whether or not he is on a target. And if he isn't, he adjusts. This is not true of selling to the degree it is true of conference leadership. The situations, of course, are different. For instance, conference leadership involves a group situation. The conference leader is not involved in a

---

[9] This research included companies enjoying national distribution as well as small companies competing in regional markets. Tangible and intangible consumer goods and industrial products were all represented. A few of the representative companies included in this research are Pratt & Whitney, Steelcase, Blue Cross–Blue Shield, Iron City Company of Pittsburgh, Hunting-Roberts of Los Angeles, Standard Block Company of Lansing, Michigan General Telephone, Norge, and Carborundum.

[10] Titles for these various roles are adapted from role titles used by social psychologists.

Selling: A Behavioral Science Approach

person-to-person situation nor is an actual sale involved. There are perhaps many, many other variables as well.

Nevertheless, in the author's opinion, the basic difference goes back to training, and the conference leader understands and accepts his role. This is supported by the concepts of "heated acting" and role playing.

ACTING AND ROLE PLAYING

In general, salesmen, like participants in discussion groups, play a restricted number of roles and enact each role with the same degree of intensity. Nevertheless, a salesman's role may, on any given day, range from minimal participation or involvement, such as saying a few words plus a few movements involved in filling out an order (motoric level) to a role involving heated acting where, in fact, the combined facial expression plus motor actions suggest substantial intensity involvement.

This concept of heated action is associated with level three of a series of situations which were selected by Sarbin to relate certain roles with intensity of enactment (organismic involvement). These roles vary from level one largely motoric action to level seven which is the ultimate in the intensity dimension and which may even lead to death. It is his discussions of levels two and three which parallel the role and intensity enactment of the salesmen in most sales situations.

Level two is described as that of the ". . . dramatic actor who performs the motions necessary for the portrayal of the role assigned to him." It is mechanical acting. The ". . . actor does not become involved; the self is relatively autonomous from the role. He must maintain a certain degree of consistency in the various response systems, which calls for more effort and precludes the degree of autonomy of the casual role." "This degree of involvement," Sarbin tells us, "is seen in many everyday interactions."[11] For instance, the employee who puts on a good front to impress the boss, the hostess who is entertaining the new neighbors, or any one of a hundred social situations.[12]

At level three the heated-acting concept is used. It describes a more automatic kind of acting than the mechanical acting of level two. Heated acting is commonly called "living the role." Here the actor behaves as if he *is* the character in the drama. "Of course, the successful actor maintains some contact with his role as actor in order to change his tempo, amplitude, intensity, etc., as conditions warrant. His involvement includes some affective (feelings) as well as motoric components. In order to portray anger, for example, the actor may work up a rage by violently shaking a ladder in the wings before appearing on the stage."[13]

It is the author's observation that in person-to-person sales situations approximately four salesmen out of ten perform at level one or between level one and level two and approximately six salesmen out of ten function at level two or less. Perhaps few situations call for the intensity enactment

---

[11] Lindzey, *op. cit.*, p. 233.

[12] For an easy-reading, fascinating, and informative account of roles people play in everyday life, see Eric Berne, *Games People Play*, Grove Press, Inc., New York, 1964.

[13] Lindzey, *op. cit.*, p. 233.

of role three. In any event, the writer has seldom made a joint call where a salesman enacted a role comparable to the *upper* ranges of level three. Role performance level, however, varied greatly among different classifications of salesmen. Route salesmen, distributor salesmen, and retail salesmen making outside calls generally operated at level one in six to seven cases out of ten and in the lower ranges of level two, three to four cases out of ten. Manufacturer salesmen, who were responsible for working with various stages of the distribution system, for example, working with distributors and also selling direct in some cases operated, by and large, at level two, or the lower level of two. Some, of course, at times operated at level one and three.

Unfortunately these observations were made when the author traveled with salesmen to gather sales case material *prior* to conducting sales training and conference leadership programs. Therefore the writer has limited research indicating the level or range of performance individual salesmen may exhibit directly after a sales training program. However, he has considerable performance data from role playing and conference leader discussion roles, which will be helpful in suggesting whether or not a properly oriented sales training program will enable the salesman to more readily play a number of roles or the same role with a greater degree of intensity enactment.

It should be established at this juncture that it is of strategic importance that each salesman have a reasonable degree of skill in portraying various roles. As psychologist Sarbin says, "It is a widely accepted postulate that the more roles in a person's behavior repertory, the 'better' his social adjustment—other things being equal."[14] To be sure, this statement could be just as valid if it read, "The more roles in a salesman's behavior repertory, the better his sales adjustment —other things being equal."

Role playing is used by the author to train salesmen to function more effectively in three forms of selling. One form is the traditional face-to-face selling situations which embraces the vast majority of salesmen selling today. The second form is the group sales situation. In this situation the salesman presents his proposal to a group of interested individuals. It is not uncommon in the industrial field, in investment selling, and in the foods field. This form is rapidly becoming more common. For instance, salesmen of Pratt & Whitney, a nationally known company manufacturing machine tools, cutting tools and gauges, are frequently called upon to present their proposal to groups numbering up to ten people who in some way may be affected by or are in a position to provide information concerning the purchase of a new piece of production equipment. Salesmen for Superior Coach, the world's largest producer of school buses, are frequently required to present a proposal to a group, for example, a school board. Salesmen selling such investments opportunities as Norge coin-operated dry-cleaning laundry villages frequently present their program to a group of interested buyers. These buyers may have banded together to form a corporation and operate a village.

The third situation involves a group of salesmen representing one

[14] *Ibid.,* p. 233.

Selling: A Behavioral Science Approach

company who present a proposal to a buying group comparable to the group described in situation two. Frequently this third role emerges when a group of specialists from one company, for example, a manufacturer of industrial machine tools, cutting tools, and gauges, have made a survey of a particular company's production needs, and after the completion of the survey, the survey team presents a proposal to a group representing officers, production people, etc., of the company surveyed.

Role playing for person-to-person selling requires two salesmen in face-to-face situations to act out certain specific roles. These roles are enacted before other salesmen who function as observers. At least fifteen minutes before the role playing takes place, each salesman selected to play a role is handed a "facts card" describing the role he is to play. This, of course, varies greatly according to the situation. This writer has given role assignments to members of a team presenting a survey a month before the role enactment took place.

This facts card may describe the role of the prospect, or it may describe the role of the salesman. A facts card describing the role of the prospect or of the customer should describe the company setting, its problems, etc., and it should describe the prospect with respect to his role in the company and provide some trait analysis of the prospect as well. The same is true of the facts card describing the salesman's role. The company and situation must be realistic and represent everyday sales situations and problems faced by the salesman.

Thus, one salesman becomes the prospect and the other plays the salesman's role. One salesman may be required to play the role of a silent and uncooperative prospect. He may be given detailed instructions such as breaking down and gradually discussing the salesman's proposal, if the salesman exhibits certain qualities and enacts certain forms of aggressiveness. In the other half of the role-playing situation, another salesman receives an instruction card describing how he should function in his sales role. He may be told how far to go in intensity enactment to jar the silent, uncooperative type of prospect into discussion. Neither role player will know for sure what instructions the other has received. But they are told to act out or play their respective roles to the hilt.

This is the role-playing situation. After allowing the role players time to study their respective roles, they come before the observers and role-play or act out their parts. The observers are the remaining salesmen in the training group. These salesmen are divided into two major groups: one group being assigned to report on the role enactment by the prospect and the other group on the role enactment of the salesman. In the case of large groups, each of the major groups are further subdivided into tables of six. Each table will elect a chairman or a reporter who will lead the group discussion of the role enactment. Later, after the group has discussed the role played, the chairman will report his group's analysis to the other groups. Normally the observing groups are not told any facts concerning the roles to be enacted other than the case itself and the fictitious names of the salesman and prospect. These names often imply the roles the salesmen are to play, for instance, the prospect may be called Mr. Silent Prospect and the salesman, Mr. Aggressive, or the pair may be called Mr. Doubtful and Mr. Problem Solver. The reporting table may be provided with work sheets giving a list of techniques the observers are supposed to identify and discuss. The possibilities, concepts, or ideas of how role playing can be used as a training tool are unlimited.

If well planned, role playing is an excellent group dynamics tool, and when used as one training device in combination with other training devices, results have been rewarding. For instance, a very successful role-playing program involved five beginning insurance agents who, in addition to the regular company training program, met from 9 until 10 every other Monday morning for a period of six months. Each took turns role playing various sales situations. Then they discussed each other's performance. During this phase of their sales training program each salesman improved considerably in the mechanics of selling. Also, each salesman developed a noticeable degree of plasticity or intensity in role enactment. The degree of plasticity achieved by this group was substantially greater than that exhibited in general by the 140 salesmen previously mentioned who had no role-playing training experiences.

Another case involved a large number, more than ninety industrial salesmen. Smaller manageable groups were obtained by holding comparable meetings in the East, Midwest, and Far West. These men represented a large manufacturer of machine tools, cutting tools, and gauges. Each salesman participated for a minimum of twenty-three days in this sales training program. These salesmen sold direct as well as worked with distributors. They were responsible for training distributor salesmen, thus the role playing in this company's case involved five situations. Each salesman role played (1) a conference discussion leader, (2) a teacher presenting a sales training program to a group of distributor salesmen,[15] (3) the member of a team presenting a proposal to a group, (4) an individual presenting a proposal to a group, (5) a man-to-man, or salesman-customer, situation.

In the person-to-person role-play situation, these industrial salesmen, like the small group of insurance salesmen previously mentioned, achieved a noticeably greater degree of plasticity than was exhibited in general by the 140 salesmen who had no role-training experience.

Further, many of these industrial salesmen showed greater plasticity in the other four roles than they did in the person-to-person role situation. In brief, they exhibited a substantially greater intensity in role enactment in the conference leadership, training of distributor salesmen, and in group-selling roles than they did in the face-to-face sales situations.

Another role-playing seminar involved a group of twelve district sales managers, who, in addition to their personal sales function, also managed and trained the salesmen in their districts. In addition, two sales managers who functioned on a national basis participated in the seminar. This program was designed for an eight-week period. Each Monday was set aside for conferences. Prior to the initial meeting, each of the district sales managers received material comparable to the manpower development chapters in this book but which was specifically designed for this com-

[15] Only eighteen salesmen of this group actually conducted these sessions. The other participants role-played distributor salesmen.

Selling: A Behavioral Science Approach

pany. This material was read prior to the first meeting. At the first meeting the writer led the conference discussion. At the end of the first day, and in preparation for the following Monday, a chapter comparable to any of the chapters in this book, but again specifically designed for this company, was distributed to the managers. Each manager was assigned the particular part of the chapter in which he was to lead a conference discussion designed to last approximately one-half hour during the next session. This same format was followed for the remaining seven weeks.

Lesson plans were substituted for role-playing facts cards. Gradually the conference leadership techniques were enlarged to where the participants were role-playing teaching in terms of sales training. Each conference leader's performance was evaluated by his fellow managers. The result was that the role-playing capacity of each of the sales managers enlarged significantly, and each developed a noticeably greater range in his intensity of role enactment. One man's change was truly remarkable.

One sales manager's behavior activity suggested qualities of being argumentative, belligerent, opinionated, and in fact doubtful of any system, idea, concept, or training but his own. In the third week of the program he was assigned a conference topic, "The Art of Listening," and a second assignment, "The Conference as an Educational Tool." Much of the material presented in these two assignments were in conflict with many of the qualities this man exhibited. After these two sessions this man related that, "this has been one of the most profound lessons I have ever had. What an opinionated person I have been." From that point on this district sales manager became one of the most promising sales trainers in the group, and as a member of discussion groups, he being well prepared, played a number of roles in the conference discussion group shifting from one to the other with plasticity, and when needed, with intensity.

From the discussion of roles above, and within the framework of the cases presented, a number of general conclusions can be drawn.

1. Approximately 80 percent of the 140 salesmen who were observed in person-to-person sales situations but who had no training in role playing lacked sufficient plasticity to play different roles at the intensity level required in selling. In other words, they functioned at level one or the upper ranges of level one or at the lower ranges of level two, as discussed above. Approximately 15 percent of these salesmen operated in the acceptable ranges of level two. Less than 5 percent of these salesmen had sufficient plasticity to reach level three—the heated-acting level.

2. Salesmen role playing in training sessions portrayed more roles and with considerably greater flexibility and intensity than did the 140 salesmen.

3. In role-playing training sessions, salesmen exhibited a significantly greater range in roles played plus greater intensity enactment in conference leadership roles, selling to a group, and as a member of a team selling to the group, than they did in person-to-person sales situations.

4. Sales managers, responsible for the training function, acquired considerable plasticity in playing various roles and in intensity of enactment through a combination of role-playing and conference-discussion training

conferences. Their flexibility was noticeably greater than that of the salesmen in general.

5. The author's final conclusion is this: From actual experience role playing proved to be an effective sales training tool. This is true of person-to-person role playing, and especially true of roles in conference leadership, selling to a group, and as a member of a team selling to a group. It must be remembered, however, that salesmen and sales managers who were involved in these sales training programs had extensive reading, discussing, and case study preparation in the "whys" of the various concepts, techniques, and strategies they were to utilize in role playing. Further, role playing was used to reinforce this prior experience and to develop motor and mechanical skills.

TENSION BINDING

In the everyday world of selling, the concept of tension binding has several implications for the salesman. It is closely related to the previous discussion of number of roles and intensity of enactment. Simply stated, tension binding is the ability to inhibit a motoric act once the stimulus for the act has been perceived.

Ability to restrict tension makes it possible for an individual (a salesman) to inhibit inappropriate role behavior. Some individuals can inhibit motoric acts for sustained periods of time, whereas others can withstand the tension for only brief periods. Social psychologists refer to those who are deficient in the ability to bind tensions as undercontrollers, that is, lack of self-control. Those who bind tension more than objective conditions warrant are referred to as "overcontrollers."

> Research shows that persons diagnosed as psychopaths exhibit the inability to bind tensions, they act on impulse, they are unconcerned about the approval or disapproval of others. Persons diagnosed as neurotic characteristically over-bind tension. They act compulsively rather than incompulsively, they are over concerned about the approval or disapproval of others.[16]

Transfer of the social psychologists' tension-binding concept to salesmanship is readily accomplished if the premise is accepted that one of the salesman's roles is to be an emotional stabilizer during the sales interview.

Salesmanship requires a high threshold of tension binding—not a low threshold. Every day each salesman may be faced with many annoying stimuli. He may fulfill or deny the tendency to act upon perceiving the stimuli. If he has a low threshold (very sensitive and quickly annoyed), he will act impulsively. With a high threshold he will act more prudently. He will be far removed from the state of easily being annoyed—a luxury, if it can be called that, that few salesmen can afford.

Having a high threshold with regard to tension binding does not mean an individual cannot exhibit intensity of enactment in various roles, nor does it mean an individual cannot at times function at the heated-acting level. A highly effective actor may have a low or high threshold of tension binding. That this is true also of the sales situation is obvious. It benefits

---
[16] Lindzey, *op. cit.*, p. 245.

Selling: A Behavioral Science Approach

the salesman to have a high threshold of tension binding so that when a prospect or customer is negative in manner, action, or word, the salesman controls his motor responses and conserves his mental resources.

In brief, the salesman has to think in terms of the "as if" dimensions.[17] When an individual has the "as if" dimension, he has the ability to treat an object, the actions of an individual, or an event as if it is something else. At times the salesman may act as if a certain act of a prospect or customer, such as a negative statement about the salesman or the salesman's company, or the product or service involved, or any event or happening which would normally be considered as threatening to one's ego or self-image, is never happening. It is a form of repression but a useful one.

EMPATHY AND SYMPATHY

Both empathy and sympathy, in varying degrees, slice across the main classes of man's emotions such as (1) primary emotions: joy, fear, anger, grief; (2) emotions pertaining to sensory stimulation: pain, disgust, or delight; (3) emotions pertaining to self-appraisal: shame, pride, guilt; (4) emotions pertaining to other people: love, hate, pity; (5) appreciative emotions: humor, beauty, wonder; (6) moods: sadness, anxiety, elations.[18]

In discussing the concepts of empathy and sympathy it will be realized that each of these concepts may relate in some way to each of the six main classes of emotions established above.

Empathy is "feeling the same emotion that is being expressed by another person, for example, feeling fear when another person shows signs of fright." Sympathy is ". . . the experience of positive emotion pertaining to the emotional state or circumstance of another person, such as the mother's feeling of protective tenderness toward her frightened child."[19]

An empathetic person can place himself in the other person's situation. He can play the role of the other individual. Or, as it is commonly expressed, he can put himself in the other individual's shoes. This, however, is not necessarily true of the sympathetic individual. The sympathetic mother may experience a positive emotion, for example, being sorry or happy because her daughter is frightened or elated but that does not mean that the mother sees the situation the same way the daughter does. To empathize, we need to perceive the situation the same way the other individual does.

More specifically, "When we have 'caught' the emotions of the other or express it in ourselves, we say that we empathize with the other."[20] But to the salesman, there is another dimension to empathy. From the discussion above, it is seen that in role playing the individual is also involved in role taking, that is, adapting to the attitude or perspective of the other. This is primarily a covert process, but in selling it may become overt, that is, when it is meaningful. Thus, "Not only must the salesman be empathetic, but he must have the ability to project this quality. He

[17] *Ibid.*, p. 238.
[18] Krech and Crutchfield, *op. cit.*, p. 235.
[19] *Ibid.*, p. 264.
[20] *Ibid.*, p. 233.

Role

must project so that the prospect knows the salesman understands his situation and problems."[21]

Psychologists Cottrell and Dymond[22] got a general picture of the abilities possessed by the empathetic and nonempathetic person through testing and other studies. Empathetic individuals were judged as emotionally expressive, insightful, outgoing, optimistic, warm, interested in others, flexible, and having had satisfactory family relations in childhood. Nonempathetic persons were judged to be rigid, introverted, non-insightful, inhibited, emotional, and subject to emotional outbursts. These nonempathetic individuals, according to the research, experienced difficulty in interpersonal relations, mistrusted others, were less well integrated, and had had unsatisfactory family relations in childhood.

Another facet to the understanding of the empathetic person is provided by Baker,[23] who studied two groups of male prisoners. One group was judged to be psychopathic and the others nonpsychopathic. Baker tested the hypothesis that male psychopaths would be less able to empathize with their cell mates than would nonpsychopaths. As one might suspect, the research verified the prediction. From the sales standpoint, the major point is that those individuals who were *fixated at the self level* have difficulty in taking the role of others. This last proposition has been generally verified by a number of other research studies.

These studies give us a good idea of what is meant by the empathetic and nonempathetic individual. Referring back to the six classes of emotions mentioned previously, it is clear this discussion has been about feelings. And feelings, yours and the other individuals, are equally important in selling and in everyday life.

Perhaps the biggest roadblock to being empathetic is the ego. The ego won't permit us to disassociate ourselves from our own particular view or position and resultant feelings and see the other person's situation. An empathetic salesman keeps this perspective foremost in his mind at all times and does not think in terms of *his* and *mine,* nor has he any tendency to think of the prospect or customer as an opponent. Rather, he understands and feels the prospect's needs as an individual. But he still wants to get at the prospect's or customer's situation with respect to employing the salesman's services or product. The individual has an emotional gate. You can attempt to push it open, you can ram through it, or knock lightly and let the customer open it. Granted that the salesman must play many roles and vary these roles with the various contacts, the empathetic individual in general will use the knock-lightly or middle-of-the-road approach. And being empathetic, according to Mayer and Greenberg,[24] is exceedingly significant. To these writers the two basic qualities, empathy and ego drive, form the cornerstone of selling.

Many salesmen construe the empathy concept to mean that a salesman can't be purposeful and positive in the sales talk. This is wrong. The salesman must believe that his product and services are best for the cus-

[21] Joseph W. Thompson, *Manager Development,* Pratt & Whitney Corp., Inc., Hartford, Conn., 1965, p. 14.

[22] Lindzey, *op. cit.,* p. 247.

[23] *Ibid.,* p. 246.

[24] David Mayer and Herbert M. Greenberg, "What Makes a Good Salesman," *Harvard Business Review,* p. 118, July–August, 1964.

Selling: A Behavioral Science Approach

tomer. If there is a difference in a product and the salesman believes his competition's product is slightly better, he still should sell positively. Are there not differences in companies and in guarantees that are important? Will not the salesman be of service after the sale? These factors can and should offset a difference in product quality or price in the long run. Thus the salesman must sell positively.

Empathy, fortunately, is for the most part a learned quality. Many individuals practice it without knowing it. But the real value found in empathy is to use this quality knowingly. Since it is such an indispensable quality, the salesman may wish to review the following ideas:

1. Review and understand the concepts of empathy and sympathy. What do they mean?

2. Review empathy as used in the contact stage of this book. Note specifically the interaction of the question forms—verification and permissive—with the direction, future, and problem-solving quarters of the contact stage. See the dialogue on page 219 for a verbal statement which suggests to the prospect that the salesman understands the prospect's situation.

3. Use the concept of empathy at every opportunity, be it social situations in the home or in business.

4. Keep intelligence information on your customers and prospects. Your observations should be planned. Make notes on your customer's and prospect's behavior after every call.

5. Don't make snap judgments about the behavior patterns of other individuals. Interpretation should follow the collection of data, not during the collection.

6. Don't be ego-involved. Look for your shortcomings. For example, have you, in all sales situations in which you are involved, looked primarily at the situation from the other individual's perspective—both his emotional and business situation?

7. Finally, follow the advice of Cottrell, who neatly tells how an individual observer can enhance his ability to play the role of another. He wrote, "Just the simple device of saying to himself, 'Now I am X facing this situation and having to deal with this problem,' seems to enhance the observer's comprehension of the perspectives, attitudes, and overt behavior of his subject." Cottrell also adds that "deliberate role-taking practice also seems to increase these observational skills."[25]

Summary

Self-image is how the individual views himself, and self is what the individual is. The salesman may view himself as honest, aggressive, fluent, smooth, self-reliant, and likable; however, he may not be.

Role is what the salesman is to do or to be. Role behavior or enactment is the doing or the action of the individual with reference to a given

[25] L. S. Cottrell, Jr., "Some Neglected Problems in Psychology," *American Sociological Review*, vol. XV, pp. 705–712, 1950.

role. Each salesman has several roles to perform. Role enactment is how well he functions and performs these roles. The role of one salesman may be to stand before a group and explain the merits of his product to that group. How he does this is the enactment of the role. Role expectation is how or what the viewer expects or anticipates with respect to a certain role.

Role perception is how you view the other person. The sales manager, for instance, may have certain role expectations with regard to the salesman's group-selling presentation. The sales manager's role perception will depend not only on how the salesman enacts his role but the sales manager's broad perceptual powers as well.

Each salesman performs a given number of roles in functioning as a salesman for his company. This is subject to observation and report. In the research involving joint calls on prospects and customers with more than 140 salesmen representing twenty-seven different companies, a number of frequently played roles were identified as ranging from information giver to the role of being an extroverted or overly expressive sales person.

By comparing the intensity of the role enactment of these salesmen against a scale of seven levels of intensity of enactment, it was determined that the majority of salesmen function at role level two or less.

In addition to salesman-to-prospect selling roles and group-selling roles, it is not uncommon for salesmen to be required to function in the role of conference leader. According to research in which approximately 120 salesmen and sales managers were observed for a total of 360 hours in conference roles, it was found that the participants exhibited a greater plasticity for functioning in various capacities within the role of conference leader than did salesmen in salesman-to-prospect sales situations. One of the major reasons for this difference is that in conference leadership there are widely accepted tools that may be used. Further, no sales are involved.

One of the best ways to train sales people to play various roles and to enact various roles with varying levels of intensity enactment is through the role-playing concept in the classroom.

In previous chapters it was indicated that the salesman should develop a coping behavior to better adapt to the emotional needs of some prospects. When the salesman exhibits a changing behavior pattern in order to cope with the prospect's activities, he is changing roles. In order to change roles and adjust to situations, a salesman has to have the ability to bind tension. Tension binding is the ability to inhibit a motoric act once the stimulus for the act has been perceived. Having the ability to restrict tension makes it possible for the salesman to inhibit inappropriate role behavior. The ability to inhibit motoric acts varies greatly among individuals. Some individuals are undercontrollers and other individuals may be overcontrollers. Salesmanship requires a high threshold of tension binding, not a low threshold.

Both empathy and sympathy in varying degrees slice across the main classes of man's emotions.

An empathetic person can place himself in the other person's situation. He can play the role of the other individual. In a word, he can put himself in the other individual's shoes. Sympathy, on the other hand, is

Selling: A Behavioral Science Approach

the experience of positive emotion pertaining to the emotional circumstances of another person. But a sympathetic person may or may not be able to place himself in the other person's situation.

Empathy and being able to project this quality to the prospect is one of the most important traits a salesman can have for successful selling. Fortunately, for the most part, empathy is a learned quality.

Chapter 6 DISCUSSION QUESTIONS

1 Describe a number of roles a salesman enacts.
2 If you describe the job the salesman has to do, for example, group selling, selling to an individual, or some other function, is this the same as saying this is a role the salesman has to enact?
3 What is the difference between role and enactment?
4 Should a salesman enact different roles with varying degrees of intensity of enactement? Would a salesman be successful if he had a middle-of-the-road level of intensity enactment for each role he enacted? Would this be true if he enacted all roles with a high level of intensity?
5 What is the relationship between self-image and role? Can a salesman's role be incongruent with his self-image? If it is, would this be a form of conflict, or would the salesman be quite happy in his work?
6 From your experience take any sales situation and describe the salesman's functioning in that role with respect to concepts of role perception, role expectation, and role enactment. Does the student on a college campus function in various roles? Assume that you are witnessing a student who is monopolizing the conversation within the group, who is jabbing his finger into other people in order to emphasize the points he is making, who is jumping on sentences, who is talking about himself and, in other words, being somewhat of a bore. Discuss what you witnessed in terms of role perception, role expectation, and role enactment. Do you think other people analyze your activities with respect to their role expectations and your role enactment?
7 What self-images do you have of yourself? Select any two friends and identify what you believe may be self-images those individuals have of themselves. Is it possible for you to identify behavior activities of those individuals that coincide with what you feel is that individual's self-image?
8 How many roles should a salesman be able to enact? What level of intensity of enactment should the salesman be able to effect? Do you think that salesmen in general have substantial plasticity in role enactment? Why or why not? Do you think plasticity in role enactment can be acquired? If it can be acquired, would this be a form of faking? Why or why not?
9 If an individual has a high level of tension binding and he exercises this high level of tension binding whenever he is faced with difficult situations, is he being a normal individual or is he being an abnormal individual? Do you have a high level of tension binding? Is this good? Is this bad? Is this true of the salesman? Why? Why not?
10 Empathy is considered to be one of the most important concepts in selling. Describe why it is important. Describe the type of salesman who can be empathetic. Describe the possible reactions of prospects or customers to empathetic sales people. Can the feeling of empathy be acquired? How?

the salesman as an educator

7

INTRODUCTION

"Educators are salesmen—or at least they should be. Educators are selling ideas and knowledge. The more effective they are as sales purveyors of their knowledge, concepts, and ideas the more effective they will be as educators."[1] In the same sense salesmen are educators, and the more effective they are as educators, the more effective they will be as sales purveyors of their knowledge, concepts, and ideas—in brief, their sales proposal.

If the concept is accepted that the salesman informs a prospect about his product, discusses problems with him, shows new uses for his product, carries information, conveys or communicates ideas to individuals with varying degrees of perception, and sells within the marketing concept, then the salesman must be accepted as an educator.

Of all the social sciences, educational psychology probably is the most profitable area of study for the salesman. Moreover, it should be added that sales managers, especially those who act as sales trainers, would be more effective if they, too, understood more about education.

"There is nothing new under the sun" is an old maxim that applies in many ways to learning. Even the ancient Greeks attempted to understand the learning process. Aristotle believed learning involved the association of ideas following the concepts of similarity, contrast, and contiguity.[2] In the centuries following, these ideas and others were explored, but it wasn't until the turn of the century that the concept of association received experimental analysis. Of special interest are two blocks of research—one completed by Pavlov, a Russian, another by Thorndike, an American. Pavlov's work on conditioning and Thorndike's work on association provided practical material and are so widely accepted in education, psychology, and the business world that the concepts appear to be just common sense. Yet Pavlov won a Nobel prize for his work, and Thorndike's work is recognized as one of the most important contributions to educational psychology of the past fifty years. Pavlov's work, as it relates to stimulus-response selling, is discussed elsewhere in this book. Here the discussion will concentrate on Thorndike's psychology of *connectionism*

---

[1] Joseph W. Thompson and William Lazer, *Pratt & Whitney Manpower Development Program*, Pratt & Whitney Corp., Inc., West Hartford, Conn., 1964, p. 1.
[2] Glenn M. Blair, R. Stewart Jones, and Ray H. Simpson, *Educational Psychology*, The Macmillan Company, New York, 1962, p. 107.

Selling: A Behavioral Science Approach

and its laws. This includes the law of effect, the law of exercise, the law of belongingness, and the law of readiness. These laws find a common root in the concept of association or connection between two or more factors.

GENERAL EDUCATIONAL PSYCHOLOGY

Law of Effect

Briefly stated by Blair, the law of effect ". . . tells those who teach that learners will acquire and remember those responses which lead to satisfying after effects. A praised response will be retained longer than one which is not praised or one which is called wrong."[3] A broader way of looking at the law of effect is given by Smith, who states,

> When a response to a situation is accompanied or followed by a satisfied feeling that response tends to be repeated; but when it is accompanied or followed by an unsatisfied feeling, the response tends to be eliminated. Our various motives demand satisfaction and when we are able to satisfy them we have a pleasant, satisfied feeling. When we fail to satisfy them, we have an unpleasant, unsatisfied feeling. . . . We tend to adopt—to learn—any behavior that leads us to goals that satisfy motives. We tend to eliminate any behavior that fails to lead us to a desirable end. And we tend to eliminate behavior that results in threats or punishment.[4]

How can this law be used in selling? Perhaps the first impulse is to say that a salesman cannot praise a prospect like a teacher can a student, but let's see about that.

A vacuum cleaner salesman is explaining to a housewife how the waxing attachment operates, and she exclaims, "Oh! You mean the airflow is changed around, so it will work the waxer brush." He uses the law of effect when he says, "Yes, Mrs. Jones, that is it," or "That's a good way of putting it," or " 'Changed around,' I'll have to remember that. It describes the idea well."

In contrast, these three replies illustrate, in decreasing order, less application of the law of effect.

1. Yes, that's what I said.
2. No, not quite.
3. No, you don't understand. You see, by changing adapters A and B the reversed airflow energizes attachment Y, two small metal gates are dropped, and the air forces the waxer head to revolve in a circular motion.

Looking back over your sales career, how many times have you had the opportunity to say in reply to a question, "Yes, that's right," or "That's a good idea," or "I hadn't thought of that," or "That's an interesting idea," or "That's a new approach," or some similar statement that makes the experience of asking questions a satisfying one for the prospect?

---

[3] *Ibid.*, p. 108.
[4] Henry P. Smith, *Psychology in Teaching*, Prentice-Hall, Inc., Englewood Cliffs, N.J., 1962, p. 280.

The Salesman as an Educator

Another practical illustration of how *not* to use the concept is given by a Blue Cross–Blue Shield salesman.[5] This particular salesman being self-centered, found it difficult to give anyone else credit for ideas, and this difficulty showed up in his sales work.

It was salesman Mr. Self-centered's third discussion in a period of two weeks with the personnel director of Preston Steel, Inc., a large manufacturing firm. On his previous calls salesman Self-centered had described to this personnel director the details of a new type of health care program and apparently it seemed it would be an excellent addition to Preston Steel's employee program. Also, during his first call or discussion with the personnel director, salesman Self-centered had casually commented that he thought the Blue Cross health care program had so many new features that it might provide excellent material for an article in the *Journal of Personnel*. Now, during the process of the third call, the personnel director commented, "You know, all in all, there are a lot of good ideas here. If we go ahead with this program, I think I'll make a case history out of it and do an article for the *Journal of Personnel*. And I think our president, Mr. Brown, would like the idea, too." The salesman replied, "Yes, I told you that on my first call."

Application of the law of effect, however, is not restricted to verbal praise situations. The law of effect operates whenever the experience is satisfying, thus, in the sales situation, whenever a prospect asks a question, raises a doubt, makes a statement, etc., and the reply by the salesman is such that the experience is satisfying to the prospect, then the law of effect is in operation. Assume, for example, that the customer inquires as to how a certain type drill could be used for drilling holes in an extremely hard metal. The salesman knows and explains to the customer's satisfaction. If, on the other hand, the salesman cannot answer the question raised by the prospect, it may prove embarrassing to the prospect or it may cause a lack of confidence in the salesman, or if the salesman gives a wrong answer, the same prospect responses as cited above may evolve. In brief, the experience would not be satisfying, and the interview may be terminated especially if the situation is repeated several times.

Not only has the law of effect application in face-to-face communication situations, but it has important implications for the sales trainer as well. It is this. The law states tht satisfying experiences tend to be repeated. Using an analogy from Michigan's ski slopes, if you want someone to start skiing, make his first skiing experience rewarding. You want to make it fun. Therefore, it is good advice to see that before the skier starts down the hill, he takes a lesson from the ski pro. When able to make some elementary turns without falling continuously, the novice may want to ski again.

Isn't this situation just as true of selling? Perhaps most sales managers would say, "Yes, I understand that analogy." But too many sales managers have failed to train their salesmen to handle sales situations adequately. The result is a bruised ego. It is small wonder that thousands

[5] Joseph W. Thompson, *Blue Cross–Blue Shield Manpower Development Program Book*, Blue Cross–Blue Shield, Indianapolis, Ind., 1963, chap. 9.

Selling: A Behavioral Science Approach

of salesmen, who could be good salesmen, are no more than good order takers. Frequently their experiences, when calling on new accounts, have been disastrous, especially to the ego. A refusal is not a rewarding experience, especially in public. Each salesman must be trained at how to get at the firm's problems, to understand and handle the prospect or customer's needs, and to be able to provide solutions to the problems and needs.

Salesmen who make regular calls on customers may see a special application of this law. The application is found in these questions: Do your customers find your sales call rewarding or satisfying? Is it an enjoyable, profitable experience for the customer? It is taken for granted the customer likes you personally, but do you, before each call, develop ideas that could be of value to the customer, either in the use of your product or ideas that may be of value to his business in general?

The Law of Exercise

To the salesman as an educator this law has the least specific application of the four principles of learning, but it does have several broad implications. This law states, "When a connection between a situation and a response is repeated, the connection is strengthened, other things being equal; but when the connection is not used over a period of time, it is weakened."[6]

Thus this law tells the salesman that infrequent calls on a customer may lead to a weakening of the connection between the salesman and the prospect. In brief, it suggests that absence does not make the heart grow fonder.

It also tells the salesman, and the sales manager, that if the salesman does not regularly use, for instance, the question techniques associated with the contact stage of the sales interview, there is a strong possibility these techniques will be forgotten. In addition to the practice of techniques, this law also has application with respect to attitude.

Accordingly it tells the salesman that if he practices a poised, mature, need-seeking, and problem-solving, emphatic sales procedure with his customers and prospects and does this in a friendly, relaxed fashion, the pattern will become a well-established personality trait.

Finally it tells the salesman that if he practices poor selling habits, he will have well-established bad habits.

The Law of Readiness

This law has many implications for the salesman. Educational psychologists frequently describe readiness as an emotional process. For instance, "once an attractive goal has been identified, to move toward it is pleasant, not to do so is annoying."[7] They also tell us that a man will

[6] Henry P. Smith, *Psychology in Teaching*, Prentice-Hall, Inc., Englewood Cliffs, N.J., 1962, p. 280.
[7] *Ibid.*, p. 281.

learn, will participate mentally, when he *wants* to and when he has the *ability* to do so.

But what determines readiness? Many factors, such as the educational level of the individual, his past experience, his emotions, his level of aspiration, his achievement, and his attitude. These variables, in varying degrees, all determine readiness.

This is where the educator starts. He receives a "package" with a certain degree of built-in readiness or the want to learn and the ability to learn. In terms of this, one of the first tasks of the educator is to appraise the student's desire and ability to learn. He appraises in terms of the skills, understandings, and knowledges required to study given material.

It is after the appraisal, however, that the real job of the educator begins. Now he must *build readiness*. He must prepare the student to learn. He presents assignments, sets the stage, arouses curiosity, in other words, appeals to the inner man. He does this by presenting *meaningful* material, that is, material of interest and material relating to the objective or goal in the situation. And he does this by getting the *participation* or the *involvement* of the student. It is in this final area where many educators and salesmen fail.

Now let's look at these concepts of education from the salesman's viewpoint. It may be easier for the educator to determine the general readiness of the individual or class to understand the subject than for the salesman to determine the readiness of the prospect to understand his proposal. The educator may give a diagnostic test, and if a student lacks background to comprehend the course, the educator may back up and prepare him. The educator also appraises the student's interest by observations and by asking questions.

It is apparent the salesman cannot give a test to appraise the prospect's or customer's readiness. But he can manage his sales effort so that it evolves around the problems of the prospect. With this approach, the question techniques used in the contact stages and throughout the sale permit the salesman to obtain the mental participation of the prospect or customer and in so doing furnish verbal and nonverbal feedback to the discerning salesman. This process permits the salesman to determine, in varying degrees, the level of the prospect's interest and understanding. It exposes the prospect's problem and situation. In this manner, not only does a salesman determine the readiness of the prospect to understand the proposal, but he *builds* a readiness of the prospect to understand. He does this by presenting meaningful material (the problem of the individual) and obtaining mental participation or, in other words, getting the prospect involved.

The concept of readiness has one additional implication for the salesman. It is a commonly accepted principle of education that once a student feels a desire to learn, the educator may need to do little more than to offer occasional guidance and encouragement. The trick, of course, to both the educator and the salesman is to establish such an attractive goal the individual being motivated will move to the goal almost on his own power.

Selling: A Behavioral Science Approach

To the educator, the student will want to learn. And to the salesman, the prospect will want to discuss the proposal. Such a goal or want setting is difficult. But it can be achieved. That is the important point.

In summary, the law of readiness establishes two related but distinct concepts. Both are crucial to selling. One is the process of determining, identifying, or appraising the individual's ability and want to learn. The other involves the process of affecting the individual's want and ability to learn. This is done by presenting meaningful material and getting the prospect to participate.

The Law of Belonging

Educational psychologist Smith writes, "When we are able to perceive relationships, the speed of learning and the permanence of attention are greatly increased. The recognition of cause and effect elements, the seeing of relationships between the parts and the total, and the perceiving of familiar elements in a new situation—all these factors greatly increase the speed of learning and the permanence of retention."[8]

Many sections in this book capitalize on the idea basic to this law. For instance, verification and permissive questions are associated with the four quarters of the contact stage, and in fact question techniques are utilized throughout the sales interview. In each case they are associated with a stage or phase of the sales interview. Cause and effect are shown in questions which will result in certain types of responses.

Throughout this book the concepts discussed are significantly related to the salesman's previous learning experiences. The concepts are so discussed that they belong to the context of learning that the salesman has already experienced.

In the same way, the salesman selling machinery equipment presents his new machinery as operating effectively within the prospect's present production system. He talks about low operating costs, but he relates this saving to profit.

In addition to the descriptions and examples above of the laws of education, the following dialogue case is given to illustrate how the various laws may be seen in operation during an actual sales interview.

DIALOGUE ILLUSTRATION—APPLICATION OF THE LAWS OF EDUCATION

CASE Ralph Benson is the general manager of the Peer-Martin Company, a manufacturer of canoes, boats, and boating equipment. The company is located on the outskirts of a city of approximately 50,000 in the state of Wisconsin.

Sales are increasing each year, and the company has enjoyed a substantial boom during the 1963–1965 period. The time is now late fall, 1965.

Benson, who has been with the company for approximately ten years, is a large man, about 6 feet 3 inches tall, weighing about 220 pounds. He is

---

[8] *Ibid.*, pp. 281–282.

The Salesman as an Educator

known as a doer. He is, supposedly, quite dogmatic and the kind of a man who doesn't change his mind easily.

Jim Tate, regional salesman of the Diamond Office Furniture Company, has heard of the company's expansion plans and has learned all of the above facts in the planning phase of this sales call. Assume the contact has been made by telephone and Benson has agreed to see Tate.

S *Salesman*
B *Benson*

1 **S** Hello, Mr. Benson. I am Jim Tate of the Diamond Office Furniture Company and I want to thank you for giving me this opportunity to see you.

2 **B** Sit down. As I told you, I have a few minutes.

3 **S** As my card here indicates (*passing the card to Mr. Benson*), my company is a distributor of six lines of office furniture and combines with that a professional service in design, color, and office flow work. And of course Mr. Benson, that is the reason I am here. I was talking to Mr. Black of the Chamber of Commerce and he told me you were thinking of expanding your plant, office, and display areas. Is my information correct?

4 **B** No, not quite. We do plan on remodeling our display area and doing some new office remodeling as well. But nothing as extensive as you evidently have heard. Perhaps in two or three years we might be working on the plant.

5 **S** Thank you for telling me this, Mr. Benson. And if I may, I would like to ask you a few questions about your remodeling plans.

6 **B** I talked about it at a recent Kiwanis meeting and I expect that is where Black heard about it, so it isn't a secret.

7 **S** Yes, he mentioned your talk, Mr. Benson. And in glowing terms as well.

8 **B** Well, that's always good to hear. I think all businessmen should let each other know they are planning improvements. It shows confidence. But go ahead.

9 **S** Mr. Benson, have you at this point developed your overall plans on what is to be done?

10 **B** Yes and no. We have plans for space and have done some overall thinking along these lines so far.

11 **S** Does that include work on color, design, layout, and such ideas?

12 **B** No, not yet. Our staff has been pretty busy with the regular work to be thinking about that. They will get to it, though.

13 **S** I suspect that the work to be done in color, design, and office work flow is exactly the type of work in which our company specializes. Have you given any thought to having an outside organization work with your people in developing your plans?

14 **B** No, not really. We have some people here who I think can do that work.

15 **S** That sounds all to the good, Mr. Benson. However, do you know the specific services that our company offers?

16 **B** Well, in a way. I did gather from what you said the type of work you do, but I don't want to get involved in outside consulting services.

Selling: A Behavioral Science Approach

17 S I can understand your viewpoint, Mr. Benson. And I'm sure I would feel the same way if I were you. Nevertheless, may I take a few minutes to illustrate the type of service that we could offer if it were needed?

18 B Sure, go ahead. I might as well know a little more about it.

This dialogue illustrates the application of three laws of learning. The law of effect, the law of belonging, and the law of readiness. Application of the law of effect is seen in a number of ways. Benson's responses are made to positive questions by salesman Tate. Tate does use a "rewarding" or "praise" concept by his statement, response 5, "Thank you for telling me this, Mr. Benson," and in response 7, "And in glowing terms as well." Further, each of Benson's replies could easily be satisfying to him. He is a dominant individual. He is the boss. He is probably quite pleased with the fact the company has expanded considerably in recent years and is now in the process of remodeling. Benson is giving information and it is being received tactfully by Tate; therefore it can be assumed Benson is not having unsatisfactory experiences by replying to Tate's questions. Referring back to the first sentence of response 5, contrast the effect if Tate's reply had been, "I am sorry to hear that," or "I guess my information wasn't too good," or "That's the way business goes," instead of the positive answer, "Thank you for telling me this, Mr. Benson." What is more, assume that at any stage of the situation Tate jumped directly into the sale by telling Benson what he could do for him. Would this be a satisfying experience for Benson?

The law of belonging is working to reinforce the law of effect. It is safe to assume that the discussion between Tate and Benson relates to Benson's business and perhaps a problem Benson is wrestling with at this moment.

At the beginning and at the end of this sale several applications of the concept of readiness can be seen. In the initial stage of the interview Tate is appraising Benson's readiness. And he is building readiness by making the material meaningful and obtaining Benson's participation through questioning. Before long Tate will be discussing such concepts as mental fatigue, physical fatigue, buoyancy in colors, work production flow as it relates to the office force, and ways in which sales appeal can be built into the display area. It is safe to assume that Benson is not ready to discuss these concepts. He does not have the background. Tate will be wise if he utilizes the best dictates of education in handling this educational process with Benson.

The reader may wish to analyze this dialogue to determine the interaction between the ten variables of the contact stage and the laws of education.

SUMMATION

How many times have you made a statement only to have the individual indicate it wasn't heard? Yet when the word or statement (stimulus) is repeated the second or third time, it is heard (perceived). In the same way, how many times have you been in the process of explaining

The Salesman as an Educator

an idea, program, or value of your sales proposal when the other individual suddenly seems to understand and says, "Let's see, you think the safety factor, low operating costs, ease of operation, and high productivity all put together will make your machine a better buy then the Air Vent machine."

Both of these cases illustrate the effect of summation, that is, the cumulative effect of repeated or successive stimuli. Summation may be either temporal or spatial. Temporal summation is a phenomenon in which a threshold stimulus when continuously applied at the same point may summate its effect to produce a response. Spatial summation is the summative effect of separate stimuli spread over space. The first situation above represents an example of temporal summation, and the second, an example of spatial summation.

It is known there are sounds so soft we cannot hear them, movements so slight we cannot detect them, and light so faint we cannot see it. Such stimuli are below the threshold of awareness. Nevertheless, stimuli of the same intensity, when repeated, may be cumulative in effect. Apparently, because there is a lag in the receptor mechanism, the receptor continues to respond even after the first subthreshold stimuli is removed. In a simple process of the second subthreshold stimuli being added to the first subthreshold stimuli, it becomes perceived. Another example may clarify these concepts further. For instance, when a stimuli has been applied to one point on the skin and the same stimuli is repeated at the same point, it is called temporal summation. When the stimuli is applied at one point on the skin and then applied to another point, it is referred to as spatial summation. It is important to note that both temporal and spatial stimuli may interact so as to reinforce or to summate the subthreshold stimuli and produce a response.

Although the summative effects of stimuli were explained in terms of physiological perception, the concept of summation can be applied equally well to the spoken word. And the concept of summation may be utilized in every type selling. Start by writing down the major appeals of your product and under each appeal list points that reinforce or support the major appeal. Take the following case of the X manufacturing salesman selling office furniture to dealers.[9]

1. The X Company has developed a number of special services for you.
   a. It offers promotional plans both at the point of sale right here in your business establishment and through local newspaper advertising.
   b. It has an effective sales training program that can be easily utilized in training your salesman to sell in the store as well as outside selling.
   c. It has developed a basic course so that your sales people can become skilled in the fundamentals of office layout and design.
2. The X Company desks are outstanding in style and appearance.
   a. There are seventeen styles to choose from.

[9] Joseph W. Thompson, *National Office Furniture Association Sales Book*, National Office Furniture Association, Chicago, Ill., 1962.

Selling: A Behavioral Science Approach

    b. There are desks provided for every situation in business.

    c. There is a wide assortment of wood finishes.

    d. More than twenty of the most popular colors are available.

    e. If special colors are desired, they may be obtained from the factory at no extra cost.

    f. They are designed by Paul McCobb, a famous name and designer in home and office furniture.

3. The X Company presells for you.

    a. Its products are nationally known for quality and functional performance.

    b. It has been in business for sixty years.

    c. It advertises nationally in business magazines.

    d. Research enables the X Company to develop the type of desks that are desired in business today.

    e. It has a promotional program designed to be used at the local level during the annual Boss Day. This past year our figures showed that over 200 secretaries had their bosses at this function.

4. Its desks and chairs are known for their comfort and work facilitating features.

    a. Each chair is posture designed.

    b. Each desk has nylon bearings to insure easy silent operation.

    c. Each desk has specially designed sectionalized storage space.

    d. Each desk has been designed to give maximum work space with its "extension platform" features.

    e. Each desk can be functionally arranged with other desks to provide beautiful as well as functional work space.

It is worth repeating that both temporal and spatial stimuli may react so as to reinforce or summate and thereby produce a response. In general, the salesman referring to the numbered appeals 1 through 4 is employing the concept of spatial summation; whereas the salesman using the lettered points is reinforcing through temporal summation.

Seldom will a salesman be interested in isolated point stimulation. Instead, he will be ahead if he uses patterns of stimulation. The fundamental of what happens at one point is not independent of what happens at another point. It would be impossible for a salesman to arrange his sales talk so that the effect of various stimuli would not interact. In fact, if he could so arrange his talk, it would be disadvantageous to do so.[10] It is the salesman's advantage to cover a number of major ideas (spatial summation) and note which are of interest to the perceiver and then concentrate or reinforce those attractive ideas with temporal stimuli.

Although temporal and spatial stimuli are concerned with the summative effect of stimuli, the concept of temporal and spatial stimuli, as used above, is supported by the educational psychologist's principle of organization.

---

[10] It will be worthwhile at this point to compare the example and case of summation above with the needs and benefits approach. Note that in the summation approach the salesman is not concerned with basic or status needs, but rather he is presenting a sales talk in "total form" —the Gestalt approach.

The Salesman as an Educator

ORGANIZATION OR GROUPING

Around the early part of this century German psychologists became interested in the organized nature of perception. Their approach became known as Gestalt, the German word for form psychology. The Gestalt approach contended that in teaching, the whole situation must be regarded as a unit rather than a series of discrete parts.[11] This school gave us two grouping principles—grouping by proximity and grouping by similarity. These two grouping principles state that other things being equal, stimuli that are in closer proximity to one another and stimuli that are similar to one another will have greater tendencies to be grouped and thereby will have more opportunity to be understood.

The very nature of organization or grouping as a learning process tells us that when temporal and spatial stimuli are combined, the perceiver has the best opportunity to comprehend the complex stimulus pattern or, in other words, the complex sales talk.

In the case of complex stimulus patterns it is difficult for the individual to organize the whole situation at once. There must of necessity be successive steps of analysis. The individual or prospect therefore fixes his attention on each part of the sales message. It is this organization or grouping process whereby the individual can cope with more material.

In practice, this concept can be tested by scattering twelve peas on a white tablecloth and seeing what happens to an individual's attention. This process succeeds in dividing the individual's attention with a resultant loss in the quality of the individual's perception. An opposite effect will result if the twelve peas are set in three clusters of four each. They will now be easily and quickly perceived.

It is not difficult to transfer the implications of this illustration to the example given above as to why spatial and temporal concepts are factors to be considered in organizing a sales presentation.

Summary

The concepts of temporal and spatial stimuli can be utilized to illustrate the summative effect of the verbal sales message. Temporal summation is a phenomenon in which a threshold stimulus, when continuously applied at the same point, may summate its effect to produce a response. Spatial summation is the summative effect of separate stimuli spread over space. To utilize this concept the salesman may need only write down the broad major appeals of his product or service (spatial stimuli) and under each appeal list points that reinforce or support the major appeal (temporal stimuli). Both temporal and spatial stimuli interact to reinforce or summate and produce a response.

The educational psychologist's principle of organization supports the concept of spatial and temporal stimuli. The grouping principle of prox-

[11] Blair, Jones, and Simpson, *op. cit.*, p. 113.

Selling: A Behavioral Science Approach

imity and similarity state that other things being equal, stimuli that are in closer proximity to one another and stimuli that are similar to one another will have greater tendencies to be grouped and thereby have more opportunity to be understood.

In this book it has been stated that educators are salesmen, or at least they should be. Educators are selling ideas and knowledge. The more effective they are as sales purveyors of knowledge, concepts, and ideas, the more effective they will be as educators. In the same sense, salesmen are educators. And the more effective they are as educators, the more effective they will be as sales purveyors of the knowledge concepts, and ideas contained in their sales proposals.

In the new world of selling, more and more business firms are following the philosophy that the salesman is an educator. But if the salesman is to educate effectively, it is important that he understand and be able to apply the laws of education. They are the law of effect, the law of exercise, the law of readiness, and the law of belonging. In general, most learning takes place through the eyes and the ears and through doing. The salesman utilizes the four laws of education to best present his proposal in terms of how and why people learn.

These laws of education are equally important to the sales manager. They are crucial to the success of any manpower development program.

Chapter 7 DISCUSSION QUESTIONS

1 Some authorities claim that man has gained more new knowledge in the last twenty-five years than in the entire history of civilization. They state that in some fields knowledge is doubling every ten years. Do you see any relationship between this knowledge explosion and the new role of the salesman as an educator? Select any product you wish and describe some of the technological changes that have taken place in the last few years.

2 Describe what is meant by the law of effect. What relationship do you see between the law of effect and the salesman educating a prospect concerning the salesman's completely new product? Is there any relationship between the law of effect and sales training?

3 Take any product you wish and describe how you as a salesman would utilize the law of effect in your discussion with the prospect.

4 Assume that you are a salesman selling a small but complex piece of industrial equipment. Describe the implication of the law of effect if you wanted the prospect to operate the piece of equipment you are selling and he failed in operating the equipment.

5 What specific implications does the law of exercise have for the salesman with respect to utilizing the problem-solving approach in selling?

6 The law of readiness has unique implications in the field of selling. Describe what they are. Do you think it is possible for a salesman to determine the readiness of a prospect? Is it possible for the salesman to affect the readiness of a prospect? How? Why would it be important?

7 The salesman is selling industrial equipment. He described his equipment perfectly, but he never applied or showed the relationship of that equip-

The Salesman as an Educator

ment to the customer's or potential customer's present production system. What law of education has he neglected to use?

8 Assume you are a salesman for skiing equipment. The company produces a complete line of clothing as well as ski equipment itself. You are calling on a small retailer who is mildly interested in developing a ski business as part of his overall retail operation. At the present time, he has no sporting goods equipment of any type. Develop a hypothetical dialogue between you and this retailer discussing the possibility of his establishing a sporting goods line in his retail store. Examine your dialogue to see which of the four laws of education you have employed.

9 Describe the relationship between the concept of summation and organization or grouping. Why is the concept of organization or grouping important to the salesman as he structures his sales talk?

the role of
maturity
conflict and
egocentrism
in selling

8

MATURITY

A description and definition of maturity is, by and large, a description and definition of good adjustment. The mature individual has survived the complexities of growing up. He has come out of this period of development with the way of life, with the attitudes and values that will enable him to pursue a series of goals compatible with society's goals. And other things being equal, it assures him happiness as well as enabling him to contribute more readily to society.

In most cases, the mature salesman will sell more and be a greater asset to his company than the immature. What is needed is a more precise description of the mature individual than the introductory statement above. Further, management is in a never-ending quest for sharper tools with which it can evaluate its sales force. The concept of maturity may provide significant evaluative guidelines for management in this effort. For the salesmen, self-analysis is needed. Man has the ability to hold himself up and step away from himself mentally and analyze his behavior activities and goals. It is a process of introspection. It, in itself, suggests maturity.

Assuming then that both management and salesmen are interested in tools of evaluation, here are some generalizations that will point out important characteristics of the mature in contrast to the immature individual.[1]

---

[1] John E. Anderson, *The Psychology of Development and Personal Adjustment.* Holt, Rinehart and Winston, Inc., New York, 1949, p. 433.

Maturity, Conflict, and Egocentrism

Orientation to Task, Not Self

A self-oriented individual salesman thinks of himself rather than the job to be done. He is ego-oriented rather than task-oriented. In varying degrees, most of us are ego-involved in all activities we perform. Our acts and feelings are centered about the self. It seems to be impossible to determine the best mix one should have of self-orientation and task-orientation. It will vary with different situations. The weight of evidence, nevertheless, indicates that in the long run the individual who is too heavily interested in his personal feelings will be a disruptive force. And management may well have to invest an inordinate amount of time in coping with that individual's behavior.

That the salesman who is predominately self-oriented or self-centered may be, in many cases, a disruptive force is seen by reviewing a management concept. Management authority Simon tells us that

> Administrative activity is group activity. Simple situations are familiar where a man plans and executes his own work; but as soon as the task goes to the point where the efforts of several persons are required to accomplish it this is no longer possible, and it becomes necessary to develop processes for the application of organized effort to the group task. The techniques which facilitate this application are the administrative processes.[2]

For instance, "if the task of the group is to build a ship, a design for the ship is drawn and adopted by the organization, and this design guides and limits the activities of the person who actually constructs the ship. The organization, then, takes from the individual some of his decisional autonomy, and substitutes for it an organization decision-making process."[3] It is self-evident that, if the ship is to be built according to its designer's specifications, all men must follow the design and specifications.

Now this analogy does not tell management it is authority unlimited, nor does it tell salesmen that they must conform; not at all. Management must have plans and ideas. It must communicate these ideas and plans to the sales force and get feedback. It is a grain of sand, an irritant to the oyster, that produces a pearl. Many ideas expressed by salesmen may be irritants to management, but they may produce great plans. But the important point is that once plans are formulated and a program is put into effect, the mature individual moves with the group. He does not adhere to his own design.

Recently, a nationally known sporting equipment manufacturer established a policy that some of its sports items would be given to competitive dealers and distributors in the same area. This was a new policy that posed a problem for some salesmen. Company salesmen had always talked exclusive dealerships. They worked closely with their customers. A number of salesmen took this decision personally. Some became emotionally involved in the situation and made such statements as, "My customers—

[2] Herbert A. Simon, *Administrative Behavior*, The Macmillan Company, New York, 1961, p. 8.
[3] *Ibid.*, p. 8.

Selling: A Behavioral Science Approach

my friends won't like this," or "I just can't do it, or we are going back on our word." This is understandable. But changing markets forces a company to change its distribution system. The decision was made because in the opinion of the management the move was in the long run best for the company and best for most dealers. Nevertheless, some salesmen rebelled. In short, a number of less mature salesman found it difficult to be task-oriented. They were being self-centered and were, as a consequence, sub-marginal in carrying out company policy.

Clear Goals and Efficient Work Habits

"Having salesmen who are able to direct themselves towards specific, clearly stated goals by following effective work habits is a dream of most sales managers," so states Paul N. Stanton, vice-president of marketing, Pratt & Whitney. He believes in a decentralized decision-making sales organization. He wants to push decisions down where they belong—with the sales organization. He wants his salesmen to plan. He wants them to establish goals and activities needed to accomplish the goals. He wants them to be territory managers. He wants his sales force to participate in presenting facts to management, for instance, facts with respect to market potential in their various areas.

Salesmen having the ability to establish clear goals and efficient work habits suggests maturity; not having clear goals and efficient work habits suggests immaturity. An immature individual starts many projects and finishes few. He goes off in many directions. His efforts are dissipated. He does not display a systematic approach to his activities. It is like comparing the adult and the child. The adult generally has better work habits than the child and therefore accomplishes more with less effort.

A program for establishing clear goals and efficient work habits is discussed in Chapter 3, "Planning and Managing Sales Effort."

Control of Personal Feelings

Control of personal feelings is related to having a high threshold of tension binding; however, it has other dimensions. In our society and times, the individual who cannot control his personal feelings is considered immature. In selling, the salesman must be mature. He realizes routing, preplanning, completing reports, making cold calls, and calling on marginal customers may be disagreeable tasks, but he performs them. He carries out the activities needed to accomplish his objectives. In contrast, a youngster, with his poorly developed sense of goals and related activities, reacts to a task in terms of its pleasantness and unpleasantness. He pursues pleasant goals and avoids unpleasant ones. He develops excuses for not pursuing unpleasant tasks.

One of Anderson's statements concerning maturity sums up nicely the two concepts of personal feelings and being task-oriented. It is especially meaningful to salesmen.

A mature person is able to work with and for people who possess traits he

Maturity, Conflict, and Egocentrism

dislikes. He encounters many persons whose traits might be changed but until he learns to ignore these and concentrate on the job to be done he does not achieve adult status. The ability to separate personal status and characteristics from skill and contribution to any activity is not achieved quickly, but comes through many experiences. It involves a willingness to use ideas and skills for the achievement of group purposes, irrespective of their origin and the ability to see the good points in others despite their undesirable traits. It does not mean an absence of feelings, but it does mean a very substantial capacity to control feelings.[4]

Objectivity

The mature, objective individual gets the facts, evaluates situations on their merits, and tends to disassociate or extricate himself from his personal feelings or biases that might prejudice him in his decisions. He uses judgment, that is, he separates the significant from insignificant and fact from value in the decision-making process. He tends to be impersonal in his decision making. For instance, an objective sales manager doesn't judge the ability of his salesmen on their appearance or whether they are extroverts or introverts or on the basis of their speech ability or other superficial traits. Instead, he judges each salesman on the basis of his intelligence, his ability to solve problems, his motivation and performance. The so-called extroverts can be poor sales performers. That is one of the most difficult concepts a sales manager has to learn in being objective in selecting personnel.

Being objective applies equally well to the salesman in analyzing his customer or his prospect or any other receiver or recipient of his sales proposal or message. Objectivity is especially important whenever the salesman is analyzing a sales situation. He must get the facts.

Acceptance of Criticism

Acceptance of criticism or suggestions for improvement is a mark of the mature individual. Probably every salesman and sales manager has been offered constructive criticism or received suggestions on ways in which work could be improved. These criticisms or suggestions may be offered in many different ways. It may be given, as the dictionary defines it, to find fault or to disapprove of a person or thing, to blame, to censure, to condemn, or to denounce. On the other extreme, it may be given in the form of a possibility. The salesman must accept both forms. For some customers the salesman is a lightning rod for raw criticism. But he must react to raw criticism in the same way he reacts to objections to his proposal, product, or company. He should welcome them. They may be important guide points for future contact with a particular individual. How criticism is given tells much about the contributor.

When the sales manager or salesman accepts criticism, he acknowledges the other's individuality and ability. Moreover, it indicates the receiver realizes that others cannot only contribute but may make more

---

[4] Anderson, *op. cit.*, p. 435.

Selling: A Behavioral Science Approach

significant contributions to a project or idea than he. One of the greatest attributes an individual can have is the ability to use the ability of others. Listen to criticisms and suggestions and acknowledge them positively, be it a personal criticism on how we talk, eat, or dress, or a criticism of a proposal presented to a prospect.

Actually the mature individual looks forward to having his final work evaluated by others. He realizes that what he says and does must come under the scrutiny of others.

As a summary example, a sales manager who is preparing a new training, advertising, or sales promotional program which his salesmen are to present to dealers should want criticism and suggestions while preparing the plan and evaluation when it is finally presented. He must be willing to take both credit and blame for what he does. One further point is this: No one can go wrong in giving credit for the ideas he is using. An immature individual is likely to be liberal with the *I*, whereas the mature individual will be liberal with the *we, Jim, Jack,* and *John.*

MECHANISMS OF ADJUSTMENT

Every salesman, every customer, every sales manager, in fact, every individual constantly makes adjustments to various situations. These mechanisms of adjustment or behavior patterns emerge when our motives are not permitted direct satisfaction. A few of the major adjustment mechanisms are *compensation, rationalization,* and *projection.* These mechanisms may not all be used by the same individual. Whenever a motive is thwarted, an individual may try one then another or a combination of the various adjustment mechanisms until he finds one or a combination that permits a reduction of tension. Adjustment mechanisms provide for a reduction of a particular tension.

Enormous numbers and shades of basic motives are involved or concerned with the process of adjustment. It would be impossible to reproduce or discuss the shades of motivation here without presenting a short course in psychology. However, there are, as Britt points out in his informative chapter, "The Strategy of Consumer Motivation,"[5] several basic kinds of factors that marketing men must keep constantly in mind if they are to understand consumers—in other words, people. Britt tells us that marketing men

> . . . have forgotten all about the following psychological facts. First of all, almost all people have terrific feelings of insecurity. With this goes fear and hate and prejudice, and sometimes desperate feelings of helplessness. Second, and closely related to insecurity, is the enormous amount of aggression and hostility which is in the unconscious thinking of most people. Third, almost all people seem to require *symbols of prestige,* in order to bolster up their ego-deflated selves.[6]

Britt's three basics provide insights as to why salesmen should be

---

[5] Steuart Henderson Britt and Harper W. Boyd, Jr. (eds.), *Marketing Management and Administrative Action,* McGraw-Hill Book Company, New York, 1963.
[6] *Ibid.,* p. 80.

familiar with the concept "mechanisms of adjustments." People do adjust through a process of compensation, rationalization, and projection. And it is important that these concepts involved in adjustment be understood so that the salesman can have a better understanding of himself as well as other people and thereby be able to adjust more readily to complex situations.

Compensation

Psychologist Cruze describes compensation as "an attempt to cover up a deficiency, either real or imaginary, by overemphasizing some other aspects of one's ability, personality, or character."[7] A physically weak individual may compensate for his inferiority (it is an inferiority in his mind) by bullying small children. On the other extreme, he may want to become a great scientist or scholar. Taking an example closer to home, the salesman may *compensate* for his *inability* to answer questions, face objections, or be subjected to an early refusal by engaging in a one-sided, salesman-oriented, pressure sales talk. Emotionally he finds it difficult to permit the customer an opportunity to voice his thinking because it may reveal a "crack in the dike." Further, it is possible the salesman has the ability to speak rapidly or well, and he is overemphasizing what he thinks is a favorable aspect of his ability as a compensation for ego immaturity.

On the other hand, the salesman may see many forms of prospect compensation. In the company decision-making process a buyer, for example, may be less important than his title or position indicates. He may not have the authority to make decisions, so he acts important in many other ways. He may tear a salesman and his company apart, somewhat like the bully in his compensation for his feelings of inferiority. It should not be inferred from this discussion that all compensation activities are harmful; on the contrary, depending upon the type of activities chosen to serve the individual's purpose, the overall effect of compensatory behavior may be beneficial, harmless, or harmful.

What the salesman is interested in, however, is how to discover whether or not an individual is resorting to compensation. The answer is, unfortunately, he doesn't. Frequently the individual does not know he is compensating for his shortcomings by engaging in compensatory behavior. Certainly the effeminate man who might smoke cigars or grow a mustache to look more masculine would heatedly deny such a suggestion just as would the salesman if it were suggested he utilizes one-way communication tactics to compensate for his inability to confront a turndown, or because of basic insecurity, or the need to be important or feel superior, or as an outlet for aggressive behavior.

Behavior activities of people are indeed a complex subject, and, to repeat, it would be crass of the author to even suggest that the salesman should be able to analyze the behavior activities of the individual in com-

[7] Wendell W. Cruze, *General Psychology for College Students*, Prentice-Hall, Inc., Englewood Cliffs, N.J., 1955, p. 484.

Selling: A Behavioral Science Approach

plex situations and ascribe reasons for the behavior. And it would be crass for the salesman to think he can analyze his prospect's emotions. In any event, the analysis aspects of a prospect's motives is not the important point involved. The important point is this: It is the author's opinion that through the study of the individual many salesmen will be able to adjust their behavior activities, a coping behavior to best appeal to the needs of the other individual. Many of the adjustments the salesman makes will be done intuitively, and many of the adjustments will be made consciously.

Rationalization

Psychologist Cruze describes rationalization as "a type of false reasoning."[8] Psychologist Dichter, writing for the business community, describes rationalization as a process that occurs when ". . . it is necessary for the [individual] . . . to explain his strange behavior to himself and to others. This he does with a host of 'rational' excuses, all of which he himself knows to be merely excuses."[9]

Dichter presents the case in this fashion:

> Take a consumer who has long dreamed of owning a certain product. Suddenly it is possible for the dream to become a reality. What will he do? According to the stereotyped picture of the American Consumer, he will immediately rush out and buy the product he has so long wanted. But research shows, in fact, that thousands of consumers, who are in the position to fulfill long held dreams, will simply continue to dream but will not act. Why? Here is a typical quote that contains the first hint of the answer. "Mother and I always wanted a boat. We talked about it for years, but we just couldn't afford it. Mother has been after me for about two years to do something about it, now that we have the money, and I always say I will, but the truth is, I keep putting it off because I don't even know where to begin." This kind of situation, filled with this same kind of conflict between desire and fear, is repeated over and over again, thousands of times each week throughout America.[10]

Thus, according to Dichter, the prospect presents a host of rational excuses, all of which he himself knows to be merely excuses.

This rationalization process, as described by Dichter, not only takes place in the case of consumer goods, but it may well apply to all sales situations. Certainly it would seem plausible that many individuals who make purchase decisions, whether it is for their company or for themselves, have conflicts between a desire to act and a fear or insecurity regarding the result. The perceptual salesman who uses a process of judicious questioning throughout the sales interview can go a long way toward alleviating the fears of the prospect.

An interesting description of the person involved in the process of finding socially acceptable reasons for behavior actuated by motives considered inferior by society is proved by Cruze. He states,

[8] *Ibid.*, p. 156.

[9] Ernest Dichter, "Teaching the Novice to Buy Your Product," *Motivations*, Institute for Motivational Research, New York, July–August, 1957, p. 8.

[10] *Ibid.*, p. 6.

Maturity, Conflict, and Egocentrism

In this case, rationalization is an adjustment mechanism used to reconcile behavior motivated by fundamentally selfish desires with the somewhat higher standards that have been established by society. The individual is able, through a process of devious reasoning, to convince himself and others (sometimes) that his behavior is a result of lofty altruistic motives, when in reality, less desirable motives are responsible.[11]

A man buying a new home is able to persuade himself that he should buy one near the golf course. He argues that although the location will make it more difficult for him to get to his work, it will be away from the traffic hazards of the city, and that his children will have plenty of room for playing and will be able to enjoy an abundance of sunshine and fresh air. He argues that his wife will have more room for her flower garden and even hints that he may be able to start a small vegetable garden. He never admits, even to himself, that the true reason for moving to the neighborhood is to make it more convenient for him to get to the golf course. It might be pointed out that his children will have to travel a greater distance to school and that this new location will seriously inconvenience his wife in her shopping activities. Since such an admission would make his behavior appear very selfish, he emphasizes the advantages for his wife and children, points out the possible disadvantages to himself, and insists that he is willing to be a "martyr" for the sake of the family.[12]

Another form of rationalization is the sour-grapes routine. This expression probably came from the fable of the fox and the grapes. In attempting to reach a bunch of grapes hanging overhead, the fox jumped and jumped and when he finally realized it was impossible to reach the grapes, he avoided admitting failure by the sour-grapes strategy: the grapes were, in any event, sour and were not good for eating. Rationalization is a universal mechanism, and in its simplest form it may be of considerable value in enabling the individual to retain a reasonable level of self-esteem. Yet if the salesman uses a sour-grapes strategy for customers, he can't reach or can't sell through such excuses that the account was "too small to really bother with" or "why should I take that kind of abuse from that guy?" he may well be "skimming the cream" in his territory

Projection

Like the terms *compensation* and *rationalization*, most people are familiar with the term *projection*. Projection is the means by which a person may protect himself by detecting in others a particular trait and characteristic in which he feels inadequate. Some businessmen use projection every day. Take a businessman who engages in misleading advertising. It was "necessary" or "the thing to do" because others do it. In short, this type of businessman says, "I am forced to do it because my competition does it." This is projection.

A used-car dealer had a series of large billboard signs perched atop nine-foot high poles that completely enclosed his car display area. In large print on each of the billboards was the slogan, "The Golden Rule Is Our

[11] Cruze, *op. cit.*, p. 485.
[12] *Ibid.*, p. 486.

Selling: A Behavioral Science Approach

Rule." One customer who felt he had been misled on the car deal in which he was involved returned to talk to the dealer. The dealer was asked what he meant by that sign and the dealer, with no hesitation, replied, "I'm doing unto my customers exactly what they are trying to do unto me." He may have truly believed that people were out to cheat him if they could, but a greater possibility was that he was projecting his basic way of doing business with others.

In summary, then, the salesman may have to cope with many prospects that utilize compensation, rationalization, and projection as mechanisms of adjustment. And, of course, the salesman may be utilizing one or more of these adjustment patterns himself. It seems evident that an understanding of these concepts will enable the salesman to have a better understanding of people—his customers.

EGOCENTRISM

As commonly expressed in psychological literature, an egocentric is one who is so wrapped up in himself that he can't get away from his own personal welfare. Thus he finds it difficult to get along with others.[13] On the other hand, Anderson speaks of the nonegocentric as one who is mature. He states, "A mature person is task-oriented rather than ego-oriented. He is oriented toward the task at hand and is interested in it rather than his own personal feelings at the moment or its effect on his own fortune."[14]

Avoiding the extreme definition of an egocentric, but taking the viewpoint, "an egocentric's thoughts are by and large on himself," and the thought that the nonegocentric is task-oriented rather than self- or ego-oriented, then the concept of egocentric can be profitably discussed within the framework of selling.

A salesman with egocentric tendencies is the one who, at the company convention when a new product is introduced, looks at the product and his thoughts are structured around himself. He thinks, "This will get me more money. It is so new, buyers will almost come after me. I will win a contest and I will go to Bermuda and those big commission checks will enable me to buy many things I want." It is apparent this thinking centers on personal status, the self, and emotional satisfaction.

Another salesman, a nonegocentric individual, may view the new company product in an entirely different way. He may look at the product and think of ways it can be improved, how the design could be changed, how his customers could use it, what problems it might solve for his customers, how it will compliment the company line, or how his sales division will benefit from the new product in meeting competition.

As expressed in the first case, the individual tends to be strongly self-centered and self-directed. The second individual tends to be task-oriented or situation-centered, since he relegates himself to the background in his approach to problems.

[13] John E. Anderson, *Psychology of Development and Personal Adjustment*, Holt, Rinehart and Winston, Inc., New York, 1949, p. 188.
[14] *Ibid.*, p. 433.

Maturity, Conflict, and Egocentrism

It is difficult for the salesman to be task-oriented and not self-oriented. Why? Because there is a constant emphasis on production, on commission, on quotas, and on winning contests. And above all, salesmen in general have not been trained to suppress their egocentric tendencies. Until recent years most sales literature glorified the so-called extroverted salesman who gave an enthusiastic sales talk; he overwhelmed a prospect with reasons why he should buy or accept his proposal. And this approach was reflected in the speech pattern of many salesmen.

In the same way, frequently the egocentric's thought pattern is reflected in his speech. It can be called self-centered or egocentric speech. And frequently the thought pattern of the nonegocentric is reflected in his speech pattern. It can be called situation-centered or customer-oriented speech.

Research reveals that egocentric speech, at least partially, is an affliction that has struck the majority of salesmen. The original research included sixty-one graduates of the class of 1947 of the University of Illinois.[15] Each participant had completed one or more sales courses as a student at the University of Illinois. They had, on the average, close to two years of sales experience when they participated in this research project. Of these sixty-one participants 94 percent believed they adjusted their sales talk to handle various sales situations. They believed they had a customer-oriented sales talk. Only 6 percent of these participants stated they used a standardized sales talk. In reply to the question, "Do you make up your own sales talk?" 69 percent answered yes and 31 percent replied they made up their talk in part. The replies to these two questions emphasize the fact that not only did the salesmen believe they did not use a standardized, memorized, or canned sales talk, but the overwhelming majority believed that they developed their own sales talk.

In subsequent research covering more than 140 salesmen (each with whom the author made one to thirteen joint calls on prospects or customers) representing twenty-seven business firms, the author found that the majority of these salesmen, like the group of college graduates, were adamant that they developed, by and large, their own sales talks and that they directed their sales talk to the needs of the prospect or customer. It is the author's opinion that these were true, honest statements. Each salesman believed he was customer-oriented. But was this borne out in fact? Throughout these sales interviews, salesmen frequently made these or similar statements: "Let me explain the qualities of our product," or "Mr. Jones, I have been selling this product for twenty years and I want to tell you my experience with this product," or "Mr. Rudder, here is a portfolio that tells the life of our company. Here on the first page is a color picture of our president and vice-president," or the salesman went on and on with a twenty-minute talk giving the technical aspects of his product, with liberal use of *I* and *we*.

At this point the reader may reproach the author for his implication

[15] Joseph W. Thompson, "What College Graduates Say about Employers' Sales Training," *University of Illinois Bulletin*, vol. 47, no. 58, April, 1950.

Selling: A Behavioral Science Approach

in the above statements that the use of the portfolio suggests a non-customer-oriented sales talk. It depends. Granted that portfolios are company sales tools which are commonly used and that they are a good sales tool, all too frequently company sales portfolios are company-oriented and not customer-oriented. The following illustration will support this point.

The president and vice-president of one of the largest trucking companies in the country built the company from a ragged postwar line to its present-day status. These two men were dynamic individuals and were truly admired and respected by the sales force. To assist the salesmen in their sales effort, a beautiful color sales portfolio with a story of company service was developed. The first two pages were large color pictures of the president and vice-president. The salesmen gave as part of their sales talk a five-minute story about the company and these men. In follow-up research, which represented personal interviews with ten prospects who had listened to a sales talk constructed around this portfolio, it was found that six out of the ten stated that the company and its officers were stressed too much. At the end of these short interviews, each of the ten participants was asked to check those statements on a preprepared list that would represent his impression of the sales presentation. Eight out of ten checked the statement, "Too much time spent talking company."

The portfolio was then changed so that the bosses' pictures were at the end of the sales portfolio. The salesmen were trained to emphasize purposefully but briefly at the last phase of their sales talk that these men were responsible for the growth of the company through their dedication to customer service, and to tie this in with what it would mean to the prospect. A group of eight individuals who had been exposed to the newly aligned sales portfolio were interviewed, and not one negatively commented on the bosses and not one of the eight individuals checked, "Too much time spent talking company."

In the first situation, the salesmen were using a company or salesman-oriented sales talk, and in the second situation with the realigned sales portfolio, they were using a customer-oriented sales talk. The difference between using a customer-oriented and a salesman-oriented sales talk in many cases isn't great, but it is the author's opinion, based on his research, that a large percentage of salesmen today are not alert to the customer's needs. They do not use a problem-solving approach. They do not use a customer-oriented approach.

Hattwick, a psychologist by training and an advertising executive by choice, comments on this problem. He describes the conflict between slipping into the egocentric predicament situation and giving a customer-oriented sales talk as natural. "Because," as Hattwick states in his excellent book, *The New Psychology of Selling,* "finding out what other people want, planning and presenting a sales story in terms of what other people want to hear—that is just the opposite of what the ego wants us to do. It runs counter to a fundamental fact of human nature which is part of all of us—our ego."[16]

[16] Melvin S. Hattwick, *The New Psychology of Selling,* McGraw-Hill Book Company, New York, 1960, p. 10.

Maturity, Conflict, and Egocentrism

The point is this. We like to have people agree with us, have the same viewpoints we have, and act pretty much the same as we act. When this doesn't happen, it tends to antagonize us. Further, the ego helps us discount what others want to hear, and instead, it encourages us to tell what we want to tell. Hattwick tells us this is natural.[17] It is normal. But it is selling the hard way.

It is important that the salesman and the sales manager squarely face the hard facts of reality—that there are certain characteristics of the selling profession that intensify tendencies toward egocentric predicament. In selling, the individual salesman is seldom in what he feels, or the customer feels, is a status position. The salesman wants to feel important, wants to be recognized, wants to feel superior, but obviously from the very nature of the salesman's role this need may not be satisfied. In fact, this unsatisfied need can indeed be a source of job frustration. Thankfully major strides are being made to give selling a status position. Today it is being recognized that selling is difficult, and it demands a professionally trained and qualified individual—an individual of intelligence and maturity—to sell effectively. Today a salesman is receiving this professional training based on transmissible skills and knowledge that have been formally acquired. He is a problem solver. He engages in purposeful discussions aimed at getting insights, gaining information, furthering understanding, and being of help and counsel to the prospect and customer. As the salesman understands his role and, what is even better, knows that other people understand and appreciate his role, there will be fewer and fewer salesmen falling into egocentric predicaments.[18]

CONFLICT

As expressed previously every motive, want, desire, and need has a goal. Physiological needs—water and food—are relatively fixed and easily obtained. Only water will satisfy the need for water, and only food will satisfy hunger. On the other hand, the more complex social needs are flexible. Status needs can be satisfied in many ways—large home, money, professional recognition, a good golf game, operating a successful business, belonging to a country club or social clubs, or holding offices in various organizations, ordering other people around, doing all the talking in a social or business situation, telling how important you are, etc. Whatever the need, it must be satisfied or it will lead to some degree of frustration and conflict. Further, needs or motives rarely operate singly but rather in combinations. It is the interplay among these motives that is important. This interplay may be the cause for indecisiveness or frustration. These conflicts are called approach-approach, approach-avoidance, and avoidance-avoidance.[19]

The approach-approach conflict exists in situations where two or more

---

[17] *Ibid.,* p. 109.

[18] Actually it is recognized that egocentric predicament does not represent the extreme ego case as identified by the term egocentric as used in psychological literature.

[19] Fred McKinney, *Psychology of Personal Adjustment,* John Wiley & Sons, Inc., 1960, pp. 63–66.

Selling: A Behavioral Science Approach

positive incentives, each of which satisfies a need, exist. Every business-man has met this problem. "Should I buy from this firm or that firm? Should I buy this product or that product?" Ordinarily the approach-approach conflict is not difficult to resolve. After a period of indecision the individual selects one alternative and forgets the other. He makes a de-cision. And that decision, it would seem, would be in favor of the customer-oriented salesman because in this situation the products are comparable—it is the salesman who differentiates the situation.

The approach-avoidance conflict is another matter. This is a situation where a goal has both positive and negative incentive properties. The re-tailer might want to stock the product, but can he move it? The salesman may want to close the sale, but will he be refused if he asks? Or the con-sumer may have a conflict in selecting between a new car or a vacation, or between repairs for his car or repairs for the home. In these situations, especially where the goal has both strong positive and strong negative incentive properties, the result is indecision and, frequently, compromise. Again it is clear the salesman's role is strategically important.

Avoidance-avoidance conflict is a situation in which an individual has to choose between two negative incentives. It is the case of selecting the lesser of two evils as expressed in the common saying, "between the devil and the deep blue sea."

Two kinds of behavior are likely to be conspicuous in this last conflict situation. One is vacillation and the other is attempting to avoid conflict by leaving the conflict situation. Usually there are many other pressures that will not permit the individual to leave the conflict situation so that the most normal process is vacillation. For instance, a salesman is re-quired by his employer to leave one territory and go to another. He has a choice of either going or resigning from the firm. Usually the individual moves to the new territory, but the result is frustration and conflict never-theless. Another example is seen in the case of a company that had an unexpected demand for its equipment. The company was months behind on its orders, yet one of the company's sales managers instructed his sales-men to promise delivery dates that were not realistic. The salesman had to choose between deceiving his customers or prospects or facing the wrath of the sales manager. The result—conflict. (It might be mentioned that this sales manager is no longer with this company.)

Another source of conflict, which is implied in the discussion above but not specifically identified, is a possibility of conflict between the in-dividual's self-concept or self and an incongruent role. From the author's observation this may be a basic reason for a salesman's success in one par-ticular sales job and for his failure in another.

Visualize, if you will, the conflict or tension springing from the pre-dicament of a salesman who views himself as honest, ethical, a family man, a churchgoer, etc., who is thrown into a role that is not in harmony with his self-concept. Assume the company he represents is not, in his opinion, honest in its advertising, doesn't really care about its customers, believes in selling regardless of the customer's needs—that volume is the only thing that pays off for the salesman—or has tricky provisions in its contracts. Or assume that this salesman is selling frozen-food plans door to door and is trained to use great emotional appeals. He knows that at times he is selling a program to individuals who probably can't afford it and, what is more, who are being overstocked. The answer is obvious: It's conflict.

On the other hand, take the case of a salesman who views himself as a free dealer, a fast talker, and an operator type, and who is completely "boxed in" by the ethical firm. He, too, may have a significant conflict between his self-image and his job. Consider also the salesman whose self-image is that he is independent, proud, self-sufficient, and who believes he controls his own destiny but he pretty much fills the order-taker category as a manufacturer salesman calling on dealers. Further, assume he doesn't understand or hasn't been trained in selling in its broader dimensions, especially the problem-solving approach to selling, and assume also that he does not understand the intricacies of face-to-face communications. The result—conflict.

Just recently the author was talking to a friend about the problems of conflicts in selling, or more specifically, how a salesman's role may be incongruent with his conception of himself. This man is a very successful manufacturer's agent, employing a staff of more than twenty salesmen. He started his career in selling door to door, and in about five years he became a manufacturer's agent. His income ranges from $60,000 to $100,000 per year. He is considered a handsome man with a beautiful, charming wife and several children. He told about the great life he has had in selling and how much he loved the field. He told about one conflict in that his job required a great deal of travel, and he felt he was away from his home and children longer than he would like. He related, however, that he had worked out everything very well, especially in recent years, and now he could spend more time with his children. But he still had a real conflict in entertainment. He paused in his story, and the author remarked, "But you seem to enjoy everything you do, and I know you like groups. Entertainment being a conflict to you comes as quite a surprise." He continued, "No, it's entertainment. You know—call girls." That came out like a bombshell. He was a heavy contributor to his church, well known in the community, and apparently a wonderful family man. He seemed to be extremely well liked and belonged to many clubs and associations and had a wide circle of friends. But the conflict was out and he said, "I had the darn thing on my mind for a long time and am glad to talk about it. But the point is, how do I handle it? I've got a few customers who expect a hotel suite, a few girls, lots of liquor and, although I am never around, I set it up. I know if I drop the entertainment I'll lose a lot of business." He took a chance; he dropped this kind of "entertainment." As you would expect he lost several accounts, but he concentrated more on managing and selling, and his total business increased. He quit taking the easy way out when he realized he was using entertainment as a crutch. Later he remarked that his attitude had changed. He felt different. He could talk integrity to his children. He could associate with his customers on a more professional basis. He never felt ashamed. He had his self-respect.

Summary

Maturity is, by and large, a description and definition of good adjustment. A mature salesman will be of far more value to his firm than will the immature salesman. A mature individual is oriented to the task, not to the self; he has clear goals and efficient work habits; he has the ability to control his personal feelings; he is objective in dealing with customer situations, and he has the ability to accept criticism. Most individuals, however mature they may be, use some mechanisms of adjustment, such as compensation, rationalization, and projection.

Each individual has many needs. The felt needs must be satisfied, or they may lead to some degree of frustration and conflict. The manner in which these conflicts are resolved are called approach-approach, approach-avoidance, and avoidance-avoidance.

One of the most overlooked conflicts that may exist in the salesman's situation is that the role he may be required to enact may not be congruent with the self-image he has of himself. This factor appears to be overlooked by most companies designing a selection program.

Chapter 8 DISCUSSION QUESTIONS

1 Mr. Frank Riley, president of the Machinery Training Corporation, made this statement, "I think maturity is one of the most important qualities a salesman can possess." Do you agree with that statement? Why or why not? What is maturity? How do you identify maturity?

2 A sales manager stated, "Show me a salesman that wants to make money, and I will show you a successful salesman." Discuss this statement with respect to the concept of maturity.

3 Is it possible that the salesman who is largely interested in money could be a disruptive force in the sales organization? Why?

4 Does an individual give up some of his autonomy when he becomes a member of a team? Explain.

5 You are an industrial salesman. Your company has told you that you are to promise potential customers delivery of various types of machinery within thirty to sixty days. You know, however, that the company cannot possibly make delivery under approximately less than six months. Could you be considered immature if you did not carry out this policy in your conversation with your potential prospects? Explain.

6 A major sporting goods company whose stock had dropped approximately fifty points on the stock market had a group of marketing consultants analyze the firm's marketing process. The consultants recommended to the company that it go from exclusive distributorships to multiple outlets in various localities. This, in essence, meant that a number of outlets would be handling that company's sporting goods line in competing areas. The company reasoned that with a greater number of outlets it would obtain a greater number of sales and thus become more solvent. Many of the company's salesmen were athletes and had built up a close personal relationship with the retailers. Many of these salesmen rebelled at the concept of selling to new outlets. They reasoned they would be betraying their former customers and close friends. In the process of its marketing

Maturity, Conflict, and Egocentrism

work, the company had advised the salesmen of what was taking place and solicited various comments from the sales force. In spite of the many negative comments the company received, it went ahead and carried out this marketing policy. Did this company's sales force have a high level of maturity? Were the salesmen justified in their actions? Did the company exhibit a mature attitude? What policy of management might be quoted to support the company's position?

7 Do you see any relationship between that element of maturity which states the individual should have clear goals and efficient work habits and the new concept of the salesman as a market manager?

8 Some psychologists claim that an individual should have the freedom to give vent to his personal feelings. Discuss the implications of this concept with respect to the salesman's success in his field. Do you think having the ability to control one's personal feelings warps an individual's personality or enlarges the individual's personality? Why or why not? Is the individual being himself if he controls his feelings?

9 Take any case from your experience and describe how you feel some individual used the concepts of compensation, rationalization, or projection.

10 Some forms of conflict can be identified as approach-approach, approach-avoidance, and avoidance-avoidance. Describe what each of these forms of conflicts involve and identify at least five ways in which each of these conflict situations can be seen in an individual's everyday life.

11 Discuss the concept that the salesman's work may not be congruent with an individual's self-image of himself. If this situation should happen from a selection standpoint, who would be responsible, the company for having selected a salesman who didn't understand the sales task or the salesman for selecting the field that didn't square with his self-image of himself?

12 What are some aspects of selling that might be considered incongruent with the average college student's self-image of himself? Considering only the new world of selling as described in this text, do you think there are any facets of selling that might not be congruent with the college student's image of himself? Could the new world of selling be too difficult for many college students? If a college student is overly interested in security, is it possible that he may find conflict in the sales area?

six
approaches
to selling

9

INTRODUCTION

Six broad approaches to selling will be introduced in this chapter. These approaches are:
1. Simple Stimulus-Response Selling
2. Formulized Selling
3. Need-Satisfaction Selling
4. Mood Selling
5. Barrier Selling
6. Depth Selling

Each approach will be analyzed, and ultimately the first five approaches will be combined to form the sixth approach—depth selling or selling in depth.

The Reason Why

There are two major reasons for understanding the component of each of the five approaches to selling and how these interact to form the ultimate approach—selling in depth. The first reason is that the salesman will be given a backdrop upon which he can better determine the accuracy of his sales effort. And if we are to have a professional approach to selling, this is enormously important. A rifleman may fire thousands of rounds at a target but never improve. In fact, he may become less and less effective. On the other hand, if after each shot a red ball is raised from the pits to indicate where the rifleman hits, he can make the necessary adjustments, provided he knows how. In short, experience is not necessarily a good teacher. Experience is a good teacher only when a system for evaluating the accuracy of the individual's efforts is devised. This is true in selling, as it is in the rifleman example, or in any other effort. For instance, the salesman must know how to get feedback and interpret that feedback, both verbal and nonverbal forms, if he is to communicate effectively. He must have a method to evaluate when he is, and when he isn't, on target.

Another reason for analyzing approaches to selling is that it develops one approach, a general theory of selling. This approach, combined with creativity, will permit any salesman selling any product to sell more effectively. The salesman selects that phase, part, or mix of depth selling that enables him to communicate effectively with each of his prospects, customers, or other individuals who may be involved in the sales process.

Hope Deferred

An unknown philosopher once said, "Hope deferred maketh the heart sick." Some sales experts believe that this parable is especially applicable in the sales area. Each day thousands of salesmen who might be called "men with lost hope" are calling on prospects and customers. These men have lost hope because they know deep down in their hearts that they do not know how to motivate people. These are the order takers who rationalize that they are doing a good job of selling when they ask the customer, "What do you need today, John?" And John responds with an order for three or four items.

Unfortunately we find some order-taker salesmen in most areas of salesmanship today. Consider the salesman who calls on the manufacturer's purchasing department, or a retailer, or distributor, or a small machine-shop operator and says, "You know, I have been calling on you off and on for three years, and we are still not getting much business from you. Could you give us a few more orders? You know, we have some new items in our line."

Many of these men who are "deselling" could be excellent salesmen, but there is a major roadblock in the path leading to professional salesmanship. It is a roadblock of lethargy that can be broken through only by a period of intensive study of sales strategy, sales techniques, and of the principles of educational psychology, general psychology, sociology, management, problem solving, decision making, and communication that are involved in selling—plus of course the application of these principles to actual sales situations and, when appropriate, an analysis of the self.

Creativity and Situation Management

It is not the purpose of this chapter to explain creativity, but every salesman should be aware that one of the greatest bars to sales creativity is habit, both physical and mental. Physical habits are developed through calling on customers in the same fashion day in and day out. Mental habits are also established in part by this routine of daily calls on customers or potential customers. More specifically, mental habits are established by the salesman's approach to selling—that is, whether it is positive or negative.

With a better understanding of the why, that is, the principles of, for example, psychology, education, and communication involved in the various approaches to selling, the salesman is less inclined to sell in a habitual way. He is more inclined to be open-minded and experimental in utilizing different ways to motivate prospects to act now.

Each salesman must be situation-management-oriented. This is a con-

Selling: A Behavioral Science Approach

cept which suggests that every contact a sales representative has with a prospective customer involves a different problem or situation. Situation management emphasizes the fact that every sale embraces a "difficulty mix" of the various factors which motivate the person to be receptive to ideas or to act.[1]

A salesman must think creatively. He must be spontaneous. He must be able to develop new sales ideas at any moment during the sale. He must adjust, modify, and change the sales structure as new problems arise.

Creative imagination is a talent which has enabled man to transcend all other animals. It is the one mental power which electronic brains cannot claim. More specifically, constructive ideation, the act of generating ideas, is the key to finding the solution to many problems—in science, in art, in professions, in public affairs, in business, and in selling. Constructive ideation is a must for the salesman.

It has been said, for example, that one-fifth of the products or services that are in use today were not known ten years ago. These new products sprang from someone's imagination. Someone had the ability to think creatively about a problem and come up with a solution.

Most great ideas were greeted with sneers and ridicule. This makes most people reluctant to come up with ideas when to do so frequently means to run the gauntlet of ridicule on the part of our peers.

To counteract this fear of ideas on his own part, Dr. James B. Conant, when he was president of Harvard University, had this motto on his wall: "Behold the turtle—he makes progress only when his neck is out."

Partly because people are a little afraid to "put their necks out" and because it is fashionable in our society to be modest, everyone has a tendency to decry his own ability to be original. This is false modesty at its best, and at its worst it leads to sabotaging of our talents.

What is the road to creativity? There are many ways in which we can learn to become more creative. One of the basic ones is given by an outstanding psychologist, Dr. Frank Kingdon of the University of Southern California. He said that "questions are the creative act of the intelligence." He tells us that when man begins to question things as they are, to ask why they can't be combined, reversed, adapted, made smaller or larger, or substituted for other things, then he becomes creative. He becomes a creative and an intelligent animal. He begins to use his reasoning and creative powers.

A great advance in formulating such questions has been made by Alex Osborn, president of the Creative Education Foundation and author of a standard book in the field of creativity, *Applied Imagination*. In order to analyze the six approaches to selling and possibly to find ways in which these six approaches may be helpful in our sales effort, here are a few of the questions he formulated as pertaining to the approaches.

How can we put these sales approaches to other uses? Can we use any of the sales techniques, strategies, approaches, etc., as they are, or could we find other uses if we modified them? How can we adapt the various sales talks to various sales situations? What other ideas do the

---

[1] Joseph W. Thompson, "A Strategy of Selling and Training for the Hotel Industry," *Hotel Monthly*, Clissold Publishing Company, Chicago, Ill., 1961.

sales approaches suggest? Do we find a parallel in the past? What should I copy from these sales approaches?

What do we do in selling now that is like the various approaches? How can we modify the various six sales approaches discussed in this chapter? How can we give them a new twist? How can we change their meanings? Can we magnify, minify, substitute, rearrange, reverse, combine the words, the systems, the strategies, etc., to give them new meaning?

We merely change, adapt, adjust, modify products, words, various things, etc., and we have another idea. In the same way, salesmen should be creative and experimental in utilizing different ideas to communicate and thus motivate the prospect to act now.

Stimulus response is the first of the six approaches to selling discussed in this chapter. It is one of the most important concepts involved in selling.

SIMPLE STIMULUS-RESPONSE SELLING

A salesman uses the simple stimulus-response approach to selling when he concentrates on things to say to prospects, hoping that as he raises a series of points (stimuli) a favorable response will be evoked from the potential customer.

Simple stimulus-response selling is linked with the simple behavior patterns of both the prospect and the salesman. Simple behavior patterns are those behavior activities or responses that occur on presentation of a stimulus with little or no hesitation. Thus stimulus-response selling can be linked with a simple decision-making process. In contrast, a period of hesitation precedes choice in most situations calling for a more sophisticated level of decision making. And this is what the simple stimulus-response approach to selling overlooks. It does not adequately allow for the more sophisticated level of behavior activities on the part of the salesman and the customer. This will become clear from the following examples.

Example of Simple Stimulus-Response Selling

For the salesman selling investment opportunities in a dry cleaning village, effective stimuli may supposedly be found in such words or phrases as "This is a real opportunity, a real money-maker," "You pay off your investment in three years and the rest is gravy," "The market is really ready for these," "Everything is coin-operated these days."[2]

The salesman who is promoting his hotel as a convention site may think he has found a favorable stimulus pattern in a glad-hander approach to the prospect and such magic words as "our beautiful hotel," "good food," "beautiful swimming pool," "exclusive night club," "good public relations," "have your convention at our hotel," or "we will give you an unlimited liquor account."[3]

The salesman selling health care programs to manufacturers may an-

[2] Joseph W. Thompson, *Norge Dry Cleaning and Laundry Village Sales Manual*, Rich Machinery Company, Grand Rapids, Mich., 1962, p. 26.

[3] Joseph W. Thompson, "A Strategy of Selling and Training for the Hotel Industry," *op. cit.*, p. 48.

Selling: A Behavioral Science Approach

ticipate a favorable prospect response through using such words or phrases as "a prepaid health care program," "peace of mind for the employees," "85% of all the business firms in Indiana who qualify have Blue Cross–Blue Shield," "it will mean greater productivity from your employees."[4]

The distributor salesman selling industrial products might be firmly convinced that the following concepts will evoke a favorable response: "Numeric control is the latest device on the market," "cutting tools that will fit right into your production plans," "we can cut costs," "we can eliminate two of your workmen," "we give service," or the salesman might say,

> Checkmate gages are what you need, Mr. P. A. They are truly precision gages. The manufacturer guarantees them because they are manufactured from high speed steel, and all thread elements are tested, and each checkmate gage is certified to meet the fullest requirements of the engineer's Bible and other industrial standard setters. And you know, of course, checkmate gages have an extended life, and these gages come in all sizes that you can possibly need. They range from X to X.[5]

The Memorized Sales Talk

In the cases above, the salesmen believe these are favorable words or phrases which will appeal to the receiver who will therefore respond favorably. He may, of course, but many times the salesman who is employing this strategy is following a standardized or memorized canned type of sales presentation. He presents it in the same way, almost word for word to every customer he contacts. And many companies provide their salesmen with a canned sales talk. For instance, one nationally known insurance company provides its salesmen with a standardized telephone interview. Salesmen are instructed to call various prospects and read from the prepared dialogue. The dialogue is extremely detailed, even including pauses. A slightly more sophisticated approach is used by other companies. They list buying motives and then list certain qualities of the product that will appeal to these buying motives. Salesmen are instructed to appeal to every major buying motive by covering every talking point with every customer. Some companies refer to this as an organized sales talk and believe it is substantially different from the canned sales talk. The author believes that both are essentially canned since they are usually memorized and given as a word-for-word sales talk.

At this point it should be clear that the author is not critical of the canned sales talk or the buying-motives–product-appeals approach as long as the salesman understands what he is doing. The stimulus-response concept is supported by psychological experiments. Pavlov's famous study on conditioning, which is mentioned in most psychology textbooks, shows that with proper conditioning or by presenting the proper stimuli an animal could soon be motivated to associate the stimulus (meat) with the

---

[4] Joseph W. Thompson, *Blue Cross–Blue Shield Manpower Development Program Book*, Blue Cross–Blue Shield, Indianapolis, Ind., 1963, chap. 3.

[5] Joseph W. Thompson, *Pratt-Whitney Manpower Development Program*, Pratt & Whitney Corp., Inc., West Hartford, Conn., 1964, p. 19.

sound of a bell and thus evoke the response of saliva when the bell was rung.

Use of Memorized Sales Talk

The salesman giving a canned sales talk hopes that the stimuli—the things he says—will "ring a bell" with the prospect. This is a simple stimulus-response pattern. Nevertheless, sales volume is produced by canned sales talks in certain sales situations (any situation involving a relatively simple decision-making mechanism on the part of the buyer such as door-to-door or route selling), and when utilized by certain salesmen (the neophyte or the salesman selling a noncomplex product or the salesman that has difficulty in adjusting his communication pattern to different prospects and to different sales situations). Although many salesmen believe that they substantially vary their sales talk for every person they call on, the record indicates this is not the case. Tape recordings of many salesmen's presentations to a prospect were made. Salesmen who indicated that they did not use a word-for-word sales talk, upon reading the transcription of their sales talk, were amazed to see the extent to which they gave practically the same talk over and over. It is logical for this to happen, for most individuals are victims of habit in almost everything they do.

A *major advantage* of the canned sales talk is, sales experts say, that it gives the salesman a regular track on which to run. He never misses a sales point. It gives him complete coverage of the topic.

Limitations of Simple Stimulus-Response Selling

Nevertheless, the salesman who follows a pure, simple stimulus-response type of selling overlooks the internal workings of the human mind. For this system to be successful it would be necessary for all individuals to react in the same way—that is, to respond to certain cues or stimuli in a set way. Krech and Crutchfield in their *Elements of Psychology,* pointed out that if we were to "allow for the finest shading and nuance of motives among . . . different people . . . we would find the number of separate human motives running well into the billions."[6] So, obviously, the *shotgun approach* which treats all people alike hits most prospects to some extent but hits few perfectly.

The *major disadvantage* is that the salesman who follows the stimulus-response method *controls* the sales interview and gives his "pitch" with little regard for the customer's viewpoint. He doesn't develop two-way communication. He doesn't get feedback. And without considering and obtaining a customer viewpoint, a great many sales opportunities are lost.

A very elementary situation will illustrate how the stimulus-response method entirely overlooks the customer's viewpoint or situation. If a salesman says to a prospect, "Let's have a cup of coffee," he hopes that his

[6] David Krech and Richard S. Crutchfield, *Elements of Psychology,* Alfred A. Knopf, Inc., New York, 1961, p. 265.

favorable stimulus will evoke a favorable response. But what is the response of the customer to this stimulus? It depends. It depends upon his needs at the moment, his general likes and dislikes, the time available, the company's policy, and perhaps a host of other factors.

Several factors, for instance, are: Does the customer want coffee? Does he like coffee? Does he want coffee now? Does he want to go out for coffee? Does he want to go out for coffee with the salesman making the request? This example is used merely to suggest that on many occasions the stimulus the salesman plans to use must vary, not only with the individual but with the present state of mind of the individual as well.

Further, this example reminds us that it is imperative for the salesman to determine what the customer wants and needs if he is to be a better-than-average salesman. The customer's or prospect's viewpoint must be obtained, and the sales talk must be given in terms of the customer's viewpoints and needs. In short, before he suggests coffee, he must find out if his prospect wants it and only then can he talk the type of coffee desired.

More on this with the discussion of the needs-satisfaction approach to selling.

FORMULIZED SELLING

In the formulized or AIDA theory, in its pure form, the salesman is trained to get the prospect's *attention,* his *interest,* then his *desire,* and finally to get *action* from the prospect. The salesman uses the AIDA approach as a series of steps.

Limitations of Formulized Selling

In general the AIDA theory to sales training has a tendency to develop a salesman-oriented rather than a customer-oriented sales talk. Like the stimulus-response approach to selling, the formulized theory also has a tendency to encourage functional fixedness, that is, the overuse of ploys, gimmicks, and canned phrases. These control devices become substituted for a purposeful communication interaction between salesman and prospect. Thus in pure formulized selling, everything the salesman does and says is directed toward first obtaining the prospect's attention; next stimulating his interest; then developing desire; and finally getting action.

For instance, the attention-getting salesman in the approach phase may use a series of phrases to accomplish the purpose of getting attention. Calling on the manufacturer-prospect he might say, "Mr. Jones, I am John Davis of Gro-Wright Industrial Distributor Company. It is nice of you to see me, Mr. Jones, and you will be pleased to know that my proposal will be a real benefit to you. And I want to assure you that you are under no obligation to buy. In fact, my call will only take a few minutes of time."

It is thought that the implication by the salesman of "no sale," "only a few minutes of time," "a real benefit to you," or the use of a gimmick

Six Approaches to Selling

will remove or reduce tension that would normally exist between the salesman and the prospect during the initial contact.

It is assumed that these particular phrases will obtain the prospect's attention-interest and as a result the prospect will see the salesman since he believes it will take only a few minutes of his time as the salesman suggested. These are pretty time-worn phrases, and more often than not they will leave a negative impression on the prospect's mind.

Another danger, and probably the main weakness of the formulized approach, is that the salesman controls. He uses external factors to get attention. He uses causative factors for attention getting for the sake of getting attention.[7] This method does not adequately allow for attention as the result of the inner forces of man. It does not allow for the very important fact that the salesman is concerned with attention throughout the sale or that mental attention is the basis of perception. The formulized approach has a tendency to treat selling as an emotional game when, instead, it is concerned with problem solving and decision making. Thus it will be seen in depth selling that the traditional mental stages are dropped and the one concept—attention—is used throughout the sales process. And if we were not concerned with perception, attention would be dropped. Why? Because once an individual's needs, wants, or problems are the focus of a sales situation, attention and interest are automatically secured. And in depth selling it will be shown that the causative factors effecting attention will be most effectively employed if they cause the prospect or customer to attend to the major ideas in the salesman's proposal. In brief, the involuntary dimension of attention is used to effect, to get, and to keep voluntary attention. It is an interactive, supportive process.

Analysis of Formulized Approach

Since the formulized approach to selling is an effective approach, and in one form or another is widely used by business firms today, a brief analysis of the formulized framework follows.

One reason why the formulized approach is so widely used is that it is not complex, and it can be easily adapted to almost any sales situation. Further, many sales managers believe that the salesman needs more knowledge on how to sell than on the why. Or, as one business executive stated to the author, "Training is expensive. We have a big investment in it and we want to make our salesmen as effective as possible in the shortest time possible. Thus our firm cannot afford the long period of study needed to comprehend fully the why of the sales process." Depending on the company, the product, the sales force, the time, and the stage of the company's development and its financial resources, each executive will have to make a decision regarding the type of sales training he will employ. But it is the author's opinion that in the long run most companies will have a more effective sales force if depth selling is employed.

Figure 3 presents the formulized theory of selling. The sales strategy for the entire sale is divided into three main areas of analysis.

[7] See causative factors in the behavioral science chapters.

Selling: A Behavioral Science Approach

The boxes represent the first area of the interview. The actual steps of the sale from prospecting to the close are represented by the boxes.

The second main area is represented by the letters A, B, C, D, and E. These letters stand for the mental states of attention, interest, desire, conviction (or confidence), and action, respectively. Each of the letters is connected to the phase or step of the interview in which the prospect is *most apt* to go through that specific mental state.

Figure 3 Formulized Selling Stages

	A	B	C	D	E
Prospecting Stage	Preapproach Stage	Approach Stage	Demonstration Stage	Objection Stage	Closing Stage
		1, 2	3, 4	5, 6, 7	8

Mental States	Prospect Decisions	
A. Attention	1. See	5. Proposition
B. Interest	2. Hear	6. Firm
C. Desire	3. Disadvantages	7. Salesman
D. Confidence	4. Advantages	8. Now
E. Action		

In the approach stage, for example, the salesman gets attention or interest or both. In the demonstration stage he creates desire. Then as the salesman answers objections, etc., the customer-prospect seems to develop more conviction or confidence in the total proposition as well as approves of the salesman's firm and its representative, the salesman himself. The close, in theory, follows.

The third major area of the sale is represented by the eight prospect decisions. Prospect decisions are closely associated with the mental stages. Whereas mental stages are psychological in nature, prospect decisions are indications by the customer or prospect that he has made, or is making, a certain decision with respect to progress in the sale.

These prospect decisions are usually vocal expressions which represent the state or intensity of the prospect's attention, interest, desire, conviction, or willingness to accept the salesman's proposition. Prospect's decisions are the other side of the coin with respect to mental stages. It is important to remember that the mental stages are *psychological* indications, whereas prospect decisions are *vocal* expressions.

For instance, when the salesman gets the customer's attention-interest, the prospect will normally make vocal decisions indicating that he is willing to see the salesman and hear the salesman's talk. In other words, he has made prospect decisions 1 and 2.

The prospect may not, of course, say, "Yes, I will hear you," or "Yes, I will see you," but he will say words that will suggest these two ideas. He may say, "I will give you a couple of minutes," or even just nod his head and say, "Uh-huh." A prospect may express the disadvantage that he sees in his present situation and the advantages of the salesman's proposal in any one of a hundred statements. The same reasoning follows for the mental stages and prospect decisions associated with the objections and close stages of the sale.

Having an understanding of these three component parts of the sale —the steps in the sale, the mental stages, the prospect decisions—a salesman has an unlimited basis for a right expression of his own individual sales strategy. It is a beginning for creative salesmanship. It is the underpinning for an *organized* sales talk. Nevertheless, the formulized approach to selling stresses how to tell and how to employ sales techniques to control the interview, and it is this emphasis which is the fundamental weakness in the formulized approach. This will become clear as the depth approach to selling is analyzed.

NEEDS-SATISFACTION APPROACH TO SELLING

Psychologist Strong, writing in 1925, advanced the needs or wants-satisfaction approach as a theory of selling.[8] He stressed the importance of finding the appeals or selling points by analyzing the product to be sold and relating the selling points to the prospect's needs—thus, satisfaction.

In a slightly more modern dress this is a customer-oriented concept to selling in contrast to the stimulus-response and formulized approaches which tend to be salesmen-controlled situations. In utilizing the pure needs-satisfaction theory of selling, the salesman must fully comprehend the customer's side of the picture. He must be customer-oriented. And the central way to do this is to be concerned with the needs of the prospect or customer.

This is low-pressure selling with high-pressure results. High-pressure selling is supposed to get results. Many salesmen strive to be high-pressured. They assume a good salesman talks a prospect into accepting the salesman's proposition. Yet psychology points out to us that the greatest pressure exerted is the pressure that comes from within the individual. The individual must want to act in a certain way. The more he wishes to act in a certain way the more pressure, but the pressure is always from within. It is a mental or psychological pressure.

A salesman cannot tell an individual that the latter needs X products or services because of certain advantages, but rather the prospect must discover these points and advantages and accept them in his own mind, and then he is more apt to respond in the way the salesman wishes him to respond.

For instance, taking an analogy relating to physiological needs, an individual generally does not eat unless he is hungry. He does not wear extra clothing unless he is cold. A salesman may present a tantalizing

[8] Edward K. Strong, Jr., *The Psychology of Selling and Advertising*, McGraw-Hill Book Company, New York, 1925.

array of food before the prospect so that his appetite is stimulated and he decides to eat. But all too frequently in presenting the array of food the salesman in a sense says, "You are hungry. Here is some good food. Eat."

Continuing the analogy, the problem in selling is finding out the type of food the prospect wants.

At first glance, it would seem that this is a relatively easy thing for the salesman to accomplish; however, it is an extremely difficult sales task because the salesman is now concerned with the perceptual powers of the prospect or customer. Since needs and experiences temper perspective, everyone looks at a particular situation or problem somewhat differently.

For instance, salesmen in the office furniture field (desks and chairs, etc.) were being trained to stress the fatigue-elimination appeal. They apparently believed this satisfied a need of the buyer, the office manager. But in research completed for the office furniture industry it was found most office managers indicated a general lack of concern about employee fatigue. During these research interviews it was found that although the managers were not interested in fatigue elimination for the sake of fatigue elimination, they were interested in how to get more work out of their office personnel. They indicated that too many people in the office force were constantly taking coffee breaks, etc., and in general they wanted to know how to get more productivity out of the "present-day type of employee."

This suggested, then, that the salesmen who were using a series of points such as fatigue elimination and employee morale might not have been effectively motivating their prospects. In fact, the salesmen, by emphasizing fatigue elimination, possibly set up negative mental barriers against the sales talk in the minds of the prospects. How much more effective would these salesmen have been if, during the interview, they had determined the specific problems of the office managers and then adapted a sales talk to the problems rather than relying on general sales points or the needs concept.

The use of specific rather than general sales points is, however, not the only problem that confronts the salesman. The salesman may be customer-oriented. He may devise and direct his sales talk to the prospect's problem. But it does not necessarily follow that the prospect will see the problem as the salesman wants him to see it, for the needs and experience of the prospect have, in all probability, set him in his interpretation of his particular situation.

Solving problems one way tends to set us to solve a new problem in the same way, provided the problem contains stimuli similar to these in the previous problems. To have the customer change his viewpoint or interpretation of his situation, we must circumvent his set. These concepts are adequately explained in the behavioral science chapters. But these last two points—determining the needs of the individual and the problem of set and perception—suggest what may be limitations of the needs-satisfaction approach to selling. Between these two words—needs and satisfaction—enumerable concepts and ideas from psychology, education, communications, and the behavioral and social sciences in general may be brought to bear on the process.

Limitations of Needs-satisfaction Approach to Selling

The needs-satisfaction theory of selling was developed largely to explain the reaction of the consumer. This theory is largely concerned with selling consumer goods such as insurance, automobiles, and door-to-door items. For instance, the vacuum cleaner salesman or the car salesman assumes that the buyer has such needs or motives as the need for comfort, the need for safety, and the need for security. Listing these needs or motives, he then itemizes as many talking points or appeals of the car or vacuum cleaner which he assumes will appeal to each major buying motive or need. The salesman in turn presents these talking points or appeals to each cutomer. Not only is this a shotgun approach, that is, treating all people alike, but it is an extremely elementary approach to needs analysis. From this example, it can be seen that the needs-satisfaction approach to selling doesn't adequately allow for the problem-solving and the decision-making process that is involved in most major industrial or business purchases made today. This is true in a structure where just one individual is involved in making a decision, or in a situation where the salesman is engaged in group selling, that is, either appearing individually before a buying group representing the purchaser, or appearing as a member of a sales team presenting a proposal to a buying group.

Then, too, the individual who thinks in terms of the needs-satisfaction approach to selling may be led into the trap of the motivational cycle, that is, once the needs of the individual are determined, it is sort of an automatic process.

Finally, the needs-satisfaction approach to selling doesn't effectively explain that complex interaction between the individual's emotional, personal, and status needs and the company's needs in purchasing a product. In this book it will be seen that the salesman is concerned with the individual's needs, not about such common stated needs, however, as love of the family, safety, food, sex, and comfort and how appeals of a product appeal to these needs. Rather he will be interested in such social, status, and emotional needs as the individual's need for recognition, the need to feel important, the need for superiority, the need for achievement, the need for an exhibitionist's attitude, the need for dominance, the need for aggression and a host of other needs. He is concerned with these needs because he must communicate with people exhibiting or having these needs. He learns to identify various behavior activities on the part of the prospect which suggest evidence of these needs, and he develops a coping behavior that permits him to cope or adjust to the individual's needs. In this way he communicates with the individual and adjusts his behavior activities to the needs of the individual. But he is always alert to the business needs of the individual or user or the firm. He is concerned with the business problems or how his product or proposal will solve problems for the buyer, and he is concerned with the individual's decision-making process. The

Selling: A Behavioral Science Approach

complex interaction of business needs and emotional needs is clearly seen at the decision-making point, for it is an individual who makes a decision and that decision is tempered by that individual's needs.

The needs-satisfaction approach to selling contributes substantially to a general theory of selling by highlighting the vital fact that man is effectively motivated through his needs—that man is motivated to satisfy his needs. It proves conclusively that in most situations the salesman who uses a customer-oriented sales talk will be more effective than will the salesman who employs a salesman-oriented stance.

MOOD SELLING

Enthusiasm, personality, and establishing a professional climate in an interview are important elements of mood selling. However, basic to mood selling is the tone of one's voice. Being able to change the climate in a sale from concern to humor by the tone of the voice is the essence of mood selling. How is this done? It is done through sincerity.

A salesman should be as sincere as a "man of the cloth." Have you not been impressed that when you talk with one of these men of the cloth you seem to feel, because of the sincerity in voice and attitude, that you are the center of his thoughts? You feel that this man of God has no problems on his mind other than yours.

The author has often wondered how these men acquired this sincerity which is so readily discernible in the tone of their voice. Recently, while visiting with a minister friend, I asked how he accounted for the sincerity that men of his profession seemed to have. After considerable discussion, he thought he could illustrate at least one important ingredient of sincerity by describing an experience that took place during his first week in the seminary. It concerned, he stated, "a man that I will never forget. He was a retired philosopher who had devoted his life to the church, but who now, in the waning period of his life, was lecturing in a seminary course, The History of Religion. And during the first week of this course he made the statement, 'If you will get a hold of an idea and believe in that idea, you will be sincere. It will affect your entire life and the lives of the people with whom you come in contact. Both you and your ministry will benefit.' "

Could this be the answer to developing sincerity in selling? Is this not a dimension needed by every salesman? In brief, if a salesman got a hold of the idea of service, believed that he is a professional, a problem solver, and had faith that he has something to offer because he is fully qualified in his area, instead of thinking in terms of income or "how can I manipulate this prospect," would not he then convey the impression of sincerity to his customers or prospects?

This concept of mood selling clearly illustrates the difference between "clown" selling and "respect" selling. The clown depends on a colorful personality. He relies on banter, light talk, and stories to establish a friendly climate for a sale.

Six Approaches to Selling

To a degree, depending on the quality of customers involved, clown selling is used and it does produce results. On the other hand, the respect salesman has a mature, friendly personality in combination with a sincere attitude, purposeful behavior, product knowledge, and sales strategies in depth; he is a professional salesman with professional dignity. He establishes a professional climate or mood during a sale. And this, combined with a sincerity that is reflected in the tone of the salesman's voice, automatically varies the mood of a sale from a buoyant aura to a subdued emotional effect, dictated by the circumstances at the moment. A salesman is required to enact many roles—and psychology tells us the mature individual can enact a number of roles.

BARRIER THEORY OF SELLING

The barrier theory of selling is best understood if the reader visualizes a series of hurdles as used in the high-and-low-hurdles track meet. These hurdles are established in the prospect's mind one at a time, and each represents something the prospect desires. It should be understood that it is the salesman who establishes these barriers one at a time in the prospect's mind. He accomplishes this by phrasing his discussion topics in such a way that he elicits favorable responses or admissions from the prospect and the prospect is forced to indicate his desires. Thus, if at the end of the sales talk, the prospect decides not to approve of the salesman's proposal, he in effect must deny all the admissions he made during the sales talk.

Barrier Theory in Action

To illustrate the barrier theory, assume that a life insurance salesman is meeting with a prospect and the prospect's wife. He has made arrangements to be in their home at eight o'clock to discuss their insurance needs. He knows the couple has three children, ages 2, 7, and 9, and that the husband is five years older than the wife. The age difference of five years tells the salesman that on the average the wife will survive the husband approximately eight years.

Assume the usual amenities have been completed and the salesman is in Mr. Jones' home discussing his and his wife's needs. In the course of the discussion with them the salesman inquires as to whether or not they are hoping that their children will someday complete college. Mr. and Mrs. Jones in all probability will indicate that this is their wish. The salesman asks if Mr. Jones also hopes or plans to be able, in some way, to help the children obtain this objective. The answer is in the affirmative.

There may be five or six other hopes, aspirations, or prospect desires that the salesman discusses in the above context. Finally he ends his discussion by asking a question concerning death. He may inquire, "Mr. Jones, from everything you have said, it seems to me that if you were to pass out of the picture, you would like to have made arrangements so that your wife and three children could continue to live at somewhat the same standard of living—or at least not have to have any drastic adjustment problems." He doesn't have to say, "Is that right, etc.;" he merely looks at Mr. Jones, nods, and remains silent knowing he will receive an answer.

It is quite obvious that it is difficult for Mr. Jones to say anything other than that he would like to see his children go through college, that he would like to provide for their college education, and that, yes, he wants to provide for the family if he were to pass away. Mr. Jones has made these and other admissions. If it is financially possible for him to increase insurance coverage so that he could provide the protection he has admitted he wants, it is more difficult for him to say, "No, I am not going to buy now." In order to say no, he would have to jump back mentally over each of the hurdles that have been set up by the salesman.

The salesman may subtly bring in another barrier. He may state, "By the way, Mr. and Mrs. Jones, you may be interested in this research concerning longevity among married people." He notes by his well-documented chart that if a wife is the same age as her husband, she will survive him by three years, $6\frac{1}{2}$ cases out of 10. He continues on with this analysis, mentioning perhaps a three-year difference, a five-year difference and perhaps a ten-year difference. The survival rate and the percentage frequency of the wife's survival is intensified with the spread of years between the husband and wife to the point when the husband is ten years older than the wife, it is almost with certainty that she will survive him by more than thirteen years.

It would seem that the admissions Mr. Jones has made, the things he has said he wants to do, and now this additional evidence will emotionally make the prospect uncomfortable if he attempts to deny all by saying no. This could be called *emotional homeostasis.*

Homeostasis

Homeostasis is a tendency of the body to maintain a balance among internal physiological conditions. Consider, for example, the case of temperature control. The typical body temperature in man is 98.6 degrees Fahrenheit. It normally stays near this point since the body cools and heats itself. If one's body temperature tends to get too high, he sweats and thereby evaporates liquid which cools the body. If his temperature starts to fall, he shivers and steps up his metabolism. Shivering burns body fuel faster and thus generates extra heat.

In addition, however, the individual may behave in such a way as to achieve a more comfortable temperature. When too hot, he takes off clothes; when too cold, he puts them on. He turns the room temperature up or down, opens or closes windows, etc. In extreme conditions of hot or cold he may expend most of his efforts in trying to obtain relief.

Another example of homeostasis is provided by the fact that our body is equipped with certain automatic mechanisms for avoiding pain. A sudden pain in a limb, for example, makes us reflexively withdraw the limb from the source of stimulation or pain. We do not think about it; we just withdraw immediately and quickly. Invariably we unconsciously tend to avoid pain or discomfort.

A further example of homeostasis, and one that we all have probably experienced, is seen in an uncomfortable or complex social situation. Sometimes when we are embarrassed, we blush or suddenly begin to perspire. In the same way, it would seem that an emotional type of homeostasis is implied in the preceding example of insurance selling. Mr. Jones claims he wants certain things for his family. He may well be too uncomfortable or embarrassed to turn around and say, "No, I am not interested in increasing my insurance."

This would be especially true if the situation involved the alternatives of purchasing a new car or purchasing additional insurance which could provide for the family's education, health, and welfare. The salesman may well utilize the combination of barrier and mood selling so that it would have a great emotional effect on a particular prospect. Without question, it may be a form of low-pressure selling with high-pressure results.

Don't forget, however, that in barrier selling the salesman may or may not be concerned with discovering each prospect's individual needs. He may believe, as many insurance salesmen do, that all prospects need insurance. In the insurance case, Mr. Jones may not necessarily desire to act as the salesman has suggested. He may not necessarily want all the things implied; perhaps he may think his children should work their way through school. He may agree with the salesman because of social pressures and the fact Mrs. Jones is involved in the sale. He may purchase the insurance, but he may be frustrated or do so with reluctance.

It can be seen that the salesman can establish mental barriers in the prospect's mind through logic and through personality. It is difficult to deny logic, and it is difficult to refute a friend. This concept may explain why many prospects find it difficult to refuse giving a particular order to friendly, good-natured Jim. As the prospect reasons, "After all, he has been calling on us these fifteen years. He has a family, etc."

The process is similar to the analogy that each individual finds it easy to refuse a stranger who asks to borrow $10 but difficult to refuse a friend, even though he would rather not lend him the $10. If he did refuse, he might be embarrassed.

DEPTH SELLING

Depth selling is a combination of the stimulus-response, formulized, want-satisfaction, mood, and barrier approaches to selling.

It involves many principles of education, psychology, and communication. It is through these principles that depth selling finds its profundity. The concept of depth selling places salesmanship on a high academic plane. It is an interdisciplinary approach. It is concerned with relationships and understanding. Above all, the salesman who comprehends and employs depth selling is engaging in a highly professional endeavor. The

Selling: A Behavioral Science Approach

man who uses depth selling is a fully functioning salesman—a professional salesman. He utilizes every concept and technique of selling as needed. He is familiar with psychological and educational principles behind the six approaches to selling. He understands how all approaches and techniques of selling may be incorporated into managing sales situations.

For instance, he realizes that every act and statement made by the salesman is a stimulus, and that the response will vary according to such diverse factors as the customer's mental ability, ethics, self-image, buying motives, emotions, and drives. He discerns how to vary the stimuli to achieve mental attention, establish a mood in a sale, obtain the customer's viewpoint, discuss his proposal or product, discuss the prospect's problems, adapt his proposal to the prospect's needs, solve prospect doubts, and complete negotiations.

An abridged depth-selling diagram follows:

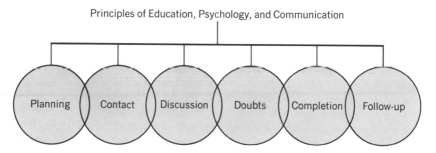

Figure 4 Depth Selling

Depth Selling and the Formulized Approach Compared

The circles in the diagram illustrate that a sale is not just a series of steps but rather is a continuous flow of thoughts exchanged between the salesman and the customer which eventually lead to a sale and a satisfied customer. In the formulized approach, the stages of the sale are referred to as approach, demonstration, objections, and close. In depth selling, we use such words as *contact, discussions, doubts,* and *completion of negotiations.* We visualize contacting prospects as professional salesmen. A lawyer contacts clients or men with whom he has business. The president of a company doesn't approach another businessman; he contacts him. The professional salesman who represents a professional company with a worthwhile product contacts other businessmen representing reliable companies. The contact is made either by telephone or in person. He doesn't use ploys to get in to see the prospect.

The difference between the words *discussion* and *demonstration* is evident. In demonstrations we think of tangible products, such as cars, re-

from the desk of J. KIM TUCCI

frigerators, data processing machines, office equipment, and industrial equipment. In discussions, we are thinking of both tangible and intangible products. We are thinking of such intangible products as investments, life insurance, Blue Cross–Blue Shield, and advertising. Whether the salesman is selling a tangible or intangible, the philosophy of depth selling is to make the value of the proposal or product tangible in the mind of the buyer. Discussion features two-way communication. Discussion encourages mental participation by the prospect, by the salesman selling proposal or product.

The very word *doubts,* in contrast to *objections,* suggests a subtle distinction between depth selling and formulized selling; however, the difference is, in fact, major. There are no objections in depth selling. The concept of objections, as traditionally discussed in selling, is the salesman against the prospect. Most companies have standard lists of objections given by prospects with standard answers for the salesman. But the fact is it is impossible to prepare a list of answers to so-called objections until you find out what each individual means by his objection. Realistically, then, in depth selling the concept of objections is not acknowledged. Instead, the salesman discusses a prospect's doubts, his beliefs, his statements, his ideas, and his concepts. The prospect wants to know; he has doubts. He is not against the salesman and the salesman is not against the prospect. This discussion can be brought to a close for now with this statement from Chapter 16 in this book. "It is impossible to have perfect communication in replying to a prospect's objections, statements, or doubts unless we fully understand what the prospect intends to communicate to us by his objections, statements, or doubts."

Prospect's decisions, as discussed in Formulized Selling, are incorporated in depth selling as well. However, just as a distinction was made between the steps of a sale being illustrated by circles in the depth-selling diagram in contrast to blocks in the formulized selling, there is a distinction between the prospect's decisions as well. In the formulized approach a stilted sales situation by stages, blocks, or chunks is found. Both prospect and salesman seem to be robots. They are engaged in a series of rough, broken happenings that take place during a sale which may lead to the sale, but there is no smooth communication pattern between prospect and salesman. In formulized selling the salesman prepares his talk to get certain prospect decisions.

The prospect decisions are the other side of the coin with respect to mental stages: mental stages are *psychological* indications, whereas prospect decisions are vocal expressions. In depth selling, the salesman judges the entire communication interaction between himself and prospect by listening and observing. He is aware of the personal, emotional, social needs, or status of the other individual, and he adjusts his behavior to cope with these needs (a coping behavior); he is aware of the distinction between these and the needs of the individual as a user of the salesman's product or service, especially as a problem solver. Finally, he understands the decision-making process that each buyer consciously or intuitively goes through before he makes a decision. Suffice here to say that depth selling weaves together in one fabric the most usable and worthwhile concepts from the stimulus-response, formulized, needs-satisfaction, mood, and barrier approaches to selling.

Summary

The six approaches to selling are simple stimulus-response selling, formulized selling, needs-satisfaction selling, mood selling, barrier selling, and depth selling. The first five approaches are combined to form depth selling.

There are two major reasons for studying these five approaches to selling and understanding their interaction and how they are combined to form the ultimate approach, selling in depth. First, the study of these approaches will give the salesman a backdrop, that is, the knowledge needed to determine the accuracy of his sales effort. This is enormously important for without the ability to evaluate there is relatively little value to experience. In order to evaluate the salesman needs feedback. He must know how to get feedback and interpret it. He must adjust his behavior according to a constant flow of feedback. He can best do this if he has the knowledge and skill needed to evaluate his sales effort and adjust when necessary.

In the second place, the combining of the five forms of selling into depth selling develops one approach, a general theory of selling, that with creativity will permit any salesman selling any product to sell more effectively.

Depth selling brings to bear on the sales situations, ideas, principles, and concepts from communication, psychology, educational psychology, social psychology, economics, management, and marketing that are basic to understanding the self and the personal, emotional, and social or status needs of others, to being able to communicate effectively with others and obtain feedback, and to developing a greater sensitivity to evaluating that feedback. In addition, depth selling develops the salesman's skill as a problem solver and a decision maker. Depth selling brings to light the important fact that two sets of problems or needs are involved in most sales situations in this incredibly complex business world today.

Initially, the salesman must analyze the problem or situation of the firm and show how his product or service will solve or improve that situation, and he must develop a coping behavior to work with the individual or individuals who are in the decision-making slot in that company. This situation is substantially different from, for example, the car salesman selling a Cadillac convertible to an individual, or the office furniture salesman selling office furniture (status) to an individual, or the life insurance salesman selling family protection to an individual. In a business situation the decision maker may be far removed from the consumption or use of the product. Thus the salesman is involved on the one hand with the problem-solving and decision-making mechanism of the buyer and on the

Six Approaches to Selling

other hand with the emotional needs of that individual, such as his need to feel recognized, to feel superior, his need to dominate, or his need for achievement, or any one of numerous other needs not directly associated with the use of the product but which must be recognized if the interaction between two individuals is to result in mutual compatibility.

Chapter 9 DISCUSSION QUESTIONS

1 Is there any value to a salesman studying the five approaches to selling which are combined to form depth selling? Why? Why not? Would you follow the same reasoning if you were thinking in terms of a door-to-door Fuller brush salesman? A door-to-door salesman of vacuum cleaners? A door-to-door salesman of aluminum windows and doors? A car salesman who makes both inside and outside sales calls? An industrial machine tool salesman? An insurance salesman?

2 What major disadvantages do you see in the simple stimulus-response form of selling?

3 Discuss the simple stimulus-response form of selling from a prospect's decision-making standpoint.

4 Formulized selling is the best known theory of selling and the most widely followed form of selling. Why?

5 Are there any disadvantages to the formulized approach to selling?

6 What is the major contribution of the needs-satisfaction concept to a general theory of selling?

7 Does mood selling adequately explain the importance of what we refer to as "personality" in selling?

8 Explain the barrier theory of selling in terms of the concept emotional homeostasis. How valid is this reasoning?

9 Does the salesman using the barrier theory of selling discuss a prospect's true needs, or does he just assume each prospect has a given set of needs? How valid is this assumption?

10 What is depth selling? Can any salesman employ depth selling?

the why
and how of
communication
10

Today salesmen, managers, educators, government, business firms, etc., are all communications-oriented—they must be. Speed, acceleration, automation, new mediums of education, new governments, new world conditions, new products, and new terms all represent our world today. Change is an everyday occurrence. With the event of world common markets and such communication devices as Telstar, selling on an international basis may become increasingly more important to the business firm and to the salesman.

Our position as world leader is at stake. It was not until after World War II that we really became concerned about foreign countries. The giant Marshall Plan which involved spending millions of dollars in foreign countries forced us to attempt to understand and accept people from other countries. This understanding and acceptance of other nations in general and their business philosophy specifically will become increasingly important to salesmen as time goes by.

Frequently today we find many business executives discussing foreign competition in industrial parts, machine tools, toys, chemicals, steel, fabrics, watches, cars, cameras, and many other products.

But what about the future? Such competition will become more and more of a sales problem. A highly skilled American salesman will be needed to sell his products in this country—not only in competition with other American-produced products, but in competition with foreign-produced products as well.

Effective communications between the salesman and the prospect will be markedly more important in the decade ahead. Before discussing each of the ingredients in the communication system, a day of an average salesman will be observed to see that he communicates with many people in many ways for many reasons and on many levels on each and every day.

A Day with the Typical Salesman

The salesman is a representative for Norge coin-operated laundry and dry-cleaning villages in the state of Wisconsin. He is staying at a downtown hotel in Milwaukee.

In the morning our salesman, Mr. Frank Hill, calls room service and orders a continental breakfast (spoken communication). While waiting for breakfast, he reads over his mail and is especially interested in a brochure describing his company's advertising program that is to appear in *Life* (pictorial communication). He turns to television and watches an animated cartoon extolling the virtues of toothpaste and listens to the announcer describing its merits (spoken and visual communication). The salesman makes a mental note not to use that toothpaste and turns to the matter of telephoning a number of company salesmen staying at the same hotel.

A waiter enters the hotel room and extends a cheerful "Good morning, sir. It is a wonderful day, the sun is shining, and it is 82 degrees." Mr. Hill acknowledges with a friendly nod of his head (gestural communication) and says, "That is good news," as he continues dialing several company salesmen staying at the hotel.

Later, fellow salesmen meet in Hill's room to discuss (group communication) the effect of a recently published city ordinance (mass communication) restricting the sale of the dry-cleaning and laundry village in certain areas in the city of Milwaukee.

Later in the morning, Mr. Hill, our salesman, meets with a group of potential investors interested in establishing a Norge coin-operated laundry and dry-cleaning village (group communications). Hill utilizes a film strip, a flip chart, and a number of the handout pieces (visual and pictorial communications). He asks the investment group to study one of the visuals of the company's description of how the village operates (communications by printed words).

One of the potential investors asks questions concerning the effectiveness of the solvent used in the Norge dry-cleaning village. Hill takes a glass container from his briefcase and hands the container to the investor. Upon opening the container, the investor notes that the solution is odorless (chemical communications—smell). Our salesman immerses various fabrics in the cleaning solution and after allowing a few minutes for the fabric to dry, he distributes the swatches among the investors for their inspection (communications by touch and visualization). The salesman wipes the floor with the newly cleaned swatches, presses the dirty swatches into a ball, and reimmerses them into the solution (communications through action). For a few minutes he shakes the bottle to resemble the kind of agitation garments would receive if they were in a Norge dry-cleaning machine. He removes the swatches and demonstrates to the investors the unusual cleaning powers of a Norge solvent.

The discussion group now adjourns for lunch. Our salesman, on seeing a customer receive a sizzling steak, smells the odor of the steak and orders a small sizzling steak. This is ideal communication: the message was sent and received. Salesmen cannot hope to equal the motivational powers of a sizzling steak, but they can go a long way in that direction by studying effective communication techniques.

SALESMEN VIEW THEIR SALES TALKS

Over the years the author has accompanied many salesmen in face-to-face calls with prospects. After many of these calls, the salesman was

Selling: A Behavioral Science Approach

asked, "How well do you think you communicated with the prospect?" Most salesmen replied that they probably did well—that they had communicated with the prospect. Seldom did they inquire as to what was meant by communication. Frequently salesmen quickly replied that they told the sales story well. This is what they meant by communication. And the fact that many salesmen believed they told their sales stories very well attests to the conclusion they did not understand the concept of effective communication. They apparently were thinking only of their message or sales talk. This is one-sided communication, as is seen in the S-R form of selling.

In general, salesmen give their sales talks well. They are good speakers; their enunciation and pronunciation are better than average. Some salesmen have flexible speech patterns, that is, they can be more or less dynamic as the occasion demands. They can apparently vary their voices in tone as well as in speed.

Yet many salesmen who have these abilities and who commented they believed they had given their sales talk well reevaluated their opinions of their sales talk as they replied to the further question, "Well, Jim, I think you speak well, too. But how effective was your sales talk in terms of motivating prospects?" "Hadn't thought of that," or "Guess I could be selling more" were not uncommon replies.

The subject of motivation was apparently another matter. It seems to be somewhat of a paradox that salesmen were fairly well satisfied with their sales talks as well as with the way they talked, but generally they were not at all sure they were satisfied with their sales talks from a productivity or motivation viewpoint. Why?

Many salesmen regard communication as a process of telling and selling. To many salesmen developing a sales talk meant incorporating as many good points as possible into their proposal or sales talk. And since the sales points are supposedly important to the prospect, the best plan of attack was to sell by telling the points to the prospect.

This is communication, but it suggests one-way communication. It is reminiscent of the sales philosophy that prevailed in the United States from 1700 to around 1950.

In the past decade, our sales executives have become more concerned with communication theory and its role in selling. It is almost incomprehensible to think that, in general, we in the sales field are just beginning to analyze the communications process when we had a communications system set in motion by a famous philosopher of 2,000 years ago.

A COMMUNICATION MODEL[1]

In his *Rhetoric,* Aristotle indicated that we had to utilize three communication ingredients: the speaker, the speech, and the audience. We may safely transpose by referring to the speaker as the salesman, the speech as the sales talk, and the audience as the prospect or prospects in

[1] Adapted from David K. Berlo, *The Process of Communication,* Holt, Rinehart and Winston, Inc., New York, 1960, chaps. 2–4.

group sales. Aristotle also told us that the purpose of communications was to persuade and that we must adjust our thoughts to the audience.

We still follow Aristotle's basic framework, but communication authorities have added some refinements. Today in the communication process we discuss:

1. Communications source   4. The channel
2. The encoder   5. The decoder
3. The message   6. The communication receiver

These six ingredients will be briefly discussed to obtain an overall view of the communication process. But emphasis will be on the *source,* the *message,* and the *receiver,* since they are basic to any sales communication system. The nervous system or other technical aspects of communication will not be considered.

All communications have a source. It may be an individual or group of individuals with a reason or a purpose for engaging in communications. It may be a sales manager or a salesman. The source has ideas, concepts, and information; therefore there is a purpose for communication. The purpose is expressed in terms of a message.

To translate the purpose into a message or language, a third communication ingredient, the encoder, is required. The encoder is referred to as a sending system of the source; it is the voice, the larynx, etc. At this point the brain, nervous impulses, etc., with respect to the formation and delivery of a message, could be discussed. Simply, the encoder is responsible for taking ideas of the source and putting them into the form of a message which will express the source's purpose. The encoder mechanism produces the word, just as hand muscles produce the written message and facial muscles produce facial expressions. In spoken communication the *channel* simply refers to the sending of a message via sound waves through the air.

So far there is a source, an encoder, and a channel. No communication will result, however. For verbal and written communications to take place, there must be a *recipient*—someone on the other end of the channel. The recipient is the prospect or customer. The recipient has a decoder. The decoder is a mechanism by which the receiver retranslates the message sent by the source. The translation will depend not only on the physical quality of the listener's decoder or hearing mechanism but also on his ability to listen and to interpret. In addition, his intelligence as well as his attitude, his verbal skill (limited vocabulary), his interest level, and the relationship of goals and physical obstacles present will affect the translation.

The prospect must listen effectively. The prospect is the other half of the communication process. Just as a salesman must talk and listen effectively, so must the prospect talk and listen effectively. Both are necessary for the most effective communication to take place. Fortunately the salesman is in a pivotal control point. With his knowledge and skill, he can, as Aristotle suggested, persuade. He can structure a spontaneous interview. He can make the interview dynamic. He can make it exciting. He can build a happy image. He can stimulate thinking. He can direct the

160

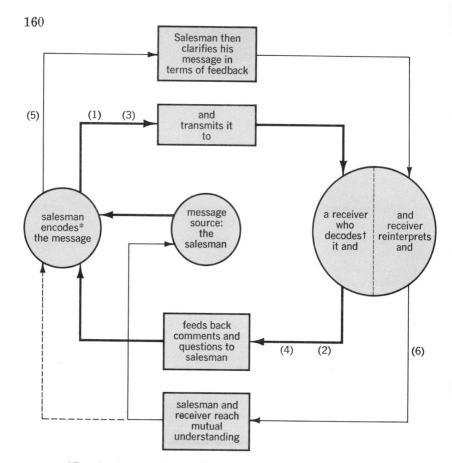

*Encoding is a technical term for the individual's speech mechanism.

†Decoding is a technical term for the respondent's thought process.

Figure 5 Two-way Communication

interview, even though prospect behavior changes must come from within his mind. The salesman's control comes, in part, through his strategy in utilizing the various parts of the communication model to "strike" the mind of the prospect.

Before discussing any ingredients of the communication system in depth, the interaction of these ingredients can be shown by the following description of a common communication situation and the diagram above of a two-way communication process.

Two college students are in the library discussing a course in logic. It is Friday night, and we find Jean and John deep in an academic discussion. Perhaps this isn't a very realistic situation, so to make it more realistic assume it is 10 Monday morning, and Jean and John are in a local coffee shop, having a third cup of coffee. John had met Jean at a dance Friday night. There is another dance Monday night, and John realized, as he watched Jean do the twist Friday night, that this was the girl he wants to take to the dance Monday night. John decides to ask her for a date. John is now ready to function as a communication source. He has a purpose. He wants to motivate Jean to accompany him to the dance Monday evening; he wants to sell her on going with him. His speech mechanism, acting as an encoder, produces a message, simply asking, "Jean, it was such a pleasure to have danced with you Friday night, and gosh! the way you can twist! What I am leading up to is that our group is having a dance tonight. May I have the pleasure of taking you?"

The message is sent through the air via sound waves. Jean is interested in what John has to say and listens intently. She hears John's message, and her hearing mechanism decodes the message. Although Jean is most anxious to go to the dance, she decides on a different strategy and orders her speech mechanism to produce the following message "Thanks, John, for the compliment—both on my dancing and for the date as well. I would love to go, but I have a term paper I must get in. I do hope you will ask me again, though."

This communication between John and Jean can be graphically seen in the two-way communication diagram. For all practical purposes, the communication process remains within the inner circle. No clarification is needed. John, as the source, developed a message. His speech mechanism decoded the message and he transmitted it to Jean, the recipient or receiver. Jean understood the purpose of the message, and she replied in terms of that understanding. On the other hand, if Jean had not fully understood the sender's message, she would have indicated this and John would then need to clarify his original message in terms of the feedback. This process of clarification and how the salesman communicates is analyzed in greater detail and with dialogue in Chapters 12 and 13. Before proceeding further, the reader may wish to refer to that discussion to obtain a detailed analysis of the two-way communication process.

From the above student-to-student conversation and an analysis of that conversation according to the two-way communication diagram, three concepts can be seen that are especially worthwhile to the salesman from a motivational standpoint. First, he must fully understand the *purpose* and the *development* of the sales message. He must develop the art of *listening effectively*. And finally, he must understand the *individual* (receiver) for whom the message is intended.

Purpose

All communication has some source. In personal selling, it is the salesman. He has a purpose, a reason for engaging in communications. He communicates to influence and to persuade—to effect with intent. He wants to effect the behavior of the prospect. This is his purpose—his target.

His target is mental behavior and eventually he hopes the physical behavior (action) of signing the order. For instance, a salesman calls on a prospect who isn't interested in seeing him or hearing his sales talk. When the salesman obtains the interview, he has, to some degree, changed the prospect's behavior. He may persuade (motivate) the prospect to

Selling: A Behavioral Science Approach

change his behavior further by agreeing to give the salesman time to present a few sales facts. But causing subsequent prospect behavior changes may be increasingly more difficult to obtain. As most salesmen will testify, the final change in the prospect's behavior—that is, buying the product now—frequently is the most difficult to obtain.

All too often sales managers have given the advice to salesmen to "go out and make calls on people and you will succeed." At a national sales executive sales rally, the speaker (a sales manager) told the group of assembled salesmen that the one key to selling was getting out and seeing the customers. One of the speaker's slogans was, "Show me a man who will call on customers, and I will show you a successful salesman." He presented statistical evidence to support his reasons. On the average, salesmen made ten calls, obtained three interviews, and made one sale. Since the salesman's commission from each sale averaged $100, each call was worth $10, with each interview being worth $33.33.

To this particular sales manager, the salesman's purpose or goal should be to make ten calls, present a canned sales talk to at least three prospects, and sell one prospect out of these three.

Making such calls is of obvious importance, but this illustration is just the opposite of the depth salesman's purpose in selling. He must effectively change the behavior of the prospect, through complete planning and through communication based on all the concepts included in this book. In the above example, it may safely be assumed that salesmen who follow the 10-3-1 concept will probably negatively change the behavior of a number of prospects. After listening to a forcefully given canned sales talk, the prospect's behavior, or set of not wanting to buy, might even be more firmly entrenched than it was prior to the salesman's call.

This salesman's image is told by Ralph Nichols, as he writes,

> It's one of our occupational diseases that's hard to cure once you are stricken. The disease: Talking too much. The occupation: Salesman. For many of us the word salesman brings to mind an image of a nattily dressed individual who talks as though he has been vaccinated with a phonograph needle. He sells ice boxes to Eskimos, and if you don't beware, he will sell you something you don't want.[2]

The salesman's regard for verbal skills is also told by Nichols. He comments:

> Many salesmen cling to the notion that one of his most valuable attributes is the ability to verbalize. He may recommend the "low-pressured sales," but we find him cultivating his voice for purposes of oral persuasion. Books on how to talk are well read in the sales field, and adult-education courses on public speaking are almost certain to be well populated with salesmen. Deep inside, many people who live by selling, lies the conjecture that glibness has magic.[3]

The examples above serve to remind us that we can get too busy mak-

[2] Ralph G. Nichols and Leonard A. Stevens, *Are You Listening?* McGraw-Hill Book Company, New York, 1957, p. 164.
[3] *Ibid.*, p. 164.

ing calls, giving sales talks, and forgetting that the purpose is to change the behavior of the prospect. And, as will be seen, this is not done through the canned, or word-for-word sales talk. A salesman cannot rely on telling the prospect, that is, just talking and just giving sales points. He must have two-way communication. He must, to a certain degree, follow the same path the psychologist attempts to follow.

What is the basic work of the psychologist? Assume the patient is a man who claims, "I just can't stand my wife." The psychologist doesn't lecture or tell the patient he must get along with his wife, and to do this he must do these things: bring her flowers on Monday, Wednesday and Friday; do the dishes on Tuesday and Thursday; and to be sure, of course, to ask the wife how she wants to spend the weekend. Not at all. Much of the work of the psychologist consists in getting a patient to specify his own goals. After the patient has specified his own goals, the psychologist tries to assist him in determining if he is acting or behaving in ways that will better or lessen his chance of achieving his goals. He must work with the patient. He cannot successfully order the patient to act in a certain way. The psychologist is not in a position of authority, but rather he is in a position of nonauthority. Any change taking place in the patient must come from within the patient on the patient's own volition.

The salesman, like the psychologist, is also in the position of non-authority. Salesmen must obtain information from the prospect on the prospect's business situation pertinent to the product, the proposal, or idea the salesman is selling. After he has elicited the proper information from the prospect, the salesman must have sufficient skills to present the solution in such a meaningful way that the prospect will want to change his behavior, that is, to act now.

An important point is now in order. It is this: A salesman who habitually gives the same sales talk, call it the canned or memorized sales talk (it makes little difference), is following the authority concept. He is attempting to force his ideas on the prospect. He is telling the prospect. Obviously this is not the most effective method since change must come from within the individual. It must be a self-determined mental process on the part of the prospect.

Just as the salesman is interested in the differences between authority and nonauthority from a prospect-salesman perspective, management is interested in this concept from an employee-management relationship. "Storm over Management Doctrine" was the subject of an article in *Business Week*,[4] and speaks to the point we have before us. According to an enlarged vocal and confident group of executives and theorists, the old classical view of authority is outmoded. The new groups are variously called "behaviorist—participationists—human relationists" and a half dozen other terms.

This new school of thought wants mutuality. It wants greater collaboration and interdependence between management and employee through the development of mutual target setting. This group says, "Work is as natural as play or rest." The degree to which men who exercise self-

[4] "Storm over Management Doctrine," *Business Week*, Jan. 6, 1963.

Selling: A Behavioral Science Approach

direction and self-control work toward ends to which management is committed will depend mostly on "satisfaction of their own ego." This group claims "lack of ambition and avoidance of responsibility" are not inherent. They believe that above-average imagination, ingenuity, and creativity in solving organizational problems are widely distributed. Finally this group favors the employee-centered management concept.

This nonauthoritarian school presents a number of important concepts for salesmen. This group would not use one-way communication. It would not use one-way authority. It wants greater collaboration and interdependence between management and employees to develop a *mutual* target-setting program. This group believes that traditional authority permits only partial utilization of intellectual potentialities of the average man. Further, they believe traditional controls and direction by management frustrates all sorts of undeveloped capacities.

Isn't it possible that the salesman who dominates, who utilizes one-way communications by giving his sales talk and doing most of the talking, utilizes only part of the intellectual potentialities of the average customer? And would it not follow that such sales talks could well frustrate many customers who may wish to express their opinions and ideas?

The views of this new school are centered in their demand of an employee-centered management. Our view is found in the concept we must have two-way communication. Our communication pattern must be customer-oriented.

We must throw off the old yoke that prospects don't want to buy, so we handle them to get them to buy. This is just as outmoded as believing that people don't want to be included in anything, so just order them to do what you want.

Purpose and Verbal and Nonverbal Feedback

It was stated above that the salesman's purpose in communicating is ". . . to influence and to persuade—to effect with intent. He wants to effect the behavior of the prospect. This is his purpose—his target." Gradually, however, this statement was modified as the process of two-way communication was interjected. It is apparent that the purpose of selling is to persuade. It is also apparent that the most effective way to do this is to have two-way communication—an intellectual interaction between salesman and customer. Meaningful verbal feedback must exist if the salesman is to assess the effectiveness of the communication process.

This is why the recognized approach in this book is for the salesman to plan his sales program so that it evolves around the prospect's needs (the firm's or buyer's business needs and the buyer's emotional, personal, and status needs). He then uses—for example, in the contact stage—verification and permissive questions to determine whether or not his planning information is correct and to obtain additional significant facts from the prospect.

Since verbal feedback is so vital to any successful communication process, some experts argue that the purpose of the sales message is to

The Why and How of Communication

obtain feedback. It is the author's contention that the salesman's purpose is to persuade—to change the behavior activities of the prospect, but that the sales talk should be so structured that the salesman obtains meaningful verbal feedback.

It is apparent that verbal feedback exists in any communication pattern. But what isn't understood by many salesmen is that nonverbal feedback exists as well. And any interpretation of verbal feedback must be made within the context of the total communication situation. What is said, when it is said, how it is said, and what behavior activities accompany the prospect's verbal message are vitally important to understanding. The salesman must listen to get verbal feedback and he must observe to get nonverbal feedback. How the salesman evaluates by observation is adequately discussed in Chapter 14. (The salesman is told to evaluate for both positive and negative verbal and nonverbal cues. In that section he is told how to appraise the prospect's behavior activities.) Here it will be worthwhile to consider another dimension of nonverbal communication. This is given by Randall Harrison in his penetrating analysis of nonverbal communication.[5] Dr. Harrison's statements will be particularly meaningful to the salesman if he will visualize that Harrison is discussing the salesman as the source of nonverbal cues and the viewer and evaluator as a prospect or customer. He writes that

> Many verbal expressions point to the importance of non-verbal communication. We say, for instance, actions speak louder than words, or one picture is worth a thousand words.
>
> In spite of these familiar cliches, non verbal communication remains an under-developed area of study. It sprawls like a huge mysterious continent, intriguing, but impenetrable. The photographer, the artist, the motion picture and television man all draw on its riches. Yet, these practitioners frequently fear to explore too far, lest they destroy its magic spell.

Certainly Harrison has fearlessly and effectively probed into the world of nonverbal communication. He gives us Figure 6 (see also Figure 7, page 167) and tells us to

> Look first at the verbal level. Both men are saying the word right. Are they saying it in the same way? No. In how many ways do the rights differ?
>
> Most people note that the man on the left, Mr. A, is asking a question; his voice will rise while Mr. B's will not. Which right is louder? Most people would say Mr. B's. Why? Because it is bigger? Why should bigness be equated with loudness?
>
> Look next at the non-verbal level. Various people project different stories into this simple scene. Differences will tell quite a bit about your personality. But equally important, most people from your culture will come to certain common conclusions. Do you, for instance, have a meaning for hand shake? Not all cultures do.

[5] J. Campbell and H. Hepler (eds.), *Dimension of Communication*, Wadsworth Publishing Company, Belmont, Calif., 1964, pp. 1–3.

Figure 6

Now let's look at some of the subtler visual clues in Figure 6. Who is more powerful? More aggressive? How do you know that? Who is more trustworthy? More honest? What makes you think so? Who is more confident? More intelligent? Who is more friendly? If this is a business transaction, who is going to come out ahead?

Harrison states,

Interestingly enough, it has been estimated that in face-to-face communication no more than 35% of the social meaning is carried in the verbal messages. What kind of decisions have you made based on non-verbal cues? If you found differences in power, trustworthiness, and competence, you made some quite important decisions. Research indicates that these may be some of the key dimensions of source creditability, which in turn is believed to be a vital element of persuasiveness. In short, whether you are persuaded or not may rest on non-verbal cues.[6]

6 *Ibid.*

The Why and How of Communication

Harrison's statement, ". . . it has been estimated that in face-to-face communications no more than 35% of the social meaning is carried in the verbal message," may or may not be equally applicable to the person-to-person sales situation. But communication writers like Harrison and others who are researching the broad area of nonverbal communication are identifying a concept that is needed to develop a general theory of selling and to explain more clearly why some salesmen are successful whereas others are not. The concept is source credibility.

Source Credibility

Source credibility is the trust, confidence, and faith the respondent has in the salesman's words and actions. In a word, is the salesman believed? This is a crucial factor in selling. The salesman represents a company. He sells, ideas, products, and/or services. His selling success is, in many instances, dependent on his credibility as a source. Why? Because the level of credibility that the respondent assigns to the salesman in turn directly affects how he views the salesman's ideas, product, or services.[7] This thought can be expressed graphically.

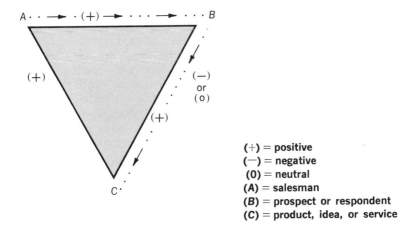

(+) = positive
(—) = negative
(0) = neutral
(A) = salesman
(B) = prospect or respondent
(C) = product, idea, or service

Figure 7

[7] For an excellent and well-researched discussion of Dyadic Interaction and Impersonal Objects see Gerald Zaltmans, *Marketing: Contributions from the Behavioral Sciences*, Harcourt, Brace & World, Inc., New York, 1965, pp. 116–122. Also, the figure above was stimulated by Zaltmans' discussion of Dorwin Cartwright and Frank Harary, "Structural Balance: A Generalization of Heider's Theory," *Psychological Review*, vol. 63, no. 5, September, 1956.

Selling: A Behavioral Science Approach

The salesman (*A*) may have positive feelings about his product, ideas, or service (*C*), but the potential customer, the prospect (*B*), may have negative or neutral feelings about the salesman's product, ideas, or services. If this is the case and if the respondent tends to view the salesman's product or service in terms of the level of credibility he assigns to the salesman, what then are some of the measurable traits, words, and actions that the salesman (*A*) can transmit to the prospect (*B*) which in turn will change *B*'s evaluation of (*C*), the salesman's product, idea, or service from negative or neutral to positive.

Some of these measurable traits and nonverbal cues are segmented in the following discussion of (1) sign language, (2) action language, (3) object language, (4) time, (5) space, (6) trustworthiness, (7) competence, and (8) dynamism.

Ruesch and Kees make the first three concepts, sign language, action language, and object language the subject matter of their book, *Non-Verbal Communication*. The authors represent different disciplines. Dr. Ruesch is a professor of psychiatry at the University of California's School of Medicine whereas Weldon Kees is a critic, film producer, and poet.

Sign language to these authors includes all gestures that are used to communicate. The gesture replaces words, numbers, or punctuation. Action language embraces all body movements that actually communicate but are not primarily meant to communicate. Object language involves the use or display of material things including the human body and its clothing. These three areas of nonverbal communication perform a mandatory function; that is, they shape or direct the other person's behavior whereas words perform an explanatory function.[8]

To the salesman this means that his posture, his actions, his gestures, and his physical appearance including his dress, are not only cues that have an important effect upon the respondent in the communication process, but they significantly determine the degree to which the respondent monitors the salesman's verbal message positively, negatively, or neutrally.

The salesman must keep in mind that the culture, the time, the communicants, and the situation all interact to determine the meaningfulness of the nonverbal cues. An individual who, for example, has a warm affection for a salesman or esteem for the salesman's company will filter the salesman's verbal and nonverbal cues quite differently than will the individual who has never met the salesman.

Take the case of sign language. A salesman may be discussing a repair job, a delivery date, the discount structure, or any one of a host of other problems, and he may signify that everything is O.K. by raising his hand and forming an "O" with thumb and forefinger. He probably combines this gesture with a facial expression. This same gesture is widely used in everyday life. It appears to be an accepted nonverbal message. It may or may not be an appropriate gesture for the salesman to use in all situations. He may be on safe ground if he uses a slight gesture of his hand, coupled with a positive nod of the head and a positive verbal message. On the

[8] J. Ruesch and W. Kees, *Non-Verbal Communication*, Berkeley: University of California Press, Berkeley, Calif., 1956, p. 86.

The Why and How of Communication

other hand, we can say with more assurance that the salesman should not gesture with a pointed finger. An extended finger, pointed at another individual suggests "I want you to," "you," "I want to talk to you," or it may imply a warning about the individual's behavior. As negatively as the use of the pointed finger sounds, the author has seen a salesman who used it effectively. He used a pointed finger to reinforce the dangers of the prospect making a decision regarding the purchase of equipment. He pointed at the prospect and stated, "I can tell you this, Mr. Ansell. Experience in other plants shows that numeric controlled machinery operates more effectively in total, and on jobs like yours, than does the manual operated machine. So it seems to me you will want to give numeric control further consideration." He got the discussion he wanted. The respondent reacted in a positive manner. The pointed finger was accepted. The prospect knew the salesman as a competent man representing an excellent company. The same salesman probably would not have been as forceful with the pointed finger if this were a cold call or with a certain individual with an overly sensitive ego.

It is apparent that sign language reinforces the verbal message and that it is a complex subject. The advice to the salesman is that he should be selective in the use of gestures, and he should not overdo them.

Action language, by definition, refers to all body movements that communicate but are not primarily meant to communicate. An individual may eat to satisfy hunger. But how he eats communicates a great deal about the individual. For instance, what messages are conveyed to the sophisticated buyer by the salesman who might bolt down his food, eat peas with a knife, hold a knife like a baseball bat in the process of cutting meat, uses the wrong fork for the salad, the wrong spoon for soup, or uses a finger to remove a food particle from the mouth? From a sales standpoint, the fact that action language is defined as actions that communicate but are not intended to communicate matters little. The point involved is that most behavior activities communicate. Just as eating communicates, so does the way the salesman walks, looks, sits, shakes hands, nods or shakes his head, shrugs his shoulders, looks at his watch, smiles, frowns, or the general expression of his face.

Visualize a prospect who has a neutral feeling about the salesman's product, idea, or service. Visualize too that a salesman is talking to that prospect, and he is verbally giving some important information about the product. This sounds like good selling. But what if the salesman combines a poorly stifled yawn with the verbal message? This salesman's total communication, although the verbal portion was positive, may leave the respondent or prospect neutral or even negative about the salesman's product. A tired, yawning salesman seldom will convey credibility.

Object language communicates, but it too must be viewed in relationship to sign and action language and the verbal message. Most material things do communicate. A diamond communicates. Its size and quality communicate. Clothing communicates, cars communicate, homes communicate. They may all tell much about the individuals. Again the meaningfulness of what is communicated varies greatly. In certain sections of the

Selling: A Behavioral Science Approach

country a large new car does not denote status, whereas in the mid-west it may. A Masonic ring communicates, but it communicates different things to different people. Further, just how obvious the individual is in his use of the ring, like all material possessions, communicates much.

The fourth and fifth concepts, space and time, are identified by Edward Hall in his book *The Silent Language* as worthy of special study in their own right.[9] As Hall puts it, "Time talks and space speaks."

Time indeed talks in the field of selling. The importance of punctuality varies substantially in different cultures. But, in general, in our culture punctuality commands respect. On the other extreme, tardiness may communicate, and rather harshly, that the other individual isn't important. It is difficult for the salesman to manage his time, other than in route selling situations, so that he can keep all appointments on time. How punctual he need be, every salesman knows, will vary with customers. However, he should, in general, use the phone if he is to be late. It is recommended that the salesman be aware that his credibility may suffer if he is overly late for appointments. The salesman is in a lesser status position. The president or a top executive may keep a purchasing agent waiting and the purchasing agent may overlook the tardiness. Yet he may perceive the behavior activities of the salesman, tardiness, as incongruent with role enactment he expects of the salesman—punctuality.

Space speaks. An executive of a company enjoying national distribution in the consumer goods field told a group of sales managers at a recent convention in Chicago that "I want my company to hire big men from 6 feet to 6 feet 6 inches." To this executive bigness was equated with dominance. And it was his observation that big men outsold smaller men. They did this, according to the executive, because they could dominate by size, that is, standing in a room with a buyer, standing at the buyer's desk, or even when sitting at the buyer's desk. He recommended that the big men get close, whenever possible, because the closer he is the more he dominates.

A big man may outsell a smaller man, other things being equal (and they seldom are), but there is no proof of this; however, in general, at least in our culture, closeness will probably have an adverse effect on the prospect. In our culture there is an accepted space between two communicants. Evans says, "In the United States, in contrast to many foreign countries, men avoid excessive touching. Regular business is conducted at distances such as 5 to 8 feet; highly personal business 18 inches to 3 feet—not 2 or 3 inches."[10]

Each salesman can demonstrate this quite easily. In the next person-to-person communication situation the salesman has, he should move closer and closer to the other individual. He will note that the respondent will perhaps lean back slightly and may even draw back a step or two. Not many people in our culture like the feeling that the other individual is crowding or pushing or falling all over him. In brief, in our

[9] Edward T. Hall, *The Silent Language*, Doubleday & Co., Inc., Garden City, N. Y., 1959.

[10] Franklin B. Evans, "Selling as a Dyadic Relationship—A New Approach," *American Behavioral Scientist*, May, 1963, p. 173.

The Why and How of Communication

culture, it is not recommended that the salesman sell as the Latin. The Brazilian may be successful in his native land wearing dark glasses, speaking rapidly, standing quite close to the respondent, and even being face to face in a heated discussion, but his actions would not have the same effect in our culture.

The final ingredients of source credibility trustworthiness, competence, and dynamism are interrelated concepts as well as being closely related to the previously discussed dimensions of nonverbal communication. In fact, no single factor can be isolated and identified as the vital agent conveying source credibility. Source credibility is a result of an interaction between two or more individuals.

Trustworthiness is identified by traits and behavior activities as they are meshed with the salesman's verbal message. Dr. Harrison has shown us that we may make decisions about trustworthiness, competence, and dynamism merely as a result of viewing the other individual. What may be a minimal cue to one may be a major cue to another. If Harrison's person A, in Figure 6, page 166, had plastered down black hair, a sneaky expression, wore dark glasses, in addition to loud, colorful clothes, the results would have been too obvious. To most viewers he would vividly transmit cues of unreliability, trickiness, and, in a nutshell, little source credibility.

In addition to cues from appearance (clothing and physical) certain traits suggest degrees of trustworthiness.[11] Such traits as just versus unjust, honest versus dishonest, reliable versus unreliable, dependable versus undependable, open-mindedness versus closed-mindedness are associated with trustworthiness.

Another dimension of trustworthiness that merits study by the salesman is the coalition concept. Since it is widely practiced, many salesmen apparently believe that they enhance their credibility position with the prospect or customer by forming a coalition with the customer against a third party, usually the salesman's firm. In carrying out the coalition or "buddy" philosophy, the salesman usually presents himself as being on the customer's side. A good illustration of this can be seen in the automotive field. Some dealers, and hopefully it is a minority, have a well-developed coalition theory. The show goes like this. The appraiser sets the price on the customer's trade-in. The sales manager must approve of the final deal, that is, the net cash outlay the customer pays for the new car. During the process of negotiations, the salesman engages in a series of coalition moves with the potential customer. He gets the low appraisal price increased. Next, he attempts to get the net final price between old and new car reduced. He may make several visits between the "hard nose" appraiser and the sales manager. On the last "preplanned" trip to the sales manager's office, he tells the buyer "Perhaps I can get another 50 dollars. I'll try. But you have a real good deal now. I don't think that he will reduce the price further." Nevertheless the salesman visits with the sales manager. After a struggle he gets another 25 dollars. He relays this

---

[11] Dr. David Berlo, a widely known communication authority, is currently doing research in trait analysis as one aspect of source credibility.

information to the buyer. The deal is made with a close bond existing between the salesman and the customer as a result of their coalition against the appraiser and the sales manager.

This same form of coalition maneuvering that exists in the automotive field exists in most industries. However, the vast majority of coalition situations are not the result of a prerehearsed coalition between firm and salesman, but they are the result of overly optimistic promises by the salesman and, more frequently, the errors of business and communication. Salesmen's promises or business errors may involve delivery dates, quality adjustments, special discounts, price changes, changes in product design, trade-in deals, price adjustments, or many other factors that are not what the customer expected. The coalition exists when the salesman represents the customer against his firm. The extreme is when the salesman's promises or claims do not materialize, and he then does everything possible (even calling the home office in front of the customer) to convince the customer that he, the salesman, will fight it out even if he has to take the case to the vice-president of marketing.

In such situations, a few successes will do much to enhance the salesman's source credibility with the customer. But it is strongly recommended, and most business executives would agree, that the salesman not cause the coalition game to happen. It may lead to a lack of credibility in the salesman's company and a loss of sales. Each salesman should have a strong sense of integrity and business ethics. Enacting a sales role within a strong integrity and business ethics framework will, in the long run, give the salesman a solid source credibility foundation with a buying company. In business today there is no need to trick the buyer.

Competence   Initial research indicates that the competent individual tends to be judged as informed, intelligent, experienced, trained, capable, and possessing a degree of expertness. To the customer viewing the salesman, competence can probably be measured best in terms of expertness. Expertness, however, must be used judiciously. Communications authority Crane, speaking about the marketeer, warns us that ". . . if the customer does not trust his intentions, his expertness may repel rather than attract, since it puts the customer at a disadvantage."[12] Why? It happens "because expertness represents power and if the person who holds such power isn't perceived as sharing the customer's interest, he may be perceived as likely to sacrifice those interests for his own."[13]

Extensive research involving some 165 salesmen in joint calls conclusively indicated that salesmen have a strong tendency to be too product-knowledge oriented. This is especially true of industrial salesmen. Most of the salesmen involved in this sample were competent; many had a high degree of expertness. But in some cases they overwhelmed the prospect or customer with product knowledge. As this happened, effective communications collapsed. Why? To enlarge on Dr. Crane's "why" above, a number of related concepts may be considered. Superiority by salesmen

[12] Edgar Crane, *Market Communications: A Behavioral Approach to Men, Messages and Media,* John Wiley & Sons, Inc., New York, p. 165.
[13] *Ibid.*

The Why and How of Communication

may damage the ego of the prospect, and, when needs are damaged, there is a tendency to project blame back to the source. Thus it isn't the fault of the prospect or respondent who doesn't understand, but, in some way, it is the fault of the salesman. Further, expertness marked by an overwhelming of the prospect's or customers—that is, the sales message is too enthusiastically given, or it isn't presented in terms of the business needs involved, or it is beyond the quick understanding of the respondent—may be interpreted in terms of untrustworthiness or lack of credibility.

On the other hand, expertness properly used is one of the main determinants of source credibility. That is why, in this book (see Chapter 12) it is recommended that the salesman plan his call, use verification and permissive questions to determine the direction of the sale and identify the needs of the firm, use a problem-solving approach, make the discussion meaningful to the respondent, and obtain his mental involvement. There is much more to the contact stage. However, this points out that the salesman must determine the prospect's readiness to communicate, for, as Campbell and Hepler say: "The amount of knowledge held in common by two interacting communicators will determine in large part the manner in which they will interact."[14]

The eighth and final fact relating to source credibility is dynamism. Dynamism has dimensions of confidence versus uncertainty, aggressive versus meek, energetic versus tired, bold versus timid, decisive versus indecisive, active versus passive, fast versus slow. From the previous discussion of confidence and expertness it can be seen that too much dynamism—that is, the type of dynamism classified as overly aggressive or overly energetic or overly forceful—will repel and reduce the salesman's source credibility. Even when dynamism is associated with expertness it may repel rather than attract. The salesman's source credibility is most enhanced when he has *balance* between the various factors that determine trustworthiness, competence, and dynamism.

In summary it can be seen that source credibility is a complex subject. It involves a host of interactive factors from the world of verbal and nonverbal communications. Much is known about source credibility, but much research remains to be done. Upon analysis, the strands of thought involving source credibility lead from discipline to discipline. The entire world of the behavioral sciences seems to be involved. Thus, at this point it may be worthwhile to give a capsule view of the overall sales process and to identify a few of the factors that relate to source credibility.

"At the outset of a sales call," Notre Dame's Edgar Crane tells us, "a receiver will judge an unknown salesman's credibility by the firm he works for."[15] This is a good start. Most companies have a fair degree of source credibility. Within moments of the contact, however, the respondent will be judging the salesman's credibility through his beliefs and feelings about the salesman's trustworthiness, competence, and dynamism. His beliefs and feelings about the salesman will be determined, at least in

[14] James H. Campbell and Hal W. Hepler (eds.), *Dimensions in Communication*, Wadsworth Publishing Company, Belmont, Calif., 1965, p. 94.

[15] Crane, *op. cit.*, p. 162.

Selling: A Behavioral Science Approach

part, from countless nonverbal cues that he will get throughout the sales interview. He will obtain cues from eye contact, purposeful behavior (such as a positive walk, good posture, a moderately firm hand shake), punctuality, use of testimonials to support statements, use of research from credible sources, use of visuals, dress (hopefully moderate), physical appearance and, finally, from the salesman's verbal message with all of its dimensions as discussed in this book.

Assume that the sale is made. What about future relations with the customer? Hovland, Janis, and Kelley give the salesman a valuable tip concerning source credibility and the salesman's future relation with the customer. They do it with a question and answer.[16] They ask, "But how do we go about assigning credibility levels to the people who attempt to persuade us?" They answer the question by stating, "One way to gain or lose confidence in the messages of a source is to check our ability to predict his behavior. If, in the past, we have been able to predict with some accuracy what he would do, we come to trust him because we feel he will not surprise us. That is, his credibility is increased. If the source seldom does as we predict, his credibility falls."

At this point the reader may wish to explore further material relating to the specific analysis of nonverbal cues and patterns of adjustment the salesman can follow in terms of these cues. This is the subject in Evaluation by Observation in Chapter 14.

Purpose and Product Knowledge

In most sales texts, lengthy chapters on product knowledge are found. This suggests the importance placed on product knowledge. And product knowledge is one of the most important ingredients in selling, for without product knowledge it would be difficult to sell in most situations, but not all.

Product knowledge in *itself* is, however, not important according to communication theory. The purpose of the sales message is to persuade. Since product knowledge is invariably an important part of any sales talk, it must also be designed to persuade. Unless product knowledge is utilized to persuade, it is not important. By product knowledge, the author is referring to any knowledge utilized by the salesman to inform the prospect regarding technical information or the value of the product or proposal to him, be it a tangible or intangible. For product knowledge to persuade, it must be presented in such a way that the prospect realizes the advantages of buying. Perhaps no one has said it better than Elmer Wheeler with his "Don't sell the steak, sell the sizzle."

Utilization of product knowledge in a sales talk depends to some degree on the sales philosophy of the salesman—that is, does he use stimulus-response, formulized, want-satisfaction, mood, barrier, or depth selling? It will vary also according to the product and the prospect. In some cases, little product knowledge will be utilized; in others, a great deal.

---

[16] Campbell and Hepler, *op. cit.*, p. 99.

The Why and How of Communication

In general, a salesman (or any individual for that matter) cannot have too much knowledge about his product or subject matter. He must know when to use his product knowledge and how much to use. The man who talks too much and who is too technical obviously will lose the interest of many prospects, but not all. The man who skips lightly over product knowledge and the technical aspects of the product or proposal may lose the interest of some prospects, but not all. The key is to adjust product knowledge to the demand and needs of each individual prospect. The following two charts, one for industrial salesmen and one representing an intangible, will illustrate the relationship between product knowledge and purpose.

Pratt & Whitney salesmen interpret product knowledge so it will have a purpose by following a principle of *benefitizing*. Benefitizing means finding ways the product knowledge or product will solve prospect problems or be of value to a prospect. Pratt & Whitney salesmen draw three columns on a sheet of paper as in Table 2.

TABLE 2   Benefitizing Pratt & Whitney's Tape-O-Matic Drill

Product knowledge	Multipliers	Persuaders
A. Simple preparation of tapes	4	1. Need a blueprint 2. Need a process sheet 3. A typewriter or hand punch 4. Any employee can do who can read a blueprint
B. Greater productivity	4	1. Fewer machines needed 2. Integrates total operation 3. Constant precision control on each unit 4. Doesn't vary with worker
C. Flexibility in changing from one drilling job to another	6	1. Immediate change (programmed instructions) 2. No farther away than the typewriter 3. Etc. 4. Etc. 5. Etc. 6. Etc.

Elements of product knowledge are listed on the left-hand side of the sheet. Each item so listed is analyzed to determine what it will do for, or what it will mean to, the prospect. Each of these points become multipliers and are projected to the right-hand side of the sheet as persuaders. Talking about the quality of construction, the ease of the tape preparation, the greater productivity of the machine or its flexibility to do a job may not be meaningful in itself. As a general rule each sales point is more effective when benefitized. Thus instead of just talking greater productivity, the

Selling: A Behavioral Science Approach

salesman specifically identifies what it will do and how it will do it for the prospect.

As seen in the following chart, Blue Cross–Blue Shield salesmen follow the same process. Instead of telling the prospect—for example, the personnel director of a large industrial firm—that the administration of BC–BS health care program is simple, he tells the prospect why it is simple and what that means to him. He states that all the prospect company has to do is send one original form to BC–BS, and then BC–BS takes over. Each claim is adjusted, BC–BS writes the claim check, files a claim form, and maintains all records, etc.

TABLE 3 Benefitizing Blue Cross–Blue Shield Health Care Program

Product knowledge	Multipliers	Persuaders
A. Simple administration for the "protected" firm	5	1. Claim eligibility 2. Adjust claim 3. Write claim checks 4. File claim form 5. Maintain records
B. Complete employee coverage	6	1. No age limits 2. No physical exam 3. Equal benefits for dependents 4. New-born members at birth 5. Simple identification card 6. Vested rights of conversion
C. Greater employee morale or *esprit de corps, etc.*	6, etc.	1. Greater employee production 2. Less turnover 3. Less operating costs through less careless work 4. Less tardiness 5. Greater public relations for the company in the community 6. Etc.
D. Etc.	Etc.	Etc.

This idea can be utilized by any salesman selling any product. One group of manufacturer's salesmen who sold automatic dishwashers to restaurants, institutions, etc., held a buzz session, placed a blackboard in front of the group, and then listed on the blackboard such elements of product knowledge as the gauge of the steel, the weight of the machines, dishwashing capacity per hour, etc. They then brainstormed to see how many persuaders they could develop from each fact concerning their product. Assuming that a restaurant has a peak customer load from 12 to 2 P.M. and from 5:30 to 8:30 A.M., this question was posed, "Just what would a machine that washed 200 dishes per hour mean to each restaurateur?" This group of salesmen developed seventeen salient persuaders concerning this one element alone. They found it would mean less dish inventory, less breakage owing to stack-up, less danger of waitresses slipping or falling in the kitchen owing to messy conditions, less turnover owing to better working conditions, fewer problems in securing dishwashers, etc.

It is highly recommended that not only should the salesman follow the process above in developing persuaders, but each salesman should provide feedback to his firm regarding unique user applications he has found for his product. It is further recommended that each salesman consistently read professional journals and trade publications in his field. Practically every retail salesman will find consumer magazines devoted to the product he is selling. Practically every manufacturer salesman will find trade publications devoted to the product he is selling. Practically every wholesale salesman will find trade publications dealing with the product line he handles as well as trade publications devoted to those stages in the market distribution system which represent his customers and prospects. Practically every specialty salesman will find trade publications devoted to the product he is selling. In brief, in this modern world of communication there is relatively little excuse for the salesman who claims he doesn't know where to get information about his product and about the user of his product, be it a manufacturer, a wholesaler, a middleman, a retailer, or the ultimate consumer. The salesman's company, of course, should make every effort to provide the salesman with meaningful product knowledge.

SOME ASPECTS OF COMMUNICATING WITH THE EXECUTIVE

At the outset, it should be made clear that there is no difference in the communication pattern which takes place between the salesman and the executive and that which takes place between the salesman and other prospects. His job is to adjust his communication pattern to each individual. Of course, salesmen who are knowledgeable about the problem-solving and decision-making process will be more effective, other things being equal, in communicating with the individual who occupies a decision-making slot in a particular organization. The purpose of this section is to call attention to the fact that the climate in any organization is established by the top executive. It is a filtering-down process. It is both vertical and horizontal in its impact. Each salesman who sells to a business firm, a corporation, or institution, has to operate within the climate which pervades a particular organization. It must be understood, however, that in the larger organization many executives have almost complete autonomy in their area of responsibility—for example, the master mechanic. Thus, the vertical impact of his form of leadership is of greatest concern to the salesman. On the other hand, whenever the salesman is presenting a proposal to a group of individuals representing various areas of responsibility within an organization, he is more concerned with the total climate that prevails in a company.

No pretense is made in this section to define or discuss executive traits (perhaps an impossible task) or distinguish between such terms as

CHART 1 Forms of Leadership, Characteristics of Leaders, Behavior Activities of Individuals under Each Leadership Form, and Guidelines for Salesmen*

Forms of leadership	Frequent characteristics of leaders	Common behavior activities under each leadership form	Guidelines for salesmen
Hard-boiled autocrat	1. Assumes full responsibility for all actions 2. Wants and expects immediate acceptance of all orders 3. Constant check on staff 4. Gives little praise 5. Determines policy and considers decision making a one-man operation	1. Submission but basic dislike of leader 2. Cliques (subgroups fail to cooperate with each other) 3. Hostility (tendency to fight and blame each other) 4. "I" feeling (frequent use of I shows selfishness) 5. Frequent buck-passing	1. Deal with top executive if possible 2. Permissive or verification question must be used submissively 3. Respect his dominance 4. Speak firmly—denote confidence but be on the humble side 5. Thank him for the interview and get to the point quickly 6. His opinion is all important
Laissez-faire leader	1. Tends to lead by being likable 2. No clear-cut goals 3. Procrastinates—has difficulty in making decisions 4. Does not encourage or discourage staff in their efforts 5. Tends to be evasive	1. Low morale, poor work, confusion 2. Considerable buck-passing and scapegoating 3. Lack of teamwork	1. More positive approach than usual 2. Really wants help, but won't admit outwardly that he wants it 3. Strong use of verification and permissive question 4. Assistance in decision making 5. A survey approach excellent here since it provides facts 6. Will find rapport for your program from staff—they want something done

Democratic leader

1. Looks on self as moderator; frequent group meetings
2. Draws ideas and suggestions from group
3. Encourages group members to set policy, goals, etc.
4. Gives praise and constructive criticism objectively

1. Friendly group spirit
2. A spirit of direction prevails
3. Much self-initiative
4. Considerable use of we and willingness to help others
5. Leader liked

1. Salesman need not start at top—in fact, best not to
2. Salesman should get help from various sources in company and let them carry the ball
3. Plan must be prepared so that it can be presented to several staff members at once
4. If top executive is contacted, be ready to work with subgroup

The benevolent autocrat

1. Is not aware he is an autocrat
2. Praises staff frequently and appears interested in them
3. Is the source of all work and decisions—establishes policy
4. Wants dependence upon himself—method of obtaining it is the crux of his autocracy (uses such expressions as "That's the way I like it, John" or "You've really got what I wanted there" or "How could you do this to me?")

1. Most staff like him, but those who see through his basic approach have little regard for him
2. Great dependence on leader as source of action, and little initiative by individual staff members
3. Individuals tend to be submissive, but not afraid—lack of individual development
4. Work output may be good and quality good

1. Like autocrat try to see personally
2. Have more freedom in use of permissive and verification question
3. Plan and problem solving must revolve around him personally. Not so apt to delegate as is autocrat—at least not initially
4. More time can be invested in developing rapport

* Ideas for this chart were drawn from four sources: Eugene E. Jennings, *The Executive*, Harper & Row, Publishers, Incorporated, New York; Glenn M. Blair, *Educational Psychology*, The Macmillan Company, New York, pp. 311–315; Aurin Uris, "Factory Management and Maintenance," July–October, 1951, McGraw-Hill Publications, New York; and Norman R. F. Maiser, "Principles of Htman Relations," *Applications to Management*, John Wiley & Sons, Inc., New York, 1952, p. 49.

Selling: A Behavioral Science Approach

administrator, leader, or executive. Here we are interested in the form of leadership effected by an individual that occupies what is acknowledged in business as the executive chair.

Books have been written on the what, why, when, where, and how of leadership. Most books are concerned with various forms of leadership and the effect of each form on the individual within the corporate structure. Most management authorities seem to concur that there is no one best organization nor is there one best form of leadership. Moreover, it must be understood that seldom does one find a *pure* form of leadership associated with an executive. A leader may be identified as predominantly one type but seldom totally. This issue is further blurred because the leader may exhibit various forms of leadership at various levels. For instance, a plant superintendent may consult with his several foremen; he may direct his secretary, and he may suggest to an assistant.

This is where the salesman starts. He is not involved in passing judgment on the various forms of leadership, but he is involved in identifying certain forms of leadership and their effect on the organization. After all, the salesman does deal with individuals within an organization and the climate that affects them indirectly affects him.

Chart 1 (pp. 178–179) is provided to give the salesman a capsule analysis of the various forms of leadership, and the effect these forms of leadership may have on the individuals within the organization. It provides guidelines the salesman may use in working within various leadership climates.

So far in this chapter customer motivation has been emphasized. Emphasis has been on how the strongly structured, customer-oriented communication system will change the customer's behavior pattern so that he may react favorably to the salesman's proposal. The fact has been stressed that in most situations the salesman can motivate best by appealing to the needs of the individual—the behavior change must come willingly from the prospect. A salesman has no authority; he cannot order a prospect to buy. He must persuade.

Product knowledge and the process of benefitizing have been discussed as having a communication purpose—to persuade. Some aspects of communicating with the executive have been discussed as well. Now to analyze one of the most important concepts in selling, the art of listening effectively.

Summary

Effective communication is crucial to selling in this world of change. There is an explosion of knowledge. It is possible that man may have gained more knowledge in the last twenty-five years than in the history of man. In some fields knowledge is doubling every ten years. Social, economic, and technological change is an everyday occurrence, and it is in this ever-changing environment that the salesman sells. He communicates with prospects in many ways ranging from pictorial to group communication, and although most salesmen are mindful of the concept of communication as such, they all too frequently think of communication as telling the sales story. This suggests one phase of communication which perhaps is the least important. It may lead to negative prospect motivation. More important is understanding that effective communication does not happen unless there is feedback. The perceptual salesman adjusts to this feedback.

Communication models are frequently described in terms of a communication source, the encoder mechanism, a message, a channel, a decoder mechanism, and a communication receiver. To the salesman the most important elements in the communications system are the source, message, and the receiver.

The salesman is the source of a sales message. He has product knowledge, verbal skills, sales experiences, and hopefully is well aware of a problem-solving approach to his customer's needs and thus structures his sales message to get feedback. He interprets this feedback in terms of both verbal and nonverbal cues.

The receiver of any message has a system of needs that determine whether or not the salesman's message is received. The most effective sales message is the one that appeals to the receiver's world of needs, presents meaningful material, and gets customer participation. In order to motivate, the receiver must be involved in the sales situation. And any salesman can involve the prospect or customer or receiver in most sales situations through good communication and a problem-solving approach to the sales situation. The salesman who has been vaccinated with a phonograph needle is very verbal but probably is the least effective salesman today. He lacks good communication and a problem-solving approach to the customer's world of needs.

An important dimension, and one that is especially important today in this world of change, is sound in the concept of source credibility. Source credibility appears to lie in the receiver's interpretation of the trustworthiness, competence, and dynamism of the salesman. There is some evidence to suggest, from a motivational standpoint, that how the prospect feels about the salesman in terms of source credibility may be more important than the verbal message itself.

It is recommended that all product knowledge be benefitized; that is, all product knowledge should be interpreted in terms of what it will mean to the prospect or customer. Otherwise, product knowledge isn't important and in fact may retard the sale.

One of the least explored areas of communication is the effect that company management has on the attitude and feelings of people within the company organization and what this means to the salesman. Forms of leadership such as the hard-boiled autocrat, laissez-faire leader, the democratic leader, and the benevolent autocrat are each identified by the characteristics of the executive or leader. These characteristics of the executive or the individual who occupy the decision-making slot affect the behavior activities of the people within the organization. Being able to identify the various forms of leadership and the effect the leader may have on his organization may provide significant guidelines for the salesman, particularly in the sales situation involving interdepartmental decision making.

Selling: A Behavioral Science Approach

Chapter 10 DISCUSSION QUESTIONS

1 Describe as many forms of communication as you, a salesman, could use in a typical day. What are the main elements of a communication model that are especially appropriate to the sales field? Select any product you wish and develop what you feel is a customer-oriented message to describe the qualities of that product.

2 What is the purpose of most communication: to persuade? to motivate? to get the prospect to sign an order? to get feedback? to develop the art of listening? to develop a two-way communication process?

3 How does nonverbal feedback enter into the communication process? Is it possible for an individual to understand another individual without nonverbal feedback? Which is most effective as a communication device, the telephone or the television? Which is most effective as a communication device, two-way television or person-to-person communication?

4 Source credibility is an important aspect of selling. If the prospect doesn't regard the salesman as having the various elements of source credibility, that is, trustworthiness, competence, and dynamism, what may happen to the communication network between salesman and customer?

5 Is it possible for a salesman to develop his personality so that he suggests source credibility? Is there any competence recognized in the verbal message that the salesman gives?

6 Assume you are a salesman selling an intangible such as life insurance, stocks, and bonds. Illustrate how you would benefitize your product.

7 What has executive leadership to do with the communication network that exists in a particular firm? How does this affect the salesman's sales effort in a particular firm, especially if his selling is across departmental lines? To which of the organizations would you rather sell—that organization which is headed by a leader who could be described as a hard-boiled autocrat or an organization headed by a democratic leader? Why did you make the selection you did? Were any of your personal or emotional needs involved in your selection?

the art
of listening
effectively

11

Listening is the other half of talking. When people stop listening, it is useless to talk, a point not always appreciated by talkers. Listening isn't the simple thing it seems to be; it involves interpretation of both the literal meaning (meaning of the words) and the intention of the speaker. If someone says, "Why, Jim, you old bum," the words are practically an insult, but the tone of voice probably indicates affection.

Americans are not very good listeners. In general, they talk more than they listen. Competition in our culture puts a premium on self-expression. Even if the individual has nothing to express, what he lacks in knowledge he tries to make up by talking fast. Many of us, while ostensibly listening, are inwardly preparing a statement to stun the company when we get the floor. Yet it really is not difficult to learn to listen effectively—just unusual.

"How to listen" experts Dr. Ralph G. Nichols and Leonard A. Stevens developed the framework for the following eight questions as a means to rate yourself as a listener. Answer each question with a yes or no. If you score from 3–5, you are a fair listener; 6–7, you are a good listener; 8, an excellent listener; and if you score 9 or 10, don't read the material following the test. If your score needs improvement, you are not alone.

WHAT IS YOUR COMMUNICATIONS SCORE?

To ascertain your communications score, try to answer the following questions. In a conversation with another individual (regardless of sex, age, or situation):

1. Do you quickly ask questions if you are not sure about the point you are conversing about? Yes—✓— No——
2. Do you believe that what the other person says is the important key to understanding? Yes—✓— No——

[1] For an interesting, effective, and penetrating analysis of the listening process, see Ralph G. Nichols and Leonard A. Stevens, *Are You Listening?* McGraw-Hill Book Company, New York, 1957.

Selling: A Behavioral Science Approach

3. At times, do you concentrate on what you are going to say rather than concentrating on what the other individual is saying? *Yes*✓ *No*——

4. Do you find fault with other people in the sense that they do not talk effectively? *Yes*✓ *No*——

5. Do you beat around the bush? *Yes*✓ *No*——

6. Do you attempt to help other individuals express their thoughts more clearly? *Yes*—— *No*——

7. Do you ever use any of the following in conversation with other individuals?

    a. Do you see my viewpoint?

    b. You don't understand.

    c. Do you understand?

    d. See?

    e. Do you follow me?

    f. Are you aware of this?

    g. This is easy to understand, isn't it?

    h. Quite true, isn't it?

    Yes—— *No*——

8. (*3 points*) Rate the following in order of importance in conversation with the other individual:

    a. Your ability to speak.

    b. Your ability to understand.

    c. Your ability to listen.

    d. Being able to restate effectively what others say.

If you answer no to the first seven questions, you are a rare individual, the perfect listener. Every yes answer means you are guilty of a specific poor listening habit. On question 8, the preferred answers are *c, b,* and *a,* in order of importance.

If your test score was 9 or 10 and you have decided not to read further on the art of listening, you will miss a discussion upon the following subjects:

1. Interest in what your prospect has to say
2. Reaction to peculiarities of fellow communicators
3. Faking of attention
4. Stepping on sentences
5. Equalizing speech and listening speeds
6. Failure to get the facts
7. Emotional deaf spots

INTEREST IN WHAT YOUR PROSPECT HAS TO SAY

Just as some individuals are inclined during social conversations to tell—to tell and to tell what they think is important, or tell what they have done, or what their children or friends have done, or tell other points related to their prestige—some salesmen are inclined to do this in sales situations. A salesman does not talk about himself, but he does tell about

The Art of Listening Effectively

his company, his product, his organization, and perhaps his ideas. The result is the same. The conversation revolves around the salesman's interests.

When a salesman is engaged in the most intimate people-to-people or person-to-person business, is it possible that he could possibly not have an interest in what other individuals have to say? How is it possible that a salesman can develop a habit of not listening when the very success of the sale may depend almost exclusively on his remembering comments the prospect or customer has made? It is easy to visualize the prospect's reaction when he has stated some facts concerning his personal situation or his firm's problems, and later the salesman makes comments that tell the prospect "with lights" that the salesman wasn't listening. Some of the answers to this paradox will be found in the following material.

In addition to the general tendencies of the salesman to tell, the salesman perhaps has further roadblocks to listening. One is that he has great drive. Many times he is so obsessed with obtaining the sale and getting his sales points across to the prospect that he sometimes forgets to listen. In so doing he frequently cultivates a habit which suggests that he has no interest in what the prospect has to say.

Recently Dr. Lewin, a communication authority and educational psychologist, had a number of individual consultations with salesmen who were attending a two-week communication and sales conference on the campus at Kellogg Center, Michigan State University. Some salesmen had several individual consultations with Dr. Lewin during this conference. Many of these salesmen evidently made some progress in analyzing their own problems and role in communication. The understanding and self-analysis made by one salesman is especially worthy of note.

This particular salesman, whom we will call Hagan, had four consultations with Dr. Lewin. During the course of these discussions, Hagan commented he thought he didn't actually listen to prospects or to individuals in conversations for a number of reasons, but two important ones stood out in his mind. First, in his own words, he thought he was rather insecure in his work—selling. Because of this he admitted that maybe he pretended to himself or was inclined to think that what the other person was talking about was rather unimportant. The second reason was associated with the first: Hagan was inclined to think he was a fairly selfish or immature individual and was therefore only interested in what people had to say when they talked about something he liked or a subject in which he was conversant.

To illustrate, he told that he and a group of his fellow salesmen had seen a Thurber play on the campus; later the group discussed the play. He enjoyed the discussion. It was after this discussion that Hagan took real stock of his own interest in what other people had to say. He objectively analyzed, and perhaps correctly, that he was reluctant to join into a discussion when he wasn't knowledgeable about the subject. The result was that in such situations he had developed a mental habit of really not listening when other people were talking.

Selling: A Behavioral Science Approach

Thus, it would appear that much of Hagan's thinking was about things that could enhance his ego, and many of his actions were behavior activities that protected his ego from being injured. Talking was his defense. When he was talking, he was all important. As a salesman he didn't have to listen to problems he couldn't solve, questions he couldn't answer, being told by a prospect, "I'm not interested."

Many times, because of our psychological makeup, we listen only to what we want to hear. This can be corrected only when the individual is aware of why he doesn't listen, or why he interprets situations to satisfy himself. He will have to want to change this behavior activity before any words written on the subject can ever help him.

An objective analysis of such concepts as status, self-image, tension binding, maturity, egocentric, incongruent, ego, role, conflict, perception, coping behavior, and other concepts from the behavioral sciences will assist substantially in understanding some of the problems involved in listening. Many of these concepts are discussed in the behavioral science chapters of this book, but in addition it is recommended that the interested individual study accepted books dealing with general psychology.

Suggestions for Improvement

Hagan, with the assistance of an educational psychologist, has given salesmen three good ideas. First, the salesman should objectively analyze whether or not he has an active interest in what other people say, and if not, he should analyze why. Each salesman must have an open mind; he must have the maturity that will permit him to hear, to understand, and to retain the spoken words (ideas, thoughts) of the other individual.

Second, implied in Hagan's comments is the thought of practice. Just as practice in not being interested in what people have to say will give an individual the habit of not being interested, practice in being interested in what other people have to say will develop a positive habit of being interested. The salesman should take just a few minutes each day, be it in a conversation with a child, an elderly person, a fellow salesman, a customer, and, regardless of the topic, concentrate on what the other individual is saying.

The third point specifically illustrated by Hagan is that with knowledge the salesman is secure in what he is doing and saying. He will be more inclined to be interested in what prospects have to say about the situation. The suggestion here is for the salesman to be firmly grounded in all phases of the sales situations. The salesman must remember that he has to manage a total situation which involves his company, his product, the buyer, the buyer's business situation, the personal and emotional needs of the buyer, and the business climate in general, and he must manage himself.

Another tip for the salesman is to become sensitive to the use of personal pronouns used by the individual. Listen for the customer's use of *we, you, us, our,* and tune in on the conversation that revolves around it.

The Art of Listening Effectively

Many times the use of personal pronouns is a cue to statements in which the individual (prospect or customer) has a particular interest.

REACTION TO PECULIARITIES OF THE FELLOW COMMUNICATOR

Most speakers, fellow discussants, customers, or prospects have one or more mannerisms which can be referred to as peculiarities. It is not unnatural for the salesman to note them, to respond to them, or even to become occupied with them to the point of eventually losing track of what the prospect is saying. The prospect may have a groaning voice, a hacking cough, a habit of clearing his throat, looking out the window, or handling papers on his desk, odd pronunciations, or distracting body movements that invite attention. In fact, the more knowledgeable one is about communication, the quicker he will see flaws in the prospect's manner of expression. This is unfortunate, in a sense, especially if the "expert" has a tendency to think negatively about these flaws, for then he is not effectively hearing or listening to the prospect's comments.

A case in point follows. The author made a joint call and listened in on a conversation between a salesman and prospect. The salesman was selling investments to a lawyer. The investment was in a coin-operated dry-cleaning village. After an aborted sales effort the salesman commented on the peculiarities of the prospect. The author commented that he, too, had noticed these characteristics. The salesman continued telling how he couldn't get the man pinned down as to how much money he had to invest or why he wanted to get into the coin-operated laundry and dry-cleaning business. He added, "I think the call was a waste of time." The fact is, though, the lawyer had mentioned that he and several of his friends were mildly interested in forming a corporation for investment purposes. The salesman had missed this cue. His attention had been involuntarily drawn to the prospect's peculiarities. Charles Irwin, a noted communication authority, states that "intolerance of another person's peculiarities is perhaps a symptom of our inability to adjust."[2]

Sometimes, Irwin comments, responses such as "the call was a waste of time" on the part of the salesman indicate a lack of maturity. Responsibility is shifted, since the salesman blamed poor communication on the prospect, when the blame rests solely on the shoulders of the salesman. Irwin tells us that in every situation the salesman must be the cushion, the buffer—always flexible, ever adjusting in the communication process, but never putting the *burden* of poor communication on the prospect. Good communication is the salesman's responsibility. Good communication isn't an accident—the salesman causes it to happen.

Suggestions for Improvement

Although the above negative reaction on the part of the salesman may be partially psychological in nature, an easy approach to an external cor-

[2] Quoted from Charles Irwin's lecture on leadership to the American Trucking Association, Kellogg Center, Michigan State University, East Lansing, Michigan, Oct. 12, 1963.

Selling: A Behavioral Science Approach

rection of this habit is to build our tolerance ratio. One insurance company psychologist recommends that salesmen role-play situations where the prospect has defects of speech, mannerisms, etc. He claims it lessens a salesman's concern of such happenings on the prospect's part; in fact, this psychologist believes that role playing may eliminate many defects or mannerisms the salesmen may have themselves.

Perhaps even more important than building our tolerance ratio is the acceptance by the salesmen of Irwin's philosophy that "the salesman must be the mature managing force in every sales situation."[3]

FAKING ATTENTION

A minister in Berea, Ohio, shocked his congregation to attention by dramatically stating that in his opinion many members of his congregation faked attention during the services. He declared that it had become the American habit to fake attention not only in church but in everyday conversation.

The minister discussed at length destruction of the inner man as the basic reason for faking attention. Such a discussion is beyond the scope of this book, but we all know that we are not supposed to give an appearance of being a poor listener, regardless of the situation. And if this minister is right that we are faking attention—that we are looking alive physically but are not alive mentally—then we may be developing a serious habit as a barrier to effective communication.

Effective listening is determined in part by the physical condition and the energy of the salesman.[4] Effective listening is hard work. It is hard to concentrate. Research shows it is characterized by increased heart action, faster circulation of blood, and even slightly increased body temperatures. On the other hand, effective listening is one of the easiest ways to acquire ideas and information.

Normally, there is much jamming of the airways. There is static in the channel. This static and jamming may be the result of physical distractions such as a telephone ringing or background talking. Or perhaps the salesman is permitting his mind to concentrate on other points, or the static may be a result of differing perception, education, and maturity of the two communicants. The result, regardless, is that both salesman and respondent are misunderstood, misinterpreted, and misquoted, and many times the salesman misses a sale.

Perhaps the fact that listening is difficult will emphasize an important point for a salesman. Realizing that it is difficult to listen, even though the sale may depend on effective listening, how much more difficult is it for the prospect to listen when many times he may have a negative thought about purchasing a product or listening to the salesman in the first place?

An understanding of the problem of listening, the difficulty in listen-

---

[3] *Ibid.*

[4] Ralph G. Nichols and Leonard A. Stevens, *Are You Listening?* McGraw-Hill Book Company, New York, 1957, p. 63.

The Art of Listening Effectively

ing, and the fact the prospect has the same problems of listening as the salesman has, but more so, will assist the salesman in finding solutions on how to overcome listening lethargy on the part of the prospect.

Suggestions for Improvement

Salesmen should recognize faked attention as a by-product of lack of interest. Faking attention may be a cover-up for the lack of discipline to listen. The salesman may not have trained himself to listen. Thus he is easily distracted. The salesman who fakes attention may well do so because he feels secure that he is giving the appearance of listening. Just as practicing negative habits, like faking attention, makes negative habits, practicing positive habits, like listening effectively, improves positive habits. Practice being an effective listener. Listen attentively. Be open-minded. Verbal and nonverbal cues that the prospect gives the salesman can lead to sales only if the salesman receives the cues. Practice concentration.

When the salesman notes cynicism on the part of the prospect, open signs of disinterest, disapproval, disbelief, or misinterpretation of what the salesman says, the salesman usually becomes discouraged and less and less effective in a sales presentation.

Surely, if these symptoms on the part of the prospect discourage salesmen, how must faked attention affect the prospect—the nod in the wrong place, the wrong explanation, or going off on a tangent. It tells the prospect the salesman is not interested.

In an analysis of many tape-recorded interviews between salesman and prospect, the author has demonstrated conclusively that a large percentage of both prospects and salesmen have a tendency to give oral signs that they are not listening. In listening to the tapes "Oh, yes—um-um—I see—or M . . . M . . ." or other similar sounds are frequently heard. Many of these oral sounds were given in the middle of sentences or in the middle of a thought or explanation on the part of the salesman or the prospect. Clearly these are some of the most obvious and most common verbal cues suggesting faked attention.

Another common faker is the nodder. This includes the salesman who nods continuously during the sale when the prospect is talking. He nods regardless of the point being made. He probably is thinking of something else, yet he continues to nod—a truly distracting mannerism.

Another tip on how to overcome faked attention on the part of the salesman and the prospect is given to the salesman by Russell Jenkins. He states that during conversations with a prospect the salesman will sustain his own attention and help the prospect to listen appreciably by making eye contact with the prospect. Eye contact, he states, has proved to be particularly helpful for the salesman who wants to keep the prospect's attention. On the other hand, Jenkins cautions the salesman not to stare at the prospect but keep on track by observing or watching the prospect. He tells us that not only will the salesman sustain attention and listen more effectively, but through the use of eye control he will catch and interpret many helpful prospect cues such as facial expression or body movements that will assist appreciably in understanding. These visual cues help the salesman to hear more—to get the total message.

STEPPING ON SENTENCES

This is a communication killer. It happens frequently. The salesman doesn't let the prospect finish. He knows what the prospect is going to say or doesn't care, or he is so ego-oriented that he jumps, verbally, into the prospect's conversation—many times in the middle of a sentence.

Salesmen having drive, enthusiasm, and knowledge find excitement in the challenge of persuading the prospect to buy. This is all on the plus side. These qualities are needed. Yet it sometimes leads to the habit of getting into the discussion before the prospect completes his *thought*. We step on his sentences—we aren't listening. As Nichols states, "Never lose faith in the ability of the talker to solve his own problems. Remember that, as the talker speaks, you are witnessing an amazing human phenomenon. He is really talking things over with himself. If you refrain from speaking up to inject yourself into his conversation, the chances are fairly good the talker will work things out for himself."[5]

If the talker—customer or prospect—cannot complete his thoughts, only half of the communication process, perhaps the least important half, has occurred. Stepping on sentences may have been accepted back in the days when the image of a good salesman was a fast-talking, hard-driving personality that fairly bubbled with the exceptional proposition he had for the prospect. By and large, he engaged in one-way conversation. He told the prospect; he dominated the conversation.

Today prospects have a different image of a salesman. They want a salesman who projects purposefulness, that is, confidence, maturity, a degree of enthusiasm. They view him as a knowledgeable, skillful, professional problem solver. They regard him as a man who isn't there just to sell, but as a man who has the ability and willingness to listen—a man who will listen to a prospect's ideas, comprehend and adapt his product or his sales message according to the prospect's situation. He manages situations.

Today, more than ever, stepping on sentences is regarded as immature behavior. This habit may cause even the most knowledgeable salesman to tarnish that aura of professionalism that is expected today, and it may cause the prospect to withdraw the welcome mat, both physically and mentally.

Suggestions for Improvement

Stepping on sentences is one of the easiest of "how not to listen" habits to correct. First, of course, each must be aware of the problem. If the problem is so simple and so obvious, it would seem that the problem could be corrected if the salesman merely asked himself, "Am I permitting other people with whom I am talking to complete their ideas before I interject my thoughts or comment on theirs?"

[5] *Ibid.,* p. 54.

The Art of Listening Effectively

Recognition of the problem is helpful, but a somewhat deeper probing is needed for an effective cure. No rationalization can be made here. The salesman must honestly face up to the problem and admit that he has a tendency to think his views on a particular problem are extremely important and, therefore, have a tendency not to let the other individual complete his thoughts. There is good reason to believe that not only salesmen, but most individuals, could stand improvement in this area. Further, it should be remembered that not only may stepping on sentences lose a sale, but that it is seldom socially acceptable.

Once the salesman has confronted himself with the analysis above and has agreed to improve, the rest is easy. Normally people modify a bad habit by restraint—by not doing it. Yet this is one habit that can be eliminated by *practicing*. Practicing is a new approach to changing this particular habit. The salesman can do this: When talking to his wife or fellow salesman, or in any one of a hundred social situations, he should make an effort to step on the other communicant's sentences. He says to himself, "I'm going to jump in whenever I can." Observing the reaction of his fellow communicant, the salesman will note the many changes that take place, from changed facial expressions to his fellow communicator's reply, "Will you please keep quiet and let me complete my thought?" Without question, he will notice that his actions have a dampening effect on the total conversation.

This novel practice approach has been used as a solution to the problem of stepping on sentences by many salesmen. It is not recommended, however, that the salesman push the practice to the point that someone will perhaps say, "Let me finish, will you?"

The general reaction of salesmen who have used this practice method is indicated by the report of one salesman. He stated that now, whenever he started to interrupt or not let someone complete a sentence, he had a sharp mental reaction to the situation. He felt ill at ease. He felt he was being boorish. He became so sensitive to the concept of interrupting someone else's conversation that when he stepped on sentences it was like ringing a bell. He claimed further that he had become more tolerant of other people during conversation and that he became more understanding of people who did not permit him to give his thoughts, but who just wanted him to listen to theirs.

Another excellent solution for improvement in this area is for the salesman to watch such panel television programs as "Meet the Press" and note how different people react. He can make mental notes on the good and poor communication processes that take place. He perhaps will be surprised at the number of public figures that don't listen effectively but who just talk.

EQUALIZING SPEECH AND LISTENING SPEEDS

Most people have heard of the missile gap, but relatively few people have heard about another, and in some ways equally important, gap—the speech rate—thought rate gap. The average prospect speech pattern will be very slow in terms of the salesman's thought processes. In general, individuals speak at the rate of 120 to 160 words per minute. There is good evidence which indicates that if thought processes could be measured in words per minute, most people would think at close to four or more times the average speaking rate. Applying this to the minimum spread between the salesman-prospect situation, there is an excess of about 360 words per minute of thought speed to listening speed. This means that both prospect and salesman have an excess of 375 words per minute of thought speed. Quite a gap!

Educational psychologists state that no attempt should be made to synchronize thought speed and speech speed. However, they do say that every effort should be made to utilize the difference between thought speed and speech speed to expedite comprehension.

Educators and speech authorities state that it is an advantage to have an excess of thought speed over speech speed. There is an important *if*, however, and that is if the excessive thought speed is utilized properly. What does a salesman do with his extra thinking time when the prospect is talking to him? The poor listener will perhaps start off listening, but unconsciously he realizes there is unused capacity and his thoughts stray to other ideas. He skips ahead of the prospect and perhaps reflects on the prospect's voice or on some mannerism the prospect may have, or look at a fly on the window or some object on the prospect's desk, or hear voices from other offices, or listen to a distant telephone ring, or any one of a hundred other possible distractions.

To the majority, the vast difference between thought speed and speech speed serves as a handicap. Yet it should bring about more effective communication. To recap, educators have stated that no attempt should be made to synchronize speech-thought rate. Rather the gap should be employed to enhance our comprehension score.

Suggestions for Improvement

To benefit from thought speed, concentration is needed, but this is difficult to achieve. Through the years, many people have weakened their powers of concentration by doing what comes naturally. They let their minds flit around.

One way to improve concentration pattern is to devote time and practice to it. If the salesman will practice listening for one, two, or three minutes an hour, ten hours a day, he can increase his concentration ability. During this one-two-three minutes an hour, he must turn his listening ability to the person talking and concentrate. It won't be easy. He should select a sound and concentrate on the sound, a voice or any other audio communication. He may be surprised how other sounds, ideas, etc., will come fleetingly into the field of his awareness, and as they fade out they will be replaced again by the dominant factor. Through practice, concentration and listening ability can be improved markedly.

The salesman must remember that shifting of attention occurs in the mental process of his prospect as well. Surely there is more reason for the prospect to shift his attention and not listen than there is for the salesman to have these blank spots. In this book many tools are given that the salesman can use to get and keep the attention and concentration of the prospect.

Another idea is to use the speech-thought gap to read between the lines to pick up all the cues given by the prospect—the facial expression, the body movement, gestures, inflection in the prospect's voice—and relate them to the spoken words. He should try to get the thought-conversation picture.

FAILURE TO GET THE FACTS

Overemphasis on listening to get the facts may be a sign of poor listening. This may sound surprising, but don't forget most people do not converse in an orderly, systematic way. And it's quite possible that by overconcentration on a fact that the total concept the prospect is trying to express may be lost. Assume the prospect is stating a number of facts about his company, his equipment, or facts about a competing model, or market conditions. The salesman listens and gets fact A; he grabs hard at it—it's secure. He grabs fact B and holds on to it. Fact C is given, but he is so busy mentally juggling facts A and B and thinking, "I've got to get the facts," that fact C may well slip by.

Good listening suggests listening for main ideas. As facts are spoken, the salesman must try to recognize the relationship of one fact to another. It will soon be realized the other half of the communication system may present a series of facts related to a central idea. The mind must be open for the central idea. The salesman goes after the ideas, not a series of memorized facts. It is somewhat like listening to a telephone operator telling us a number is Calumet 4–4671. We think of CA . . . and by that time the numbers have gone by and we ask the operator to repeat them. On the other hand, if we listen to the operator say "Calumet 4–4671," make a mental note of 4–4671, and then jot down the number on a pad of paper, Calumet will be easily remembered. Further, if we listen for the total number, a pad of paper won't be needed.

As a sales illustration, however, follow the reasoning of prospect Armstrong as he gives his views on one of his company's marketing problems. Armstrong's company handles a long line of builder's supplies, ranging from bricks, lumber, windows, and doors to kitchen equipment.

Armstrong begins, "One of the problems we have in our business is price and a movement to the suburbs, lack of remodeling on old homes, new homes being built in huge tracts rather than just individual houses being built. I suppose you have a price problem, too. In fact, I guess most businesses do. We think in terms of 40–50 percent markup on most lines in our business. We have to have a high markup to cover our many services. You know, we have a pretty good-size sales force that makes direct calls on contractors. But also we get into direct selling on homes."

If the salesman is a facts man, he gets the facts—price, suburb, lack of remodeling, new homes in the suburbs, etc. He neglects to look for relationships and for ideas. He neglects to see that Armstrong may be saying that if the salesman had a new wood kitchen line that his salesmen could handle and fit into the home developer's market, he and the salesman could talk business. But the facts man will perhaps concentrate on markup.

Many times, the salesman listens to the facts so that he can come up with a rebuttal. When Armstrong mentioned a 40–50 percent markup, the salesman perhaps shrewdly plotted a devastating rebuttal, if this was something he could *successfully* challenge. He may even have gone so far as to interrupt and say, "Oh, no, Mr. Armstrong. You have to realize that with our line, although we only have a 33⅓ percent markup, you will get a greater volume, so you need less markup because the total profit is greater."

Suggestions for Improvement

The salesman will listen for main ideas and try to recognize relationships to the various facts presented. The preceding example presents a situation where the speech rate–thought rate gap can be used advantageously. A move into the suburbs means distance but also a concentrated market. Large builders mean doing business with one firm, but its buying power will be very great. Large building means speculative building by the suburban developers. Large building tracts mean that salesmen do not contact the individual home builders directly. Lack of remodeling means loss of sales; new homes mean more sales. Housing developments mean large sales opportunities if the product can be sold to the housing developer. Markup is not important; it is not a crucial reason for doing business with the salesman. Frequently price takes a back seat if the salesman solves problems.

EMOTIONAL DEAF SPOTS

For most people there are words that excite them emotionally. When this happens, listening ability may be impaired. The individual concentrates on the emotionally charged word. Take the case of the salesman on a straight commission. In order to sell to the markup or price customer, he may have, in the past, many times cut his commission. When such a salesman hears the word *markup*, it may well be an emotionally charged word—it is a sore spot—an area of tremendous sensitivity. The result may well be that the prospect's statements after the word *markup* are not heard. The salesman concentrates for a moment on the charged word. The result: a blank spot in the communication process.

Many other examples are found in everyday life. If you are a great Johnson man, how do you react to Goldwater's name? Do you grow deaf? "Not much, just a little bit," you say? It only takes a little bit to impair hearing and listening ability. We all have some cherished complexes and ideas. When someone strikes one of our treasured ideas, often we freeze up or think of a devastating answer. This is the end of listening. In the same way a salesman may have blind spots when a prospect mentions a competing product, a competing salesman, a poor model his company built last year, shortcomings of his product, price depression, those damned Democrats, the elimination of tariffs, or the name Kennedy.

Here is another example from the sales field. During a sales meeting

The Art of Listening Effectively

attended by the author, a group of salesmen selling gas kitchen installations charged electrical kitchen installation salesmen of giving kickbacks or discounts or both to contractors who installed electrical kitchens in new homes. There was no actual knowledge of whether this was true or not, but the gas salesmen were extremely bitter about the situation. Some of the gas salesmen took pride in telling how they, in no uncertain terms, told or implied that the builder was taking a bribe. From the tone of the discussions, it was obvious that actual arguments between builders and salesmen had resulted from this situation. Some of the salesmen who had been calling on certain builders for a period of years were blinded by the thought that these men might be taking kickbacks from electrical salesmen. They were so blinded that in many cases communication and personal relationships were practically severed.

Suggestions for Improvement

Recognizing the hot spots is not enough. The salesman should, of course, know the words that apparently cause him to stop listening or the words that will get a "rise" out of him. But more important, he must objectively analyze why the words or phrases upset him.

In the case of Armstrong it is entirely possible the real reason that he was affected by certain words was simply that he hadn't been successful in selling. Whenever the customer mentioned price, market, kickback, or some related concept, perhaps the first thing he thought about was giving the prospect a price concession out of his commission. There are numerous salesmen who cut their commissions in order to sell. Little wonder it is a blind spot.

In the group sales discussion concerning the gas versus electrical situation, two concepts were discussed. One was the motto, "Reasonable men always agree if they understand what they are talking about," and the second a related point made by Bertrand Russell who said, "The degree of one's emotions varies inversely with one's knowledge of the facts—the less you know, the hotter you get." During a discussion of these two concepts, salesmen began to discuss the problem as reasonable men should. They believed they had a tendency to get "hot under the collar" because they did not have a solution to the problem. The gas salesmen were fighting with the builders, trying to get them to change their ways with respect to taking kickbacks from electrical appliance salesmen. Gas salesmen, at the discussion, resolved to forget all about the so-called kickback situation and concentrate on selling; after all, the real goal of the builders was to sell homes. They agreed that not every buyer wants an electric kitchen, nor does every buyer want gas kitchens that are obviously alike. If the builder has two homes—one having an electrical kitchen and related equipment and the other a gas kitchen and related equipment—in all probability he will have an easier time selling the two homes if both were not exactly alike than if both were gas or both were electric. In brief, the salesmen concentrated on the prospect's problem and how they could solve that problem rather than being blinded over a certain word or situation. Now quite obviously, a rebate, if this were the case, became unimportant when the gas salesmen discussed the builders problem—selling more homes.

Selling: A Behavioral Science Approach

Summary

Salesmen communicate with many people in many ways, for many reasons, and on many levels on each and every day. This communication may range from gestural communication to group communication or to pictorial communication.

Communication is a two-way process. It involves both the sender of the message and the receiver of the message. This compounds the difficulty of effective communication. The prospect must listen effectively, for he is the other half of the communication process. Just as the salesman must talk and listen effectively, so must the prospect talk and listen effectively.

Fortunately the salesman is in a pivotal control point. With his knowledge and skill he can persuade; he can structure his sales talk utilizing the best in the communication process. The message must be developed so it has a purpose that is meaningful to the receiver (the prospect) and permits the prospect to participate. The salesman communicates to influence and persuade, to effect with intent. He wants to affect the behavior of the prospect, for this is his purpose, his target. He wants to change the behavior pattern of the prospect, both the prospect's mental behavior and eventually his physical behavior. In order to accomplish this, the pressure of the change must come from within the prospect. This tells the salesman he must develop a customer-oriented sales message, one that will strike the mind of the prospect. Employing a customer-oriented approach means the salesman is aware that he must manage each situation. He must be aware that two major sets of needs—the buyer or respondent's personal or emotional needs and the needs of the buyer's firm from a business perspective—are involved in each sale. In brief, good communication is essential if the salesman is to cope with the emotional needs of the respondent and present a message as to how the buyer's firm can profit using the salesman's product or service. Each salesman must effectively benefitize product knowledge.

The art of listening effectively is one of the most important concepts in selling. Listening is the other half of talking. When people stop listening, it is useless to talk, a point not always appreciated by talkers.

Insights into the salesman's listening ability may be obtained by analyzing his (1) interest in what the prospects have to say, (2) reaction to peculiarities of fellow communicators, (3) tendency to fake attention, (4) tendency to step on sentences, (5) ability to utilize the differences between speech and listening speeds, (6) art of not getting the facts, and finally (7) not being aware of emotional deaf spots.

Chapter 11   DISCUSSION QUESTIONS

1   One communication authority says that the art of listening is far more important than the art of talking. Defend his statement.
2   Do you regard yourself as a good listener or as a good talker? Why? Why

have you made the decision you have made? What experiences have suggested to you that your choice is correct?

3 Why is it considered poor communication quickly to ask questions if you are not sure about the point you are conversing about? Are there any exceptions to this rule? Explain.

4 What are the implications in the communication system between salesman and prospect when the salesman frequently uses such statements as, "Do you see my viewpoint?" "Can you understand?" "Do you follow me?" "See?"

5 If we accept the minister's statement as true that most Americans fake attention during church services, what implication does this have regarding the emotional needs of the churchgoers? What implications does it have for a minister?

6 Can the minister be regarded as an educator? As a salesman?

7 Would you consider most ministers as good listeners? If so, why? If not, why not?

8 Can you think of any ways in which an individual can improve his listening ability? Would the same advice apply to salesmen?

9 What is meant by the concept of stepping on sentences? Why is this an affliction that many salesmen appear to have? Discuss this statement with respect to the needs of the salesman.

10 What is meant by emotional deaf spots? Why are some people emotionally involved with certain words? Do emotionally charged words help the listener get the total message, or do they have a tendency to lessen the individual's ability to listen effectively?

11 Discuss Bertrand Russell's statement, "The degree of one's emotions varies inversely with one's knowledge of the facts—the less you know, the hotter you get."

the contact

part one

12

INTRODUCTION

Through planning, investigation or precontact work, information is obtained about each potential user or prospect for the salesman's product or services. This information can be personal or impersonal. Personal information ranges from the potential user's own code of ethics and his traits, to his hobbies or the part of the country of which he is native. Impersonal information concerns the business the prospect represents—his position in the company, the products manufactured, the company's market position, the company's financial position, etc., and may even include information regarding the future of the company.

Normally the first prospect-salesman communication mix comes in the contact phase of the sale. The investigation, planning process, or precontact work does not bring the salesman into direct contact with the customer. When he has his first contact or actual interview with the prospect, he sometimes wants to verify information during the first few minutes. He does not accept as fact all the information he has obtained. He must verify it when necessary by observation and questioning.

This last statement answers the question, "Just why does the salesman contact the prospect?" The answer is simple. He wants to get all the information possible. He wants to discover whether or not the prospect can use his services or his product. The information he desires is that information which will assist him in effectively determining the prospect's situation.

Some salesmen, an industrial distributor salesman for example, may state at this point, "Look, my company is a great name. Users of our products and industrial buyers in general are pretty smart people. They know their business. So why not merely say to the prospect or customer, 'Pratt & Whitney's cutting tools are used by 80 percent or 14,000 of the manufacturing firms in Michigan. The tools are widely accepted because they do the job the company wants done. Would you like to program Pratt & Whitney cutting tools into your production system?' "

This approach is comparable to the retail sales clerk asking the customer, "Is there anything else?" and getting the usual "No, I don't think so" reply. There are obvious reasons why this thinking doesn't square with

---

[1] At first glance, much of the material in this chapter may appear to be directed to the salesman making cold calls or initial contacts with prospects; however, it is equally applicable to the sales situation where the salesman has, over the years, built up a close personal relationship with the customer.

The Contact: Part One

the facts as they are today in the industrial world and in the business world in general. A few of the reasons are that in all probability the prospect, and in some cases, the regular customer:

1. Doesn't really know the salesman.
2. Doesn't really know about the salesman's company.
3. Doesn't really know about the products, services, or the value of the services and products the salesman's company can offer.
4. Doesn't know or isn't aware of his company's needs. (In this incredibly rapidly expanding and changing business world, company needs may be altered dramatically in a relatively short period of time.)
5. Has a whole world of personal, emotional, or status needs that in many instances are related to company needs.

These five points illustrate several of the situations which arise in the contact stage. They further focus attention on the salesman's goal in the contact stage of getting information relevant to the prospect's true needs and true situation. Herein lies the real difficulty with which the salesman is confronted in the initial stage of the sale.

Each prospect's personal needs, each company's needs, and each situation will vary considerably. Moreover, the interaction between company needs and the prospect's status needs is incredibly complex, as suggested by this statement from the industrial sales field concerning the prospect's needs.

Frequently the industrial salesman is called upon to manage a situation that has a multitude of nebulous variables. First, each salesman should be sensitive to the climate existing in the "prospect" firm. It is understood that the tone, the quality, the drive, the enthusiasm, the integrity, the morale of the staff and, in fact, the total "climate" existing in a particular firm filters down from the type of leadership exercised by the "top" man. Is he, on the one hand, an autocrat, or on the other extreme, a democratic leader? Under each leadership form, various situations exist that are important to the salesman. (See Communicating with the Executive). Then the salesman must understand that this "climate" may or may not be compatible with the needs and self-image of each individual who is under a particular form of leadership. Each individual (at times this is compounded when a number of individuals are involved) has personal, emotional, and status needs, for example, the need to feel important. And if this need isn't satisfied under a particular form of leadership, emotional conflict may result. And, in addition to the prospect's personal needs, each salesman must remember that the prospect, for example, a shop superintendent, may be only dimly aware of PW or he may just plain dislike PW or on the other hand, he may obviously prefer PW over other companies, or he may not be aware of the role that machine trading, financing, etc., can play in a successful machine shop modernization program, or the situation may involve some individual in a position of decision making authority who may have some close personal reason (ethical or unethical) for doing business with a competitor of PW.[2]

2 Joseph W. Thompson, *Pratt and Whitney Manpower Development Program*, Pratt & Whitney Corp., Inc., West Hartford, Conn., 1964, p. 22.

Selling: A Behavioral Science Approach

It is apparent that unraveling or coping perfectly with some situations may be an impossibility, but it does not alter the fact that these situations exist and somehow the salesman must work in this complex world. The author's only claim is that through an awareness, the salesman will be more sensitive to the behavior needed to cope with complex situations. This awareness must begin in the planning stage, because cues as to the prospect's personal needs, firm's needs, and the situation are many times uncovered during the salesman's planning, precontact or investigation work and are verified through questions and through observations early in the contact stage.

As has been mentioned, the contact stage represents the beginning of person-to-person communication between the salesman and prospect. But much is involved in this process. This process will, therefore, be analyzed through the following subject matter development.

1. Set, Readiness, and Empathy
2. An Overall View of the Contact Stage
3. Contact General Strategy
4. Ways of Making a Contact
5. Ten Variables of Any Contact
6. Question Forms and Two-way Communication Diagram
7. Dialogue Cases
8. Four Quarters and the Ten Variables of the Contact Stage
9. The Techniques Approach and the Removal of Sales Tension

SET, READINESS, AND EMPATHY[3]

Set

Every salesman and every customer has mental and perceptual sets. Set is a pivotal component of the broad concept of perception. As a rule-of-thumb definition, perception refers to the act of perceiving or being aware, whereas set affects what will be perceived and how it will be perceived. Each individual brings to any given situation various expectations that substantially affect his interpretation of and reaction to stimuli. Or as Krech and Crutchfield comment, "The perceiver's state as he encounters any given stimulus pattern is never completely neutral. In a word, he is set to perceive something more or less specific. . . ."[4] What does this mean to the salesman? It means this: Whenever the salesman contacts a prospect, the salesman must be aware that the prospect is set for a particular thought process, or he is set to receive a particular organization of stimuli. For instance, after hearing the word *Pratt* he is set to hear the word *Whitney*. In everyday language, after an individual hears the word *salt* he is set to hear the word *pepper*.

These mental and perceptual sets of the individual are determined

---

[3] Before beginning this section, it is recommended that the reader review the more technical discussion of set, readiness, and empathy that is given in the behavioral science chapters.

[4] David Krech and Richard S. Crutchfield, *Elements of Psychology*, Alfred A. Knopf, Inc., New York, 1961, p. 96.

by the individual's experiences, values, and emotions. A salesman is not expected to change the individual's basic adjustment of life, but the salesman can affect whether or not a particular set will be brought into play at a given moment. It is clear that if the salesman uses a salesman-oriented canned sales talk, he will reinforce and bring into play a prospect's negative set toward salesmen. For instance, what is, at least from the text of the letter of Figure 8 (see page 202), the set of Saginaw Steering's purchasing agent Fred M. Cooper, with respect to the poorly prepared salesman, the friendly glad-hander salesman, the "big deal" salesman, the time consumer? The answer is clear. Mr. Cooper's set is negative.

On the other hand, if the salesman follows the problem-solving approach recommended in this book, he will bring into play favorable prospect thought processes or sets. Apparently purchasing agent Cooper would be mentally receptive to seeing a purposeful problem-solving salesman.

Another way of viewing the prospect's thought processes or set—one that is remarkably well adapted to explaining what may be the prospect's state of mind as the salesman contacts him, as well as what the salesman can do to favorably affect the prospect's thought processes or set—is the educational psychologist's concept of readiness.

Readiness

Readiness is one of the most frequently referred to concepts in educational psychology. And in the author's opinion, it will become one of the most frequently referred to concepts in sales psychology.

Set and perception are involved in any discussion of readiness, but readiness can be adequately discussed without referring to these concepts. Readiness, in its simplest form, states that an individual will learn, that he will participate mentally, when he *wants* to and when he has the *ability* to do so.

Readiness is determined by numerous factors such as the educational level of the individual, his past experiences, his emotions, his level of aspiration, his achievement, his ego drive, and his attitude. In varying degrees, these variables all determine readiness.

This is where the educator starts. He receives a "package" with a certain degree of built-in readiness, the want to learn and the ability to learn. Each educator must appraise the individual's ability to learn through tests, examining the individual's records of past achievement by performance of a task and by questions. He appraises an individual's want to learn through questions and observations. Each educator knows that he can actively change an individual's *lack of want to learn* to *positive want to learn* through the simple process of presenting *meaningful* material and structuring the work to be done so that student *participation* is obtained. The effective educator involves the student mentally and physically.

This, too, is the salesman's situation. He contacts prospects, each of whom has a varying degree of built-in readiness or the want to learn and the ability to learn. Like the educator, what better way is there for the salesman to affect the prospect's readiness than by discussing meaningful

Selling: A Behavioral Science Approach

SAGINAW STEERING GEAR DIVISION

GENERAL MOTORS CORPORATION

SAGINAW MICHIGAN 48605

TELEPHONE 517 754-9111

WE ARE BUSY AT SAGINAW STEERING GEAR

MAY WE RESPECTFULLY ASK YOUR COOPERATION in making our plant a more efficiently run organization?

Here's how you can help us (and perhaps speed up your own busy day) - -

CONFINE YOUR VISITS TO THOSE OCCASIONS WHEN YOU HAVE A SPECIFIC REASON FOR CALLING - -

> An inspection or engineering problem
> A service call
> A call which we have specifically asked you to make
> or
> A sales call which you feel will be of benefit both to
> you and ourselves

Routine calls don't benefit anyone, we feel, and serve only to delay really important business. WE RECOMMEND THAT AN APPOINTMENT BE MADE in advance of your visit to make certain you will see the man you need, and without delay.

DON'T SPEND ANY TIME WITH PEOPLE IN OUR ORGANIZATION OTHER THAN THOSE WITH WHOM YOU HAVE SPECIFIC BUSINESS. If you feel that you really need to see more than one of our people, please arrange any additional visits through our receptionist to assure prompt connection.

HELP US TO MAKE THE MOST EFFICIENT USE OF THE TIME OF OUR PEOPLE BY CONFINING YOUR VISIT TO THE BUSINESS AT HAND. We receive about 200 callers each day. This means that unless each visitor confines his visit to the business at hand and concludes the matter quickly, our people will lose a large portion of their working day, with the result that their regular work is not done and other callers are held up unnecessarily.

Please do not misunderstand our purpose in directing this request to you. This Division has to rely on all the products and services offered by our Vendors, both old and new, to maintain our organization and continue our expansion. With your cooperation we intend to grow with resulting benefit to you and ourselves. Thanks.

Fred M. Cooper
FRED M. COOPER
Purchasing Agent

MANUFACTURERS OF POWER AND MANUAL STEERING GEARS — TILT WHEEL STEERING — UNIVERSAL JOINTS — PROPELLER SHAFTS — STEERING LINKAGES — TRANSMISSION CONTROLS — FRONT END SUSPENSIONS — HIGH EFFICIENCY BALL BEARING SCREW AND SPLINE ASSEMBLIES

---

material (the potential customer's problems) with the prospect and thus obtain his viewpoint and his mental participation. Just as the educator involves the student, each salesman must involve the prospect—orally and mentally. The problem-solving approach, reinforced by appropriate questions, effectively involves the prospect. Not only do questions get mental participation, but they uniquely enable the salesman to begin an appraisal of the prospect's readiness (his want and ability) to understand the salesman's proposal, idea, or concepts.

The Contact: Part One

From the discussion above, it is reasonably evident that set perception and readiness are fundamental concepts involved in most forms of sales activity. A third concept, empathy, is equally important.

Empathy

more

One point of view describing empathy is found in the psychologist's term "similarity to the perceiver." A leading handbook of social psychology states that the most similarity there is between perceiver and the perceived person's object, the greater degree of understanding, empathy, and identification that is possible. In simple terms it means being able to put oneself in the other individual's shoes. And it means that the potential purchaser is strongly disposed to buy from the salesman who fully comprehends his side of the picture.

In describing empathy authors Krech and Crutchfield stress feelings. "Empathy is feeling the same emotion that is being expressed by another person, for example, feeling fear when another person shows signs of fright."[5] Mayer and Greenberg also use feeling as a central factor in empathy. They use a unique and understandable analogy to describe the nonempathetic salesman in contrast to the empathetic-feeling salesman.

> A parallel might be drawn in this connection between the old anti-aircraft weapons and the new heat-attracted missiles. With the old type of ballistic weapon, the gunner would take aim at an airplane, correcting as best he could for windage and driftage, and then fire. If the shell missed by just a few inches because of a slight error in calculation or because the plane took evasive action, the miss might just as well have been by hundreds of yards for all the good it did.
>
> This is the salesman with poor empathy. He aims at the target as best he can and proceeds along his sales track; but if his target—the customer—fails to perform as predicted, the sale is missed.
>
> On the other hand, the new missiles, if they are anywhere near the target, become attracted to the heat of the target's engine, and regardless of its evasive action, they finally home in and hit their mark.
>
> This is the salesman with good empathy. He senses the reactions of the customer and is able to adjust to these reactions. He is not simply bound by a prepared sales track, but he functions in terms of the real interaction between himself and the customer. Sensing what the customer is feeling, he is able to change pace, double back on his track, and make whatever creative modifications might be necessary to home in on the target and close the sale.[6]

In addition to the descriptions above of empathy, there is another dimension which may be implied in the discussions but is not specifically stated. Not only must the salesman comprehend the customer's situation, but his behavior activities must be such that he causes the prospect to feel

---

[5] *Ibid.*, p. 264.

[6] David Mayer and Herbert M. Greenberg, "What Makes a Good Salesman," *Harvard Business Review*, July–August, 1964, pp. 119–120.

204

and to know that the salesman understands his situation. The salesman must project the quality of empathy.[†] Empathy is the heart not only of the contact stage but of the entire sale. Visualize a small intercore circle within each of the circles illustrating the various phases of depth selling in Figure 4 (see page 152). Color that intercore circle red. Empathy is so important that every salesman must firmly keep this concept in mind throughout the sale.

In summary, a salesman establishes empathy when he fully comprehends and feels the prospect-customer situation and when he acts in such a way that the prospect-customer knows and senses that the salesman understands.

AN OVERALL VIEW OF THE CONTACT STAGE

Figures 9 and 10 provide a general framework for the contact stage. Inputs 1, 2, and 3 describe what the salesman does as well as what the salesman represents as a human being. Outputs 1, 2, and 3 describe the prospect's or customer's feelings and responses to the inputs or stimuli.

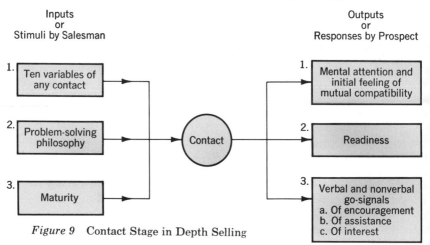

Figure 9 Contact Stage in Depth Selling

(I) 1. As inputs, use of the ten variables will depend upon each situation. In some situations the salesman will incorporate most of the variables and in others only a few. For instance, he might not use both verification and permissive questions in every interview. It will depend on the total situation, that is, the prospect or customer's status needs, the company's business needs, and the amount of information the salesman obtains during the planning stage. It goes without saying that when the salesman is contacting a friend or a customer he has serviced over the years, he will use fewer variables than will the salesman making a cold call.

[†] Fortunately this quality, as explained in the behavioral science chapters, can be acquired. There are ways in which the salesman can let the prospect know that he does understand the prospect's situation.

The Contact: Part One

(I) 2. Each salesman must have the philosophy that he is contacting new prospects or customers in order to define problems and to provide solutions to those problems. Through problem solving, the salesman can most effectively present meaningful material and get mental participation with a resultant degree of prospect readiness.

(I) 3. The concept of maturity is reflected in the salesman's total adjustment to life. This concept is fully described in the behavioral science chapters.

(O) 1. Through inputs 1, 2, and 3, certain prospect responses or outputs will evolve. In depth selling the salesman isn't interested in attention for the sake of attention, or the utilization of causative forces to secure attention; rather he wants intellectual attention. He wants the prospect's mind to focus on a problem, not a gimmick. Thus, through judicious and flexible use of the various contact variables, he obtains mental attention. Especially important here is the use of the verification and permissive questions. These question forms are described in detail later in the chapter.

(O) 2. As previously indicated, readiness is one of the most important concepts involved in education. This concept states that an individual will learn when he wants to and when he has the ability. This is one of the crucial issues in selling. The salesman, like the educator, is involved in determining the degree of individual readiness, that is, the prospect's want to learn, to listen, and his ability to do so. The salesman, like the educator, is also involved in the process of how to affect the individual's want to learn. He does this by presenting meaningful material and having the prospect participate in the discussion. The salesman in the contact stage uses verification and permissive questions to achieve this goal.

(O) 3. A salesman doesn't judge the output of his efforts through prospect decisions. During the contact stage in the traditional approach to selling, the prospect will supposedly make prospect decision one, "I will see you," and prospect decision two, "I will hear you." In depth selling, the salesman communicates with the prospect. He receives verbal and nonverbal feedback in this communication process. He gets cues or signals of encouragement, assistance, and interest. This communication process is a much broader concept than the prospect decision approach.

CONTACT GENERAL STRATEGY

The general strategy in the contact stage as outlined in Figure 10 is to get information and to give information. The salesman plans to give brief information about himself, about his company, and to get information about the prospect's situation and the prospect's needs. As a result of this input-output strategy, the salesman will obtain the prospect's mental attention and affect the prospect's readiness to participate. Problem solving is emphasized here.

Only through customer or prospect participation can the salesman have control of the interview. If the customer does not participate mentally, it is impossible for the salesman to control the interview. Too frequently, too many salesmen think of control as a one-sided telling process.

Selling: A Behavioral Science Approach

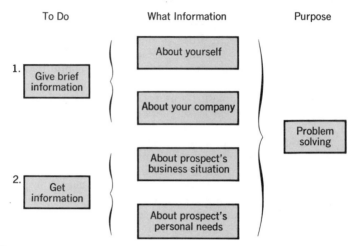

Figure 10 General Contact Strategy

It is true the salesman has control of the interview in a "talking" sense, but this is not the control that is necessary to achieve a successful sales process. Only when the customer or prospect participates mentally, orally, and physically in an interview does the salesman control the interview. Because without participation the prospect's attention will be fixated elsewhere.

Questioning gets participation which is one of the cornerstones of readiness. Participation means satisfaction for the prospect's ego. As the prospect talks and gives his comments and ideas, the salesman can feed information into the discussion. It is through this control—through prospect mental participation and through prospect discussion—that the salesman can change prospect behavior. Finally, a problem-solving approach exists only when the salesman is engaged in the process of getting and giving information.

WAYS OF MAKING AN INITIAL CONTACT

There are many ways in which the salesman can initially contact the prospect. Most of the commonly used methods are briefly described in this section. Many of these methods can be used in combination with the author's philosophy of the contact stage as expressed throughout this chapter.

The Personal Call

Regardless of the method used to make initial contact, the end result is a personal call on the prospect. The recommended way to contact the prospect is given in the section devoted to the ten variables of any contact. The following example is given only to illustrate the personal call which is followed in many fields—the curiosity approach. In general, the curiosity approach is not recommended; however, its appeal is used frequently by life insurance salesmen. It is illustrated here by a health care insurance program salesman:

The Contact: Part One

S   I am Frank Hill, district representative for the Blue Cross–Blue Shield. If I could give you some information on how Blue Cross–Blue Shield could enhance your employee relations program at no cost to you, you would be interested in hearing about it, wouldn't you?

The next monologue illustrates how it might be used by the industrial salesman.

S   Mr. Hillman, I am Frank Hill, a representative of the Honeywell Industrial Supply Company. If I could give you some information on how Brighton's cutting tools could cut your production cost and give you more precision work at no additional cost to you, you would be interested in hearing about it, wouldn't you?

The Introduction

The introduction from a mutual friend or a satisfied user of the salesman's products and services can be, depending on the circumstances, one of the most effective means of obtaining an interview with a company executive or anyone in a position to affect the purchase of the salesman's product.

There are a number of ways in which a salesman can utilize the introduction concept. He may have a satisfied customer (whom the salesman knows as a friend of Jim X) write a note on the back of his personal card saying, "Jim, this will introduce Frank Hill of the Honeywell Distributing Company to you. He has done some nice work for our company, and I thought you would be interested in talking to him." After the salesman has obtained the interview, he simply hands the card to the executive or to the supply room clerk or to whomever he is contacting and states, "Mr. X of the Dover Company was kind enough to write a little note on the back of his card."

The salesman should never ask for a recommendation. The business executive, the satisfied customer, or friend, or whoever it is should never be put in a position of saying he is recommending the salesman. In the example above, the satisfied customer stated that Frank Hill's service had been of value to his company. True, this is a recommendation, but Hill did not request it. Many times the satisfied customer will include a recommendation if the salesman handles the situation judiciously. For instance, Hill of the Honeywell Distributing Company has come to know Mr. X fairly well over the past few months, through his professional services and the quality of his company products. At the end of a recent service call, he states:

Hill   Mr. X, I have been interested in making contact with the Ronald Machinery and Tool Company for some time now. Do you happen to know Jim Franks, the purchasing agent, or Ed Snyder, the plant superintendent?
Mr. X   Yes, I do. I know both of them, Frank. Is there something that I can do for you?
Hill   Yes, indeed. Would it be possible for you to write a note on the back of my card introducing me to one of these gentlemen?
Mr. X   Well, what should I say?

Selling: A Behavioral Science Approach

Hill Oh, you can say anything you want. For instance, "Jim, this will introduce Frank Hill of the Honeywell Company,"—just a sentence or two like that.

Other than a personal introduction, one of the finest forms of introduction is by letter. If a satisfied customer is willing to write a letter of introduction to another executive in another firm and refers to his company's success with the salesman's product and his services, the salesman has one of the finest introductions he can obtain. Such an introduction should assist considerably in obtaining the initial interview.

The Telephone

The telephone is usually considered to be a fairly ineffective means of making a sale. In fact, most experienced salesmen indicate it is impossible to make any type of a difficult sale over the telephone. It does, however, have considerable value in obtaining the initial interview with the prospect. For example, if a salesman has a large number of new prospects in his territory, he may initially wish to use the telephone to screen out those who are the least interested. He can then concentrate on those who appear to be most interested in the salesman, his company, or his product. Obviously the telephone is used regularly to arrange appointments with present users of the salesman's product or service.

Here are four brief general recommendations concerning the use of the telephone. The mix will vary according to the call the salesman is making—a cold call, a service call, or a user call.

1. The telephone approach must move rapidly. The salesman's introduction of himself, his company, and why he is calling must move quickly. The opening should only be a short sentence and should perhaps end in a leading question which invites a yes reply.

2. The salesman must get to the objective of the telephone call quickly. Brevity is permissible over the phone which might not be permissible in the personal interview.

3. The telephone approach must be aggressive without seeming to be so. Again, the short question which would invite a yes answer is the best method of "getting home" if the salesman is using the telephone to get an appointment.

4. After he has announced his name and business, the salesman should speed up the conversation. If a prospect is going to cut him off, in all probability it will take place just at the introduction. Therefore the salesman should hurry and reach the point at which a yes answer is forthcoming.

The above suggestions concerning the telephone as a contact technique also suggest the disagreeable aspects of using the telephone and the ease with which the prospect can state no.

The Sales Letter

The sales letter, be it from the company or the salesman, needs no explanation. It is merely a method that is used to smooth the salesman's way for the contact. Many salesmen or companies write letters to prospective customers mentioning their services and the reason for the letter. Often the salesman telephones and asks the prospect if he has received the particular letter. If he has, they discuss it; if not, the salesman briefly mentions the purpose and content of the letter. If the prospect indicates some interest during the telephone conversation, invariably the salesman follows through with a personal call. Some salesmen eliminate the telephone call and refer to the letter during their initial personal contact with the prospect.

The Two-call System

The two-call system is widely used. This is a system where a salesman calls on a prospect merely to leave some information with him and then calls back at a later date to discuss it. A distributor salesman, for example, may leave a brochure describing a new product, machinery trading, tax benefits, finance plans, and then tell the prospect he will be back in a week to discuss this with him. Many times the two-call system is an opener for the survey method.

The Survey Method

The survey method is widely used. It is used by such companies as Burroughs, National Cash Register, and International Business Machines, by restaurant equipment salesmen, life insurance salesmen, and in fact by most salesmen in one way or the other.

This approach involves two sales. The first sale results when the salesman receives permission to survey, to check, to research, or to gather information on some phase of the potential user's business in which the salesman can be of service to the customer or prospect. It is a problem-exposing and problem-solving method of getting new users. It is, of course, even more readily employed with current accounts than with entirely new accounts. Proof of real sales ability in using this system is, however, in getting original business. Here are two sample dialogues which illustrate the survey principle. One is taken from an industrial firm's manpower development book, the other from an office furniture sales training manual.

Dialogues Illustrating Survey Method or Contact

DIALOGUE 1   INDUSTRIAL SELLING

S   Mr. Franklin, I've read in the *Trade Press* that Brattin has been getting a number of new contracts, especially in the missile field. Is this—
R   Sure have, and damned happy about it. We have tough competition.
S   I suppose in a way that's when business is the most satisfying—when you get it in the face of tough competition.
R   Yes, that's how we feel about it. We don't ask for any quarter.
S   Mr. Franklin, is it permissible for me to ask you about the dollar value or unit size of the new contracts?

R Oh, some of the news has been published in the *Trade Press*, as you know, Smith, and of course it's enough to keep us real busy.

S Mr. Franklin, that's good news. And of course I've been wondering, since your company has been plowing ahead in the contract field, whether you were thinking in terms of replacing equipment or adding to your present machine tool equipment?

R No, not at the moment. But it's always a possibility.

S One of Pratt & Whitney's services, Mr. Franklin, is an equipment audit. I know, of course, that you are completely up to date and familiar with your entire equipment; but once in a while we have found that by surveying the company's equipment with respect to its relationship to the jobs being done, we come up with an idea here or there. We of course make a report of this to you. But also, Mr. Franklin, we are always getting requests from small machine shops for used equipment. It is entirely possible that we could be of service to you and to some of our smaller accounts if you should decide to invest in new equipment.

DIALOGUE 2   OFFICE FURNITURE SELLING

(*The first stop is at the receptionist's desk.*)

Salesman   May I speak to Mr. Turner?

Receptionist   Who should I say is calling, please?

S Mr. Frank Hill of the Bronze Office Furniture Company. (*Receptionist calls Mr. Turner.*)

R Mr. Turner is busy now. He can see you in about thirty minutes if you care to wait.

S I would be pleased to wait. I have a few telephone calls to make, so I will go down to the drugstore and be back in about thirty minutes.

R You may use this telephone if you don't talk too long.

S Thank you very much, but I wouldn't want to inconvenience you. I think one or two of my calls might be on the lengthy side. I'll be back in fifteen or twenty minutes.

S (*Twenty minutes later. Salesman walks to receptionist's desk.*) By the way, you might want to give Mr. Turner my card if you have an opportunity. (*Salesman then sits down next to two other waiting salesmen.*)

R (*Ten minutes later.*) Mr. Hill, Mr. Turner will see you now.

S Thank you. (*Proceeds to Turner's office.*)

S Hello, Mr. Turner. I am Frank Hill of the Color and Design Division of the Bronze Office Furniture Company. I want to thank you for giving me this opportunity of seeing you. (*He is friendly, poised, and positive, but doesn't rattle off his opening statements. He gives the customer a chance to talk, pauses at times, lets the customer tell him to sit down, shakes hands if the customer wishes. In short, the salesman manages the situation.*)

T That's OK. Sit down, please.

S My call won't take long, Mr. Turner. I was just talking to Mr. Ralph Bond, sales manager for the Presto Company, and he told me that you are expanding your operation, and also that you are adding several salesmen to your organization. Did he give me correct information?

The Contact: Part One

T   Yes, that's right.

S   Well, I am glad I am on the right track. Because of your expanded operations I thought you might be interested in our planning service. Do you know of the Bronze Office Furniture Company, Mr. Turner?

T   No, I don't, and although I said I could see you, with the shifting of quarters and the other problems we have here now, I'm pretty busy.

S   Yes, I knew you were busy when I called on you, and strange as it may seem, that was the very reason I called on you. But I will need a few more minutes to determine whether or not we can be of service to you. May I have up to ten minutes to discuss our planning service?

T   That will be OK. I can give you ten minutes.

S   Thank you, Mr. Turner. I will come right to the point. Am I right in understanding that in addition to hiring several new men and expanding operations generally, you are also moving into larger office space?

T   Yes, we will be moving in about two months to the fifth floor of this building.

S   Have the new office quarters been decorated as yet?

T   No, we just aren't that far along.

S   Have you decided on the type of office equipment you will need for your new offices and additional staff?

T   No.

S   Just one final question. Will you be adding secretaries or rearranging your secretarial pool or your office force to handle the increased work because of expanded operations?

T   Well, no, we haven't done too much thinking on this.

S   Mr. Turner, the three questions I have asked, in a sense, explain our service, a service we refer to as three-dimensional office planning. We plan office layouts for the best possible work production flow. Our company recently completed an office procedures study for the Foremost Company and Mr. R. Ralph Jones, the manager, estimated that we had improved office efficiency close to 20 percent. (*The salesman uses an attractive brochure that outlines the three services.*)

T   That sounds good, but we aren't a very large firm, and we really don't have office procedures problems.

S   I didn't mean to imply that your company has problems, but rather that if we came in as consultants we might be able to make some suggestions that would result in greater work efficiency. In some cases, our studies have resulted in better office morale, too. On the other hand, it is entirely possible that even if we analyzed your operation, we wouldn't find anything that could be improved.

The second service is planning production flow based on functional as well as attractive office furniture. Basic to this idea is maximum utilization of space. We realize that space is an investment to you, so our service is designed to help our clients utilize every possible foot of space. (*The salesman pauses but makes no comment.*)

T   That sounds good.

S   The third service, Mr. Turner, is largely that of color and design and blending the first two services into a personality or office climate adapted to

Selling: A Behavioral Science Approach

the needs of your personnel and the customers who may call on you. In other words, we are concerned with the image that employees as well as customers may have of the firm owing to its office procedures and, of course, the appearance of its offices. Mr. Turner, are there any questions you have about these three services?

T   No, I think I have the idea in mind.

S   OK. Now, Mr. Turner, may I ask you just two more questions before I leave?

T   Sure, go ahead—shoot.

S   First, Mr. Turner, I want you to know that our service is free, other than a maximum charge of $100 for our costs. With that idea in mind, I would like to ask you these two questions. First, if an organization such as ours were to analyze the needs of your business from the standpoint of examining your office procedures, layout, and color and design needs, is it possible that we could save your time from the myriad of details that are connected with a construction program such as yours?

T   Yes, I guess you could.

S   Second, you mentioned previously that you had not yet selected the colors for your new offices.

T   No, we haven't. That is taken care of by the building superintendent. The offices will be painted before we move in.

S   I see, Mr. Turner, but is it not possible that selection of the proper colors to blend with the office furniture you now have, and the office furniture you might need to add now and in the future, would give you a better overall working climate in your new offices?

T   Yes, quite logically it would.

S   Now this is precisely what I would like to do. I would like to spend some time in your office, becoming familiar with such things as which girls handle what and why; whether the offices are arranged in a logical fashion for accessibility to files; staff accessibility to the office people; in fact, everything concerned with quality production flow in the office. And we even consider such minor points as elements that may be distracting, for instance, to one or more secretaries. In one organization we rearranged the desks of several secretaries and eliminated about 75 percent of the conversation that was going on.

T   Well, we have a problem there and it might be good for an outsider to do this. But, Mr. Hill, you mentioned a free service and a fee of $100. Now, what's the gimmick?

S   No gimmick! All we want to do is survey your needs and then present a plan to you based on our survey. Our company will charge you a maximum of $100 for this service. We hope, however, that if you need office furniture you will purchase it from our company. And the $100 is deducted from your investment in office furniture. In addition to the expectation that we can provide whatever office furniture you may need now, we also look to the future. As a result of a survey, we might find that through a planned replacement program you may need a limited number of desks now, but as time goes on and you replace older furniture according to a planned program, we hope that we'll obtain that business as well. Does that sound fair to you?

T   Yes—yes, it does, but I'm not really sure.

S   Perhaps these illustrations of our service and some of the programs we have done will relieve your mind with respect to our services. Here are a few of the programs we have completed and the names of the companies as well. (*Salesman thumbs through the portfolio illustrating things the company has done for various firms.*)

S   Mr. Turner, I would like to have your permission now to go ahead and plan this survey for you and present the complete plan to you within one week, with the understanding that you are under no obligation to buy from us now or in the future. If you will introduce me to your office manager, I can begin this afternoon.

T   Well, we really don't have an office manager. One of the girls, an executive secretary, pretty much handles the work in the office. I'll tell her that you're going to be doing some work here. You say our maximum bill will be $100 and that you will present a complete plan to us?

S   Yes, I will. When I return to my office this afternoon, I will dictate a letter setting forth the condition we have discussed. It should be here for you to-morrow or the following day.

T   Well, that does sound businesslike. . . .

TEN VARIABLES OF ANY CONTACT

Whenever a salesman is making a call on a new prospect, experience shows he should give serious consideration to incorporating most of the following concepts in his initial contact with the prospect. The variables used will depend upon the situation, of course. The discerning salesman will recognize that many of these variables are also used, in modified form, in contacts with regular customers.

1. He should state the customer's name. With a regular customer the salesman may say, for instance, "Hello, Ben."

2. He should, without question, mention his own name. Not with an old friend or regular customer, of course.

3. It is advisable he mention his company's name. Not with a regular customer, of course.

4. It is advisable that he thank the prospect for the interview.

5. It is advisable, if possible, that the purpose of the call be stated.

6. He should exhibit a degree of purposefulness through his actions and statements.

7. He should have in mind questions (permissive) to *get* information.

8. He should plan questions to verify (verification) precall information or assumptions he has made concerning the prospect's or customer's situation.

9. He should establish a climate of mutual compatibility.

10. Finally, he should, if possible, make some form of a statement that will assist in establishing the first shade or slight degree of empathy between himself and the prospect.

The use of each variable is illustrated later in this chapter. The con-

Selling: A Behavioral Science Approach

tact variables are also analyzed as part of the four quarters of the contact stage in Chapter 13. But two of these variables, the use of permissive questions and verification questions, need further discussion so that their utilization in the following dialogues will be clearly understood.

Question Forms and Two-way Communication Process

Two basic question forms are used in the contact stage to obtain effective customer mental participation. One is the verification question and the other is the permissive question.

A verification question is used to verify the accuracy of (1) information a salesman has gained in the precall or planning process or (2) general assumptions the salesman has made about the prospect's or customer's situation without specific fact gathering.

Oftentimes in fairly complex sales situations or where the sales volume warrants it, a reasonable amount of fact gathering regarding the prospect's or customer's situation is done by a salesman during the planning or precontact stage as specific preparation for the actual contact. Reinforced with this information the salesman may, during the first phase of the contact stage, make a statement about the prospect's situation. He will then ask a question to verify the truth of the statement.

For instance, the industrial salesman may state, (1) "Mr. Ryan, I understand you are planning on constructing an addition to the west side of the plant to house more cutting equipment. Is my information correct?" This will give the prospect an opportunity to amplify or verify the salesman's statement. This feedback tells the salesman whether or not he is on the right track. It will also furnish guides to the prospect's wishes regarding further discussion of the particular subject raised by the salesman. The logic of this thought is soundly supported by the process seen in Figure 11, "Two-way Communication," page 215.

In contrast, it is not uncommon for the experienced salesman to make certain assumptions about a prospect's or customer's situation with little actual planning or gathering of specific precall information. As an illustration, the paper supply salesman or the salesman selling office record forms may make the assumption that a particular business firm is using certain materials or forms in its record-keeping process. It is clear that in these cases a salesman still has to determine the accuracy of his assumptions. To do this, he may have to ask a direct verification question early in the contact stage, such as, "Mr. Jones, are you using the XYZ type forms in your office procedure work?"

Continuing the verification example (see number 1 above), assume that the prospect has replied in the affirmative: (2) "Yes, that is correct." The salesman then asks permission to ask a question like (3) "That is good news, Mr. Ryan, and may I ask you a few questions about the building project?" The salesman could, of course, have stated, "May I ask you a few questions about your production needs," or cutting needs, or gauge needs, or any one of fifty other ideas and concepts relating to the products he is selling and the customer's or prospect's situation. He doesn't say,

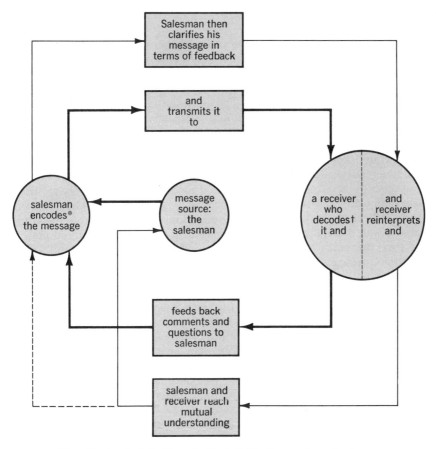

*Encoding is a technical term for the individual's speech mechanism.

†Decoding is a technical term for the respondent's thought process.

Figure 11   Two-way Communication

"Mr. Ryan, I will need some facts about your production program." The latter is a direct statement which may be offensive to the prospect. With the permissive question, it is difficult for the prospect to deny or resent the salesman's question when prefixed by, "May I?" It should be remembered that the salesman should always identify what he is asking questions about. He never should make the blunt statement, "May I ask you a few questions?" There may be a substantial difference in the prospect's reaction to these two statements.

The reader is now asked to examine the statements identified by numbers 1, 2, and 3 in the text above, and relate those statements to Figure 11. Next, assume however that the prospect Ryan replied to the salesman's question 1 above; (4) "No, that is a way off yet." This feedback is not what the salesman expected. He adjusts, however, by clarifying his original message in terms of Ryan's statement. The salesman states, (5) "Well, thank you, Mr. Ryan, but is the project something that can be talked about now, or is it too far in the future?" Ryan listens and reinterprets. He replies, "Oh, no. There has been reference to it in the *Trade Press,* but it is six months off." Thus Ryan and the salesman reach an understanding on that particular point. This clarification process is identified by the outer circle of Figure 11. The salesman's next statement may again throw the communication pattern into the clarification process or the communicators may clearly understand each other. This pattern is illustrated by the inner circle.

In addition to the functions performed above, verification and permissive questions bring about some remarkable outputs. They enable the salesman to use a problem-exposing and problem-solving approach with all the ramification therein related to prospect responses and feelings. As has been indicated previously, each educator knows that he affects the readiness of the individual to learn by presenting meaningful material and involving the individual in the process. What is more meaningful to the prospect than a situation about what is happening in his firm at the moment? What involves the prospect more than a question about these happenings and his responses to this? Do not verification and permissive questions suggest to the prospect that here is a salesman who understands his situation?

In view of Saginaw Steering's purchasing agent Cooper's open memo to salesmen in Figure 8, doesn't it seem logical that the salesman who makes regular calls on customers, for example, monthly calls, could profitably use these questions? Why not ask, "Jim, are any new jobs being bid on?" Or, "Are there any changes in your production equipment needs that are important from a gauging standpoint, etc.?" Thousands of questions could be asked. Each salesman can design appropriate questions according to the situation. And if thousands of questions are asked, thousands of sales will be made.

DIALOGUE CASES ILLUSTRATING THE TEN VARIABLES OF THE CONTACT STAGE

Three cases are presented. In Case 1, the hotel salesman is selling an intangible, "The Cultural Growth of the Family through Dining Out." In Case 2, an office furniture salesman, who could be representing either a manufacturer or a retailer, is selling a combination of his design and layout service and office furniture—an intangible and a tangible product. In Case 3, the industrial distributor salesman is selling a tangible industrial product.

CASE 1 *Cultural Growth of the Family through Dining Out—the Contact Stage*[8] A hotel sales representative is calling on the personnel director of a local manufacturing firm employing some 300 men and women. About 200 are blue-collar and 100 are white-collar workers. The hotel he represents

---

[8] Joseph W. Thompson, "Increasing Hotel Sales Effectiveness," *The Hotel Monthly,* pp. 10–12, 1963.

The Contact: Part One

is a fine, modern facility with three dining rooms. The hotel sales representative is contacting the personnel director to discuss the advantages of establishing a program of company gift certificates and awards entitling recipients to a family dining out at the hotel. This is part of the hotel sales campaign to promote a new concept—the cultural growth of the family through dining out.

S refers to the salesman's comments, and R refers to the respondent in the communication process.

DIALOGUE A

S   (1) Mr. Owens, (2) I'm Bill Smith (3) of the Delta Hotel, and (4) I want to thank you for seeing me.
R   Not at all. I have recommended your hotel to some of our visitors.
S   That's nice to hear, Mr. Owens, and we appreciate your recommendations. In a way, my call today is to get your thoughts or opinion about a new plan we have called "the cultural growth of the family through dining out." (5) We are hopeful you, as the personnel director of Smith Company, will be interested in the program. (6) Have you heard about this program, Mr. Owens?"
R   No, I haven't.
S   Very briefly, it is a program designed to call attention to family benefits through dining out. We are particularly emphasizing how the poise and confidence of children and young people is prompted through family dining out. As you know, of course, family dining out has many other advantages ranging from "togetherness" value to better understanding between teenagers and family. Does that idea sound logical to you, Mr. Owens?

In Dialogue A salesman Smith has used variables (1) name of prospect, (2) and (3) identified himself by name and company, (4) expressed an appreciation for the interview, (5) stated the purpose of his call, and (6) asked a verification question. In addition, his call was purposeful. Whether mutual compatability and some degree of empathy was established is always a question. It would appear, however, that Smith's statement, "That's nice to hear, Mr. Owens, and we appreciate your recommendations," suggests that salesman Smith comprehends how mutual compatibility is established.

DIALOGUE B

S   (1) Mr. Owens, (2) I'm Bill Smith of the (3) Delta Hotel, and (4) I want you to know I appreciate this appointment.
R   That's OK. I had some free time, so I'm glad to see you.
S   Thank you. And I'm simply calling on you (5) to see if the new program we are promoting, called the "cultural growth of the family through dining out," could be adapted to your employee relations program.
R   Well, what did you have in mind?
S   I understand that your company gives its employees annual Thanksgiving and Christmas gifts as well as a series of service awards to employees for five, ten, or twenty years of service. I understand, too, that you have a stock award given at retirement as well. (6) Is my information correct?

Selling: A Behavioral Science Approach

R Yes, it is, and we feel our award program is a very important part of our employee relations program.

S I see. If I may, Mr. Owens, (7) I would like to ask you a few questions about your employee relations awards.

R Sure, go ahead—we're pretty proud of it.

S I was wondering if you had ever given any thought to changing or modifying your awards program, that is, only from the standpoint of the type of gift given to the employee?

R Well, we do change our awards from time to time, especially Christmas and Thanksgiving gifts. We have never changed the retirement program, in which we give stock in the company. Actually, from time to time we have discussed this. Perhaps we should give stock in the first years instead of the last. In any event we are changing, and I believe that was your question.

S Yes, sir, and the reason for the question. . . .

In Dialogue B Smith has used variables (1) name of prospect, (2) and (3) his own name and name of his company, (4) has made an expression of appreciation for the interview, (5) stated the purpose of his call, (6) used a verification question, and (7) he used a permissive question. Again the tenor of the dialogue suggests a purposeful Mr. Smith. Smith is making the discussion meaningful, and he is getting prospect mental participation.

Dialogues A and B illustrate the fact that the salesman adjusts his remarks to the customer's comments. Even in the contact stage he must converse in a logical, orderly manner. However, regardless of what the customer says, the hotel sales representative will eventually cover two important points during the contact stage: (1) He will briefly describe what is meant by the cultural growth of the family through dining out and (2) He will ask questions concerning the company's service awards. In brief, he will set the stage for a problem-exposing and problem-solving sales interview.

In these dialogue illustrations the salesman's comments concerning the cultural growth of the family could be first or the subject of the company's service awards to employees could have been first. Don't forget—the salesman must adjust his comments so that he is in tune with the prospect.

CASE 2 *Office Furniture Salesman—The Contact Stage*[9] Salesman Jack Hall, office furniture salesman, has just heard or read that the French Company is expanding its operations, had a profitable year, is adding new lines, is moving to new quarters, is adding a new partner, or any one of a multitude of possibilities which suggest change or expansion.

S refers to the salesman's comments, and *R* refers to the respondent in the communication process.

S (1) Mr. Jones, (2) I am Jack Hall of the (3) Eveready Office Equipment Company. John Jules of the Shearer Company told me you are constructing an addition to your present building to house some new office personnel.

[9] Joseph W. Thompson, *National Office Furniture Sales Manual*, National Office Furniture Association, Chicago, Ill., 1962, pp. 12–13.

The Contact: Part One

R   Yes—that's right, but it's sometime in the future yet. We haven't started building.
S   I see, but if I may, (4) I would like to ask you a few questions about your new expansion program.
R   Well—yes. What did you have in mind?
S   As you probably gathered, Mr. Jones, the business of the Eveready Office Equipment Company is office furniture, and we would like to be of assistance to you in planning your new offices. (5) Have you developed a plan, as yet, concerning the quantity and type of office furniture you might be needing?
R   No—no, we haven't. Not as yet.
S   Mr. Jones, it would be a pleasure to explain a survey service we have for analyzing the various problems that are associated with equipping and planning the layout for new offices in an expansion program such as the one you are undertaking. (6) May I show you a few facts concerning our approach to planning office equipment and layout?
R   Well, I don't have a great deal of time, but—OK, go ahead.

The reader is now asked to determine what variables are being identified by the numbers 1 through 6 in the case above.

CASE 3   *Industrial Distributor Salesman of the Emerson Supply Company—The Contact Stage*[10]   This is a routine call by a distributor salesman. The prospect is Mr. Arnold, the shop superintendent of a machine shop employing twenty to thirty men in the machine shop proper. The call takes place in the Cleveland, Ohio, area. The Emerson Supply Company is a local firm and is fairly well known in the area.

S refers to the salesman's comments, and R refers to the respondent in the communication process.
S   It is a pleasure to meet you, Mr. Arnold. I am Frank Hill of the Emerson Supply Company, and I want to thank you for seeing me as a supplier of Pratt & Whitney cutting tools and gauges.
R   That's okay. Sit down, won't you?
S   Thank you. This is quite a comfortable chair.
R   Yes, I have always believed in a relaxed sort of feeling and these big chairs give it, I believe.
S   They do indeed. But I don't want to become so relaxed that I don't get to the purpose of my call, so I will come right to the point. It is this. If it is to your advantage to do so, we at Emerson Supply Company are hopeful you will consider using Pratt & Whitney new Checkmate gauges in your machine shop production work. But before we can discuss whether or not it is to your advantage, Mr. Arnold, it would be helpful if you would take a few minutes to comment on your gauge needs.
R   What do you want to know?
S   Specifically, may I ask you a few questions about the major machining jobs now under work orders in your plant?
This dialogue has several unique implications. The straightforward,

[10] Joseph W. Thompson, *Pratt-Whitney Manpower Development Program*, Pratt & Whitney Corp., Inc., Hartford, Conn., 1964, chap. 5.

Selling: A Behavioral Science Approach

direct, honest comment "If it is to your advantage to do so . . ." has customer appeal. Isn't that why the salesman is there? Why not tell the prospect? But note the implication of that statement. The implication is let's get the facts, and if it is to your advantage, fine. And if not, we won't attempt to sell to you. This salesman is indeed customer-oriented and is probably establishing mutual compatability and certainly some degree of empathy. May not the prospect think, "This man understands my position." Is the salesman putting himself in the prospect's shoes?

THE TECHNIQUES APPROACH AND THE REMOVAL OF SALES TENSION

Many sales managers train their salesmen to use, and many skilled salesmen do employ, ways to remove or relieve sales tension quickly during the initial stages of the interview. Some salesmen and the sales managers believe that during the opening phase of an interview there is a noticeable feeling of tension on the part of the prospect with regard to the salesman's call. The tension supposedly springs from the prospect's belief that the salesman is up to something. Further, men of this school prepare their sales talks under the assumption few prospects enjoy the thought of a salesman calling on them.

This school of thought suggests the salesman should, early in his opening remarks, eliminate or relieve tension by bringing into play one or more of the following ploys: (1) the salesman may assure the prospect there will be no high pressure tactics used; (2) that the call will not take much time; (3) he may use the prospect's hobbies as an ice-breaking technique; (4) the salesman may quickly present a profitable idea; (5) he may use a mutual friend's name, just as a tension reducer, or he may use it as an introduction; (6) he may talk about hypothetical situations or ask the prospect's advice about a particular problem; (7) the salesman may use humor; and (8) he may flatter the prospect.

The following dialogue puts to use several of these techniques which are supposedly designed to get the prospect's attention, interest, curiosity, and remove sales tension. A salesman who follows the techniques approach would walk into the prospect's office with a breezy flair and perhaps say:

DIALOGUE A

S Mr. Owens, I'm Bill Beavertail of ABC Industrial Supply Corporation. I was talking to a mutual friend of ours, Ralph Adams of the Paramount Company, and he was telling me about the wonderful production systems and controls you have developed for Bullard.

C Thank you, but the company had a fine production program before I came here.

S From what Mr. Adams told me, you are just being modest. But in any event, I am here to tell you about some new Pratt & Whitney cutting tools that not only could cut costs but also give you more precision work. I think it would really be profitable to Bullard and would only take me about five minutes to see if you are interested.

221

The Contact: Part One

DIALOGUE B

S I'm Bill Beavertail of ABC Industrial Supply Corporation. Ralph Adams of the Paramount Company told me about your fine new production program, and this is why I'm calling on you. I have several cutting tools that could fit right into Bullard's program to cut costs and still increase precision output, and I'd like to take about five minutes of your time to tell you about it.

In these techniques and approaches, Beavertail has designed his sales talk to get attention and interest through curiosity and through removing sales tension. It is entirely possible he will arouse Mr. Owen's curiosity. However, he hasn't followed the strategy of getting information. Rather, he is telling-controlling the situation through high pressure. And although some prospects may react favorably to this approach, it can be safely assumed that the majority of prospects will be more negatively impressed than positively. For example, how would Saginaw Steering's Cooper react (see Figure 8, page 202)?

Further Analysis of Tension Reduction Approach

Although the techniques approach is in general poor selling and has caused many potential buyers to react negatively to salesmen, it is possible for salesmen to use a number of the tension reduction concepts within the structure of a salesman-oriented approach. Two dialogues will be utilized. One will illustrate the misuse and the other the correct use of several tension reduction concepts.

CASE 1[11]   The salesman is calling on a potential customer for Red-Duck Hunting Coats. This prospect operates a leased sporting goods department in a large retail store. He is aggressive and the sports department is doing well. The sporting goods phase of the department store is not heavily advertised but probably gets its business as a result of the heavy traffic flow drawn to the department store.

A cursory examination of the sporting goods department shows a line of sporting goods in the average to low-price range. You get a feeling it is a bargain department. You find golf clubs, a great array of spinning equipment and fishing gear, water skis, diving equipment, guns, etc.

For purpose of this example, the salesman's possible discussion over the telephone has been omitted. It is assumed that the salesman is making a cold call; the amenities have been completed and he is walking into the manager's office.

DIALOGUE A

S Good morning, Mr. Lamp, I am Frank Hill of Brunswick Sports Division and I appreciate having this opportunity to see you. I know how busy you must be, but I can assure you this call will be well worth your while. In fact,

[11] Joseph W. Thompson, *You and the Brunswick Sports Division*, Manpower Development Program, Brunswick Co., Chicago, Ill., chap. 1, pp. 11–17.

Selling: A Behavioral Science Approach

it won't take long—perhaps a minute or two—to discuss my proposition with you.

C I see.

S Did you know that Brunswick has now created Brunswick Sports Division to handle its complete sports line? Some of our lines are MacGregor, Zebco, etc., but today I particularly want to talk to you about Red-Duck. It is a fast selling line that I think will go well in your department.

C I am pretty well set.

S Sure, but don't you know about Red-Duck? Let me buy you a cup of coffee so I can have five or ten minutes of your time to tell you about Red-Duck.

DIALOGUE B

S Mr. Remington, I am Jim Honer of Brunswick and I want to thank you for this opportunity to see you.

C That's my job. What are you selling? Selling bowling balls?

S No, no bowling balls, but if you wanted a gross I wish I were. Actually, I am with Brunswick Sports Division and of course, that's why I am here—to talk about your sports line. I have a few folders here I would like to leave with you. (*Salesman places several folders on prospect's desk.*) But before I do, may I ask you a few questions about your fall merchandising plans?

C Sure, go ahead.

S Mr. Remington, have you planned a fall promotional program yet on any particular lines or items you are planning to push?

C No, not yet.

S It's possible then, Mr. Remington, that this particular material may be of interest to you.

Dialogue A is a salesman-oriented sales talk. It suggests the fast talking, extroverted, quick-deal salesman. In direct contrast, Dialogue B depicts a customer-oriented, mature, problem-solving salesman. He does suggest the few minutes of time concept with his statement, "I have a few folders here I'd like to leave with you." Some sales experts may consider this the use of a gimmick; however, it is the author's opinion that any material of this type which is specifically part of the sales interview is not to be considered as a gimmick. In addition, it must be remembered that Jim Honer moved quickly into a purposeful sales call. Yes, he got attention partly because of the folders, but mostly because of the question, "But before I do, may I ask a few questions about your fall merchandising plans?" In brief, Jim Honer did an excellent job of selling.

Summary

The contact is the first action stage of the sales process. Normally the first prospect-salesman communication mix comes in the contact phase of the sale.

Planning for each sales call is essential. In situations where complex sales analysis is needed or the dollar value of the sale is large or for other strategic reasons, the salesman may engage in an extensive fact-gathering campaign prior to making the initial call on the prospect. In some cases little preplanning work will be done. How much to do is a matter of judgment. The salesman must invest his time to best bring about the development of his market opportunities, especially in his work with individual customers. Most salesmen, however, spend too little time in fact gathering.

In general, other than the second phase of the survey call or the call on regular profitable customers or where the power structure is with the salesman's company or where the salesman has been asked to make a call on the prospect or solve a problem or give a service, the salesman should expect each prospect to have a negative set toward any salesman. This concept focuses attention on the salesman's need to convert this negative set to positive readiness. This process is not difficult. It is just frequently misunderstood.

Each of the ten variables of the contact stage may affect a prospect's set toward the salesman but two variables—verification and permissive questions—are especially designed to change a negative set to positive readiness. Readiness is the educational psychologist's concept which describes the individual's want and ability to learn. In education as in selling, positive readiness is developed by presenting meaningful material and getting the individual to participate. Not only do verification and permissive question forms affect readiness, but they permit the salesman to determine the prospect's ability to learn and his want to learn. In brief, two broad areas are involved in readiness. One is the appraisal of the individual's want and ability to learn and the other is how to affect the individual's want and ability to learn. Other outputs of these question forms are that they help the salesman to establish a climate of mutual compatibility and some degree of empathy.

Viewing the contact stage as involving inputs by the salesman and outputs by the prospect will give the salesman an excellent overall view of the contact stage. The salesman utilizes all or part of the ten variables of the contact stage as inputs in each sale. The number of variables and how they are used will depend upon the situation. Each situation is different. Each variable is important.

A constant input in every sales situation is a problem-solving philosophy which gives an impression of maturity. All inputs by the salesman should be regarded as obtaining outputs or responses by the prospect. These responses are mental attention and mutual compatibility, readiness, and verbal and nonverbal signals. The salesman may view those responses as forms of feedback. And it is feedback that enables the salesman to determine the accuracy of his sales effort.

Chapter 12   DISCUSSION QUESTIONS

1   Just why does the salesman contact a prospect or a regular customer? Does the salesman have the same purpose in mind when he contacts a

Selling: A Behavioral Science Approach

regular customer as when he contacts an entirely new account? Explain.

2 Why should the salesman understand the concept of set, readiness, and empathy? Explain each concept and how understanding these concepts would be important to the salesman.

3 Describe the two major question forms identified in this chapter.

4 Specifically identify the relationship of these question forms to the concept of set, readiness, and empathy.

5 Is it possible for a salesman to utilize a verification question without any extensive personal preplanning work for a particular call? How?

6 The author states that questions give the salesman a shortcut to good two-way communication. Do you agree or disagree with this statement? Explain.

7 Develop a dialogue and analyze in terms of a two-way communication diagram in this chapter.

8 How could the salesman use the letter that Saginaw Steering's purchasing agent Cooper wrote to salesmen as an asset in the sales interview? Write a dialogue illustrating your concepts. (Assume, of course, that the salesman has utilized Cooper's memo to salesmen as part of his contact stage.)

9 Could Cooper's set be an advantage to the new salesman? To the experienced salesman? In what way would the set be a disadvantage to the new salesman or to the experienced salesman?

10 What relationship do you see between the pure tension reduction approach and the pure canned sales-talk approach?

the contact

part two

13

THE FOUR QUARTERS AND THE TEN VARIABLES
OF THE CONTACT STAGE

Each sales situation is a fluid and flexible sequence of events. Dialogues A and B (see pages 217 and 218) illustrated this principle of selling. Although each sales situation may vary, there is a basic order to the sales interview, especially the contact. This order is established by the introduction, direction, future, and problem-solving phases of the contact stage.

Introduction

The introduction phase is the initial contact. It is the first face-to-face meeting between the salesman and the prospect. Just as there are accepted ways of functioning in any social situation, so are there certain ways of functioning in a sales situation. For instance, in any social situation involving an introduction of two people, most individuals expect certain verbal statements to be made accompanied by certain behavior activities on the part of the three people involved. In brief, each individual is set to receive (hear) certain verbal stimuli and set to view certain behavior activities. Why not say and do what the individual expects?

That is why it is important that the salesman identify the customer, himself, and his company, thank the prospect for the interview, and, if possible, state why he is there. Further, the salesman should present some degree of purposefulness by his overall demeanor. He should be positive but not overly so. He should be enthusiastic but not overly so. He should be friendly but not overly so. He should have good diction but not overly so.

In a nutshell, it is recommended that the salesman follow a middle-of-the-road strategy. After determining the degree of mutual compatibility or rapport existing, the salesman's role enactment and the intensity of that role enactment should vary according to the demands of the situation.

Direction

How does the salesman determine where he will "go" in each sales situation? Normally most salesmen have a preset track, or plan, on which

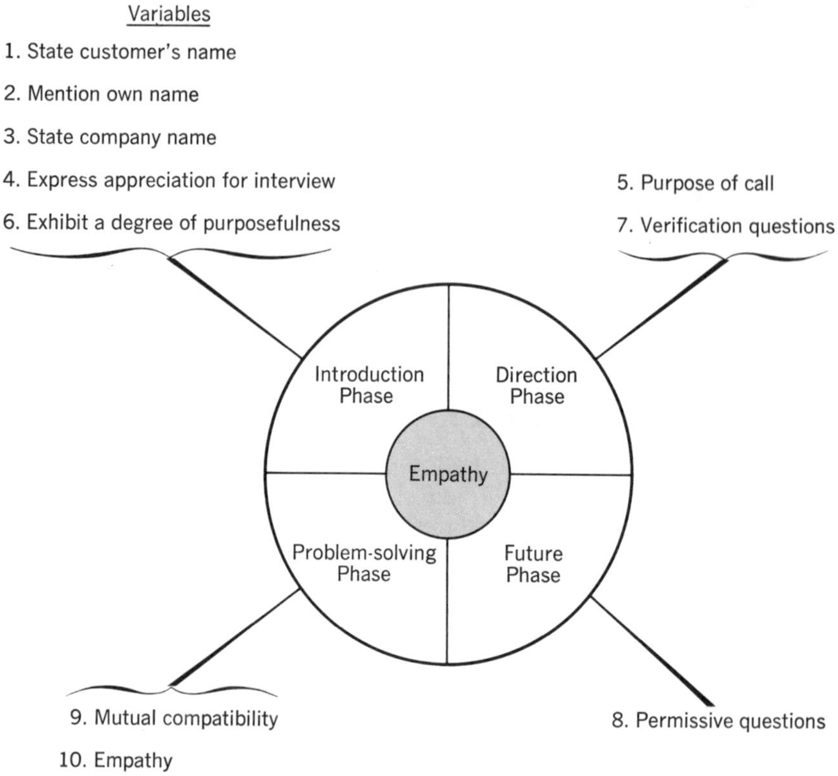
Variables
1. State customer's name
2. Mention own name
3. State company name
4. Express appreciation for interview
6. Exhibit a degree of purposefulness
5. Purpose of call
7. Verification questions
Introduction Phase
Direction Phase
Empathy
Problem-solving Phase
Future Phase
9. Mutual compatibility
10. Empathy
8. Permissive questions

Figure 12 Four Quarters and Ten Variables of the Contact Stage

they expect to run. This is all to the good. It is an excellent place to start He must, if possible, obtain information about the prospect as well as the prospect's firm. He must, if possible, have a specific reason for making this call. The purpose of the call determines the direction initially. However, through verbal and nonverbal feedback the salesman may get information from the prospect which will change the direction of the sale. If a salesman has product knowledge, if he is sincere, and if he has the ability to communicate this to the prospect or customer, he is prepared to change direction during the sale.

Many salesmen find this concept difficult to comprehend, yet it is basic to a customer-oriented selling philosophy. Many salesmen are concerned that the prospect might state that the information he has is in error in part or total. But isn't this precisely what the salesman wants to hear? How else can he adjust unless he is put on the track by the prospect or customer? Visualize if you will the poor communication that results if the salesman assumes he is correct and proceeds to give his sales talk.

Future

As stated each salesman has a plan or direction established before he contacts a prospect or customer. On the other hand, if he accepts the principle that what he thinks the prospect wants or needs may be quite different from what the prospect actually needs or wants, he will automatically plan to get information that will enable him to shift gears or change direction. To do this in the contact stage, the salesman uses verification and permissive questions.

Verbal and nonverbal prospect responses to these questions tell the salesman if his assumed direction is correct or in error. If his preplanned assumptions are correct, he proceeds in his intended direction. If they are in error, he changes direction.

It must be understood that the salesman may alter directions several times during the course of the sales interview. The entire sales interview should be regarded as an adjustive process. It is an intellectual and emotional interaction between the salesman and prospect. Each exchange of knowledge and feeling may call for a change in direction.

Problem Solving

"A problem," Webster states, "is an unsettled matter demanding solution or discussion, and requiring considerable thought or skill for its proper solution or discussion."[1] And the solution to a problem lies with a decision, followed by an appropriate series of actions. It is evident that problem solving is not restricted to the contact stage. Discussion and decision identify problem solving as a process that permeates the entire sales interview.

Why then the emphasis on problem solving in the contact stage? There are two reasons for this. First, the emphasis is needed to point out that the salesman who plans in terms of solutions to problems will have a natural process working for him. Considerable evidence indicates that businessmen have a propensity to avoid or put off grappling with a problem, but once the process starts there is a "mechanism of behavior-persistence" that tends to keep the individual working at the problem.[2] Thus the salesman who brings a problem into focus or who presents possible solutions to the problem develops a team member of the decision maker. Second, the salesman who is not alert to problem exposure and problem solving during the contact stage may quite easily overlook obvious solutions. This danger is uniquely illustrated by Norman R. F. Maier, an authority on problem solving.[3]

Figure 13 illustrates four solutions to a problem, represented by routes leading from the starting point to the goal. Note that if one travels route 1-3-5-9, the only opportunity for reaching the goal is to choose path 11 rather than path 13. If a person retreats to path 5 he can reach the goal by traveling by paths 7 or 9. However, if a person retreats to the starting point, four solutions become possible. These solutions become

[1] *Webster's Third New International Dictionary*, 1961, p. 1809.

[2] Herbert A. Simon, *Administrative Behavior*, The Macmillan Company, New York, 1961, pp. 94–95.

[3] Norman R. F. Maier, *Problem-solving Discussions and Conferences: Leadership Methods and Skills*, McGraw-Hill Book Company, New York, 1963. This book is recommended reading for most salesmen, but it is especially recommended for the sales manager or conference leader.

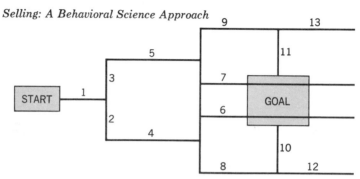

Figure 13 Problem-solving Approach

quite different as illustrated by the fact that the number of common paths change (the change from odd-numbered to even-numbered paths).

The reader will recognize that complex problems are often solved not by persisting in pursuing a certain path but by making an entirely new start. *Solution possibilities are richest if one returns to the starting point of the problem.* This is difficult to do, however, because once one experiences progress along the path toward a goal, it is difficult to give up the gains and start over. Nevertheless, it is apparent that the best solution can be found only with a thorough exploration of many and different possibilities.

Assume salesman Smith believes that X company has equipment that is obsolete and can profitably be replaced. Assume further Smith has learned that X company has had a number of government contracts, and recently several large shipments have been returned to the X company marked "rejects." The salesman decides to contact an X company executive who is in a decision-making slot and attempts to sell the executive a new machine which can reduce rejects because it is a precision machine. He may make a sale. He may not. He may miss a number of facts or possible solutions to the reject problem by following the 1-3-5-9 route.

First, rejects are a symptom of a problem and not necessarily the problem. It may be a matter of poor inspection. Poor inspection may be due to certain individuals, for example, marginal employees, or due to the work situation, for instance, work layout, lighting, etc., or the inspection problem may be lodged in the group, that is, the group structure or social organization. Each situation will call for substantially different solutions.

Or assume in the example above, salesman Smith's machine (a numeric control Tape-O-Matic, which is an automated piece of equipment) would replace three older machines with more precision work and with a greater output. Thus the company could discharge under these circumstances at least two employees. In this situation, a decision to buy the new machine might raise a new problem that would be more difficult for the salesman to cope with than the original problem of selling the Tape-O-Matic machine.

Many times it is easy for the salesman to justify the investment involved in a machine through laborsaving, tax credits, special depreciation allowances, etc. But what about the firm's ability to retain the men dis-

The Contact: Part Two

placed? What about unions? What about the company's image in the community? What about new work standards because of greater output? What about employee morale? What if there is a shortage of this type of labor being displaced rather than a surplus? Finally, what if the employees involved in the situation were old-time employees, or one happened to be the father-in-law of, say, the shop superintendent who is making the decision? Again, the salesman who takes the 1-3-5-9 route may not get the necessary facts. Maier's diagram forceably exposes the tragedy that the salesman who does most of the talking is, moment by moment, proceeding down a narrow path providing no turn-around position and one that leads to a sign marked "dead end."

Agreed then that the salesman must begin the problem-solving process in the contact stage, but how does he go about it?

Each writer appears to bring a somewhat different viewpoint to bear on the problem-solving process. Nevertheless, one descriptive scheme appears throughout most literature on the subject of problem solving. Time and time again writers stress the importance of fact finding,[4] preparation,[5] identification,[6] inquiry,[7] as the initial steps in problem solving.

From the identification of the problem and the fact-gathering point on, the problem-solving process varies considerably among writers. One of the most meaningful process is described by management authority Peter Drucker.[8] In brief, he identifies the process as:

1. Defining the problem. What kind of problem is it? What is its critical factor? When do we have to solve it? Why do we want to solve it? What will solving it cost?

2. Defining expectations. What do we want to gain by solving it?

3. Developing alternative solutions. Which of several plans offers the surest way to avoid things that are unexpected?

4. Knowing what to do with the decision after it is reached.

One authority, Hodnet, describes the phenomena of problem-solving quite vividly and lightly. He states,

Learning to solve problems is like learning to play baseball. You learn to throw, to catch, to bat, to run bases, to execute all sorts of refinements of these basic skills. You do not learn to play baseball. You learn the basic skills separately and you put them together in new combinations for every game.[9]

On the other hand, it is known that this skill will vary among individuals. As Krech and Crutchfield point out, "The natural history of one creative problem-solving process differs from that of almost every other

[4] Joseph D. Cooper, *The Art of Decision Making*, Doubleday & Company, Inc., Garden City, N.Y., 1961, p. 261.

[5] David Krech and Richard S. Crutchfield, *Elements of Psychology*, Alfred A. Knopf, Inc., New York, 1961, p. 395.

[6] Edward Hodnet, *The Art of Problem-Solving*, Harper & Brothers, New York, 1955, p. 11.

[7] Max Black, *Critical Thinking*, Prentice-Hall, Inc., Englewood Cliffs, N.J., 1946, p. 248.

[8] Peter F. Drucker, *The Practice of Management*, Harper & Brothers, New York, 1954, p. 1.

[9] Hodnet, *op. cit.*, p. 194.

Selling: A Behavioral Science Approach

one. The difficulty and complexity of the problem, the capacity of the problem-solver, his work habits, his store knowledge, his motivation, his personality, all influence the sequence of events which, taken together, we call the creative problem-solving process."[10]

In any problem-solving process, the salesman is also interested in the decision-making mechanism as well. A decision means a cutoff point. Thus it would seem that any discussion of this subject should be deferred until the completion phase of the sale is reached. Nevertheless, since decision making is a process, that is, it is the result of solutions to problems, and since decision making and problem solving are closely interrelated, it is worthwhile to examine the concept briefly at this point.

Decision making As in problem solving there are substantially different opinions regarding the decision-making process. Dwight Joyce, Glidden Company president, remarks, "If a vice-president asks me how I was able to choose the right course, I have to say, I'm damned if I know."[11] George Terry believes a decision to be "the selection of one behavioral alternative from among two or more possible alternatives."[12] John Golver simply states a decision to be "the choice of alternatives, based on judgment."[13] Richard Owens formally states a decision is a formation of an opinion or a conclusion, the termination of a controversy, or the making of a choice between possible course of action or between persons.[14] On the other hand, Erwin Bross presents a rather elaborate decision-making mechanism.[15]

In all probability, however, most executives intuitively or by plan ask the following four questions during the decision-making and problem-solving processes.

1. "What is the risk in implementing this decision?" Here the decision maker must simply evaluate on the one hand what may be a loss by implementing a decision, and on the other hand what gains will accrue to the company.

2. "Will this decision involve the least effort with greatest results and with least disturbances to an organization?" Here the decision maker has to look at the decision in terms of the size of the job to be done. In brief, he doesn't want to take a magnum shotgun for a sparrow-size problem or a slingshot for an elephant-size problem.

3. Each decision maker has to ask himself, "Is this the moment? Is this the time?" There are times when action or a solution to a problem may be delayed for weeks, months, or even years. Recently a nationally known company's stock dropped from sixty points to eleven points. This

[10] Krech and Crutchfield, *op. cit.*, p. 395.

[11] John McDonald, "How Businessmen Make Decisions," *Fortune*, vol. 52, no. 2, p. 85, August, 1955.

[12] George R. Terry, *Principles of Management*, Richard D. Irwin, Inc., Homewood, Ill., 1953, p. 106.

[13] John G. Golver, *Business Operations: Operational Research and Reports*, American Book Company, New York, 1949, p. 12.

[14] Richard N. Owens, *Introduction to Business Policy*, Richard D. Irwin, Inc., Homewood, Ill., 1954, p. 115.

[15] Erwin D. Bross, *Design for Decisions*, The Macmillan Company, New York, 1961, p. 221.

company had many serious problems including low morale. It was time for dramatic action. The company couldn't delay in making decisions.

4. A final question each executive must consider before making a decision is, "Are our financial and human resources adequate in terms of what has to be done?" In brief, does the company have the money to do the job and does the company have the human resources to do the job?

To the salesman this decision-making process means that the more positive supportive information relevant to the four points above he can feed into the discussion process, the easier it will be for the decision maker to make a decision, other things being equal.

Summary

There is no one way to sell. But there is an acceptable framework of proven principles, ideas, and concepts that the salesman can employ to develop his own way of selling. This broad framework is graphically spelled out through the relationship of the ten variables to the four quarters of the contact stage.

The four quarters of the contact stage are introduction, direction, future, and problem solving. The variables are (1) the customer's name, (2) the salesman's name, (3) the company's name, (4) an expression of appreciation for the interview, (5) a statement to identify the purpose of the call, (6) a degree of purposefulness, (7, 8) the use of verification and permissive questions, and (9, 10) a climate of mutual compatibility and empathy.

The introduction phase is comparable to the social amenities of any social situation. Variables 1, 2, 3, 4, and 6 are specifically identified as being employed during the introduction phase.

The direction phase represents what the salesman plans to do and expects to happen based on planning. Variable 5 (the purpose of the call) and variable 7 (the verification question) are closely allied with the direction of the sale. Each salesman has a purpose for contacting the prospect, and that purpose directs the call initially. Through a verification question the salesman determines the accuracy of his purpose. If the verification question determines that the salesman's purpose for the call was correct, then the present direction of the sale becomes the future phase of the sale. The permissive question permits the salesman and the prospect to reach a mutual understanding concerning further discussion. Should the salesman's planning be incorrect, the verification question will determine the incorrectness of his information. When other questions elicit the correct information, the salesman moves to the future phase of the sale.

Problem solving is the fourth quarter of the contact stage. The direction and future phase of the sale always revolve around a problem. When the problem or the situation has been identified, the salesman is automatically in the future phase of the sale. The problem may be minor or it may be major; nevertheless, any situation that can be improved should be

Selling: A Behavioral Science Approach

regarded as a problem situation. Prospect problems involve the prospect; they are especially meaningful to him. Discussing these problems establishes a feeling of mutual compatibility between salesman and prospect. If the salesman projects an image of understanding the prospect's situation, a feeling of empathy may be established. Being empathetic and projecting this quality to the prospect through maturity and a problem-solving approach is the heart of every sales situation.

CASE 1 *Franklin Machine Shop* The Franklin Machine Company is a potential buyer of Pratt & Whitney machine tools, cutting tools, and gauges. This potential user operates a combined marine dry dock and machine shop. The machine shop does all the work required by the dry dock, but a fair amount of its work comes from general machine shop business. The company employs about fifteen machinists year round plus a number of helpers. Most of the equipment in the shop is in good condition; it is fairly stable, and has been in operation quite a few years. Apparently the company bought a number of machines, drills, lathes, etc., between 1939 and 1945 and then again bought additional machine tools through 1947 and 1952. The company, until about ten or fifteen years ago, was housed in a wooden building with a planked floor. Not only is the new brick-exterior, concrete-floor building much larger than the old building but it also boasts of being fairly modernistic in structure. The company's balance sheet picture financially is only fair, and it is of perhaps average or less than average in its profit structure. Recently the company has been obtaining a substantial number of subcontract work on government contracts supplying parts for manufacturer's finished products.

Franklin, Sr., is president of the machine shop and Franklin, Jr., is the general manager, a position he has held for approximately ten or more years. Young Franklin appears to be more aggressive, and perhaps he is the one responsible for the increased flow of contract business.

DIALOGUE 1

The salesman is Frank Hill of Wheel & Grind Company and he is making a cold call on Mr. Franklin.

1 **S** Good morning, Mr. Franklin. I am Frank Hill of Wheel & Grind and I appreciate having this opportunity to see you. I know how busy you must be, but I can assure you that this call will be well worth your while. In fact, it won't take long, perhaps a minute or two to discuss my proposition with you.

2 **R** I see.

3 **S** Did you know that Wheel & Grind has created a new line of Checkmate thread gauges?

4 **R** No, I didn't.

5 **S** Well, it's a great line and this is what I especially wanted to talk to you about, the new Checkmate gauges. It is an item which I think will work out well in your shop.

6 **R** We are pretty well set on gauges.

7 **S** Sure, but you don't know about these gauges. Tell you what, let me buy you a cup of coffee so I can have five or ten minutes of your time to tell you about the new Checkmate line.

233

The Contact: Part Two

DIALOGUE 2

Salesman John Hildon of Brown & Bratton is making a cold call on Mr. Franklin.

1 **S** Hello, Mr. Franklin. I'm John Hildon of Brown & Bratton. I want to thank you for seeing me, especially so because it's close to five o'clock.

2 **R** Okay, what did you have on your mind?

3 **S** Not much. I just wanted to introduce you to Brown & Bratton's Checkmate gauges. They are really great. Here is a brochure announcing these new precision tools. What do you think about them?

4 **R** I heard about them. I guess they are okay, but we are in good shape here. We've got another distributor who keeps us pretty well stocked. Besides your people are high on the stuff. What is the price?

5 **S** We are high, Mr. Franklin, but we're competitive now. Checkmate gauges have been reduced 25 percent.

6 **R** Still high. We pay less than that and we can't operate at a profit here paying Brown & Bratton a long dollar for everything. We have to cut costs.

7 **S** Mr. Franklin, Checkmate gauges are a quality item and they cut your costs so that you have a lower cost than you have using lower-priced items.

8 **R** That may be, but we are pretty well set now. When you have something else that's new, stop in and see us. Things are changing so fast now and we always like to keep up with improvements from time to time.

9 **S** Sure will, Mr. Franklin. Brown & Bratton is a leader so I'll be back from time to time.

DIALOGUE 3

First Call

1 **S** Hello, Mr. Franklin. I'm John Hildon of Osborn & Osborn and I want to thank you for the time you are giving me.

2 **R** Well, that's our job to see salesmen, so let's take it from there.

3 **S** Mr. Franklin, here is one of Osborn & Osborn's new Checkmate thread gauges. I say new in the sense that our former very fine gauges are now manufactured with even greater accuracy standards. Each gauge is certified to be equal to or better than the tolerance requirements of H-28, the engineer's Bible, as well as other military and industrial standard's publications.

4 **R** Well, most companies manufacture good gauges. By the way, how much are yours?

5 **S** That's one of the plus features, Mr. Franklin. Osborn & Osborn has not only improved the gauges but has reduced them 25 percent. I'll look up the price quotations here. Mr. Franklin, what are some of the gauge sizes that you most consistently need?

6 **R** We tap a lot of different size holes, but let's say size 12.

7 **S** Let's see, here's a list on size 12.

8 **R** Not too bad, but still high.

9 **S** Well, you know, Mr. Franklin, considering the quality, we think it is a very reasonable price. But, Mr. Franklin, may I ask you a few questions about your current machine shop orders?

10 **R** Sure, go ahead.

11 **S** Have you received any new government contracts in recent months?

12 **R** Sure, we have quite a few.

13 **S** Do the type of contracts you have received call for more precision work than in the past?

14 **R** Sure, they're getting tougher and tougher.

15 **S** And of course, Mr. Franklin, that means possible rejects if a few items even in a large supply aren't up to standards.

16 **R** Yes, that's right, that's a possibility.

17 **S** Mr. Franklin, Osborn & Osborn's stock in trade isn't selling a particular unit to a customer but knowing as much as possible about the customer's needs so that we can suggest, to the best of our ability, the correct unit. For instance, Mr. Franklin, I think it is quite difficult for me to suggest that you purchase two or three sets of our gauges, or to tell you specifically why you should have them unless I have the facts. Further, it is possible you might not need them. With this idea in mind, Mr. Franklin, I'd like to make a survey of your gauge needs and present a report to you. Would that be all right with you?

18 **R** Well, I suppose so, but what do you have in mind?

19 **S** In brief, it is this, Mr. Franklin. I'd like to look over some of the jobs being done now and see if there are any gauges or for that matter other nonproductive items that I could recommend which would enable your men to do more productive work.

20 **R** Well, when would you want to do that?

21 **S** I could start tomorrow morning, Mr. Franklin, or better still I could start a little preliminary work right now if it would meet with your approval.

22 **R** Okay—who do you want to talk to? And by the way I want to make it very clear that I don't want anybody's time tied up for any long period of time or any of our production work to be disrupted.

23 **S** You can be sure, Mr. Franklin, I will not in any way interfere with your work program.

Second Call

1 **S** Hello, Mr. Franklin, beautiful day isn't it?

2 **R** Yes, indeed, more sun than I've seen in a long time.

3 **S** Mr. Franklin, the complete report is here.

4 **R** (*Smiling*) It looks impressive, but is it any good?

5 **S** Yes, I think so, but you will have to be the final judge. The first page presents in outline form some of the facts contained in the report. I would like to go over the outline briefly and present in capsule form some of the major ideas involved.

6 **R** What's this going to cost me?

7 **S** Nothing, Mr. Franklin, there is no charge for the service. It is a pleasure to do so and I appreciate your giving me the opportunity to do it. More than anything. . . .

8 **R** Okay, I'm trying to kid you a little bit.

9 **S** I understand, Mr. Franklin, and actually I appreciate that. The first item here pertains to gauges. According to your supervisor you have six major

The Contact: Part Two

jobs in operation now or that will be put into operation before long. On page 10 of this report there is a list of the jobs now in operation and a recommendation with respect to gauges.

QUESTIONS

1. What variables of the contact stage do you find being used in the above dialogues?

2. Can you distinguish the four quarters of the contact stage in each of the dialogues?

3. Where in the dialogues above do you find the variables of the sales being misused? Rewrite the dialogues so that they are better examples of good selling.

CASE 2 *Lobby Case—Contact Stage* Press and Press salesman John Owens is sitting in the reception lobby of the Exceptional Machine Tool Corporation. About ten other salesmen like Owens are talking to each other, but two or three are reading trade magazines.

Suddenly the receptionist (switchboard operator) calls out, "Mr. Owens of Press and Press, Mr. Speed will talk to you."

This electrifies not only Owens but also most of the salesmen in the lobby. Speed is the master mechanic and is known among the salesmen as Speedy. He had, it seems, a propensity for giving short interviews. "To the point" was his rule.

Now it seems, Owens reflected as he walked to the lobby telephone, "This bird has a new wrinkle—now he stops you in the lobby." Owens gingerly picked up the phone and hesitantly said, "This is Owens of Press and Press. Did you call?" Speedy replied, "Yes, and I'm damned busy. What did you want?" In a flash, Owens thought, "What in the hell do you think I want? I want to see you," but he reflected a moment and said:

Mr. Speed, . . .

QUESTIONS

1. Analyze the above case from a problem-solving viewpoint.

2. Then write out four different statements you could make to complete Owens' last statement—"Mr. Speed, . . ."

3. Why do you think the salesman thought and acted as he did?

4. Before long salesmen may be screened in the lobby of a company by television. The television set would be, for example, in the purchasing agent's office. The salesman could see the purchasing agent, and the purchasing agent the salesman. The salesman would be called to the television screen in a lobby booth. Do you see any difference between this situation and the phone situation? Would the salesman use the same tactics? Why? Why not?

CASE 3[16] *James Wentworth, Distributor Salesman* James Wentworth, a young salesman for one of Pratt & Whitney's distributors, was recently promoted to a larger and more difficult territory in recognition of his successful record. The previous salesman for this territory had experienced considerable difficulty due primarily to inefficient sales methods.

On the new salesman's first call at the shop superintendent's office of a

[16] Adapted from Kenneth B. Haas, *Case Problems in Salesmanship*, Prentice-Hall, Inc., Englewood Cliffs, N.J., 1953.

large manufacturer of retail appliances, the "super" began to "pan" the former salesman. He recalled how he never was around when the buyer wanted to see him, how he used high-pressure selling methods, how he made promises that were never kept. The super concluded by saying:

"There must be something wrong with your company when they allow men like that to represent them, don't you think so?"

QUESTIONS

1. Evaluate the attitude of the super.
2. What should the salesman say?
3. Should the salesman view this as an opportunity rather than a problem?
4. Should the salesman "knock" the former salesman?

Chapter 13   DISCUSSION QUESTIONS

1　What is the relationship between the four quarters of the contact stage and the various question forms?

2　How does product knowledge permit a salesman to change direction in the sale?

3　Once the salesman has identified the future course of the sale in the contact stage, does he stay on the same track throughout the sales interview? Why? Why not?

4　In what way does the techniques approach and the removal of sales tension concept differ from the concept of using questions during the contact stage?

5　If the salesman uses a canned or memorized sales talk, is it possible for him to have a problem-solving approach to selling? Why or why not?

6　Explain your answer to question 5 in terms of the problem-solving diagram illustrated in this chapter.

7　What is the relationship between problem solving and decision making?

8　In what way does understanding the decision-making process permit a salesman to sell more effectively to the decision maker?

9　If the salesman has low source credibility, as described in Chapter 10, "The Why and How of Communication," is it possible that this may be one of the major reasons why he may never get into the future quarter of the contact stage?

10　Why in this chapter is the emphasis on problem solving in the contact stage when problem solving is a process that permeates the entire sales interview?

discussion
that
motivates
part one

14

INTRODUCTION

In previous chapters the importance of customer or prospect participation has been emphasized. Obtaining prospect participation was singled
out as one of the most meaningful concepts involved in the customer-
oriented, problem-solving approach to selling. Without customer participation, mental as well as physical, the salesman finds it difficult to sell
effectively. Why? Because only through the exchange of ideas, thoughts,
beliefs, and feelings between salesman and respondent can the salesman
truly adjust his remarks to "strike" the respondent's mind and heart,
thereby enhancing the possibilities of the prospect changing his behavior
pattern if needed.

Further, the complexity of the communication problem was exposed
in Chapter 10, "The Why and How of Communication." That chapter
established the many variables that affect both the salesman's and the
respondent's message sending and listening ability. Both the prospect and
the salesman are concerned with verbal and nonverbal cues from the other.
This difficulty of sending a perfect message and having perfect reception
from a motivational viewpoint is compounded by the fact, as psychologists
tell us, that the shades of human motives run into the millions.

In spite of this, the salesman is interested in these shades of human
motives and during the sales interview, he attempts to obtain cues regarding the other individual motivations—cues that will direct and guide him
in his sales effort. He is not so crass, however, to believe that he can, or
that he needs to, adjust his sales message to embrace all shades of human
motivation. But he must do everything possible to communicate with the
other individual effectively so that he has an opportunity to adjust his
message to best bring about the desired prospect behavior change. The
degree to which a salesman will accomplish this will depend upon the per-

ception, sensitivities, abilities, sets, role sensitivity, tension-binding ability, etc., of both the salesman and the respondent.

Fortunately, even though meaningful two-way communication is difficult, the salesman has a vast array of materials, ideas, and concepts from the behavioral sciences on which to draw for assistance in his sales effort. One of the most profitable areas of assistance to the salesman is the field of general educational psychology.

GENERAL EDUCATIONAL PSYCHOLOGY

Educators are salesmen—or at least they should be. Educators sell ideas and knowledge. The more effective they are as sales purveyors of their knowledge, concepts, and ideas, the more effective they will be as educators.

Educators understand they must have a proper attitude toward teaching. Like the salesman, they should have many qualities, for example, maturity, a high threshold of tension binding, the ability to communicate, and many other qualities as discussed in the behavioral science chapters. But to be most effective, they must want to be educators—they must find it rewarding and fun. They must let the student know they enjoy it. Enthusiasm, as every salesman knows, is contagious.

Educators use a variety of tools, techniques, and principles to exchange ideas or impart information. They are often classified according to which of the following four actions predominate: telling, discussing, showing, performing.

TELLING, EXPLAINING, OR LECTURING

The telling or lecturing method is commonly used in education. In its pure form, it is recognized by one-sided communication. It is the process of an educator telling facts, ideas, concepts, and principles to students. It is a formal discourse about a subject in which the student participates—as a listener.

The lecture method is commonly recognized as one of the weakest ways in which to communicate knowledge. An outstanding lecturer may effectively "educate" by this process; nevertheless, it has many drawbacks.

The greatest failure of the lecture method is its format. It is not designed to involve the student as an active participant. Frequently he becomes a listener and all too frequently a passive one at that.

Just as the lecture method has difficulty for the educator, it has difficulty for the salesman and even more so. The educator has a captive audience. Students are more or less required to listen. If the student doesn't listen, he may fail a future examination. Not so with the salesman as an educator. His prospect or customer not only is not required to listen but, in most cases, is inclined not to listen effectively.

The lecture method can be compared to the stimulus-response or canned sales talk. The salesman does most of the talking. He engages in one-way communication with all its obvious disadvantages.

Discussion That Motivates: Part One

DISCUSSION

The discussion method is widely used by educators. In contrast to the lecture method, the discussion method is considered by many educators to be an ideal educational tool. The discussion method is sometimes referred to as a conference-type activity. It includes all those activities which tend to develop an interchange of ideas between the instructor and students and between the students themselves. A mutual interchange of experience and thoughts takes place with the objective being the solution of a problem or the development of a logical conclusion.

Discussion, with all of its implications and with all its educational tools, principles, ideas and concepts, is one of the most distinguishing features of depth selling. This is the approach to selling that every salesman must use in the new world of selling.

SHOWING OR DEMONSTRATING

Most salesmen use visuals of one form or another such as brochures, models, portfolios, films, flip charts, etc. This is important, since the old adage you have to "show to sell" is well grounded in psychological fact. Psychologists have shown that on the averge people remember 10 percent of what they hear, 50 percent of what they do, and 90 percent of what they see and *participate* in. There is considerable discussion regarding these percentages since learning is difficult to measure; nevertheless, the comparison clearly illustrates the importance of seeing and doing. It is only logical then that if the individual gets impressions, understanding, and learning through the eyes and through doing to the extent they do, the salesman should use visualization and participation as tools to reinforce verbal discussion. Research shows that visuals promote both mental and physical participation, center and keep the prospect's attention, and increase the prospect's confidence in what the salesman is saying. Proof or hard facts in visual form make it easier for the customer to understand the proposal presented by the salesman; it makes the situation tangible in the mind of the buyer; and it gives the salesman an opportunity to break the monotony of the sale and put forceful action into it.

Showing or demonstrating is always accompanied by telling or explaining. To the sales trainer, as an educator, a demonstration may be used to show various contact methods, to indicate where the salesman should sit, to show how visual materials may be used, to show the various ways a salesman should use a pen or pencil during an interview, or any one of numerous other sales techniques. The showing or demonstration method portrays actual procedures and operation of a particular technique or sales tool. It may, for instance, center attention on the actual manipulation of a model in some sales demonstrations. Demonstrations give meaning to facts and thus help prospects understand the salesman's proposal.

Whenever a salesman has a tangible product to sell, he is actively engaged in showing or demonstrating the properties of the product to the prospect. For instance, whenever the industrial salesman demonstrates a Tape-O-Matic, a Kellering machine, gauges or cutting tools, he is vividly

Selling: A Behavioral Science Approach

proving the quality of his company's products. He is proving how and why they will do the job. He is presenting hard facts. They can't be denied.[1]

A demonstration of any product must, if possible, always be associated with the potential user's needs. Thus, the salesman shows not only how his product operates, but he must be alert to every possible relationship between the product being demonstrated and the user's total situation—his total production or equipment needs, his finance plans, his tax situation, his profit situation, his depreciation needs, and in fact the state of business conditions in general. In a nutshell, he should be alert to any pertinent fact or sales mix that will facilitate the sale.

Alert is a key word for a salesman to remember when showing or demonstrating. A demonstration is only one sales tool to be used advantageously. The salesman must get feedback. He must communicate—he shouldn't just lecture. He shouldn't just show, but he should have a participating demonstration both mentally and physically with the potential user. Herein lies another basic selling point: There is no difference between selling a tangible and an intangible product if the salesman accepts the theory that the whole idea in selling is to make his proposal tangible in the mind of the buyer. The best advice for the salesman is don't develop "functional fixedness" and become a demonstrator.

Dialogue Illustration of Demonstrations

This actual case as it happened at Detroit's 1964 national convention for the American Society of Tool and Manufacturers Engineers will illustrate the ineffectiveness of a one-sided demonstration. At the company booth of a well-known industrial manufacturer, one sales engineer was effectively demonstrating how his company's automated machines machined various forms of pieces of steel. About every half hour he began a new lecture combined with a demonstration showing how the machine functioned. He would put a block of steel in place, adjust the various instruments, program instructions into the machine, push a button, and the machine began to operate. At most demonstrations he had a good audience. During the second day of the convention the national sales manager of the company watched the sales engineer demonstrate this automated piece of equipment. After the demonstration, the following discussion took place:

NSM   *National Sales Manager*
SE   *Sales Engineer*

NSM   That's a mighty fine demonstration, Jim.
SE   Thanks, Frank. The people seem to enjoy it. Getting pretty good crowds as you see.
NEM   Yes, indeed. But do you think there is any way that we could make your demonstrations even more effective?
SE   I suppose so, but what did you have in mind?
NSM   Your question is the answer—use questions. It sounds pretty simple, but that's what I have in mind. For instance, do you think if you, prior to giv-

[1] Joseph W. Thompson, *Pratt & Whitney Distributor Manpower Development Program,* Pratt & Whitney Corp., Inc., West Hartford, Conn., 1965, p. 26.

Discussion That Motivates: Part One

ing the demonstration, talked to a few of the men who stopped by to see the demonstrations about the type of steel, etc., they are using in their machine shop operations and also got them to ask a few more questions about the machine, your demonstration might be even more effective from a sales stand-point? In brief, I'm asking you to get the participation of the viewers in any way you can. You think about it and I'll stop by and check with you on it in a few hours.

This is what the national sales manager heard the next time he watched a demonstration.

SE (*Stepping out a pace or two from his machine, and extending his hand to a Mr. Johnson—each man attending the convention was issued a badge which stated his name and company in large print—and looking at the badge.*) Let's see, you are Mr. Johnson of the Cubular Rivet Company. Let's see, that's in . . .

P Jamestown, Ohio.

SE Oh, yes, Mr. Johnson. What kind of work are you doing in your plant at the present time?

P Oh, actually we are doing a lot of deck engine work.

SE Any particular type of deck engine work?

P Yes, we are actually building the deck engines from the castings up.

SE (*Turning to another viewer, the sales engineer quickly asked the same type questions. By this time there was a fair-size group watching and listening to the conversation. He turned to the group.*) Gentlemen, I have quite a few different sizes of blocks and shapes of steel here. Would anybody like to pick out one that resembles the type of work he is doing in his plant now? (*About eight to ten of the viewers looked over at the steel blocks and one man said, "What about this one here?" Pretty soon the men were talking back and forth about the type of work they were doing in their plants.*)

All right, we will work on this one. (*Then he quickly explained how to program the machine with tape and how simple it was. Before he began the operation, however, he turned to the group.*)

Are there any particular questions at this moment? (*He answered a few questions and after about five minutes of cutting, he stopped the machine and turned to the gentleman, who had selected the piece of steel.*)

Mr. Smith, what did you say your major work in your plant is at this time?

P We are doing a lot of machining for one of the large new jet fighters. It is a government contract.

SE I see, pretty rigid specifications then.

P Yes, everything's got to be in the range of very close tolerances.

SE What do you think about the operation of this machine, as it applies. to the type of work you are doing now?

After this customer-oriented demonstration, the national sales manager approached the sales engineer and said, "It's pretty obvious, Jim. You don't need me around here at all."

Dialogue Illustrations (continued)

As a further example, this is how a salesman selling an intangible—

Selling: A Behavioral Science Approach

his hotel accommodations and services—might demonstrate his product. The first example, "the cultural growth of the family" concept is a continuation of the case presented in the contact stage (see Chapter 13), and the second dialogue shows how the same salesman could demonstrate his product—his hotel—as the site for a convention. A third dialogue illustrates a demonstration of the intangible aspect of a proposal by the office furniture salesman—whose product is a tangible. The ideas presented in the following three dialogues plus the demonstration dialogue previously given can be employed by most salesmen whether they are selling a tangible or an intangible.

DIALOGUE EXCERPT *Cultural Growth of the Family through Dining Out*
S Yes, Mr. Owens, we have different price ranges for the different dining rooms. Although there is an overlap in prices between the dining rooms, there are three distinct general price levels. Here in dining room A . . . (*Salesman points to the picture of dining room A. This is the use of the visual. Or if the salesman wishes to put more showmanship and color into his visuals, he may through preparation show the prospect special models or images of a factory, which could be placed at tables where the company employees would be dining. Or he could show pictures of a specially designed dessert for company employees.*)

DIALOGUE EXCERPT *Selling a Hotel as a Convention Site for a Business Meeting*
S Mr. Davis, you mentioned that you will be having a number of brainstorming sessions during the conference part of the convention. Do you think this conference room (*shows a picture of special conference room*) would be suitable for this session?
C It looks unique, especially with that beamed structure.
S Yes, and I had in mind that we could place a series of large pictures on the wall, depicting man's progress through the ages. It sounds appropriate to me for the creative thinking or brainstorming session, and I know we have them at the hotel.
C Good idea. It surely would lend atmosphere.

DIALOGUE EXCERPT *Office Furniture Sale*
S Mr. Turner, each office we have designed for you was actually set up in our display area and analyzed with these questions in mind. Page 4 of our survey shows the result of that testing. (*Use of the visual. Whenever a salesman uses visual materials, they must be handled like any demonstration. The visual materials must be used in such a way that the ideas that are contained therein can be interpreted in terms of buyers' business needs.*)
S This cutaway of the seat will clearly show the six-way construction involved. (*Use of model or cutout.*)

PERFORMANCE

Utilizing the performance method, the educator allows the student to learn by doing. He performs. The performance method is usually preceded by telling and showing and is accompanied by explaining and more showing for some students. The salesman utilizes the performance concept by actually having the prospect write out some figures, for example, his interpretation of figures with respect to cost. But like the educator, the salesman should first engage in telling, discussing, or showing the prospect some of the cost factors which he wants the prospect to write out or perform. Not only does the prospect obtain a better understanding of the cost factors involved, but the salesman has an excellent occasion to evaluate the prospect's comprehension or understanding.

In each of the educational methods—telling, discussion, showing, and participating—the educator realizes the student learns by participation. He learns through his eyes, ears, voice, motor skills (writing), or his sense of touch, taste, and smell (in some cases).

Generally the educator may best educate by appealing to all of the learners' senses. Thus, whenever possible, the educator uses visuals—films, flip charts—to present ideas. He uses reading materials. He uses a blackboard. He has the student write out material whenever appropriate. He discusses. He asks questions. He gets the individual involved.

From long experience the educator knows that by using the discussion method he may combine all the educational techniques which permit him to convey his ideas easily to the students and to receive ideas from them in like manner. This is education. It is *precisely* what the salesman does in discussions with the prospect or customer. Now to examine the educator's use of questions. Question forms are among the most versatile and effective tools in the educator's arsenal. This statement applies equally well to selling.

THE ART OF QUESTIONING—THE COMMON DENOMINATOR OF EDUCATION AND SELLING

Introduction

During the first few minutes of the contact stage, verifying questions are used by the salesman to test the accuracy of the salesman's knowledge concerning the prospect or his company. Permissive questions may be employed at this time as a way to request permission to ask questions.

In selling, just as in education, questions must be asked at the right time. In education they must be used to guide and control the development of the topic, subject, or philosophy that is being discussed. In selling they must be used to guide and control the development of the sales situation. To the salesman, the main test of a good question is the extent to which it helps to attain his objective in each sales call.

As previous dialogue examples show, verifying and permissive question forms were asked at the right time in the contact stage and were used to guide and control the development of the sale. The direction and future of the sale is determined by the prospect's or customer's responses to the salesman's verification and permissive questions.

On the other hand, questions utilized in the discussion phase of selling are more developmental in nature than those asked in the contact phase. But in each phase or stage of selling, a question must be selected,

Selling: A Behavioral Science Approach

worded, and used according to the purpose the salesman has in asking it. In the discussion phase questions are mobilized to:

1. Obtain greater prospect mental attention
2. Increase and intensify prospect mental interest
3. Open discussion about a subject
4. Provoke thinking about a subject, idea, or concept
5. Accumulate data in the form of the prospect's ideas, concepts, thoughts, and facts
6. Assist the salesman and prospect to arrive at conclusions
7. Develop further discussion of a subject
8. Direct the prospect's observation
9. Change discussion trends
10. Obtain prospect's participation
11. Evaluate the prospect

Developmental and Evaluative Questions

In developmental questions the salesman uses how, why, and what. These are questions which open discussion, provoke thinking, assist in developing a subject, obtain continuous prospect mental attention, and even intensify prospect interest. Evaluative questions permit the salesman to accumulate data, facts, ideas, and concepts; to arrive at conclusions; to direct observations; and to change discussion trends.

There is no absolute, well-defined line identifying developmental questions and evaluative questions. The purpose, the characteristics, the flavor, the properties, and the features truly overlap just as the circles in the stages of the sale overlap. Nevertheless, a useful purpose is served by drawing some distinction between developmental questions and evaluative questions.

The greatest difference between developmental and valuative questions is this: Developmental questions do not beg a yes or no answer. It is difficult for the prospect or customer to reply to a how or why with a word. On the other hand, the greatest area of common bond between developmental questions and evaluative questions is that both obtain greater prospect participation.

Moreover, used in combination, both question forms tell the salesman where he is going and how to get there. Evaluative and developmental questions are the salesman's compass and sales map. When the individual takes an automobile or private plane trip across the country he uses a map and compass. He uses them in combination to check direction, to verify landmarks, and to check location and progress with respect to time and distance. In selling, the salesman must know where he is at all times, know where he is going and then make frequent use of questions to find out whether or not he is getting there.

Developmental questions illustrated Dialogue A reviews the use of permissive and verification questions in the contact stage. Dialogue B illustrates variations in developmental questions and how these variations are designed to accomplish the purposes of developmental questions, that

Discussion That Motivates: Part One

is, to open discussions, promote thinking, to develop a subject, to obtain further attention and to intensify interest.

S *Salesman*

R *Respondent*

DIALOGUE A *Industrial Distributor Salesman*

S Good morning, Mr. Jones. I'm Tom Hunt of Block & Block.

R Yes, come on in.

S A beautiful day, isn't it?

R Yes, it is. It is very nice.

S Mr. Jones, I appreciate having this opportunity to see you.

R It's all right. What's on your mind?

S Block and Block, Mr. Jones, and how we may be of assistance to you in your present drilling needs. However, I will need some general information from you to see how and, for that matter, whether or not we can be of assistance. With this idea in mind, (1) may I ask you a few questions about the type of steel you are now using and the tolerance needed in your drilling operations?

R All right. Well, yes. Go ahead.

S (2) First I should ask you if you have heard about the new diamond point drills?

In Dialogue A, Tom Hunt used a permissive question, (1) "May I ask you a few questions about the type of steel you are now using and the tolerances needed in your drilling operations?" This was followed by a verification question, (2) "First I should ask you if you have heard about the new diamond point drills?"

Question 1 asks permission to ask questions. Question 2 tells the salesman whether or not the prospect is knowledgeable about diamond point drills. From his planning work or experience, he was reasonably sure the prospect was familiar with the drills. However, before talking drills and relating diamond point drills to the prospect's problems, salesman Hunt decided to verify his information.

DIALOGUE B *Blue Cross–Blue Shield Salesman*

S Good morning. It's a pleasure to meet you, Mr. Arnold. I am Frank Hill and I want to thank you for seeing me as a sales representative of Blue Cross–Blue Shield.

R That's OK. Sit down, won't you?

S Thank you. This is quite a comfortable chair, isn't it?

R Yes, I have always believed in a relaxed sort of feeling and these big chairs give it, I believe.

S They do indeed. But I don't want to become so relaxed that I don't get into the purpose of this call. You are busy, so I will come right to the point. It is this: If it is to your advantage to do so, we at Blue Cross–Blue Shield are anxious to have you consider starting the Blue Cross–Blue Shield program in your plant. But before we can discuss whether or not it is to your advantage, Mr. Arnold, (3) it would be helpful if I could ask you a few questions about your present employee benefits program?

R I don't see why you can't. I believe we have it published in one of our pamphlets, but go ahead.

Selling: A Behavioral Science Approach

S (4) Do you at the present time have some type of medical care program for your employees?

R Yes, we do—a fairly substantial one.

S Off hand, Mr. Arnold, (5) what are some of the major benefits for your employees under your present medical care program?

R As I mentioned, it is rather comprehensive. Some of the major benefits are . . .

In Dialogue B point 3 is a permissive question. Frank Hill's ". . . it would be helpful if I could ask you a few questions about your present employee benefits program?" is requesting permission or getting an indication from Mr. Arnold to continue the sales discussion and ask questions. With question 4 Hill is verifying whether or not Arnold's company has a medical care program for its employees. Hill is verifying information he has about the company to be sure that he is on the right track. These two questions are clearly in the contact stage.

With question 5, however, salesman Frank Hill makes a transition from the contact stage and establishes the future perimeter of the sale. Question 5 is clearly a developmental question. Why? Because it is marked by a how or why concept. It does not beg a yes or no answer. It provokes thinking and begins to develop a subject of substantial interest to the prospect. The prospect is describing his medical program to the salesman. He is talking. He is participating. The discussion has his mental attention.

DIALOGUE C *Industrial Distributor Salesman Regular Customer Call*

S It's good to see you, Mr. Kravis, and I want to thank you for giving me this opportunity to discuss Hunt and Hunt's gauge analysis program with you.

R Sit down. And yes, I appreciate your coming.

S Thank you, Mr. Kravis. (1) I hope it isn't too presumptuous of me to ask you whether you have had time to read the brochure describing Hunt and Hunt's gauge analysis program that I sent to you?

R Yes, I took time to look at it and found it rather interesting.

S That is good to hear. (2) What were some of the ideas in the program that seemed worthwhile to you?

Dialogue C tells of a salesman who sent the prospect, Mr. Kravis, a brochure describing his company's gauge analysis program and who later called to make an appointment. He is now making a personal call on the prospect.

This salesman, in contrast to all our previous dialogue situations, is starting his questioning series with a clear example of the verification type question. There is no doubt that he is verifying whether or not the prospect has had time to read the brochure (1). And in Dialogue C, in contrast to Dialogues A and B, the salesman is omitting the permissive-type question and forging directly into his sales talk.

Even though this salesman has moved rapidly into the last part of the contact stage, his discussion represents good communication. His questions are entirely appropriate in view of the circumstances and the prospect's reception. It is seen, too, that the salesman is courteous by his, "I hope it isn't too presumptuous . . ."

The succeeding question (2) "What were some of the ideas in the

Discussion That Motivates: Part One

program that seemed worthwhile to you?" is solely a developmental question. This question promotes discussion, promotes thinking, and develops a subject. The interest-getting qualities of the question are evident.

Evaluative questions illustrated   To review, evaluative questions have been designated as those questions which assist the salesman in ascertaining the prospect's viewpoint or understanding of statements, facts, ideas, or opinions expressed by the salesman during the sale. Through evaluative questions the salesman can specifically question the prospect's or customer's understanding, feelings, or opinion regarding an idea that the salesman has presented.

Evaluative questions also serve the purpose of accumulating data, arriving at conclusions, directing observations, and changing discussion trends. But again the *primary function* of the evaluative question is to get the prospect's or customer's reaction to the salesman's comments.

In Dialogues C and D, a specific statement or idea expressed will point out this function of evaluative questions, but the salesman must be aware that evaluation by questions does not necessarily give him a total interpretation or analysis of the prospect's reaction or emotions at the moment. Evaluative questions are most effectively used as analytical tools when they are used hand in hand with personal observations of the prospect. This will be discussed after Dialogues C and D have been analyzed.

DIALOGUE C (continued)

S   That is good to hear, Mr. Kravis. What were some of the major concepts in the gauge analysis program that seemed worthwhile to you?

R   One thing that surprised me is your idea to use a team to analyze a company's gauge problems and that you then present a complete gauging program for a customer.

S   Yes, Mr. Kravis, that viewpoint is shared by many other business executives. But here is how it is done. This chart gives the entire sequence in step-by-step form. Here, . . .

R   Well, that's something.

S   Etc.

R   Etc.

S   Mr. Kravis, (1) have I made clear that the automatic gauging combinations can be varied and adjusted to give each industrial firm the specific automatic control of each process they need and thus become more fully automated?

OR

Assume that during the discussion Kravis asked the salesman: "How can the Air-O-Matic gauging system be used in conjunction with a boring transfer machine?"

After explaining how this can be done, the salesman uses the evaluative question by asking: "Have I adequately answered the question, Mr. Kravis?"

DIALOGUE D

The reader is asked to visualize a Blue Cross–Blue Shield sales situation in which the salesman is explaining that under Blue Cross–Blue Shield's new health care program, each company can have almost any

248

Selling: A Behavioral Science Approach

combination program it desires. In brief, the programs will be tailored to fit the needs of the prospective business firms. After the salesman's discussion, the prospect comments, "Uh huh!"

The salesman uses an evaluative question by asking:

S   Mr. Arnold, have I made clear that Blue Cross–Blue Shield has numerous health care combinations and that these combinations can be varied and adjusted to give each industrial firm the specific health care program they desire?

Or if after replying to a prospect's question, he wants to determine the effectiveness of his answer, he uses an evaluative question when he merely asks:

S   Have I adequately answered your question concerning tailored benefits, Mr. Arnold?

In these examples, the salesman is evaluating whether or not he has made an adequate explanation to the prospect. He is asking the prospect a specific question regarding the quality of his explanation and whether or not the prospect has understood.

The Concept of Burden

Besides the evaluative qualities, a unique and very important concept is found in the evaluative questions. It is the concept of *burden*. The salesman has assumed the burden of understanding. He asked the prospect, "Have I (the salesman) adequately answered your questions?" or "Have I adequately explained the X concept?" or ". . . have I made clear?" He has not said, "Do you understand?" or "Do you follow me?" or "Do you see?"

Where is the burden if the salesman asks, "Do you understand?" "Do you follow me?" or "Do you see?" What is implied to the prospect in these three statements? The implication is clear. If the prospect doesn't understand, he is short on mental agility. Each individual is reluctant to admit that he does not understand something that has been explained to him. This is evident to the experienced educator who knows he seldom will have a discussion from the students if he puts the burden of understanding on the students. This is especially true if the question concerning understanding is directed to a specific student rather than the group.

Other evaluative questions commonly used in error are:

"See my point?"
"Isn't that true?"
"Simple, isn't it?"
"Right?"
"That's obvious, isn't it?"
"Do you get what I mean?"
"You agree, don't you?"

Compare the seven negative evaluation questions above with the concept of burden as illustrated in the positive evaluative question, "Have I made this clear?" and to such related questions as:

"What do you think of this idea?"

Discussion That Motivates: Part One

"Is my assumption correct, Mr. Jones?"
"Have I answered your question, Mr. Smith?"
"Have I adequately explained the X concept, Mr. Hogen?"
"Let's see if we get the same results?"
"Have I omitted anything?"
"Is there anything I didn't cover?"

The next series of brief monologues and dialogues show how evaluative questions or development questions are used to direct observation, to change discussion trends, to accumulate data, and to arrive at conclusions.

To direct the *prospect's observation,* the salesman emphasizes a specific point previously discussed. He asks, for instance, "What do you think of the tailored program idea, Mr. Smith?"

By means of selective questions, discussion may be shifted from one topic to another the salesman wishes to explore, or in some cases discussion moves away from an area the salesman does not wish to discuss further. A situation where the salesman is discussing, for instance, the specific production capabilities of his machine and he believes it would be wise to move on to another topic provides a good example of the shift of subject. He may inquire, "Mr. Kravis, many executives tell us they are especially pleased with the flexibility in set-up time of the Tape-O-Matic. Does the flexibility feature seem of particular interest to you?"

The salesman may arrive at conclusions by asking a question such as "Do you think the automatic gauging system for your machines X, X^1, X^2, and X^3 will give you the controls you want toward your automation?"

Finally, accumulating data is accomplished whenever the salesman requests quantitative information from the prospect. He does this by inquiring:

S   Mr. Kravis, from our previous discussion am I right in assuming that your machine shop produced around 4 million dollars in orders last year?
R   More or less.
S   In producing these orders, Mr. Kravis, what was the approximate hourly usage of your machining equipment?
R   About six hours per day.
S   That is a lot of floor time. How does that compare to your milling equipment?
R   Etc.

EVALUATION BY OBSERVATION[2]

In the previous discussion the salesman evaluated the interview by developmental questions and evaluative questions. Pure developmental questions expanded the scope of the prospect's discussion, especially with the "how" and "why" question forms. Evaluative questions were used to

---

[2] The general approach followed in this section, especially the diagram illustrating various positive and negative responses of the prospect or customer, was stimulated by Harold C. Cash and W. J. E. Crissy's chapter "Tactics for Conducting the Sales Call," in *The Psychology of Selling,* vol. 5, Personnel Development Associates, Station A, Flushing, New York, 1962.

Selling: A Behavioral Science Approach

reveal subtly the prospect's understanding or reaction to sales points made by the salesman.

Nonverbal Behavior Activities

What the prospect or customer says is tempered by the tone of his voice and his physical responses (nonverbal behavior activities). The emphasis here is on the nonverbal, not the verbal, responses of the prospect. See the appendix of this chapter for a more complete work sheet based on both verbal and nonverbal prospect reactions.

TABLE 4   Nonverbal Behavior Activities[3]

Awareness level	Positive cues		Negative cues	
Voluntary (conscious)	a. b. c. d.	(Block 1)	a. b. c. d.	(Block 3)
Involuntary (subconscious)	a. b. c. d.	(Block 2)	a. b. c. d.	(Block 4)

By and large, Table 4 is concerned with nonverbal prospect responses. However, at times, for clearer explanation reference is made to verbal responses.

The positive and negative cues in the analysis refer to the customer's statements and his actions. The customer may make positive statements, or he may make negative statements; he may have a positive attitude, or he may have a negative attitude. The voluntary and involuntary parts of the table refer to the idea that the positive or negative statements, or the positive or negative actions, of a prospect may be voluntary (consciously known) or they may be involuntary (unconscious or subconscious).

Block 1 represents those activities or behavior patterns which are positive-voluntary. Voluntary behavior patterns are those reactions which are consciously made by the prospect. These reactions or behavior patterns tell the salesman he is making contact in the communication process. He is striking the mind of the respondent, and the respondent is consciously letting the salesman know it.

Block 2 pertains to those behavior patterns or reactions classified as

---

[3] A more elaborate form for the analysis of verbal and nonverbal cues is given on page 256 in this chapter.

positive-involuntary. These reactions tell the salesman he is making contact and that he is striking the mind of the respondent, but the respondent is not deliberately projecting this message or image to the salesman.

Block 3 refers to those behavior activities or reactions classified as negative-voluntary. In this situation the respondent wants the salesman to know that he hasn't "zeroed" in. The salesman isn't striking the mind of the prospect.

Block 4, negative-involuntary, represents those behavior patterns or reactions which tell the salesman he is not making progress in the sale; however, the respondent may not intend to convey this image or message to the salesman.

A word of caution Before determining ways in which the analysis above can be used to define the sales process and thereby develop an effective interaction between salesman and respondent, a word of caution.

The above approach to reaction or behavior pattern analysis is subjective; the effectiveness of the analysis is in the "eyes of the beholder." It depends on his perception, judgment, maturity, or in general, his adjustment to life. Obviously, if, for example, a branch manager and a salesman were to make a joint call on a prospect or customer, their evaluation of the prospect's behavior pattern or reaction may differ somewhat.

Nevertheless, this does not detract from the usefulness of this form of analysis. Compare this analysis by observation with the question process presented in the contact and discussion phases of the sale. Surely there is some difference of opinion as to how, when, and where the various question types could be used, but this does not detract or limit their usefulness. From the author's research, the majority of more than 500 salesmen believe that an analysis of the question approach sharpens the perception of their roles in selling, and the question approach enables them to be more flexible and adaptive to various situations.

Without repeating the analysis of the individual as given in the behavioral science chapters, it is known that the more aggressive salesman will interpret the prospect's reactions or behavior patterns and statements more positively, whereas the less aggressive salesman will interpret or classify reactions less positively. Looking at it another way, the optomistically inclined individual is liable to place a greater positive value on positive-voluntary reactions than will the more cautious salesman. Thus each salesman must appraise, identify, or assess his own personal adjustment to life and temper his evaluations of the respondent's behavior patterns in view of his own perceptual and emotional framework. An individual must first know himself and thereby gain insights into the behavior patterns of others.

For instance, how sensitive is a salesman to varying social situations? The more sensitive each salesman is to happenings in these situations (the interaction between individuals and between the individual and the group), the more sensitive he will be to cues or behavior activities or other individuals. He doesn't judge, he adjusts.

Another example for consideration: A salesman, while talking to an individual, notes that the individual frequently refers to his watch. What

252

cues should the salesman get from this? Should he stop talking and tell the individual, "You must be in a hurry, and I will, therefore, move on." Or should he interpret this as just a mannerism, and think, "What I am saying is too important for some individual not to be interested in." Or would he regard this as merely one more cue that must be considered as part of the total situation? If the salesman is talking about the merits of his product and the individual prospect picks up the phone and calls someone on what appears to be a minor call, or if he fidgets unnecessarily, or nervously "works" paper on his desk, what should these cues tell the sensitive salesman? Should he be hurt and leave, or should he adjust his sales talk. If he decides to adjust his sales talk, how should he do it?

One of the purposes of this book is to present material to the salesman as a guideline to assess his own behavior patterns as well as that of the respondent, and to make the necessary adjustments. The more obvious the changing behavior pattern of the other individual is, the easier it is to discern or identify. The more subtle the changing behavior pattern is, the more difficult it is to discern. For instance, it is quite easy to determine the difference in music notes when the difference is great, but the finer the shadings of differences, the greater the difficulty of identification. The knowledgeable, sensitive person in the field of music, however, would discern the note differences easily.

As a case in point, what tactics should be used when the salesman recognizes a reaction he classifies as negative-involuntary, such as doodling, rearranging items on a desk, looking out the window, slight negative nodding of the head, frowning, turning away? If the cue is missed by the salesman and he continues along the same pattern, the respondent's reactions may move to negative-voluntary. If the salesman receives a cue and shifts subtly to points of greater prospect interest, the prospect reaction may become positive-involuntary or even positive-voluntary.

Note that the requirement in this situation is to shift subtly. Salesmen have a tendency to shift their tactics abruptly when faced with a negative-involuntary reaction. Frequently he brings new and perhaps more powerful sales ammunition to bear on the situation, only to miss completely. Had he shifted slightly in his approach to an area of mutual interest, he might have more readily sustained the prospect's mental interest.

The analysis above provides some general connotations and cautions on handling various situations. Now attention is turned to a more specific analysis of each block of reactions: positive-voluntary, positive-involuntary, negative-voluntary, and negative-involuntary.

Tactics for Positive-Voluntary and Positive-Involuntary Behavior Patterns

Perhaps the most voluntary positive statement the individual can make is "Yes, let's go ahead." Right here the salesman has made the sale. It probably is the last positive-voluntary statement of a series of such statements or behavior activities the respondent has made in the discussion from contact to the completion of negotiations. But it is the end, and the salesman should stop talking. He shouldn't let the flush of accomplishment carry him on to a talking marathon and talk himself out of a sale. This can happen, as many salesmen know.

This same flush of accomplishment can occur when the prospect sends a series of positive-voluntary reactions during the sale. These signs may so stimulate the salesman that he talks on and on and exhausts a particular sales point. Or he may raise points that aren't pertinent, or that may raise a doubt, and the prospect could be talked out of a sale. The more observant salesman may have tried a trial dose during the series of voluntary positive reactions.

Four positive-voluntary signals or cues are listed below. What should the salesman do in each case?

1. The prospect takes notes.
2. The prospect nods his head affirmatively at the right time.
3. The prospect leans forward or moves closer to a visual the salesman may be showing.
4. The prospect has a general facial expression that denotes alertness and interest in the discussion.

In the case of positive-involuntary behavior patterns, the respondent is unaware of his responses to stimuli. The salesman wants to reinforce the stimuli that developed the positive response, and so his strategy is to continue along the same path.

An example of this is a salesman selling Smith-Corona electric typewriters to an office manager. The manager states, "Well, you have a good typewriter, but I can buy for a lot less at a discount house." This isn't new to the experienced salesman Davis, who replies easily, "Yes, you can, Mr. Morgan, but there may be a few other facts that are important to you. We don't sell out of boxes. We are a typewriter company, so we take each typewriter out of the box and give it a complete check-out before we deliver. When we deliver you can be assured that all the keys and the electric mechanism are perfectly synchronized."

At about this time a slight smile appears on Mr. Morgan's face. Because salesman Davis notes this positive-involuntary reaction, he continues with "And, Mr. Morgan, we give a full year's guarantee including free maintenance." Now, Davis notes a slight nodding of Morgan's head coupled with a more understanding look and slightly increased smile. He continues: "Mr. Morgan, just in case you were to have a mechanical failure when important correspondence or invoices or orders had to be typed, you would have to wait for the other seller's machine to be sent to a branch office and back. It would take a month, perhaps six weeks, but we could deliver another machine to you as quickly as you call us and at no cost either."

"You have a real point there that is pretty important," Morgan comments.

"Well, thank you, Mr. Morgan," Davis states, as he now notes that Morgan's whole demeanor is in keeping with his positive-voluntary verbal statement. What does Davis do? If he is alert he uses a trial close. That's selling!

Tactics for Negative-Involuntary Behavior Patterns

Negative-involuntary reactions are unconscious behavior mechanisms of the prospect. They are the result of the interreaction between salesman and prospect and are unconscious behavior activities by the prospect. They are more subtle negative responses than are voluntary negative reactions.

Negative-involuntary reactions are frequently seen in the sales interview. Examples are the prospect who glances at his nails, looks out the window, watches a fly zoom around the room, fidgets, makes an unnecessary phone call, doodles excessively, or glances at his watch frequently. Other things being equal it is obvious the salesman is not making progress. In fact he is probably losing ground. But the prospect does not yet openly, consciously, or intentionally express his disinterest or disapproval.

These cues tell the salesman to change sales points. If, for example, an industrial salesman is calling on the manager of a medium-size business and he observes, as he is explaining some concepts basic to understanding numeric control, that the prospect's reaction is negative-involuntary, he will quickly, but easily, shift gears. He may change to the idea or the concept of how the small machine shop could advantageously use numeric controls.

Tactics for Negative-Voluntary Behavior Patterns

The difference between negative-voluntary and negative-involuntary behavior patterns, like differences in positive-voluntary and positive-involuntary behavior patterns, is a matter of degree. But whenever the salesman doesn't adjust to negative-involuntary cues, this frequently leads to the negative-voluntary action and statement, "No, I am not interested, and I just don't have any more time to talk about it."

What to do must be preceded by an analysis of why the *negative-voluntary* reaction developed. If the salesman continues along the same track that brought about a minor negative-involuntary reaction, a voluntary negative reaction could develop. Obviously it is common sense to note the minor negative-involuntary reaction and adjust rather than permit the negative-voluntary situation to develop.

USE OF INDIRECT QUESTIONING

Many times a sales representative must interrogate the prospect if he is to discover personal yet important information about the prospect or the company he represents. Throughout the interview the salesman should judiciously use the questioning process. But if he is attempting to discover the financial position of the company or the prospect's image of himself, his code of ethics or his attitude concerning an employee, the salesman must exercise extreme care in the questioning process. He should not use direct questioning to obtain what the prospect might regard as personal information.

Indirect questioning is the process of asking questions in such a way

Discussion That Motivates: Part One

that the individual being questioned is placed in the safe position of giving the views of others rather than his own. The salesman, however, interprets the things the prospect says as a reflection of his own viewpoint.

This form of questioning is seen in the following monologue. Assume that a health insurance salesman wants to get some perspective about the personnel director's feelings concerning unions and their particular health plans. During the interview with the personnel director he might use indirect questioning in this manner:

S   Mr. Lewis, I know you are in contact with personnel directors of other large companies, and I wonder what they say about union health care programs in general? That is, how do they seem to feel about union health care programs?

With direct questioning it seems safe to say that the salesman will get less honest answers than when he uses indirection. Surely the prospect's replies to indirect questioning may be more realistic than to the direct question. He can express more openly his true view, since he in a sense is saying, "These are the views of someone else." In fact, the use of "someone else" may permit the prospect to unleash some of the bitter feelings he may have about some situation. This relates to the concept of ventilation, as discussed in the behavioral science chapters of this book.

The unleashing of the prospect's true feeling may permit the salesman to get to the real core of the reason why the prospect may not buy. This concept will become clear through the analysis of the following sales situations.

A salesman who sells automated equipment wants to get some perspective about an executive's feelings concerning unions, automation, and men being replaced by machines. He might interrogate or use indirection in this manner:

S   Mr. Lewis, I am sure that from time to time you have talked to other executives about automation and resultant manpower replacement and perhaps even problems with unions because of this.

C   It's kind of a problem.

S   I'd appreciate it, Mr. Lewis, if you could give me an idea of what other executives around the country are talking about with respect to this problem.

OR

S   Mr. Lewis, in your association with other businessmen, I suspect you talk about general business conditions and how the automotive industry is going to fare in the country.

C   Yes, we take a go at that from time to time.

S   From the tenor of these discussions what would you say executives in the Detroit area are thinking?

Compare the dialogue above with a direct approach:

S   Mr. Lewis, what is your opinion of unions with respect to automation?

OR

S   What view do you and other executives of your company have with regard to future business conditions?

Selling: A Behavioral Science Approach

TABLE 5 **Analysis Work Sheet for Examples of Respondent Reactions, Verbal and Nonverbal**

Awareness level	Positive	Negative
Voluntary (conscious)	Verbal cues 1. 2. 3. 4.	Verbal cues 1. 2. 3. 4.
	Nonverbal behavior cues 1. 2. 3. 4. (Block 1)	Nonverbal behavior cues 1. 2. 3. 4. (Block 3)
Involuntary (unconscious)	Verbal cues 1. 2. 3. 4.	Verbal cues 1. 2. 3. 4.
	Nonverbal behavior cues 1. 2. 3. 4. (Block 2)	Nonverbal behavior cues 1. 2. 3. 4. (Block 4)

Summary

Discussions that motivate effectively and advantageously from a sales perspective must be customer-oriented. In addition, the discussion must be so structured that it appeals to the status needs of the individual. Good discussion is a complex problem as numerous variables affect both the salesman's and the respondent's message-sending and -listening ability. Both the salesman and the respondent are concerned with verbal and non-verbal cues from the other. Thus sending a perfect message and having a perfect reception from a motivational concept is a complex matter. Nevertheless, there is much the salesman can do so that his discussion with the prospect will motivate. One of the most profitable areas of assistance to the salesman is the field of general educational psychology.

It has been established in this book that the salesman is an educator, at least from a functional standpoint. The salesman is involved in the telling, discussing, showing, and performance methods of instruction. If the salesman uses a canned, one-way communication sales talk, he is involved in the same process that the educator is involved in when he lectures. It may or may not be effective.

The discussion method is widely accepted by educators as one of the best methods to educate. The discussion method is comparable to the conference-type activity. It includes all those activities which tend to develop an interchange of ideas between the salesman and the prospect. The discussion method is basic to depth selling.

Normally whenever the salesman has a tangible product to sell, he is involved in showing or demonstrating how to utilize a particular product. Demonstrations do give meanings to facts and help the prospect understand the salesman's proposal. However, a demonstration should always be associated with the potential user's needs. Invariably a demonstration is accompanied by a process of telling or explaining. If this telling or explaining process revolves around the prospect's problem, the demonstration will be effective. But it will be most effective if the salesman combines a demonstration with the discussion concept.

Many times the salesman utilizes performance as a method of educating the prospect in how to use a product. If a salesman is selling a product that the individual can use, for example, a typewriter, the sales effort will be far more effective if the individual has an opportunity to operate the typewriter. This is true of most sales situations.

The individual learns through seeing, hearing, talking, and through his motor skills. Generally the salesman will best educate if he appeals to all of the buyer's senses. He can do this best in most situations by utilizing all of the educational methods, that is, telling, discussing, showing, and participating. Whenever possible, he will use visuals; he will ask questions; he will have the individual perform, for example, writing out material or figures whenever appropriate. The best way to educate is to get the individual involved in a problem or situation. As indicated in the behavioral science chapters, the salesman utilizes the laws of education—the law of effect, the law of readiness, the law of exercise, and the law of belonging.

The art of questioning is a common denominator between education and selling. Salesmen use developmental and evaluative questions. Developmental questions stimulate the respondent in the discussion process to enlarge on the topic under consideration. These questions are especially identified by the use of how and what. They do not beg a yes or no answer. In fact, it is often difficult to reply to a developmental question with a simple "yes" or "no." Evaluative questions are designed to permit the salesman to judge the effectiveness of his discussion or explanation. In the evaluative process the burden for good communication is always on the salesman. Evaluative questions must be used so that the burden of understanding is placed squarely on the shoulders of the salesman.

In addition to evaluating the sales situation through developmental and evaluative questions, the salesman also evaluates by observation. In most two-way communication processes, what the individual says must be

Selling: A Behavioral Science Approach

interpreted in terms of nonverbal behavior activities as well. Thus the salesman is alert to four blocks of responses. He is interested in voluntary positive cues and voluntary negative cues on the one hand, and involuntary positive cues and involuntary negative cues on the other. The ability to get and analyze nonverbal cues within the context of the total communication process is especially valuable to the salesman. But it must be remembered that this approach to analyzing behavior patterns is subjective.

A final method that the salesman can use to obtain information is through the process of indirect questioning. Indirect questioning is a process of asking questions in such a way that the individual being questioned is placed in the safe position of giving the views of others rather than his own. Frequently what the prospect says in reply to an indirect question may be a reflection of his own viewpoint.

Chapter 14   DISCUSSION QUESTIONS

1   Take a stand pro or con and discuss the statement made in the book that salesmen are educators.
2   Describe each of the basic methods of teaching in terms of how each can be used to advantage by the salesman.
3   Which salesman, the salesman selling an intangible or the salesman selling a tangible, can most effectively weave the basic methods of teaching into a sales presentation?
4   What are the basic principles a salesman must keep in mind if his demonstration is to be effective?
5   What relation do you see between the use of visuals in a sales situation and the demonstration concept?
6   Define what is meant by developmental questions. Give three examples of how you would frame a developmental question in your everyday discussions with a friend. Do the same thing for an assumed sales interview.
7   What is the major difference between developmental and evaluative questions? Define burden in terms of how it might facilitate the flow of communication between prospect and salesman.
8   Describe what is meant by nonverbal cues. What classification of nonverbal cues do you think are the most difficult to ascertain? Why?
9   What is the basic purpose behind the use of indirect questions?
10   Complete the analysis work sheet for example of respondent's reactions giving both verbal and nonverbal cues. See the appendix to this chapter.

discussion
that
motivates

part two

15

DRAMATIZATION OF THE SALES PROCESS

Dramatization or showmanship is colorfully described by sales authority Greif as ". . . the priceless ingredient that gives your sales story impact. It literally makes your product or service speak for itself; it fires the sales message to your prospect."[1]

The futility of one-way communication—the one devoid of feedback—has been recognized in previous chapters. Questioning is the backbone of the sales communication message. Verification and permissive questions are used in the contact stage. The discussion phase is marked by the extensive use made of developmental, evaluative, and indirect questioning. And although questioning is one of the most important concepts in selling, the salesman must not forget there are a number of other effective sales aids available—sales aids that put action into the sales interview.

It is known that the communication message employing stimuli directed to the prospect's needs, wants, and interests is the one most apt to be received by the prospect. It gains the prospect's mental attention. Not only, however, must the message be designed to obtain the prospect's or individual's mental attention, but it must be designed to *hold* the prospect's mental attention throughout the interview. A communication-oriented sales talk does this, but there are other external stimuli that also determine what the prospect will perceive and the extent to which he will perceive it.

External stimuli may be plus factors in holding attention, or they may be negative factors. Distracting mannerisms are negative factors; they hold attention after turning attention away from the sales message. On the other hand, dramatization, visuals, moving visuals, and showmanship words are important devices for directing and holding attention to the particular points, ideas, or concepts that the salesman wants to communicate.

[1] Edwin C. Greif, *Modern Salesmanship: Principles and Problems*, Prentice-Hall, Inc., Englewood Cliffs, N.J., 1958, p. 250.

Yet visuals may be distracting if used too frequently or if they are the wrong kind. Or they may even be a negative factor when used with certain individuals under certain circumstances. An investigation of the external factors affecting attention will help the salesman avoid traps in the use of physical sales tools, such as portfolios, brochures, surveys, and models.

An important rule of depth selling is that any form of dramatization that is used by the salesman must be employed only to enhance the communication process. Causative factors used to get attention for attention's sake will, in most instances, destroy the communication process. Some of these external or causative factors affecting attention are involved in the concepts of shifting of attention, intensity, and size, and in contrast, repetition, and movement.

ATTENTION

Attention is a commonly discussed topic. It appears in most books dealing with public speaking, letter writing, education, drama, television, and salesmanship.

Despite its importance and its general application, sales books apparently overlook several of its most promising characteristics as a field of study. All too frequently writers state that the sure way to success in selling is to follow the procedure of first getting the prospect's attention; second, developing his interest; then creating desire; next, establishing conviction; and finally, closing the sale. Thus a salesman in quick succession takes a prospect through these five mental stages. The concept of mental stages in itself appears to be well-grounded in psychological literature. But the way the process is used in selling is subject to serious questioning. In sales literature the emphasis is on getting attention via external control rather than on attention resulting from the inner forces of man. Numerous references are made that the salesman gains attention through external factors such as enthusiasm, handing the prospect a model, stating that he will only take a few minutes of the prospect's time, or that there need be no concern for a sale because, as the salesman comments, "I'm not here to sell you anything," or "This proposal will be of real value to you," or some combination of these ideas.

Concentration on the external forces which effect attention overlooks the inner man; his motives, needs, wants, desires, and wishes which are more important in selling as determinants of mental attention and keeping attention than are causative factors.

Moreover, in most sales literature the discussion on how to get the prospect's attention is restricted to the approach stage of the sale. Such discussion omits the essential fact that attention is a vital part of perception and understanding and that the salesman is concerned with the prospect's attention *throughout* the sale.

Much of the advice given to salesmen on how to get attention stems from the fact that an individual's attention is known to shift rapidly. At any given moment our sense organs, eyes and ears especially, are bombarded by a multitude of stimuli all vying for attention. Yet only a few of these stimuli get a clear channel. We can focus our attention on only a few stimuli at any one time. Man cannot comprehend everything in a situation completely and at once. Man has finite limits to his perception. The fact that man is limited in what he can comprehend or include in his perception at one given moment is the main necessity for shifting attention from one stimuli to another. Thus since attention is focused on a few stimuli at a time, other stimuli are relegated to the background. Such stimuli are not clearly perceived. They are in the vague, hazy, or marginal area of perception. What may be essential stimuli at one moment may be marginal the next and vice versa.

Many of our everyday experiences testify to this. At a football game, we normally concentrate on the backfield, not on the line. More particularly, the man with the ball has our attention. Other players are in the background. They are in a marginal area of perception. We may be cold or we may be wet, yet these discomforts are relegated to the background during the play. At the height of a dramatic play, for example, the Scat Back in a breakaway run, we may receive a lusty slap on the back from an excited individual behind us, but we are hardly aware of the blow.

At the completion of the play, as the football carrier fades out of awareness, the noise, cold feet, the slap on the back, and other stimuli come back into focus.

As an analogy, the football game example overstates the case for concern regarding shifting of attention as it applies to the sales interview. Whenever the salesman gives the customer the ball by talking his problems, his needs, or his situation, he gets and holds the prospect's attention reasonably well. Nevertheless, educational psychology tells us an individual cannot concentrate for any sustained period of time. The salesman must consider the factor of shifting of attention, both his and the prospect's, during the sales interview.

From this it seems that attention is capricious, shifting here and there, never resting long on one subject or object, or never continuing long in a single direction. Nevertheless, there are a number of principles which determine what will capture attention and, what is even more important from the sales point, what will hold it.

Motivation is a term which conveniently enables us to link together the individual's needs, interests, attention, attitude, set, and values. Motivation is a powerful determinant of what we will perceive and upon what we will focus our attention. What is of greater interest to the individual than his own needs, his own situation, his own wants, his own problems, and his own ego? That accounts for the emphasis in this book on a customer-oriented, problem-solving, need-satisfaction theory of selling as an *attention-gaining* and an *attention-holding* strategy rather than the traditional approach to selling.

The power of the "interest state" of the individual as an attention-selecting force is clearly seen in the college classroom. An instructor only needs to say, "We are now going to discuss the sex habits of the American female," and a dormant freshman will come to attention and be ready to discuss the problem vigorously. The ornithologist is interested in birds, the geologist in rocks, and the businessman in his business; therefore the salesman's strategy is to motivate, through a process of interaction be-

Selling: A Behavioral Science Approach

tween the salesman and prospect, centered on the prospect's social needs and his business needs.

Since motivation is discussed elsewhere in this book, attention here will be limited to the external forces which attract attention. But before proceeding to that subject, a brief discussion of voluntary and involuntary forms of attention may be helpful.

Involuntary and Voluntary Attention

There is no sharp dividing line between the two concepts of attention, nor can one say irrefutably that one situation refers to voluntary and the other to involuntary attention. Therefore there is overlapping in the two concepts, but they do illustrate a point of importance to the salesman.

Voluntary attention refers to those situations where an individual has the freedom to select and focus his attention to what he wishes to attend. It is more concerned with the factors relating to man as a thinker, a reasoner, a problem-solver, a decider, or in other words, where the locus of motivation is—in the mind.

In contrast, with involuntary attention, the person is less an agent in selecting the focus of his attention and is more a pawn of other forces that demand what he is to attend to. A hungry person's attention is drawn irresistibly to the aroma of coffee or the display of food in the bakery window in spite of what he wishes to attend to voluntarily. In the same way, an individual may voluntarily wish to attend to a stimulus, for instance, a point just made by a salesman, but his attention is drawn elsewhere by other stimuli that compel, direct, attract, or demand his attention. Therefore it would seem that a salesman must judiciously use the tools of attention getting so that they become devices or means to *fortify* the voluntary attention of the individual and never become *disruptive* influences as is suggested by the more razzle-dazzle devices aimed at attention for the sake of attention.

The value of such causative forces as intensity and size, contrast, repetition, movement, isolation, novelty, and incongruity as factors to attract and hold attention will vary considerably among prospects. It will depend upon the prospect's intellectual and emotional adjustment to life. It will depend on his maturity, attitude, intelligence, habits, value; it will depend on his position, the product, the company.

Again it must be stressed that the causative determinants of attention will be most effectively employed if they cause the prospect or customer to attend to the major idea in the salesman's proposal. In brief, the involuntary dimensions of attention are used to get and keep voluntary attention. It is an interactive process.

Intensity and Size

Big, loud, and bright are forces that direct attention. The full-page ad in *Life* attracts more attention than the one-page ad. A shot from a cannon attracts more attention than the shotgun. The billboard with one thousand lights attracts more attention than a ten-light sign. In general, whenever two stimuli are competing for attention, attention will be focused on the bigger, louder, or brighter stimulus.

It is not being recommended that all salesmen be over seven feet tall, wear red jackets, or carry flashlights, but it is being suggested that salesmen realize the value of intensity and size as factors in directing and holding attention. The salesmen must be cautious, however, of a trap in the misuse of these concepts.

A case in point is the salesman using a sales portfolio that has large print next to small print. The prospect may perceive the large print. He may not perceive the small print. When a page of the sales portfolio contains both large and small print, the large may be a continuous disturbing factor to the communication process. The large print may direct the prospect's attention to such a degree that the salesman may have to point to the smaller print to direct the prospect's attention away from the large print.

Frequently salesmen using sales portfolios have a series of colorful headliners on each page. Each of these headliners are supported by copy in small print. Many salesmen use the headline as a major attention-getting force and verbally support the main concept. In brief, the salesman provides the copy. He does not expect a prospect to read small print. The headliners are excellent, especially if the salesman's verbal support is designed to get two-way communication.

Contrast

Big, loud, and bright suggest contrast. But here the role of contrast in directing attention refers to a *change* in the stimulus to which the individual has become adapted. Immediately the change itself captures attention. The change or new stimulus may be a lesser stimulus or a greater stimulus than the original stimulus.

For instance, you are driving along the highway and your car is performing smoothly, but suddenly it develops a slight ticking. You are aware of this at first, but in a few minutes it becomes unnoticed. Then perhaps a backfire or another sound may capture your attention. This role of a greater stimulus in attracting attention has been dramatically demonstrated to most partridge hunters. Witness the hunter walking through the woods meditating on the peace, quiet, and beauty of the area and suddenly he is shocked into attention by the roar of partridge wings close by.

As another example, most people have had the experience of sitting in a quiet room reading when someone suddenly turns on the radio. Immediately the reader is aware of the radio being on, but after a while it becomes unnoticed. Then if the radio is shut off, it again becomes noticed. This is the contrast of a lesser stimuli. This final example illustrates how a stimuli is perceived both at the onset and the termination point. Both require attention because there is contrast. There was contrast when the radio was turned on and contrast when it was turned off.

Each salesman can profitably employ contrast as an attention-holding device in many ways. Questions provide contrast. A visual provides contrast with previous actions. The salesman can vary his sales talk so that

Selling: A Behavioral Science Approach

there is contrast in his tone and words. Even the momentary pause (silence), a lesser stimuli, has attention-getting power.

This last point, the pause, can be an extremely effective communication device. It is subtle. Many times the prospect must be prompted or encouraged to comment, but more often than not, good discussion will evolve and will flow along profitable lines if the salesman is customer-oriented in the preparation of his sales approach and if he pauses from time to time. The pause at a meaningful point in the conversation is a cue for the respondent to comment.

Repetition

Repetition may be viewed profitably from three related considerations. The first is that repetition enhances understanding. We learn by repetition. It is not known specifically, however, how many times an idea or concept should be repeated to enhance understanding. Nor is the best "time lag mix" between repetitions known. It is known that repetition aids learning in most situations, other things being equal. Although it is impossible to predict with accuracy how many times a salesman should repeat a particular idea to assist the prospect to gain a clearer understanding of the proposal, the salesman can, by judiciously eliciting feedback and by correctness in interpretation of that feedback (both verbal and nonverbal), receive cues to prospect's understanding. The salesman, of course, adjusts to the prospect's needs and to the situation.

A second side to repetition is that a stimuli repeated twice has a better chance of "striking" the mind of the prospect. This is particularly so if the original stimulus was projected during a period of waning attention. If this were the case and if the second stimulus was received, it becomes perfectly clear the second stimuli will assist the prospect to gain a better understanding of a salesman's message. It is a matter of the law of averages. Nevertheless, the salesman is selective in repeating the stimuli.

This leads to the third side of repetition. Psychologists tell us that the second stimulus will support or reinforce the first stimulus. This is the 1 + 1 equals 2 process previously discussed regarding temporal stimuli. Repetition increases the individual's sensitivity to the particular stimulus. That is to say, the second or third time a particular stimulus is presented to a prospect, the more sensitive he is to receiving the particular stimulus. In the preceding sentence you probably noticed that the word *stimulus* was spelled "stimlus," but perhaps you did not notice its misspelling in the sentence preceding that one until your attention was directed to it.

Another way of explaining this increased awareness of the second stimuli is that a repeated stimulus is a more intense stimulus. Every hunter knows that two shots in succession are more apt to attract attention than one shot, and three rapid shots even more so. Repetition has an intensifying or compounding effect.

In view of the foregoing, salesmen may wish to repeat important points two or three times during the sale, depending upon the cues the salesmen receive. This is especially true if their concept or idea is complex.

Discussion That Motivates: Part Two

In the completion stage of the sale, the concept of repetition is utilized when the salesman summarizes the main ideas in his proposal.

Movement

Psychologist Morgan explains that "human beings, as well as most animals are quite sensitive to objects that move in their field of vision. Our eyes are involuntarily attracted to movement in much the same way as a moth is attracted to a flame."[2]

Advertising specialists make abundant use of movement as an attention getter. Some of the most effective advertising signs contain movement or what the advertising men refer to as "advertising in action." Sometimes we are almost involuntarily drawn to view a particular sign. It goes without saying that these signs should be so designed that they not only get involuntary attention, but they should be so structured they get voluntary attention as well. In short, attention for the sake of attention is not the most effective advertising.

To the salesman, movement is used as a communication device as well as for attracting and holding attention. A gesture, raising of an eyebrow, nodding of the head, a thoughtful pose, or a slight smile may be critical to holding or losing attention or enhancing or detracting from the verbal message.

When appropriate, many salesmen subtly flip a page of the portfolio, point to a pertinent fact, hand the prospect a visual, take an item from the inner pocket, remove an item from his briefcase, and thus utilize movement to get and hold attention. One Blue Cross–Blue Shield manager utilizes movement effectively by moving his chair a little closer to the prospect. This manager tells us that in some situations, especially when he is using a visual, he may have his chair beside the desk of the prospect and, as he senses the prospect's increased interest, he intensifies his own actions. He leans forward just a little more and inches his chair a little closer. His observation of this action is that invariably ". . . it intensifies a prospect's interest in the proposal."[3] He believes that his own more intense actions, plus moving his chair closer to the side of the prospect, suggests his enthusiasm for the Blue Cross–Blue Shield program. Such enthusiasm, he tells us, begets enthusiasm.

In the same sales manual we find that "one of the most effective uses of movements in the sales interview is through the moving visual—a pencil."[4] This is illustrated in the following dialogue.

DIALOGUE ILLUSTRATIONS OF HOW TO USE A MOVING VISUAL

S Mr. Bronson, a quick way to get an overall look at this proposal would be for me to write down the figures for the various plans we have under con-

---

[2] Clifford T. Morgan, *Introduction to Psychology*, McGraw-Hill Book Company, New York, 1956, p. 165.

[3] Thompson, *Blue Cross–Blue Shield Manpower Development Program Book*, *op. cit.*, chap. 8, p. 2.

[4] *Ibid.*, chap. 8, p. 3.

Selling: A Behavioral Science Approach

sideration. (*Simultaneously with this statement the Blue Cross–Blue Shield salesman takes a pad of paper from his brief case and begins carrying out his idea as he continues.*) Perhaps it would be best if I drew three lines on this sheet of paper and labeled them plan A, plan B and plan C. Under each plan we can write in the figures for the varying cost of rooms, medical care, etc. It will give us a concrete idea on what the different plans entail.

Here is how the hotel salesman makes use of a moving visual in his sale of his hotel as a convention site.

S I'll write these figures down for the range of prices for each of the dining rooms so that we will have the specific amount involved for each of them. If we served X wine to five at the dinner, the cost would be $—— and without wine, $——. You are thinking in terms of 600 persons, so that would make it $—— with wine and $—— without wine.

Provided that the materials are meaningful and well-organized, the use of a moving visual in this way will obtain not only attention but also prospect participation, both mentally and physically.

Industrial salesmen make frequent use of the pencil to draw plans, designs of a particular piece of equipment, etc., and to support highly technical points, such as the various types of metal coatings on a drill head or what "floating zero" means on a Potter and Johnson. The author has made joint calls on prospects with many industrial salesmen and has yet to see the time when the use of a pencil, as described above, has not added immeasurably to good two-way communication.

ISOLATION, NOVELTY, AND INCONGRUITY

Isolation, novelty, and incongruity are used extensively for their attention-demanding qualities as are intensity, contrast, movement, and repetition.

When properly used, isolation has strong attention-getting properties or qualities. It is effectively used in advertising by a single printed word on a white page or a single printed white word on a black page or the single diamond lying on a black piece of velvet. Salesmen selling a long line of items have long practiced placing one product at a time on the display pad. In fact, a general rule is to minimize the number of items shown to the prospect at a given moment, unless a large number of items or units can be used to reinforce or illustrate a point the salesman is making.

Novelty refers to something new, different, fresh, or unusual. It is change or innovation. Perhaps the two most widely demonstrated effective uses of novelty are seen in ladies' new hats and in the first car of a series, such as Ford's Mustang. For the young, perhaps the Beatles, a widely acclaimed musical group in 1964–1965, should be mentioned. But like all novelties this group faded into the hinterland only to be replaced by other novelty entertainers. Salesmen use novel or new approaches to many situations if they are given an opportunity or encouraged to do so. The author has found salesmen on the whole to be quite creative in discovering the new ways to sell their product. For example, one successful industrial cutting tool (drills) salesman carried five different quality of drills (all looked very much alike) in a small leather case the size of a pocket bill-fold. Four of the drills were of like quality and like price. One drill, how-ever, was high quality and higher-priced. During the course of an interview with a potential user, this salesman reaches into his inside coat pocket, takes out the pocket billfold, lays out the drills, and asks the prospect to select the drill that he thinks will drill the most holes. After the selec-tion of a drill, the salesman inquires, "Now, Mr. Jones, do you think you would be willing to have that drill used in your machine shop?" Regard-less of the drill selected by the potential user, the salesman has made a strong point. If any of the four like-quality drills are selected, the sales-man points out that the drill selected plus the other three will not have the lifeline to drill as many holes as the more expensive drill. If the pros-pect selects the best drill, the salesman merely compliments the potential user on the selections and compares that drill to the others and, depending upon the situation, uses any one of twenty different ways of asking for the order.

Although the author does not believe in the use of novelty items in selling, they can be used effectively and usually without any danger of offending the prospect if they are specifically tied in with the sale and permit the salesman to make a smooth transition from the novelty item to the purpose for his sales call. Two such situations follow:

A large manufacturer of air-conditioning equipment provided its sales-men with small Japanese-made, battery-operated fans. These fans resem-bled and were about the size of a boy scout flashlight. When the salesman called on a potential buyer for a small air-conditioning system, he gave the fan to the potential customer, turned it on, and referred to this as the old-fashioned method of air movement. He quickly made the transition from the battery-operated fan to the modern air-conditioning system.

The second case involves a large industrial supplier of overalls, gloves, and related work clothes. One of this company's special services is the repair of work gloves. This company found that since most workmen were left-handed, work gloves for the left hand were worn out but considerable wear remained in the right-hand glove. In initial contacts with the shop superintendent, for instance, the salesman handed the superintendent a worn glove and explained the reasons why this took place. They also showed the superintendent what a reconditioned glove would look like. Even though the superintendent may not have been interested in the mending service, it gave the salesman a good transition into the service aspects of the call.

Other than new or unique ways of professionally demonstrating or displaying a product or service, or communicating an idea or proposal, attempts to capitalize on the concept of novelty as an attention-getting and an attention-holding device may prove disastrous in many instances. Take the case of the few companies which provide the salesman with

Selling: A Behavioral Science Approach

cleverly made, and more often than not, cheap toys or jokelike devices to give to the prospect in the initial call. One of the poorest examples of novelty, or perhaps incongruity, was found in the company which had its salesman hand prospects a little package inscribed with the words "Sure Fire Mosquito Killer." On opening the package the prospect found two blocks of wood with a note inscribed, "Catch mosquito, put mosquito between blocks, and bring the blocks forceably together." The salesman then followed up this so-called attention getter with a little joke and, of course, "My real reason for being here is this." From that point on he went into his canned sales talk.

Another case is found in a sales manager whose company manufactured refrigerators. This sales manager had a sales meeting, got before his salesmen, and showed how he used his large oversized red suspenders to get attention. He actually showed the salesmen how to put the thumbs behind the suspenders—one to stretch them out and another to cover them up, etc. No comment is needed on such tactics, but the illustration does suggest some of the things done in selling at various levels.

Incongruity—the woman smoking a large black cigar. This is novel. This is different. But something incongruous has the added dimension that it does not correspond to what is thought to be right, proper, or reasonable at the moment.

Incongruous acts or stories are basic to most humor. Things are funny when they have a twist in them which is unexpected. We laugh at things that strike us as illogical or peculiar. We laugh at the comedian when he unexpectedly breaks some highly rigid rule of conduct. Incongruity is a basis for many of the commercials seen on television.

It is not recommended, generally, that a salesman resort to incongruous acts to get attention. Nevertheless, depending on the time, place, and individuals involved, incongruity can be used as a tension reducer. The author witnessed this very unexpected turn of events during a sale.

Industrial salesman Foster had had, in the past few months, a number of discussions with a potential buyer for an automatic gauging system. Salesman Foster believed that he knew the potential buyer well. On this particular call Foster appeared to be well on the way to obtaining a purchase order. Foster had been talking to the potential buyer for approximately thirty minutes when the telephone rang. It was an emergency call. The potential buyer made a number of calls to other administrators in the plant. The time involved was about twenty minutes. When this buyer finally turned to Foster to continue the discussion, he appeared to be quite upset and discussed the problem that had come up. Foster listened and then reviewed a few of the high points of the past discussion and gave the potential buyer a visual to examine. However, both the verbal and nonverbal cues told Foster that the potential buyer was not listening. It was at that moment that Foster did the unexpected. He reached in his briefcase and gently rolled a golden golf ball across the potential buyer's desk. He casually remarked, "You know, Jim, I read in the paper that your son had recently won the junior golf championship at your club, so I thought I'd bring this along for him." The potential buyer smiled and commented that his son, Jim, would certainly appreciate the golf ball and he stated, "Now, where were we?" Foster made that sale.

Admittedly Foster took a chance. He had come prepared to give the golden golf ball to the potential buyer at the end of the sales call, but he changed his plans. Foster felt that if he could continue his discussion, he could make that sale and that, if he put it off any longer, one of his competitors might get the inside track. He stated, "The idea just came to me, so I reached into my bag, pulled out the golf ball, and did it."

SHOWMANSHIP THROUGH ACTION WORDS

Some people are colorful; others are pretty commonplace. The same is true of sales demonstrations and discussions. The sales representative with showmanship puts color, enthusiasm, and creative ideas into his sales talk when needed and to the degree needed. His portfolio, pamphlets, or visual tools are unique. He uses movements, contrast, intensity, and size. He uses action and showmanship[5] words. He uses yes or customer-oriented words in his sales talk and his actions; his voice and his enthusiasm give life to the words.

The industrial salesman states, as he gestures toward the proposal portfolio lying on the prospect's desk:

S   All the facts show that this program with numeric control specifically adapted to your X1 and X2 machines plus automatic gauging will give you an outstanding, integrated continuous flow production system.

The office furniture salesman states:

S   Mr. Turner, this installation will put you ahead of your competition. It will make your customers take notice that they are doing business with an aggressive, energetic, business-seeking organization.

OR

S   Mr. Turner, will you compare these two swatches for color and texture? Which of these swatches do you think would be more indicative of an action climate in your business offices?

Compare the above section with the less colorful, negative dialogue which follows:

S   This program will leave no doubt in anyone's mind that you want a good production system. It appears to me that your employees will not look unkindly upon this plan.

OR

S   Mr. Turner, I don't think I'm far wrong in the claim that our installation will leave no doubt in people's minds but that they are dealing with an aggressive organization. It may probably be an error to assume . . .

A few other negative words too often used by salesmen are *fault,*

---

[5] It has been firmly established in the behavioral science chapters that the mature salesman can play a number of roles with varying degrees of intensity of enactment.

failure, discourage, wrong, can't disappoint, improbably, omission, unable, afraid, wait, adjustments, only covers, don't believe it covers, regulations, and *costs.*

One sales manager asked, "What kind of salesman makes those negative statements?" He claims that only the meek, negative, or untrained salesman would consistently utilize such words. He emphasizes further that the salesman that uses the less colorful, negative dialogue doesn't believe in his company program or himself. He lacks self-confidence and is not sales-oriented.

Compare the negative words to these positive ones: *yes, certainly, right, will do, encouraging, success, immediately, right away, accurate, correct, complete coverage, total program, full service, your security, skilled,* and *investment.*

As another example, the industrial sales representative is using colorful, positive language if he states:

S   Yes, I think you are correct. I, too, feel confident that with the positive production system established through this program a very favorable Franklin Company image will be projected and established in the minds of your customers.

He is less colorful when he says:

S   It seems improbable to me that with this program we would go far wrong. In fact, it would be a disappointment to me if we were unable to generate a satisfactory image on the part of your customers toward this program. If they visit the shop you would think they would obtain a good look at what you are doing.

PAINTING THE PROSPECT INTO THE PICTURE

Whether the salesman is selling a tangible or intangible, he must convey a mental picture of the situation as it will exist in reality. He must structure his communication with the prospect in such a way that the prospect will be able to see himself enjoying or benefiting from the use of the product or the ideas the salesman has advanced.

Advertising experts know how to utilize this principle. An examination of any magazine demonstrates that the potential customer or user is usually shown as owning and benefiting from the products. The potential customer is shown at the helm of the cabin cruiser or boat; he is shown where the "yellow went," and the young lady using X perfume always has many admirers.

Dialogue Illustrations

Now to show how the salesman can utilize this idea. A health insurance salesman is discussing industrial health care programs with the per-

Discussion That Motivates: Part Two

sonnel director. He paints Mr. Franklin, the personnel director, into the picture by:

S   Indeed, Mr. Franklin, that's a sound idea. I haven't thought of it, but giving your employees a complete health care program for Christmas is a first in employee relations. No other company, at least in this area, has done this to my knowledge. So let me add on to your idea by asking you: Do you think this would be a good subject for publication purposes—perhaps one of the industrial personnel journals?

OR

S   Mr. Franklin, here are some typical letters and brochures sent by various companies to their employees announcing the beginning of a Blue Cross–Blue Shield health care program by the company. (*These brochures may, for instance, have a picture of the president of the company on the front of them, or they may be signed by the president of the company or include pictures of the administrative staff, including the personnel director.*)

The industrial salesman may paint the prospect in the picture by stating:

S   Mr. Seldon, the facts show that this proposal will contribute heavily toward giving you a dependable, highly productive, but low-cost productive system. It is a forward-looking investment.
R   Yes, I believe it would, but I think I should talk this over with several others in our plant.
S   That's a good idea; however, may I suggest that if you personally think this is a forward-looking program and a program that is going to be of great benefit to your firm you might want to submit a proposal to them for their consideration.
R   Hadn't thought of that. What do you have in mind?

OR

S   Mr. Seldon, let's assume for a moment that you have decided to go on gauge control and thereby integrate your present equipment into a highly flexible, automated productive system. Do you think that such a program, known of course to potential contract users of your plant, might favorably affect their decision to give their business to your company?

The office furniture salesman may paint the prospect into the picture (assuming, of course, that the prospect is with the salesman at one of the company's showrooms) as follows:

S   Mr. Turner, this mock setup was designed to give you an overall look at the design, etc., we proposed for your new central offices.
R   Well, it certainly doesn't have that cluttered look we have now.
S   Yes, Mr. Turner, it was designed to be roomy and give the appearance of roominess. If you would like to stand or sit over here, you'll get a good view of the overall spaciousness and beauty of the proposed central office. In fact,

Selling: A Behavioral Science Approach

standing about here, you'll get a good view of what your customers will see when they come into your office.

R Well, it does have a nice overall look.

S Yes, the design, the modular furniture, and the color scheme were planned by expert stylists, so everything is in harmony.

Here is another example of the office furniture salesman painting the prospect into the picture.

S Your office furniture has been planned around a conference room theme. The new William Vining functional furniture has been used so that it all can be quickly shifted to a conference room setup. And as I recall, you mentioned that you plan on having a staff meeting every Monday morning.

R Yes, that's right, I do.

S Are there any ways in which we can restructure this setup to make it more practical with respect to your conference needs?

This final example shows a hotel convention salesman painting the prospect into the picture.

S Here is a color picture of the Caesar Room. This room with its elegant tasteful decor, would be very suitable for your association's final dinner. What do you think of it?

R Well, it's nice all right and I think the women would like it.

S Yes, we get some very fine comments. By the way, we usually have the head table about here. Would that be suitable? I think—since you plan to have thirty or forty persons at the head table—you might want to have two tables like the arrangement we had for the Masonic convention last year.

R You know, I'm a Mason, and I wonder if I know any of those people at the head table.

HOW TO HANDLE THE INTERRUPTED INTERVIEW

Many times salesmen are confronted with this situation: They have talked to a prospect for five, ten, fifteen, or twenty minutes when there is an interruption, by a telephone call or by someone entering the office. The prospect may then be engaged in a distracting conversation.

When resuming the sales talk, after the interruption, the strategy followed by the salesman will vary according to what he believes is the intensity of the distraction. He will watch closely for the prospect's reaction and will analyze the prospect's statements as indicators of the degree of distraction. In brief, he will be sensitive to both positive and negative verbal and nonverbal cues.

How would you assess this situation? The salesman has been discussing a specific plan with Mr. Franklin for about twenty minutes and the telephone rings.

S (*Gesturing toward the door*) Shall I leave? (*It may be a good idea to suggest leaving. It does show courtesy on the salesman's part and also empha-*

Discussion That Motivates: Part Two

sizes the importance of the prospect. In most cases, the prospect will tell the salesman to remain seated. Nevertheless, if the prospect later has to ask the salesman to leave because it turns out to be a private conversation, he will feel free to do so and neither the salesman nor the prospect will be embarrassed.)

R No, that's all right. (*The prospect talks five minutes on the original call and then makes three more calls after this for a total of twenty minutes. Obviously the call was important.*)

S I hope the news wasn't too bad, Mr. Franklin. (*This is poor technique. The salesman should never mention the prospect's or customer's telephone conversation. The prospect may think it is none of the salesman's business.*)

R No, it wasn't too bad. You have to expect some bad news, however, and it seems that it comes in every day.

S Well, Mr. Franklin, we were just discussing some of the numeric control features we could incorporate into a tailored production plan for the Franklin Company and such a plan would give. . . . Have I interpreted our discussion correctly?

R I guess so.

S Also, we discussed that, in addition to the numeric control program, Pratt & Whitney electronic control for Kellering machines looked good to you. Is this . . . ?

R Uh-huh.

S I see.

From the tenor of the prospect's statements and from a general observation of the prospect's physical indication of interest, the sales representative does see. He believes that Mr. Franklin isn't following him. What should he do? He has used the question technique effectively. He posed two questions but decided when the prospect interrupted his question with an "uh-huh" not to use a successive or third question. He evidently suspected the prospect would again say uh-huh or yes or make some similar remark.

What else can he do? He wants to bring the individual's attention back to the important elements of the proposal. He wants to get the customer to participate mentally and physically in the sale.

Fortunately there are a number of specific techniques and strategies that can be used. The methods used may be classified as verbal, nonverbal, or a combination of both.

Verbal techniques are:

1. Repeating the last statement made prior to the telephone call.
2. Reviewing some high points from the total previous discussion.
3. Employing both evaluative and developmental questions.
4. Making a forceful statement.
5. Discussing a subject of mutual interest.

Nonverbal techniques are:

6. Visuals of all types.
   a. Handing the prospect a product, picture, a model, a statement

Selling: A Behavioral Science Approach

of notes taken during the interview, use of a portfolio, or any visual item that will draw attention away from the interruption.
   b. The salesman's proposal.
7. Movement
   a. Body movement (action of all types).
   b. Writing down facts, drawing, or making an illustration of what the salesman and the prospect are discussing.
   c. A salesman may just sit and wait until the prospect turns his mind back to the sale. Actually there is no movement involved, but it is a nonverbal cue to the prospect that the salesman is waiting to discuss the proposal. In some situations such a strategy has value.
8. Combination of verbal and nonverbal.

The previous discussion of the psychological concepts of contrast, repetition, reinforcement, intensity, and size should be kept in mind for the following discussion of ways to use verbal and nonverbal stimuli in handling the interrupted interview.

Last Statement Approach or Review of Several High Points

S   Just before the telephone call, I had said . . .

OR

S   Just prior to the call you mentioned your interest in . . .

OR

S   Mr. Franklin, we were just discussing the combined tax benefit and the new depreciation allowances.

In the case of the interrupted interview, psychological principles suggest that the salesman should review a number of high points from the previous discussion regardless of the time duration. Why? Because any interruption causes a change of attention and calls for a review of facts. This of course will vary with the listener and the situation. Nevertheless, it is good advice to the salesman since he can, in the course of the review, more clearly identify the degree of the prospect's attention. Reviewing or use of other techniques are especially necessary when the telephone conversation has lasted three, four, five, or more minutes and when the prospect was apparently engrossed in the conversation.

In reviewing the important points, the salesman may profitably question the prospect to make sure that he (the salesman) is getting the same answers that he got before. These answers will guide the salesman as to the time he might spend on reviewing the high points or tell him if he should use more dramatic tactics.

Use of Questions in the Interrupted Interview

The question is one of the most versatile of all sales techniques. In the interrupted interview, evidence of this is again seen as the salesman uses questions to bring the prospect mentally back to the sales situation. The salesman may use developmental or evaluative-type questions:

S   Mr. Franklin, we were just discussing the fact that numeric control was ideally suited to one-piece runs. How does this flexibility idea fit into your future production needs?

OR

S   Just prior to your telephone call we were discussing how Vining's modular design provides great flexibility in combining office furniture. Did I clearly explain how this would give you one basic furniture design, although you would be adding furniture from time to time as your office force expanded in the next three years?

Using Visuals

Sometimes a more forceful method than the question technique is needed to bring the prospect's mind back to the sales situation. Handing the prospect a pertinent visual encourages participation. Handing the prospect a visual forces participation. Frequently it is easier for the prospect to concentrate on a visual than on a question. The salesman may use a portfolio, a pamphlet, or a model. He may even use the pad of paper on which he and the prospect had jotted figures prior to the telephone call. For instance, as the industrial salesman hands the prospect the "written" visuals, he may say, "Here are some of the figures we jotted down with respect to tax and depreciation benefits that will accrue to you with an investment in a Tape-O-Matic." "Here is the numeric control program we have outlined to date, but a couple of additional thoughts came to my mind. I can jot those down here." Or the health insurance salesman may state: "Here are some of the figures we jotted down with respect to the cost of the three different programs for your employees."

A Forceful Statement

The forceful statement technique is one calculated to jar the prospect back into the sales interview. Some sales authorities recommend that the salesman use it in a situation where the sale has been about completed and then the interruption occurs or when the interruption is of such a nature that the prospect is mentally distant to the salesman's discussion. The salesman might say:

S   Mr. Foster, I am certainly pleased to have you agree with these points. I, too, think plan number 3 would be the best investment. I will be most happy to submit a complete plan to you for your approval in about one week. Would that be satisfactory with you?

This last technique should be used with care. In most cases there is little question that it will mentally and perhaps physically bring the customer back into the interview. However, it is also possible that such a statement might jar the prospect too much with the end result being a salesman on the way back to his office without a signed contract.

Selling: A Behavioral Science Approach

Marginal Techniques

The tactics of discussing a problem of *mutual interest,* waiting for the prospect to recognize the salesman and finally having the salesman ask for a later interview, are all marginal techniques, but they are used by many salesmen.

Some authorities recommend that when a prospect has engaged in an apparently serious lengthy telephone conversation, it is well to discuss a subject of mutual interest. For instance, proponents of this method would suggest that the salesman talk about deer hunting, golf, or some subject he knows is a subject of interest or the prospect's hobby. The salesman could gesture to a painting on the wall and turn the discussion to it but only if it were a particular painting professionally known to him and the prospect. The word *professionally* overstates the case, but it does emphasize the fact that the salesman should not talk about a subject if there is a possibility he is going to be exposed as a "talker" and not a "knower."

There are those salesmen also who believe that after an interruption it is best to sit and wait quietly until the prospect focuses his attention again on the salesman. A brief wait may be desirable, although any wait beyond twenty or thirty seconds may seem like an eternity to most salesmen and, for that matter, to most prospects. On the other hand, the author has been with a salesman where he waited approximately five minutes after a telephone call interrupted a conversation; the prospect then turned to the salesman and practically continued the sales discussion at the point where it had been interrupted. Obviously there may be many schools of thought concerning time and the concept of waiting.

Finally, there are those sales managers and salesmen who believe that whenever the interview has been interrupted by a serious telephone call or an interruption of another nature, it is best for the salesman to step out of the picture. They claim it is desirable for the salesman to ask for a later appointment. Their reasoning is that if the customer is visibly disturbed, the salesman will, by carrying on the interview, eventually reach a point of no return—a point where the prospect will say no, and this may end any sales opportunity he might have in the future.

It would seem that a salesman should never push a prospect to the brink or practice the art of brinksmanship, but it would seem that the salesman should probe to ascertain the prospect's degree of interest before he makes the decision to ask for a future interview. In many cases it appears salesmen use the later-interview strategy as a crutch to save getting into a difficult sales situation at the moment.

Summary

Dramatization is that priceless ingredient that gives a sales story impact. And although the emphasis in this book has been on the problem-solving, questioning, customer-oriented approach, skillful dramatization can support the salesman's message. Dramatization must be used judiciously. It must not detract from the theme of the discussion. It must not attract attention for the sake of attention.

As causative factors the salesman can use intensity and size, contrast, repetition, and movement as attention-getting devices, but must be wary of isolation, novelty, and incongruity.

A strongly structured stimulus pattern attracts attention and keeps mental attention. Some people are colorful and others are pretty commonplace. The same is true of sales demonstrations and discussions. The sales representative with showmanship puts color, enthusiasm, and creative ideas in his sales talk when needed and in just the right degree. His portfolio, pamphlets, and visual tools are unique. He uses movement, contrast, intensity, and size. He uses action and showmanship words. His actions, his voice, and his enthusiasm give life to the words.

The salesman may dramatize the sales interview by painting the prospect into the picture. This is done when the sales discussion is structured so that the prospect can see himself enjoying or benefiting from the use of the product or idea the salesman is discussing.

Few interviews are completed without being interrupted. There are many techniques that the salesman can use to handle the situation effectively. The interruption such as a telephone call may bring good news to the prospect or on the other extreme, bad news. Regardless of the reason for the interruption or the news that has been conveyed to the prospect, the salesman must regard any interruption as possibly sidetracking the communication process. Normally after an interruption, especially one lasting five minutes or more, the prospect's mind does not again immediately focus on the salesman's presentation. The prospect may be in another world. There are many techniques the salesman can use in such a situation. Most of them could be considered as methods of dramatizing the situation so that the prospect's attention is focused again on the sales situation. The salesman may repeat the last statement he made prior to the telephone call; he may review a number of highlights from the total previous discussion; he may use the question technique; he may employ both evaluative and developmental questions; he may use a forceful statement; he may use visual tools; he may talk of a subject of mutual interest; or he may just sit and wait until the prospect turns his mind back to the sale; or he may excuse himself and ask for a later appointment.

Chapter 15 DISCUSSION QUESTIONS

1 Is there any conflict between the idea that one of the objects of the salesman's verbal message is to get the prospect's mental attention with dramatization when used for attention-getting purposes includes using causative factors? Explain your stand.

2 As a student, has your attention shifted away from the subject matter of a lecture? If so, can you explain why it happened? What can the student do

Selling: A Behavioral Science Approach

and what can the teacher do to center the student's mind on the lecture material or classroom topic? Is there any difference between a student-teacher relationship and a salesman-customer or salesman-prospect situation with regard to getting attention?

3 Both intensity and size demand attention. It should follow thus that the loud-speaking and big salesman 6 feet 6 inches tall would be more effective than the smaller man and the man with moderate voice tones. Discuss.

4 Which is the more important stimuli to use in a sales situation, the employment of a lesser stimuli or the employment of a greater stimuli? Discuss your answer.

5 If the salesman understands the concept of repetition and its value in the communication process, what are two or three tactics the salesman may use at various stages during the sales interview to communicate effectively?

6 Discuss why such words as *yes, certainly, right, will do, encouraging, success, immediately, accurate, correct,* etc., are more positive than such words as *fault, failure, wrong, can't disappoint, omission, unable, afraid, don't believe it covers, regulation.*

7 In which situation is it easier for the salesman to sell—in the case of the sales interview in which the prospect has been interrupted but the prospect received favorable news, or in the situation where the prospect has been interrupted and received unfavorable news? Which of the techniques for handling the interrupted interview do you think the salesman utilizes in the normal interview? Why? Why not?

9 Selecting any product or using any situation from your experience, write a dialogue that will paint the other person into the picture that you are attempting to sell. For instance, assume you are trying to convince your friend to take a ski vacation with you between terms. He, on the other hand, is thinking of Florida. Or, assume you are a salesman for a large resort that is talking to a group of fraternity houses concerning the possibility of their using the resort between vacation periods. What dangers do you see in the use of the forceful statement?

solutions to prospect doubts

part one

16

INTRODUCTION

In previous chapters, depth selling, communication, planning, problem solving, contact, and discussion phases of selling were analyzed. The doubt, or so-called objections phase, is the subject matter of this chapter.

No salesman goes through the contact and discussion stages of the sale and then sits back and waits for the prospect to raise objections as is implied by the statement "the doubt or objections phase of selling." Each experienced salesman knows that the sale is a continuous and integrated whole. But for purposes of analysis each phase or principle of selling must be segmented.

Objections or doubts may be raised by the prospect or customer from the first moment of the contact until the final completion of negotiations. These objections or doubts are significant and of value to the salesman. They give him direction. They enable him to communicate and to solve deep-rooted problems and obtain total prospect participation. Objections or doubts are prospect problems. The prospect is involved with them. Each individual gives his own problems and needs his *undivided attention.*

Objections, Please

"Objections, please," should be the viewpoint of the salesman toward any objections the prospect may raise. Without *statements, questions,* and *comments* from the prospect, it is impossible for the salesman to ascertain fully his *doubts, beliefs, interests,* and *confidence* concerning a proposal.

And regardless of the objection or doubt voiced by the prospect or the point in the sales interview (contact to completion of negotiations) at which the objection or doubt is raised, as a general rule, the salesman should discuss that objection or doubt at that moment. Depending on the

Selling: A Behavioral Science Approach

situation there may be exceptions to this rule (see Price in this chapter).

The preceding statement, "Without statements, questions, and comments from the prospect, it is impossible for the salesman to ascertain fully his doubts, beliefs, interests, and confidence concerning a proposal," suggests, for the salesman, that the term *objections* may be a misnomer. Why? In many cases the prospect may have doubts the moment the salesman walks into his office. These doubts may continue throughout the sale and may vary from emotions concerning the sales representative's personal manner or tone of voice to doubts concerning the validity of statements the salesman may be making. These doubts are expressed in many ways, both verbally and nonverbally.

The alert, sensitive salesman wants the prospect to express his feelings, his thoughts, his beliefs, or his doubts. He will facilitate this process. He does not visualize these doubts or objections as placing him on one side of the issue and the prospect on the other.

The Set-answer Approach

The concept of meeting objections, as used in selling for more than fifty years, has had a tendency to condition or set salesmen to think in terms of techniques of handling objections. He has been trained to give a specific answer to a specific objection. This can be called the set-answer approach.

This approach has one basic flaw. It does not necessarily follow that what the customer states is what he really means, nor is it possible for one set answer to an objection to be equally meaningful to all prospects. Thus a more accurate way to handle objections is to qualify or to determine specifically what the individual means by his statement. This can be accomplished through a process of clarification. Or, in other words, the salesman questions the prospect or customer to determine the root meaning of the objection or doubt.

The clarification approach to handling objections or doubts requires the salesman to get feedback by communicating in a mature, professional manner. The clarification process is consistent with a problem-solving approach to selling. However, a philosophy of techniques or a set-answer approach, suggests a one-way communication process—a control or forcing of a prospect to accept the salesman's view. This is pressure selling that is usually associated with a canned or formulized sales talk.

Objections and the Two-way Communication Process

In a nutshell, each salesman must recognize that *it is impossible to have perfect communication in replying to prospect objections, statements, or doubts unless what the prospect intends to communicate by his objections, statements, or doubts is fully understood by the salesman.*

As an illustration, what does the prospect mean when he says to the salesman selling an industrial machine, "Your costs are too high"? This could refer to cost of anything from the initial price of the equipment, its operational cost, installation cost, or cost of changing productional runs to the relative use the purchaser would have for the equipment. Thus, before the salesman replies to the prospect, he must be reasonably sure he knows what the prospect intends to communicate by his objection or doubt; otherwise, the salesman cannot receive the prospect's message and he cannot, in turn, strike the mind of the prospect. This entire process is clearly seen in the two-way communication diagram, page 160.

Visualize the disruption to the communication process as the salesman gives an excellent reply to the prospect's statement, but he hasn't answered the prospect's real question. Communication is sidetracked. And the salesman becomes one who just doesn't understand with all of the sales implications therein.

A GUIDELINE FOR HANDLING OBJECTIONS

Before proceeding further with this discussion of objections, a framework will be provided as a guideline for this phase of the sales interview. For the situation-management, customer-oriented salesman the framework is as follows:

1. He understands that there are both business and personal reasons as to why a prospect may voice objections or make statements, comments, beliefs, etc.

2. He understands the "why" concept which is used to clarify the prospect's statements, doubts, objections, or questions.

3. He understands the various tactics that can be used to handle these so-called objections once they have been clarified.

4. He understands that the procedure for handling objections, statements, beliefs, or concepts will vary according to the individual's personal, emotional, or status needs. In brief, the method used will be tempered by the prospect's predominant traits. This concept is explained in Chapter 17.

Some Business Reasons for Objections

1. Each individual wants to understand fully the details of the salesman's plan and how it affects his firm, his position, and his organization.

2. Each individual wants to be sure that he needs the specific program or product that the salesman is recommending.

3. Each individual wants to be sure that the salesman's services, the product, and the services of the salesman's company will have the advantages claimed.

4. Each individual wants to be sure the salesman's plan is timely, that is, that it will fit into his total operational program at this time. Above all, the prospect wants to be able to justify the investment, time, and risk the salesman's plan requires. He wants to be sure it is the best possible solution. (It is recommended that the salesman reread problem solving and decision making as discussed in Chapter 13.)

5. Each individual sometimes raises objections from the standpoint of how the salesman and his company will carry out, physically and finan-

Selling: A Behavioral Science Approach

cially, the plan presented, because he does not have confidence in the salesman personally or in his company.

Some Personal Reasons for Objections

1. Each individual wants to *feel* that he is a partner in the conversation with the salesman.

2. Each individual wants to *feel* that his opinions are respected—that he is important.

3. Each individual wants to be satisfied in his own *mind*, regardless of what the salesman thinks.

4. Each individual wants to *feel* that the decision to act is his own decision.

5. Each individual wants to *feel* that the salesman's professional and moral standards are those of an individual whom he personally would like to meet and with whom he would like to do business.

All of these reasons for objections are emotional in nature. They spring from the personal, emotional, or social needs of individuals. The intensity or degree of each status or personal need will vary with each individual. It is significant that, on the one hand, business needs for objections were discussed and, on the other hand, personal needs were identified as a source of objections. It is apparent that these two sets of needs interact at all times in all sales. This is, however, advantageous to the salesman employing depth selling. He satisfies both sets of needs. He understands their interaction and through high fidelity communication he gets verbal and nonverbal feedback which permits him to adjust to the complex interaction between the individual's personal needs and the needs of the business firm. It seems it would be impossible for any individual, whether it is a businessman making a decision concerning a product or equipment purchase for his company or the individual making a decision to buy an item for his personal use, not to have that decision significantly influenced by his emotional or personal needs.

The Process of Clarification

In previous chapters, the importance of the question technique has been firmly established. In fact, it has been stated, "It is the one most important sales tactic the salesman can employ in the verbal portion of the communication process."

In the contact stage verifying and permissive question forms were introduced. In the discussion stage developmental, evaluative, and indirect question forms were brought into play. Now in the doubt stage the why question form will be used. It is the hub of the *clarification* process.

The why concept is utilized in two ways. In the basic method the salesman responds to the customer's objection with a simple "Why?" Used this way, it puts the customer on the defensive. But, even so, many times it assists in clarifying what the prospect means by his statement.

Solutions to Prospect Doubts: Part One

In the second approach the why concept is used as a refined, courteous, questioning device designed to facilitate the flow of ideas between the sales representative and the prospect. And what is perhaps even more important, it enables the sales representative to clarify effectively—to get to the root reasons behind the customer's statements or objections.

A few examples will show the difference between the set-answer approach, the "basic why" approach, and the "refined why" (refined-questioning) concepts. Here are several objections or statements that have been heard by most salesmen at one time or another.

Several Common Objections

1. "I'm not interested in a preliminary or survey plan."
2. "Your costs are too high," or "You just keep on raising the price," or "Your price is too high."
3. "I want to talk it over with some other people."
4. "We use or stock other products."
5. "I'll think about it this fall."

To each of these so-called objections the sales representative may reply (1) with a set answer which has been prepared for the specific objection, (2) with the basic why approach, or (3) with a refined why approach.

The danger of using the prepared or set answer has been previously explained—the prospect may not specifically mean what he said. Nevertheless, this approach is followed by some of the largest companies in the United States.

As an example, one large corporation requires its salesmen to list all objections they hear from prospects. Set answers are prepared for these objections. They are incorporated in the company sales manual and each salesman is required to memorize an answer or answers for each objection. This, the company feels, is an excellent procedure[1] because every salesman has the information at hand with which he can handle any situation. But the memorized-answer approach may lead the salesman into the trap of giving canned answers to objections. Dialogue 1A illustrates the set-answer approach and its danger.

The basic why method is commonly used. If a salesman followed this method to each of the objections above, he would merely ask why. This forces the prospect to answer. It puts him on the defensive. But putting the customer or prospect on the defensive has a major disadvantage. Some individuals might resent a salesman's terse "Why?" Thus the salesman should use this technique judiciously.

Refined questioning, in contrast to the set-answer approach and the why approach, has no disadvantages, although it is not so forceful as the why. Compare the set-answer and the basic why technique with the refined-questioning approach in the following dialogues.

---

[1] It would be far better, in most training situations, if the salesmen learned rather than memorized.

Selling: A Behavioral Science Approach

Dialogues Illustrating the Clarification Process

Assume that Horton of Smith & Smith, an industrial distributor, is attempting to interest an executive in a preliminary survey.

DIALOGUE 1A

S I am fully confident we could save a great deal of your time if we had your approval to make a survey of your present equipment and then present you with a preliminary plan for your specific replacement needs.

R No, I don't think I am interested in a survey.

S That's because you probably are not familiar with all the advantages of having a survey of your production system (or a survey of your equipment productivity) made.

The dialogue above is a good example of how not to handle a prospect's negative-voluntary statement. Horton assumed he knew why the prospect said he was not interested in a survey. He gave the prospect a rather dogmatic answer, which perhaps was a prepared set answer. Many individuals would react negatively to the salesman Horton in the above situation.

Instead of this salesman-oriented handling of the objection, here is how the basic why and the refined why, customer-oriented concepts would be employed.

R No, I don't think I am interested in a survey.

S (1) Why?

OR

Mr. Davis, (2) is there any particular reason why you are not interested in the survey plan?

OR

Mr. Davis, (3) I would appreciate hearing your viewpoint on preliminary plans, if I may.

OR

I am sorry to hear that, Mr. Davis, but (4) it would be helpful to me if you could tell me whether it is the survey or preliminary plan concept in general or Smith & Smith in particular in which you are not interested.

Is there a difference between the why concept as used in 1, 2, 3, and 4? The answer is yes. Number 1 illustrates the use of the basic why method, whereas 2, 3, and 4 show how the refined why may be used.

The next dialogue is a continuation of Dialogue 1A. It will demonstrate how a salesman may, by proper questioning and discussion, reveal the reasons for the objection. Prospect Davis has replied that he was not interested in a survey.

Solutions to Prospect Doubts: Part One

DIALOGUE 1B

S I am sorry to hear that, Mr. Davis, but it would be helpful to me if you could tell me whether you are not interested in a survey or preliminary plan concept in general or Smith & Smith in particular?
R Oh, I suppose it is both.
S I am sure, Mr. Davis, that you have a specific reason for feeling as you do. Would it be possible for you to comment further on the survey idea?
R Well, OK. I have had a few problems in the past with companies and what they say they are going to do and what they do. I have had a few salesmen tell me they want to make a survey of some nature and that's the last I hear of them, or it's a mess, or someone just wants to be nosey. Also, it really takes an accomplished man to come in and make a survey of our equipment and production. It has to be someone skilled in that particular area.
S I see, Mr. Davis. Am I right in assuming then, that if you had a survey done of your gauging situation and equipment situation, you want to have it done by an organization that is reliable? You want the man doing it to be competent in the field, that is, one who is trained to present a worthwhile preliminary program to you, and you want it done with little, if any, disruption in the work process?
R Yes, I think that's it, more or less.
S Thank you, Mr. Davis. I can understand, . . .

With the proper questioning Horton has now exposed the real thinking behind Davis's objection to a preliminary plan or survey; that is, Davis had been disappointed in the past with the results of other survey attempts. Also, he thinks it takes a really competent man to do it. And above all, he doesn't want work or staff disruption.

From this point on, it would be much easier for Horton to explain his competence in the field, the reliability of his company, and also show the prospect how the survey would be done with little or no work interference. Horton may assure Davis that he will have to go to just one, or just a few, people in the organization to get all the facts he would need to come up with a particular program or plan. Perhaps it would mean talking only to the master mechanic, or to several machinists, or the general manager, plus some time inspecting equipment.

In summary, it is seen in Dialogue 1B that each of Horton's questions results in what may be termed "agreeable clarification." It is difficult for the prospect to become annoyed with the salesman asking courteous questions such as "I am sure that you have a specific reason for feeling as you do. And would it be possible for you to comment further on the survey idea, Mr. Davis?" or "I would appreciate hearing your viewpoint on that, Mr. Davis."

On the other hand, the why concept will elicit responses which may not necessarily reflect the prospect's opinion. Furthermore, the prospect may be just as terse in his reply to the salesman as the salesman's "Why?" was to the prospect.

So far in this chapter, two of the three component parts of the doubts phase of selling have been examined. Reasons why the prospect raised objections have been analyzed and concepts that can be used to clarify or explain a prospect's statements, doubts, objections, or questions have been illustrated.

Each of the several common objections or doubts previously listed may be clarified by the same process used in Dialogues 1A and 1B. *It is understood that the salesman clarifies whenever he is not reasonably confident that both he and the customer or prospect attach the same meaning to the objection or doubt.*

TACTICS FOR HANDLING OBJECTIONS

After an objection or doubt has been clarified, or if the salesman is reasonably sure he knows the prospect's intent, he will answer the objection. Any salesman who has product knowledge, knows the prospect's situation, knows his own company's policies, its strengths and weaknesses, knows his competition, knows his markets, and understands and practices selling in depth will be able to communicate effectively with the prospect concerning any valid statement that the prospect voices during the interview. It must be understood that if no need exists, it is impossible to handle objections or statements related to need. Most prospect doubts, statements, or objections, however, are answerable. The following five tactics give the salesman a workable system for handling this phase of the sales interviews. Four of the techniques are used after the salesman has clarified the prospect's objection. The first tactic described, however, is intended to eliminate any need for clarifying a prospect's objection.

1. Forestalling Objections
2. Direct Denial
3. Indirect Denial
4. Compensation
5. Boomerang

Each technique will be described and illustrated with dialogue as well.

Forestalling Objections

Many sales specialists believe it is a good idea to eliminate doubts or objections before the prospect has an opportunity to express them. This process is called forestalling. It is especially applicable for frequently heard objections or doubts. It is thought that once a prospect raises an objection or doubt, regardless of how well the salesman answers it, the prospect may be reluctant to accept the answer.

In support of this concept the psychologist might add, "Many people resent being told—no matter how nicely—that they have made a wrong assumption."

To forestall objections, the salesman *does not* raise the objection and then answer it, but rather he eliminates the objection by weaving the fabric of his sales talk in such a way that he presents material and evidence that eliminates the objection. The prospect never voices the objection. Normally, should the salesman desire to do so, he can forestall most valid objections that are frequently raised by prospects.

For instance, assume a salesman has often heard the objection that his company is frequently increasing prices. To forestall this, the salesman never lets this doubt be raised but instead eliminates or circumvents the situation before it is stated by the prospect. The salesman may say:

S Hunt and Hunt is very proud of its low-cost services and product pricing. The fact is it has held increases to a minimum. Taking the base year 1959, we see that prices for X products have risen by 12–14 percent. On the other hand, Hunt and Hunt has raised its prices only 3½ percent.

Or take this hypothetical situation of salesman Wallace for Ford's Mustang. Assume Wallace has frequently heard that the Mustang has been involved in accidents because it isn't stable at high speeds. Salesman Wallace is concerned about this false objection, and he decides the best course of action is to forestall it. It is about 10 A.M. and a prospect is looking at a Mustang in the company's showroom. Salesman Wallace approaches the prospect. This excerpt from a sales dialogue will illustrate how Wallace forestalled the above objection.

R It is a good-looking car.
S Yes, Mr. Blank, from what people tell us and from what we read in the magazines the Mustang design has indeed captured the hearts of most people. They like the comfort too. (*Wallace is now opening the door to the car.*) How about your slipping behind the wheel here and seeing for yourself how comfortable the Mustang really is?
R This is a surprise. . . .
S By the way, not only has the Mustang been rated tops in all of these plus features we have been talking about, but its roadability is something unique. Research tests which are documented in that portfolio show (*gesturing towards the large portfolio on a nearby desk*) that because of Mustang's unique styling, structural build, compactness, weight, it has been proved to be one of the safest cars on the road.
R That sounds rather interesting. I think I will take a look at those research data.
S Fine, and after you have glanced at that, I hope you will take time for a quick run so that you can feel that Mustang performance.

As the Ford Mustang dialogue shows, the salesman has forestalled or answered the objection before it was raised. Frequently objections are, however, voiced by the prospect and answered directly and immediately by the salesman. A prospect or customer voices an objection and the salesman, based on his experience and judgment, classifies the objection, statement, or doubt as vague, true, or false. If the prospect's statement or objection is vague, the salesman follows the why or the refined why clarification process. After the true meaning of the prospect's statement or objection is ascertained, the salesman judges the objection to be true or false. If an objection is false, the salesman uses a direct or indirect denial.

Selling: A Behavioral Science Approach

If the objection or statement is correct, the salesman uses the compensation or boomerang method.

Direct Denial

Direct denial is used when a statement made by the prospect is false. It is used by some salesmen when they want to deny forcefully a statement the prospect has made. It is recommended that the salesman assume the prospect raised the objection in good faith. He may have heard it from another competing salesman, another executive, or union representative or from any one of a hundred sources. He has a reason for voicing the doubt; it is an honest objection.

Assume the prospect made the statement, "I heard that you give better deals to some companies than to others." Utilizing the direct denial idea, the salesman would reply:

S   Mr. Davis, you are wrong. We take great pride in living up to a rigid code of ethics. We give the same service, same prices to all of our customers. Here, let me show you what I mean with some of the material I have in my portfolio.

Making this statement and showing the prospect the evidence that neither he nor his company gets involved in prices and "deals," the salesman will frequently satisfy the customer or prospect. If the source of the false information is a competing company or salesman, the salesman's straightforward denial will weaken the unethical salesman's position. In fact, if the prospect is an ethical individual, he might disrespect the other salesman for the types of offers or statements which may have been made.

The direct denial, however, has a major disadvantage. Few people like being told that they are wrong. Yet some sales authorities believe that in matters where the ethics of a firm are being questioned, the salesman should take a strong stand.

The recommended stance for the industrial salesman is to deny directly any false statement concerning the integrity of his company. But the direct denial must be so structured that it will not offend the other individual. It must not be forgotten that although the prospect's objection is false, it is a simple matter of his being misinformed or not getting the facts. Thus, in contrast to the example above, "Mr. Davis, you are wrong," the salesman could, and in most situations it is strongly recommended that he do so, make any of the following statements:

S   Mr. Davis, this is wrong. We take great pride in living up to a rigid code of ethics. . . .

OR

S   Mr. Davis, I am afraid I have to take definite issue with you on that point.

OR

S   Mr. Davis, I believe you have been given some incorrect information. . . .

Solutions to Prospect Doubts: Part One

Indirect Denial

Like the direct denial, the indirect denial is used for objections the salesman judges to be false. With the indirect denial technique, the salesman never directly tells the prospect that he is wrong; instead, he understands the prospect's views, doesn't get defensive, but does correct the false statement.

Continuing with the objection above, when the prospect says, "I have heard that you give better deals to some companies than to others," the salesman would reply:

S I can understand your saying that, Mr. Davis, since we do have substantial variances in final or net prices. It varies with the trade-in, special features or design, or in other words, the price varies as in a car situation. It varies with the optional equipment ordered. We adapt each product or each program so that it meets the needs of each individual firm. However, I can assure you, Mr. Davis, that no firm in my territory receives a better price than another firm investing in identical products or an identical program.

No sales representative should attempt to overexplain or protest too much. He should discuss away the prospect's doubts through an honest, straightforward statement of his own thinking and his company's policies.

Compensation Method

When the customer's objection is valid, the salesman uses the compensation method. He must present some factors to justify or offset the objection.

Assume that during the sales interview the prospect tells the office furniture salesman, "Let's see, you want $200 for your chair. I like your chair, but I can get an Expand chair for less." This is true, and if the salesman uses the compensation method, he would agree with the prospect, but he would attempt to justify the rationale for the difference in price.

S Yes, Mr. Marker, you can buy the Expand chair for approximately $50 less than ours. And, Mr. Marker, the Expand chair is a good chair; however, for that additional $50 investment in a Jennings chair you get precision workmanship and the best possible leathers that improve in beauty as the years roll by. And the Jennings chair is guaranteed ten years. We guarantee that the leather will not chip or crack. . . .

The next dialogue illustrates the clarification principle combined with the compensation method.

R Jim, I like to do business with you but I can get that desk for less someplace else.
S Do you mean exactly the same desk, Mr. Turner?
R No. It is an XYZ desk, but it is just about like yours.
S Yes, Mr. Turner, the XYZ desk is a good desk and the price is lower than ours. I believe the price per desk is approximately $27 less than ours, but by investing $27 more in the Vining desk you are getting X gauge steel. . . .

Selling: A Behavioral Science Approach

In short, the salesman justifies the difference in price by reminding the prospect of the difference in quality.

Sometimes the compensation method is referred to as the "yes, but" or offset technique. The reason for these terms is self-explanatory from the foregoing dialogues.

Boomerang Method

This method is also used in the case of reasonably true objections. But in contrast to the compensation method, the salesman now takes the statement made by the prospect and converts that statement into a reason why the prospect should buy.

In this case, Harper, an industrial salesman, is discussing numeric controls, a form of automated industrial equipment. To utilize the boomerang method, he would reply to the prospect's statement in this way.

R Numeric control is just too far in the future for us.
S That's the very reason why you should invest in numeric control. You have heard the expression, "Time waits for no man." Well, that's the way it is with progress in business. Especially in machine shop business. If you don't move now, you will be too far behind in the future. Your competition will always be ahead of you and you know what that means—lower costs . . .

OR

R I just can't afford to spend money for a numeric-controlled machine.
S Mr. Plant, that's the very reason why you should invest now. If you can't afford a new machine, how can you afford to have a high-cost operation or miss out on some new contracts because of high unit costs?

Discerning salesmen will quickly see that as standard operating procedure the boomerang technique doesn't sound like professional selling but is more suitable for the fast-talking, overpowering-type salesman. Nevertheless, many firms do train their salesmen to use the boomerang method. They claim that a forceful throwback to the customer of an objection shows superiority and ability to handle a situation, that it is a good motivating tool, and that customers like to have positive salesmen who make positive assertions—especially when there is doubt in the prospect's mind. This may all be true in certain situations and with certain prospects, but this method should be used with care.

A Reminder

Every salesman must remember that the question technique is basic to clarification. To illustrate, a review of the following hypothetical objections will be helpful.

1. "I'm not interested in a preliminary plan."
2. "Your price is too high."
3. "I want to talk it over with some other people."
4. "I'm going to think about it."

Solutions to Prospect Doubts: Part One

5. "I've been doing business with X company for some time," or "I have had C. M. Machines for a long time."

6. "I have heard that you give better deals to some companies than to others."

On analyzing these objections, it is clear it would be difficult to have one prepared answer for these comments. Each of these objections must be clarified before it can be answered, since each prospect will have a different meaning behind his particular objection. Just what does a prospect mean when he says, "I am not interested in a preliminary plan"? Or what does he mean when he says, "Your price is too high"? Too high for what? Or, "I want to talk it over with some other people." What people? Why? When? What in particular does he want to talk over? Or, "I'm going to think about it." What does he want to think about? Is it the price? Is it the time? Is it the company? Is it the salesman?

Or take the statement, "I have had C. M. machines for a long time." What's wrong with that? It's not an objection. It's perhaps a good company with good products, and the salesman should want to find out why the prospect has been doing business with that company for some time. It could be that his brother-in-law is the sales manager, or they could be paying some executive $500 for services rendered, or it could be service or quality or company reputation.

Take the statement, "I have heard that you give better deals to some companies than to others." What does the prospect or customer have in mind? Can the salesman afford to risk replying to this statement before he identifies what is specifically meant? Why not inquire, "This comes as a surprise to me, Mr. Blank. What do you have in mind?"

In brief, then, whenever the salesman has doubts about what the prospect means, it is advisable that the salesman discuss the statement or objection with the prospect. After the prospect has clarified why—for instance, he thinks the price is too high—then the salesman justifies or denies as the case may be. The salesman must remember that some objections, feelings, or beliefs of some individuals remain hidden. The salesman has to smoke out these concealed facts into the open.

PRICE

Price is one of the most discussed problems in business today. Generally companies attempt to produce the quality product they want at the lowest possible price. This is true whether a company's strategy is to produce the highest possible quality and project this image to the marketplace or whether the company's strategy is to produce a relatively low-quality item. Frequently the problem for the salesman is that a competing company may produce a lower-quality item that compares favorably in appearance to the high-quality product but sells at a lower price.

Most companies add a markup to the basic cost to cover all other costs including marketing. Many companies adjust their price, of course, to competition and according to business conditions. But *in general* there is much truth in the old saying, "You get what you pay for." The mistake made in many cases by the salesman and the customer is comparing basic prices and forgetting the quality, workmanship, guarantees, and service of all forms (transportation, location, repairs, instructions for operation, and installation) are all elements of price.

It is quite easy for the discount house to sell a Smith-Corona electric typewriter for less than the established typewriter retailer who has a full line of service and gives a guarantee. The discount house sells out of a box, or the typewriter is still in the box when the customer receives it. The retail company adjusts the typewriter, inspects it, delivers it, and is responsible for all maintenance for a certain length of time. If the customer's typewriter breaks down, the full-line-service company representative will repair on the spot or give the customer a loan typewriter. Not so with the discount house. The customer buys the product as it is. If he has a problem, he ships it back to the manufacturer, or he takes it to the typewriter repair shop and pays for the repair. On the other hand, it is difficult for one discount house to sell a quality typewriter in competition with another discount house which may be selling a foreign-made, lower-quality typewriter.

Price is relative. Some individuals want quality, others do not. What do you pay for your shoes? Your suit? Your car? Some people buy economy cars; others buy high-priced cars. In brief, not everyone wants to pay a higher price regardless of what they get.

Now the salesman's job is this: He must justify the higher price. He is a problem solver. He can explain what his product, his company, and his service can do for the prospect. He must perform this function when he is in competition with a lower-quality item of the same type he is selling or one of comparable quality selling at a lesser or equal price. The salesman makes a difference. In most cases, if he has to rely solely on price, then that salesman has nothing to offer. He is not a salesman.

Assume there are 500 people all buying shoes. Shoes look alike but are not comparable in quality. The lines sell for $10, $12, $14, $16, $18, $20, $22, $25, and $35. Not everyone wants $10 shoes, nor does everyone want $35 shoes. Assume that 50 of the 500 buyers above think in terms of shoes around $16 or $18. If the salesman can explain quality, comfort, etc., he could shift most of these 500 buyers $2 one way or the other. And he may shift several to $35.

The same analysis holds good for the industrial buyer. Equipment varies in price. The salesman will not sell to everyone. But assume there are 500 potential customers of equipment. The prices are $18 to $35 per unit. Assume most buyers lean toward the price of the $18 unit. An efficient salesman will convert more buyers to $22 and $30 units than will the less efficient salesman. He must, of course, justify price in some way such as quality, workmanship, solutions to problems, or service of all types. This is selling.

HANDLING THE PRICE SITUATION

Many salesmen feel that the price situation is the hardest of all to handle. Yet, in some respects it is easier to sell high-priced products than low-priced products. Mentally the salesman never has to apologize for price. He can take pride in knowing the customer or prospect has bought the best. Seldom, with the purchase of quality, does the consumer, the business firm, or the industrial buyer become dissatisfied. On the other hand, many business firms, many consumers, and many industrial firms have become dissatisfied with lower-priced, lower-quality products.

The salesman should not forget, however, that some customers will be better satisfied with lower-priced merchandise, others with higher-priced products. The important point is that the salesman should solve the customer's problems, not his commission.

The following are a number of points specifically related to handling the price situation. It is recommended that the salesman:

1. Sell quality
2. Break price down into small units
3. Talk investment and profit
4. Build a mental bridge

Sell Quality

The salesman should never apologize by action or statement for price. The salesman should never say, "We are asking $X for this product." This sounds apologetic and suggests that the salesman is ready to bargain.

To sell either quality lines or lower-priced lines, the salesman uses the strategy and tactics discussed in previous chapters, but it is important the salesman remember that the same stimulus words will not sell both low- and high-priced items. If the salesman is selling a low-priced item, for example, a low-priced desk, he should talk about the fact that the chair is a good substantial item for its price and point out its good qualities. On the other hand, if he is selling a high-priced wooden desk, he should talk quality. He should talk about the sculptured design, highest quality wood, fine precision workmanship. Dialogue illustrating how to sell a low-priced product as well as a high-priced product is given in the discussion on Building a Mental Bridge, later in this chapter.

Break Price Down into Small Units

Two illustrations will be given, one of a retail furniture salesman and the second from the industrial field. In the first illustration the salesman is selling a $200 chair and the customer is thinking of buying a lower-priced chair from his competitor. He combines the compensation method with breaking the price down into small units in this fashion:

S   Yes, the Expand chair is a good chair, and you can get it for approximately $50 less than the Jennings chair. However, Mr. Turner, I would like to mention to you that for the additional $50 investment in this chair you will be getting precision workmanship, the best possible leathers that will never chip or crack. Furthermore, when you think of the fact that you will have this chair in your office approximately ten years, then your investment would be no more

Selling: A Behavioral Science Approach

than $5 a year or less than fifty cents a month for all the extra quality that you can see and the extra quality that is in the basic construction of the chair.

The second illustration is taken from the industrial field. This salesman is selling a $10,000 Tape-O-Matic.

S Yes, Mr. Jones, I can understand your concern about a $10,000 investment, but let's take a look at this from an investment standpoint. The initial investment is $10,000, but the minute you invest in this machine the government gives you a 7 percent tax credit. Or in other words, $700 refund on the taxes you will pay this year. This is cash savings to you. Your investment in the Tape-O-Matic now becomes $9,300, and as you know, there is a special depreciation allowance of 20 percent given by the government for all investments in capital goods. Depreciation is granted on the original investment. Therefore your depreciation allowance is $2,000. I'll jot these figures down on this pad of paper here. Is it all right, Mr. Jones, if I assume that your corporation or your company is in the 50 percent income tax bracket?
R Well, that makes us pretty prosperous, but we would like to be there, yes.
S That $2,000 depreciation then means a $1,000 tax savings to you at the end of the year. So far, your total savings amount to $1,700. At the end of the year in which you have purchased investment equipment, as you know, you are allowed the normal 20 percent depreciation on the depreciated balance of $8,000. That is a $1,600 depreciation credit. Following the same reasoning we used before, this decreases your tax liability by another $800. Actually then, before you begin to use this machine, you are purchasing it for $7,500. This is now your initial investment. Do you agree on these figures, Mr. Jones?
R Yes, that looks okay to me.
S Now, in addition, a Tape-O-Matic will cut your costs in these seventeen areas. (*Salesman itemizes them.*)

Before long the salesman breaks the price down to a per-hour-usage basis that is, of course, a significantly small amount.

Take the Ice Out of Price by Talking Profit and Investment

In the example above, the industrial salesman talked investment. It is good practice for the salesman to talk investment and not talk about spending money. In the same example, the salesman could have broadened his discussion of investment to include profit as well.

Talking profit means telling the prospect what the product will do for the user in terms of lowering cost or increasing sales and thus enhancing the user's profit picture. It is relatively easy for the industrial salesman or the salesman selling equipment to convert the qualities of his product into the profit picture. But what isn't understood is that the salesman selling nonproduction goods can also talk in terms of profit. The following is taken from the National Office Furniture Association's Sales Training Manual, Chicago, Illinois.

Talking profit means telling the customer what your installation of office

Solutions to Prospect Doubts: Part One

furniture will do for him and his office. Tell him about the increased efficiency, the morale, better relationship with customers, etc. Tell him, too, how efficiency will be improved and how as a result turnover may be reduced.

These factors are all related to profit. Investment in office furniture explained in terms of what it will do for the business firms takes the ice out of price. Also, the salesman can make a strong point by comparing the firm's investment in each square foot of office space, plus salaries of its office personnel with its investment in office furniture. It is clear the salesman can emphasize that a relatively small investment in office furniture will give the company more mileage out of its investment in space and people.[2]

This sales book also tells the office furniture salesman that whenever he is selling office furniture to a manufacturer who has showrooms, he should interpret the office furniture as being just as important as production machines in the factory. It tells the salesman that showrooms or offices where the customer meets the product are just as important as the machines in the factory, since it is the showroom where the product is sold.

Building a Mental Bridge

Most salesmen are confronted with the problem of selling two or more price lines. They find it difficult to sell one line without deselling the other. A possible solution to this dilemma is found in the concept of building a mental bridge. Building a mental bridge refers to showing a prospect a low-priced and a high-priced product in such a way that if the customer decides not to buy the high-priced product, he can feel free to go back and buy the low-priced product. This suggests that the salesman never compare the two products, unless he is specifically requested to do so. Rather he gives good positive talking points for the low-priced product and good positive talking points for the high-priced product. To explain this concept, two illustrations will be used. The first is from the office furniture field and the second involves a retail sale of a pen, but the concept applies equally well to all forms of selling. For instance, the salesman selling a lower-priced product may state:

S   This is a fine desk, Mr. Turner. It is one of our biggest selling lines. Our customers have been getting years of good solid wear out of this desk. Here's why: It has the X gauge steel even on these pull-out shelves. . . .

On the other hand, when the salesman is selling the higher-priced desk, he says:

S   I believe, Mr. Turner, this is the finest desk on the market. If you stand back here, you can see its sculptured design. I think you can feel the warmth

---

[2] Joseph W. Thompson, *National Office Furniture Sales Manual,* National Office Furniture Association, Chicago, Ill., 1962, p. 39.

of wood, and of course, as you look at the grain, you see a different picture every time you look. There's no monotony to an X brand wooden desk. And if you look closely at this overhang, you will notice it is a product of precision workmanship. . . .

The salesman could be showing low-priced steel versus high-priced steel, or low-priced steel versus low-priced wood, or high-priced steel versus high-priced wood, or high-priced wood versus low-priced wood. Neither the product nor the combination makes a difference; it's just good advice for the salesman to think positive selling points for the low-priced and the high-priced product or line.

The following will illustrate the wrong way to compare low- and high-priced desks. It will also suggest why it is a good idea to use positive points for both lines:

S This X desk is made by the Brown Company. It's a good company, but the desk is just put together with nails and glue. It feels pretty solid but it doesn't have the workmanship that goes into the White line. That White desk is a real desk—solid wood, not veneer like X. . . . (*This shows the danger of deselling one line in contrast to another.*)

Isn't it possible that Mr. Turner might be somewhat embarrassed to buy the low-priced line even if he wanted it? Also, hasn't the value of the low-priced line been lowered? Why buy a "glue and nail" desk? Now for the right way:

S Yes, this X desk is a good buy. Our customers tell us that it's a lot of desk for the money. It is manufactured by the Brown Company, a well-established company with a fine reputation for standing behind their products.

Or, for high-priced desks:

S We believe this is the finest desk of its type manufactured today. When you have a White desk in your office, you have the ultimate in executive desks. Only finely grained wood, finished with precision craftsmanship, is used in these desks. It is called the sculptured line. What do you think of the workmanship, Mr. Turner?

R It's really a beautiful desk, but perhaps I should stick with that "all-around best buy" in the Brown line. This might not look right in my office.

The next example is of a retail sales person using the concept of building a mental bridge in the sale of a low-priced pen in contrast to a high-priced pen.

S Mrs. Jones, this pen is our best-selling pen. Many of our customers have mentioned that it writes smoothly and seems to be trouble-free. Would you try it, please? (*Passes pen to customer.*)

C Yes, it is nice.

Solutions to Prospect Doubts: Part One

S Glad you like it, Mrs. Jones. By the way, what are you planning to use the pen for?
C Oh, it's to be a gift, my . . .
S Well, Mrs. Jones, before you decide perhaps you would like to look at several other pens. This is a lifetime pen—it has a solid X point; its case is . . . It will never leak. Would you like to try it?
C Yes, I would.

In the pen sale three points stand out.

1. The salesman did not desell the low-priced pen. He sold it as a good pen. He made the customer want that pen. He emphasized all of its good qualities.

2. On the other hand, the salesman sold the high-priced pen and never deemphasized the low-priced pen. He brought out the positive qualities of the high-priced pen. He did not compare one pen with the other. He did not say, "This good pen has this, and the cheap pen has this."

3. He asked a very sensible question. He found out the use of the pen—was it for a gift? If it is for a gift, he knows that close to 90 percent of all gift pens are more expensive pens.

Summary

The objection stage of selling may be a misnomer. A more logical approach may be for the salesman to think of objections as statements, comments, requests for information, or inaccurate statements by the prospect that need clarification, rather than as objections that the salesman is going to handle.

With the clarification concept, the salesman asks questions or uses the why concept. After an objection has been clarified, or whenever the salesman is reasonably confident that he understands specifically what the prospect means by his objection or statement, he will use the direct denial, indirect denial, compensation, or boomerang techniques. If the objection is false, he uses the direct or indirect denial; and if the objection is true, he uses the boomerang or compensation methods.

Forestalling is the process whereby the salesman eliminates the prospect's or customer's objection before it is stated. It is used for objections that the salesman expects to hear frequently.

Price is one of the most discussed problems in business. Many salesmen feel that the price situation is the hardest of all to handle. The salesman must remember that some customers will be more satisfied with a low-cost product, and others will favor a high-cost product. It is recommended that the salesman remember to sell quality, to break price down into smaller units, to talk investment and profit, and to build a mental bridge. The depth salesman will solve the prospect's problem and not be concerned with his commission.

Selling: A Behavioral Science Approach

Chapter 16   DISCUSSION QUESTIONS

1   Is there any particular reason why a salesman should have a philosophy of "objections, please"?

2   Explain why the term *objections* may be a misnomer.

3   What is the difference between the set-answer approach and the clarification process?

4   Thinking in terms of the business reasons for objections as listed in this chapter, in what way would the salesman's knowledge of the decision-making process as it is described in the contact chapter assist the salesman in communicating with the businessman?

5   If personal reasons for objections are emotional in nature, is there any way in which the salesman could forestall such objections?

6   Specifically what is meant by the process of clarification?

7   Are there any advantages to forestalling doubts or objections?

8   Assume that the prospect has raised the true, honest objection that your price is too high. Is it possible that all of the tactics for handling objections could be utilized in one way or the other to handle this objection?

9   Salesmen state that price is one of the most difficult problems they have in selling. If this is true, why is it true? Should price be a major problem in sales situations?

10   You are debating between purchasing a ten-dollar and a fifteen-dollar tennis racket. The fifteen-dollar tennis racket is the higher-quality racket and of noticeably higher quality than the ten-dollar racket. The salesman points the fine features of the fifteen-dollar racket and he tells you that the racket will last you approximately five years with fairly rough and steady play. He then reminds you that you are talking about one dollar per year to own a fine racket or about two cents every time you play tennis. Would you be impressed with such reasoning? Would it cause you to buy it?

solution
to prospect
doubts

part two

17

KNOWING THE PROSPECT

Prospect knowledge, a basic of selling, refers to the salesman's ability to analyze and adjust to the various prospects he encounters. In brief, the salesman adjusts to the emotional and personal needs of the individual. Frequently these needs are reflected in characteristics of an individual. And although a list would be almost endless if an attempt were made to account for shades of differences among people, a general list of characteristics can be compiled.[1] Such a list can be most helpful as the salesman develops his ability to identify and adjust to individuals exhibiting certain characteristics. The shades of differences among prospects can be more easily gauged. This form of analysis helps the salesman become sensitized to people. What is more, it perhaps emphasizes the importance of placing the burden of good communication on the shoulders of the salesman. This is where the burden belongs. It is not up to the customer or prospect to adjust to the salesman, but rather it is up to the salesman to adjust to each prospect in each situation.

Each sales situation has two broad dimensions. One is the firm and the firm's problems and needs; the other is the human element—the prospect and his needs. For instance, every potential user of industrial equipment has some form of a manufacturing process. The process may be long or it may be short. It may be complex or it may be simple. The production output and capacity will be modified from time to time. In any case, a solution or key to why a company should purchase new equipment always exists. In most cases, the decision to buy is made by an individual. Knowing the prospect will assist each salesman in his effort to solve the problems of each firm.

Each individual may exhibit many characteristics or traits. Table 6 lists ten general characteristics which bulk large in an individual's psy-

---

[1] The reader may wish to review the discussion of needs in the behavorial science chapters before beginning this section.

chological makeup. This analysis suggests ways in which the salesman can adjust to each individual. It presents a rule of thumb for the industrial salesman to follow to assist him in his adjustment process with different prospects. The vast majority of the concepts and techniques that have been discussed in previous chapters can be utilized by the salesman in working with any one of the individuals listed in Table 6.

TABLE 6   Prospect Characteristics and Techniques to Use

  I. To handle objections
  II. To complete sale

Prospect characteristics	To handle objections	To complete sale		Comments
		Buildup closes	Clincher closes	
1. Silent				
2. Procrastinator				
3. Glad-hander				
4. Slow or methodical				
5. Pugilistic or argumentative				
6. Timid or overcautious				
7. Ego-involved or opinionated				
8. Skeptical or suspicious				
9. The grouch				
10. Impulsive— changeable				

Techniques for meeting objection	Buildup closes	Clincher closes
1. Forestalling objections	1. Compliment	A. Assuming prospect will buy
2. Clarification	2. Continuous yes	B. Ask for the order
3. Direct denial	3. Summary	C. SRO
4. Indirect denial	4. Emotional	D. Minor point
5. Compensation	5. T account	
6. Boomerang		

PROSPECT CHARACTERISTICS AND TACTICS TO USE

Table 6 is designed to emphasize that the salesman must not only change roles, but he must have a range of intensity enactment of each role in managing human situations. This table is not complete since it will be advantageous for the salesman to think through the process of meeting objections and to select methods he would employ with each individual.[2]

---

[2] It is recommended that the reader defer completing Table 6 until after Chap. 18, "Completing Negotiations," has been analyzed.

Solutions to Prospect Doubts: Part Two

In addition, this table combines techniques for completing negotiations with the techniques of handling objections. Frequently when doubts are voiced by the prospect and are successfully analyzed and answered to the satisfaction of the prospect, it is a good time to complete negotiations. Salesmen, however, have a tendency to feel mentally satisfied when they have answered the doubt and do not then adequately think about completing negotiations.

Here are a few traits or characteristics which certain prospects may exhibit. It is understood that any one individual has many traits, but in this discussion it is assumed that the characteristics identified represent the dominant characteristic exhibited by a specific individual.

The Silent Prospect

There are certain individuals who are reluctant to discuss their situation or even the point the salesman is making. Thus it is difficult for the salesman to obtain an oral response. It is especially difficult to get this individual to commit himself. He may be silent because he doesn't know how to converse; that is, he has little to say. He may be silent because he is a thinker, or it may be a lack of confidence, or perhaps the individual is unusually cautious. The salesman may never know why the prospect is silent.

Coping behavior A variety of questions may be used to obtain a response from the silent individual. Questions requiring his opinion or asking him to amplify on various points may be especially helpful. If possible, the salesman can show a visual and obtain participation from a prospect by asking him questions about it.

The salesman should be careful not to be impatient in waiting for an answer. Sometimes silence is golden. When the salesman pauses or asks a question, he should expect an answer or response. If none is forthcoming, it may be helpful for the salesman to look at the prospect and wait for an answer. Sometimes the salesman may need to talk about topics that are of interest to the prospect but may be irrelevant to the salesman's reason for calling on the prospect.

The Procrastinator

There are many people who procrastinate; that is, they find it difficult to make decisions. This individual is more than just an undecided prospect; he is one who would rather put something off because change is difficult for him. This prospect makes statements similar to those of the undecided buyer such as, "Let me think it over," or "I'll call you in a few days," or "I will have to talk it over with X, Y, and Z." Procrastinators are extremely cautious and wish to look at other alternatives before they decide. Even after examining other alternatives, they find it difficult to make decisions.

Coping behavior It is recommended the salesman be positive, self-assured, and dramatic but not overpowering when selling to a procrastina-

Selling: A Behavioral Science Approach

tor. The salesman may subtly suggest that the prospect has the ability to make decisions. Showmanship and visuals may be helpful. It would be wise for the salesman to summarize important sales points several times during the interview. He reinforces his sales talk through repetition. The T-account close may be especially helpful with this prospect in completing negotiations. Finally, it is suggested the salesman review the problem-solving and decision-making process discussion in Chapter 12.

The Glad-Hander, Talkative, or Overenthusiastic Individual

This prospect sells the salesman rather than the salesman selling him. The salesman has been calling on the glad-hander for two or three years but never has been able to complete negotiations. The salesman likes him and he apparently likes the salesman. This individual will frequently agree with much of what the salesman says and will at times compliment the salesman and even comment on the fine company the salesman represents. In fact, he may even comment that he wants to do business particularly with the salesman. However, the glad-hander gets off the track frequently and talks about things irrelevant to the sales situation.

Coping behavior The salesman must be alert at all times to lead the prospect back to the sales proposal or situation. He should always be alert to say, "By the way, that reminds me. . . ." He should keep on the track, be brief, summarize his points, and above all not try to meet the prospect's enthusiasm but rather feed him material about which to be enthusiastic. When communicating with the overly enthusiastic individual, there is a strong possibility the salesman doesn't sell the things he can do for the prospect or the prospect's company but rather concentrates on being a "fine fellow."

The Slow or Methodical Individual

Many times salesmen overlook this individual, believing a slow reaction indicates a lack of interest or lack of ability to think and communicate. Salesmen are apt to be too rapid in the communication process even when they recognize this individual as a real prospect. There is no relationship between an individual being methodical and having the ability to communicate and think. For instance, an individual may be methodical because he has a strong need for autonomy, that is, to resist influence or coercion; or he may have a strong need for order, that is, a need to arrange, to organize, and to be scrupulously precise; or he may have a strong need for cognizance, that is, an inquiring attitude to explore, to look, to listen and inspect.

Coping behavior The salesman must really slow down and accept the prospect's speed. He should be painstaking and careful in examining details; this individual is likely to be detail-minded. When asking a question, the salesman should wait patiently for a reply. The individual may be mentally juggling a number of variables before he replies. In brief, the salesman allows the prospect to set the pace. Restudy the art of listening in Chapter 11.

Solutions to Prospect Doubts: Part Two

The Overcautious or Timid Individual

This individual appears unsure of himself and consistently appears to seek someone else's advice. The author has worked with a trade association executive who refers many matters concerning conventions to his wife. He is sure she fully represents the women's viewpoint in his association and that women are all-powerful. He is also sure that he has little knowledge of the educational function of a program or the aesthetic value of particular programs for women, so he defers to his wife's judgment for advice in these areas. Another trade association executive whom the author knows depends almost entirely on his assistant. His assistant is actually the decision maker. In the same way some individuals always defer to others in a group for a decision or to other more vocal or more dominant individuals in the company situation.

This individual may be merely insecure or have a strong affiliative need, that is, a need to form friendships, associations, and to cooperate and converse socially with others; or he may have a strong need succorance, that is, the need to seek aid, protection or sympathy, to be dependent; or he may have a strong need deference, that is, to admire and willingly follow a superior, to cooperate with a leader, to serve gladly; or he may have a strong need infavoidance, that is, the need to avoid failure, shame, humiliation, ridicule, or to refrain from attempting to do something that is beyond his power or to conceal a disfigurement. Quite obviously a combination of these needs and others may well explain the person's timidity. The needs of an individual may be fused into an almost unexplainable pattern.

Coping behavior The salesman should concentrate on evidence and facts such as sales portfolios, testimonials, visual materials, tests, and lists of satisfied users. Sometimes, the salesman must build the timid individual's confidence so that he will realize he has the facts on hand on which to base a decision, and the ability to do so.

The Ego-involved or Opinionated Individual

This individual apparently knows all the answers. He knows all about the salesman's company and product before the facts are presented. He wants to control the interview. He thinks his own judgments, opinions, and predictions are best and reacts negatively to suggestions and advice. The following discussion may be helpful in understanding this individual.

Each individual has a degree of need achievement, that is, the need to overcome obstacles, to exercise power, to strive to do something difficult as well and as quickly as possible. This is an elementary ego need and it alone may prompt any action or need for recognition: a self-forwarding attitude, a tendency to excite praise and commendation, to demand respect, to boast and exhibit accomplishments, to seek distinctions, social prestige, and honors of high office; a need exhibition, the need to attract attention to one's person, the need to excite, amuse, or shock others, or the need for self-dramatization. The opinionated person may have a strong need to dominate, to influence or to control others, to persuade, to dictate,

Selling: A Behavioral Science Approach

to prohibit, to lead, to direct, to restrain, or to organize the behavior of a group.

Coping behavior   In general the main rule to follow in dealing with the strong-ego individual is to make him feel important. This is apparently what he needs, so the salesman caters to him. The salesman never gives his ideas as being conclusive, but he seeks the prospect's advice, counsel, and opinion. The salesman can control the interview and do the guiding by presenting facts and ideas in a purposeful but permissive fashion. The salesman must be permissive in his entire attitude. Conflict in personalities may be expensive from sales standpoint; the salesman adjusts to the ego-involved individual.

The Skeptical or Suspicious Individual

This individual seems to have a negative answer to everything. He knows the where, when, and why about everything you discuss. He may feel very strongly about specific points, for instance, cost, delivery, quality, etc. He is difficult to work with, and it is difficult to communicate with him.

Why is an individual consistently skeptical or suspicious of others? There is no one answer to this situation. But it is possible this individual has a need to dominate, to receive recognition, or to feel superior. He may have a strong feeling of need rejection, that is, the need to snub, ignore, or exclude, to remain aloof and indifferent; or the cause of his attitude may be need defendance, that is, the need to defend himself against blame or belittlement, to justify his actions, to offer extenuations, explanations, and excuses, or to resist probing.

Coping behavior   In coping with the skeptical individual the salesman emphasizes facts. This person has a tendency to argue and to be steadfast in his opinions. It is recommended the salesman use logic and syllogistic reasoning. He should hide nothing. No product is perfect. If the product has limitations it may be well to point out these limitations before this individual has an opportunity to voice them.

The Grouch

At the outset of an interview, the salesman must never say to this prospect, "How are things going?" That is all the grouch needs to begin telling him that nothing is right, his health, his job, his friends, etc. After twenty minutes of this pessimistic outlook even the salesman begins to think things are indeed intolerable. The grouch is always ready to relate rumors concerning the financial condition of all business firms; he expounds on how the Democrats or the Republicans will ruin the country, on how we are on the verge of socialism or communism, and on how we may be headed for total destruction now that China has the atomic bomb. He is the extreme opposite of the individual having a pollyanna outlook.

Coping behavior   As difficult as it may be, it is recommended that the salesman hear the grouch out. The salesman must have patience. He

305

must be buoyant. He must be optimistic and give this individual constructive ideas. Above all, the salesman must not absorb his pessimism. A strong offense is the best defense with this individual. The salesman shows him how, with the program of action recommended, his product will solve some of the grouch's problems.

The Impulsive, Changeable Individual

This person is usually a rapid talker and sometimes is abrupt in his speech. He is just as changeable as he is rapid. This individual may have a strong need achievement or need recognition or need exhibition or need dominance or need contrariance, that is, to act differently from others, to be unique, take the opposite side, etc., or in other words, it is extremely difficult to say why this individual is impulsive and changeable. Apparently, he takes pride in being impulsive and changeable.

Coping behavior It is recommended the salesman speed up his sales talk, omitting unimportant details whenever possible, and maintain the rapid tempo.

But the salesman must be sure he presents sufficient facts so that the prospect knows what he is deciding; otherwise, he is apt to change his mind completely. Perhaps it would be well to push this individual slightly and pin him down with facts. It is recommended the salesman think in terms of spatial summation and then when he observes an interest pattern on the part of the prospect he can reinforce each of these interest patterns with temporal stimuli. It is recommended the salesman be alert for trial closes early in the sale with the impulsive, changeable individual.

The Pugilistic or Argumentative Individual

The pugilist apparently wants to argue. He wants to take issue. He may make cutting or sarcastic remarks concerning the salesman, selling in general (peddlers), the salesman's product or company. Frequently he takes a stand for the sake of arguing. He is usually insincere and tries a salesman's patience.

Why do some prospects or customers exhibit pugilistic tendencies toward the salesman? Again there is no one answer to this, but it must be remembered that the salesman goes to the prospect, and in some prospects' minds the salesman is of a lesser status position. Thus he may be a lightning rod for their feelings.

In spite of his actions this individual may be quite insecure, or he may have a need to dominate, to influence or control others, to dictate; or he may have a need aggression, that is, to belittle, harm, blame, accuse or maliciously ridicule a person, to punish severely; or he may have a need contrariance, that is, to take the opposite side, to act differently from others; or he may have a need superiority, that is, to have power over things, people, and ideas.

Coping behavior There is one thing a salesman shouldn't do when dealing with a pugilist; he shouldn't argue and be pugilistic in return. The salesman can be purposeful; he can be firm and stand his ground, but he must have a high threshold of tension binding.

It is helpful, but difficult, if the salesman will give this individual some recognition.

Summary

To the salesman prospect knowledge means being able to analyze and adjust to the various prospects and customers whom he encounters. He adjusts according to the status or emotional needs of the individual. Frequently these needs are reflected in characteristics of an individual.

As previously discussed in the behavioral science chapter, an individual may have a need for order, that is, to be scrupulously precise; he may have a need for superiority, that is, the need to achieve and to receive recognition such as social approval and high social status; he may have a need for achievement, that is, a need to overcome obstacles or to exercise power; he may have a need for exhibition, that is, to attract attention to himself, to excite, to amuse, to thrill others; he may have a need to defend himself against blame or belittlement or to justify his actions; he may have a need to dominate, that is, to influence or control others, to persuade, to prohibit or to dictate; he may have a need for aggression, that is, to assault or to injure, to belittle or to harm, to accuse or ridicule other people; he may have a need for abasement, that is, a need to surrender, comply, and accept punishment. And although such a list would be almost endless if an attempt were made to account for shades of differences among people, a general list of characteristics can be compiled. The list in this chapter merely represents certain prospect characteristics that the salesman may identify as being dominant with one particular prospect. The prospect may be silent, he may be a procrastinator, he may be a glad-hander, he may be slow or methodical, he may be pugilistic or argumentative, he may be timid or overcautious, he may be ego-involved or opinionated, he may be skeptical or suspicious, he may be a grouch, or he may be impulsive and changeable.

By being able to identify certain traits in individuals, it is possible for the salesman to develop a coping behavior that will permit him to communicate best with that individual.

Chapter 17 DISCUSSION QUESTIONS

1 How does knowing prospects assist the salesman in handling objections they may state or doubts they may have?

2 Take any of the major prospect traits identified in this chapter and associate that trait with some individual you know. In the same way, identify a second individual having a different major characteristic. Thinking of

Solutions to Prospect Doubts: Part Two

these two individuals, identify the characteristics and then discuss whether or not you would use the same tactics in discussing a problem with each of them.

3 What is meant by the term *coping behavior?*

4 Is it possible for a salesman to have a coping behavior and be able to adjust to different individual needs, and still have a true personality?

5 Why must the salesman adjust and not the prospect?

6 Why is it difficult to work with an ego-involved or opinionated individual?

7 Would you classify the impulsive, changeable individual as mature?

8 An individual prospect is a slow, methodical talker. He keeps an extremely orderly desk. What needs might you associate with this individual?

9 Does the needs analysis as described in this chapter help the salesman become sensitized to people? If so, why? If not, why not?

10 What is the difference between the firm's problems and needs and the salesman's problems and needs?

completing negotiations: strategies and tactics

18

INTRODUCTION

This is the culmination of the problem-solving interview. It is the end of the decision-making process. Decision making means cutoff point. This is it—the completing negotiations stage of the sale.

This is the final stage of the salesman's depth approach to selling. The contact, discussion, dramatization, and doubt stages of the sale have been analyzed. The salesman is now ready to complete the sale.

As a researcher into sales problems, the author traveled with more than 140 different salesmen representing twenty-seven companies selling many different products (both tangible and intangible) and was present as an observer while the salesmen sold. And the most universal areas of difficulty, say these salesmen, are the initial contact with the prospect and the completion phase of the sale. In brief, salesmen believe they do well in the discussion and doubt stages, but they have difficulty in contacting prospects and getting the prospect to say, "OK, let's go ahead now." This is understandable. In both the contact and the completion phases of selling, each salesman with each prospect has to overcome a very realistic hurdle.

This is especially true when the salesman is a stranger in the initial stages of the sale. He is attempting to get information, sell himself, and relax the customer all at once. Thus he may be requiring the prospect to make some abrupt changes in his thinking and feelings during the contact stage. Each salesman tries to make the required change for the prospect to be as easy and gradual as possible to ensure success. Nevertheless, there is a tendency for the first stage of the sale to be somewhat unsettling to the prospect, and it invariably presents problems. It is apparent why the discussion and doubt stages of the sale, in contrast to the contact and completion phases of the sale, are easily handled by the salesman. During the contact stage the ice is broken and the discussion flows easily along lines dictated by good two-way communication. Prospect and salesman are locked in a normal communication pattern. There is no danger in the conversation; the prospect is not concerned with being sold or having to make a final decision. He is discussing plans and problems that are of interest to him, and he is raising questions and receiving answers. The law of effect is in operation. But the discussion is leading to the need for a decision.

The salesman has been talking to the prospect for some time; therefore the final decision should not represent an abrupt change. This point is well taken and suggests the importance of structuring the sales discussion so that the decision to buy does not require an abrupt change for the prospect or customer. The final action by the prospect will not involve the psychological turmoil associated with abrupt change if the sales representative has used a problem-solving, customer-oriented approach.

In theory, the salesman starts off by having limited information about the prospect's business needs or situation, but during the sales interview he gets information and gives information. The entire communication process is designed to expand and enlarge on the customer's ideas and concepts throughout the sale, and finally the salesman begins to narrow the sale down to a focal point—the decision to buy. In general, this focal point—the decision to buy—will not give the salesman great difficulty if he has used a customer-oriented communication pattern during the sale, and if the plan that evolves from the discussion represents the prospect's plan.

In addition to understanding and employing, where necessary, all the tactics and strategies presented in previous chapters, the salesman will be constantly alert for opportunities to use trial closes, buildup closes, and clincher closes. In this chapter, the various trial, buildup, and clincher closes will be described and illustrated with dialogue.

TRIAL CLOSES

The old story that Samson slew 10,000 Philistines with the jawbone of an ass and that salesmen have killed thousands of customers exactly the same way appears to have some merit. Some salesmen, especially those who use a simple stimulus-response type of selling, do kill potential customers by talking on and on in an interview, thinking they have to give the prospect the complete story. They seem to think that they have to tell the customer everything they know, but obviously sometimes it's best to stop and close the sale.

When feasible, a good rule for the salesman to follow is to try several trial closes in every sales interview. Here is how a trial close looks in dialogue—after five to ten minutes of discussion.

DIALOGUE EXCERPT 1 TRIAL CLOSE

S   Yes, Mr. Kelly, it is my firm opinion that plan A which includes numeric control for your Widget machine plus automatic gauging for the X^1, X^2, and X^3 units will give you a top integrated production system. Although . . .

Selling: A Behavioral Science Approach

I   I see.

S   And although such a statement is one of judgment, it does represent the best judgment of the combined survey team and their experience and United's experience as to what will work best with your present production system.

I   Well, yes, I understand that.

S   Well, Mr. Kelly, we'd be most happy to move ahead with this program within two or three weeks. What do you think? (*This last sentence by the salesman is a trial close. The trial close is an attempt to close. The salesman may hope to close, but he does not expect to close. He does not expect to close in the same sense as if he were using closing techniques later in the sale. It is entirely possible that at this point the prospect might say, "Yes, we could think about that," or "We could work out something." But more realistically, the prospect might want to discuss the entire plan further.*)

Here is another brief example. Assume that the industrial salesman has been talking to a prospect for about fifteen to twenty minutes. The sales representative has explained, in about fifteen minutes, the various combinations available in gauging equipment.

DIALOGUE EXCERPT 2   TRIAL CLOSE

R   Well, for some time I have been looking for a new plan, a new idea that would move us toward a more automated production system, and plan A sounds like it has considerable merit. (*A prospect's statement of this nature is a "buying signal" [positive voluntary] and it may be an ideal point at which to attempt a trial close.*)

S   Thank you, Mr. Smith, and assuming that we can tailor the specific program you want, was there any particular time you wanted to put a plan such as this into effect?

Following are examples of other positive voluntary statements made by the prospect which indicate a salesman could try a quick trial close. An industrial sales representative has actually made a previous call on a buyer and presented some facts to him. On the second call—say after ten minutes of discussion—the buyer makes any one of the following statements, and the salesman then tries a trial close.

R   1. The plan looks pretty good.
    2. I like the idea.
    3. There don't seem to be too many problems involved.
    4. Your sales program looks real good.

S   I am most happy to hear you say that, Mr. Smith, and if you are ready to go ahead with the plan, we certainly are.

The next two examples are from the office furniture field. Dialogue 3 shows the salesman employing two trial closes. In this case, the salesman is attempting to get the buyer to make a trip to the salesman's company showrooms.

Negotiations: Strategies and Tactics

DIALOGUE EXCERPT 3   TRIAL CLOSES

S   Yes, Mr. Turner, I can see that you aren't interested in a complete analysis of your central office, but you mention that you had been thinking about replacing six or eight desks.
C   Well, we do have quite a few that should be replaced.
S   That's always good news to the office furniture man and I would like to take you to our display offices and show you what we have. You might find exactly what you want. Could you go down this afternoon? (*Trial close*)
C   That sounds good, but we don't have to replace them immediately.
S   I see, Mr. Turner, and of course we would be most happy to show you our display room whenever you are ready. As you know, there are two basic desks —wood and steel—but there are many different types of wood and steel desks. I notice that you have both in your main office. Do you have a preference for either wood or steel?
C   I just don't know. Some of the girls seem to like wood and some steel.
S   We have found that many companies have a mixture of wood and steel desks, but on a number of occasions after management has seen the complete line of desks available in wood or steel, they begin to think of one particular make as being best suited for their offices. And as I mentioned, Mr. Turner, whenever you are ready to take a look at the desks we handle, I will be most happy to pick you up and take you down to our display office. On the other hand, it might be presumptuous of me to think that you want to see them.
C   No, no, I would like to look at them.
S   Well, I'm free whenever you are, Mr. Turner, and if you're free sometime tomorrow, I would be most happy to pick you up. (*Trial close*)

In the next example the sale has been going on for fifteen minutes. The salesman has explained a great deal about his company, products, etc., and the customer says:

DIALOGUE EXCERPT 4   TRIAL CLOSE

C   Well, I have been thinking of doing something with our office furniture.
S   I see, Mr. Turner. Perhaps it would be helpful if you were to look at the complete line of desks in our display room. We could set up a model that would simulate your present office and you would then get a good idea of what your office would look like with new furniture. Would that be all right?

Through the above dialogues it can be seen that the trial close is a closing technique in itself. When it is used early in the sale, it takes on the appearance of being strictly a trial close. In such a case the salesman may not expect to complete the sale, but rather hopes to complete it. Obviously some factors in the sales situation suggest the salesman press a little for a close. Regardless of the analysis of the term *hoping* or *expecting*, many times the trial close permits the salesman to take the prospect's "temperature." Other things being equal, the more time the salesman has spent *discussing* the plan with the customer, the more the trial close becomes a straightforward closing technique.

Selling: A Behavioral Science Approach

EIGHT BASIC CLOSING TECHNIQUES

In addition to the trial-close idea, there are eight basic techniques for the final closing of a sale. Five of the basic techniques are called buildup closes, and the other three, clincher closes.

The Buildup Closes

Buildup closes refer to presenting or rephrasing the major concepts, points, or ideas that appear to be important to the prospect in capsule form at the end of the sale. These closes are the compliment technique, the continuous-yes technique, the summary strategy, the emotional close, and the T-account close.

The compliment technique   With this strategy the industrial sales representative flatters or compliments the prospect:

S   It is obvious from this discussion and the appearance of your machine shop that you are very forward thinking and that you are ready to use ideas and adjust them to your own program. So I would appreciate your telling me, Mr. Big, how well do you think the XYZ units could fit into your system?

By giving the master mechanic credit for using new ideas and attempting to develop new programs and advance new ideas in his shop, the salesman compliments the prospect and this, like the barrier technique discussed in Chapter 9, may make it more difficult to say no to the particular plan. It is always difficult to say no to credits. The compliment technique may be especially effective when used with the ego-oriented individual. But it must be used with care.

The continuous-yes technique (sometimes called the "continued-affirmation method")   When using this technique the salesman plans a summary so that the customer answers with a series of yeses. The idea behind this technique is that several yeses from the prospect will make it much easier for him to give the final yes. It may be advisable to employ the continuous-yes technique with certain individuals, but the salesman should be judicious in using the technique with certain other prospects. Three brief dialogues are used to illustrate the continuous-yes technique. The first is from the industrial field, the second from the office furniture field, and the third from the hotel field.

DIALOGUE EXCERPT 1

S   I understand that you want to think it over, Mr. Smith, but from our conversation it seemed that you thought the automatic gauging on X^1 would give you the control you need in that spot in your shop. Am I right on that, Mr. Smith?
R   Yes, that's correct.
S   Also I assumed you thought the five precision cutting capabilities of X looked good to you. Is my assumption correct?

R You're okay there.
S Etc.

DIALOGUE EXCERPT 2

S I understand that you want to think it over, Mr. Turner, but from our conversation it seemed that the White office furniture line was almost designed for your needs. I believe you mentioned that the modular aspects of this line would enable you to be extremely flexible in adding new furniture as your company expands, and also it would facilitate your interchanging the furniture between offices. Is that right, Mr. Turner?
C Yes, yes, I did like that idea.
S And I think, Mr. Turner, we agreed that the addition of four desks, six chairs, and three file cabinets give you an overall attractive central office, and that the furniture we would add now would be part of our planned replacement program. Perhaps I'm wrong in stating that you actually wanted to begin a planned replacement program.
C No, no, I want to begin one, but . . .

DIALOGUE EXCERPT 3

S I understand that you want to think it over, Mr. Owens, but from our conversation it seemed the "cultural growth of the family" dining-out concept as it would be used in your present plan would be significant enough for publication in one of the personnel journals. Do you still believe that, Mr. Owens?
C Yes, I certainly like the idea.
S I think too, Mr. Owens, we agreed dining out would help people appreciate the art of living and make them more receptive to the enjoyment of shared experiences. Am I right on that?
C Yes, that's right.
S Also, it would take a burden off the housewife—she would not have to prepare a turkey at home; it would help develop social graces in the children, perhaps help them develop better family relationships; it would give the family a new type of experience and, in fact, even give the family a better image of the corporation. Perhaps something in our discussion made you believe these goals were not attainable?
C No—no, I think they are attainable and I think we should probably go ahead with this. Perhaps there are one or two little points in the back of my mind.

The summary technique Here the salesman takes four or five points in which the prospect indicated interest and presents them in summary form. The difference between the summary and the affirmation technique is simply that in using the affirmation technique the salesman pauses and interrogates the prospect concerning the various statements that he has made, whereas in the summary technique there is no pause. The salesman merely presents a number of major points in summary or capsule form. With the summation strategy, the salesman is making good use of the psychological concepts of repetition and reinforcement discussed in previous chapters.

DIALOGUE EXCERPT 1

S Of course, Mr. Smith, this is an important decision and you want to make sure you are making the best possible decision for your company—a decision that will be of benefit to you now and in the future. That is why I'd like to comment on some of the points you and I have discussed. We agreed that the adaptability of numeric control would enable us to construct a production program that would give you the degree of flexibility that you need now and in the future. Please correct me if I am in error, but I believe you thought a . . .

DIALOGUE EXCERPT 2

S Of course, Mr. Owens, this is an important decision and therefore to make sure you are making the best possible decision, you may want to take a few moments to run over some of the major concepts we discussed. I believe we more or less agreed that the plan would have new dimensions in the personnel field, that its total cost to you would be in line with what you are doing now in the form of gifts and awards. I think too that you thought it would accomplish one basic plan that you have in mind—to upgrade your supervisory people, to help elevate them to a higher social level and perhaps in so doing make them even more understanding and better employees. Also . . . I think the total plan is certainly in keeping with the climate or image that you want your employees to have of your firm.
C Yes, I think that's right.

The salesman should note that in the two dialogues above illustrating the summary close, the salesman did not specifically ask the prospect to reply, whereas, as is seen in the two dialogues illustrating the affirmation method, the salesman asked the prospect a series of specific questions.

Although there is a distinction made between the affirmation close and the summary close, the salesman should recognize that the summary close will be used most effectively if he observes the prospect for nonverbal cues and if he pauses at times regarding the points he is summarizing to let the prospect agree either by a nod of the head, a gesture, or a spoken word, or some combination of verbal and nonverbal cues.

The emotional close This close is used extensively by life insurance salesmen. If used properly, it can be a strong motivating factor, but it must be used with care. This is especially true of the industrial sale. In industrial selling it may be possible to use this method with smaller accounts, for example, when the shop superintendent has a feeling he knows every man on the assembly line.

DIALOGUE EXCERPT 1

S I understand your viewpoint, Mr. Smith, but why put off this important decision and all it will mean to you, your company, and your employees? I know what the automated plan would mean to your employees and perhaps

Negotiations: Strategies and Tactics

I am thinking more of your employees than anyone else. Of course, on the other hand, many executives say that what is good for your employees is good for your company. . . .

DIALOGUE EXCERPT 2

S Of course, Mr. Davis, but this might be the time to make a decision. We have discussed fully all phases of the program, and I know your real concern is for your members. From everything you said, you want your members to be truly guests in our hotel. And I can assure you, Mr. Davis, that everyone of your members will get the gracious treatment you want them to have. I have shown you on our organizational chart that the small details which provide for the comfort of your guests come under the direct authority of our sales department. Yes, Mr. Davis, your people will be treated as they want to be treated in our hotel.

The T-account close or balance-sheet tactic Another tactic, and one that is extremely well-suited to the concept of completing negotiations, is the T-account strategy. To utilize this concept, the salesman may take a pad of paper from his briefcase and draw a large T on the page. On one side he will list "To Act" and on the other side "Not to Act." The following monologue is an example of how an industrial distributor salesman could utilize the T-account concept. This concept permits the salesman to use judiciously all of the buildup closes, all of the clincher closes, or any combination he desires. The T-account close is, in general and in the author's opinion, the most effective closing concept a salesman can employ for handling complex situations.

S Certainly, Mr. Smith, I can understand your desire to think further about this program. From everything you said it is obvious you want the best possible production program for your company. You want to come as close as you can to a 100 percent plan now and yet have one that is going to be effective in the next ten years. Thus, Mr. Smith, it might be helpful to you in arriving at the decision if we took just a few minutes to review a few of the facts we have discussed. I would like to list on the left-hand side of this sheet the reasons why you should act now. On the other side of the sheet we can list the reasons not to act now. As you give the facts to me I will jot them down. Perhaps I could start off by rementioning one of the points you made earlier as a reason not to act. As I recall, you mentioned . . . (*The salesman begins to jot down his ideas and the prospect's ideas and puts them on the proper side of the T account. Obviously, before long the list on the right-hand side far exceeds the list on the left-hand, both qualitatively and quantitatively. The industrial salesman just sits back.*)
S Mr. Smith, these are the facts. The decision is entirely up to you. What do you think?

The buildup closes are not always effective if the salesman does not use one or more of the clincher closes in combination with them.

Selling: A Behavioral Science Approach

The Clincher Closes

Clincher closes are nudging closes and are used in combination with one or more specific buildup closes. The term *nudging* is used since many times it is the last little effort of the salesman that clinches or finalizes the sale.

The following clincher closes are combined with the buildup closes by:

A. Assuming or implying that the prospect is going to buy or by simply asking for the order
B. The SRO or standing-room-only close
C. The minor-point technique

Tactic A This tactic is combined with the summary-close method in the following dialogue.

S I think, from what we have said, Mr. Smith, that our plan has everything you want in the way of a forward-thinking, automated program. Am I right on this?
R Yes, I believe it does.
S Well, Mr. Smith, shall we go ahead with the plan now? (*Here the salesman has asked for the sale. He has used tactic A. He should stop talking and let the prospect reply. But like many salesmen, he continues. He has more to say.*)
S You don't have to worry about a thing. We will work out the final details on delivery, installation, and other things of this nature. Later we can confirm this by letter.
R Well, I—uh—I still don't know.
S Is there anything I haven't made clear, Mr. Smith? (*Evaluative question*)
R No, not really.
S Perhaps I should review briefly some of the major ideas we have talked about. We pretty much agreed . . . (*Summary*)
S Am I right on these points, Mr. Smith?
R Well—yes.
S I think then, Mr. Smith, we are in agreement on all the major points concerning this idea. We could go ahead and have the total program developed for you and put into effect within three weeks. Would three weeks be satisfactory to you? (*Tactic A*)
R Yes, I believe that's about right. Three would be about right.

The next dialogue represents an office furniture salesman combining the summary and implied-consent close.

S Our plan for your office has everything you want in the way of new office furniture, doesn't it, Mr. Turner?
R Yes, yes, I believe it does.
S Well, Mr. Turner, why don't we fix it up now? If you will just authorize this contract, we can go ahead with our plans for modernizing your office.
R Well, I, uh, I still don't know.

Negotiations: Strategies and Tactics

S I see, Mr. Turner, but why don't we look over this contract and go over the details of our agreement with you concerning the trade-in of your present office furniture, and in that way, we can see if we are in agreement on all the fine points. It will only take a few minutes. We agreed on $X for your present equipment, is that right, Mr. Turner? *(The salesman proceeds to go over the details of the agreement.)* I think we are in agreement on everything then, Mr. Turner. Now all you have to do is write your name in here *(motioning to the contract)* and begin modern office living. We can deliver your units in three days. Will that give you time to organize the moving here in the office?

R Yes, I believe it would.

Tactic B Another nudge or clincher close is the SRO—standing room only—or the offering of an inducement to the prospect if he buys now. Like all other clincher closes, this technique can be used with any of the buildup methods.

INDUSTRIAL SALESMAN

S I know from our discussion that this tailor-made ABC Machine Shop program, and this automated gauge program specifically designed for you has everything you want in the way of a new type production program. You and I have carefully discussed the present needs of the ABC Machine Shop and its future needs with respect to the more precision work that you are getting now and that you will be getting in the future. We've even discussed your goals, aspirations, and aims for this company. I believe it would be a wise decision to put this plan into effect now, so that the installation and change-over can be done during the holiday season. What do you think?

The point made in the above SRO technique is simply that if the ABC Machine Shop executive does not act now, he cannot put this plan into effect and take advantage of the holiday season. The SRO technique is also used in many cases in trading of machines, in delivery dates, price increases and in any other situation in which the prospect would gain something by acting now and losing something if he were to wait. Thus the SRO technique can be utilized to advantage in discussing depreciation and tax benefits.

Tactic C After using one or two of the buildup closes, either individually or in combination, the salesman can use a minor point as a clincher close. In the following dialogue the minor point will be used in combination with the summary and emotional close. The decision maker has said, "There is this matter of the various groups we have in our organization. I had better think it over a bit more."

S I can understand your wanting to think everything over or reflect on any decision you are going to make. But is there anything in particular you want to think over in this instance? Is there anything I haven't made clear?

R No, no, I don't think so. *(This is a buying signal. It is a good point to ask for action—"Let's fix it up now.")*

S Mr. Smith, you and I have worked out these plans very closely to give

you the best possible program for your company, your employees. . . . I believe we agree, too, that there would be no special problem with the union group. You did agree that the plan was satisfactory, didn't you, Mr. Smith?
R Yes—yes, I approve of the plan in general. (*Buying signal. Why not close?*)
S Mr. Smith, may I ask you a question here?
R Sure, go ahead.
S Mr. Smith, have you ever purchased a new car and then felt sorry you purchased it?
R Yes, I thought about the payments a number of times after I bought a car.
S Yes, we both have. But I am thinking of the pleasure, the comfort, and the security one feels when driving a new car. Have you ever felt sorry about that?
R No, I haven't.
S Mr. Smith, that's exactly what I have in mind regarding the. . . . Add this to the actual solid values that accrue to the firm and then I am sure you will look and be able to say, "It is a good decision." In fact, Mr. Smith, this is a powerful statement to make, but just recently in the March issue of *Production*, Mr. Dunn, president of the New Way Corporation, stated that "a company pays for new equipment such as numeric control each day they don't have it; it pays for itself and it puts profits into the company's pocket." He was talking about lost productivity, turnover, rejects, setup costs, labor costs, repair costs that take place as productive units become less efficient. More than this is involved, however. Mr. Dunn stated that even if the equipment is in good condition you can't afford to operate with it because your competition today is constantly upgrading its productive units. I think he has a strong point here. What do you think?
R Well, I've got to agree with him, especially the way he's put it. (*Let's close here.*)
S We of course want to put this plan into effect as soon as possible since the sooner you have it in, the sooner you begin to reap the benefits from it. Are you free to make this change-over in September or would October be better? (*Finally the minor-point close is used.*)

PROSPECT CHARACTERISTICS AND CLOSING TACTICS

Each of the buildup closes can be used in combination with each of the clincher closes, and in most cases it is the combination of methods that is most effective. The author recommends that in most situations the salesman will be most effective if he does not use just one method. Here is why. The compliment, the continued-affirmation, the summary, or the emotional-buildup closes used alone may be too obvious and thus offensive to the discerning individual.

A compliment, for instance, is best used in combination with another buildup method. Most individuals like to receive compliments but the overuse of such a concept suggests poor judgment on the salesman's part and is normally distasteful to most people.

The summary method is best employed if the salesman pauses at appropriate intervals and permits the prospect to comment. A pause by the salesman is more subtle than a question, and it may be more effective. In any event, the summary method is best used if the prospect has an opportunity to comment on the salesman's summary.

The continued-affirmation method used alone may suggest a high-pressure approach by the salesman. Further, few people enjoy being interrogated about every concept or idea being presented.

The purely emotional close is, in the author's opinion, the least desirable. It doesn't suggest professional salesmanship. It suggests that the salesman is using tactics to force a prospect to buy against his will.

On the other hand, since the T-account close permits the salesman to use each of the buildup closes or to combine them in any form he wishes, the T-account close is the most effective method to use.

It is suggested that the reader now return to Table 1, Chapter 17, and then list a first-choice and second-choice closing technique for each prospect. After listing these choices, the reader should try to list the methods of meeting objectors that might be employed with each prospect.

Summary

This is the end of the problem-solving interview. It is the cutoff point. It is the decision-making point.

Salesmen identify the contact and completion stage in the sale as areas of most difficulty. This is understandable because in both the contact stage and the completion stage, the prospect has to make a significant change in his behavior pattern. In the contact stage, the salesman may have to change the prospect's set from a negative one to a positive one. In the completion stage the salesman is asking the prospect to make a decision now. One reason it is difficult for buyers to make decisions is simply that all the facts are not known, and sometimes the salesman does not represent source credibility. Nevertheless, if he has structured his sales interview according to the principles set forth in this book, the salesman should have considerably greater success completing negotiations than he would have normally.

It is recommended that the salesman try a number of trial closes throughout the sales interview. A trial close represents an attempt by the salesman to close the sale although he may not expect to complete negotiations. The advantage of the trial closes is that they represent purposeful behavior on the part of the salesman and permit the salesman to evaluate, at least to some degree, the intent of the prospect with respect to making a decision. In brief, the salesman determines the feelings and thinking of the prospect more accurately with trial closes.

In addition to trial closes, there are eight basic closing techniques. Five of these basic techniques are called buildup closes and the other three, clincher closes. The buildup closes are the compliment technique, the continuous-yes technique, the summary strategy, the emotional close, and the T-account close. They are called buildup closes, since the salesman is reinforcing the discussion he has had throughout the interview by selecting the most important concepts and presenting them in capsule form to the prospect. Buildup closes are a process of reinforcement and a process of repetition. Clincher closes are nudging closes. They are always used in combination with buildup closes by assuming or implying the prospect is ready to buy, using the standing-room-only close, or by using the minor-point technique.

These eight are best used when they are employed in combination rather than in one single system. The summative effect of these various stimuli will help to eliminate any doubts the prospect may have with respect to making a decision now.

Chapter 18 DISCUSSION QUESTIONS

1 Why should the contact stage and the closing stage of the sale present problems for the salesman? That is, why is it more difficult to motivate the prospect in the contact stage and the closing stage?

2 Is there any particular reason why the salesman should try several trial closes before he actually gets into what he feels is the closing stage of the sale?

3 What is the major purpose of using buildup closes?

4 Would the continuous-yes technique be more effective with the ego-oriented individual or the procrastinator? Why? Why not?

5 Do you see any relationship between the summary technique and the psychological concepts of repetition and reinforcement?

6 Is it possible to use an emotional close with an industrial purchasing agent? Why? Why not?

7 A salesman is talking to a shop superintendent. He tells the shop superintendent that in order to get delivery on the equipment he desires in six months from now, he will have to order it now. Which closing technique is he employing? Why might the technique be effective?

8 Is there any reason why the T-account tactic may be the most effective closing technique discussed in this chapter?

9 If you were to select one closing tactic that would be suitable to use with the largest number of prospects described in the previous chapter, which closing technique would you use?

10 What relationship do you see between prospect characteristics and utilization of various closing tactics?

a manpower development program

19

INTRODUCTION

This chapter is designed to be read by the student, by the salesman, and by the sales executive. It is assumed that the student is interested in manpower development, since he will be employed by a company which hopefully will have some form of a manpower development program. This chapter will give the student insights as to the why of the company training program. Through reading this chapter it is anticipated that the salesman will better understand his role within his company's manpower development program. Thus learning will be facilitated. Finally, it is hoped the sales executive will find this chapter helpful in evaluating, planning, and executing his company training program.

The sales executive has a moral responsibility to do what he can to establish a climate in his company within which each salesman can realize his full potential.[1] This is not a one-way process. Each salesman should want to realize his full potential as well, but management must lead. That is one of management's obligations.

The surest way for a man to realize his full potential is through education. Education gives man dignity. Education is a great motivational force, perhaps one of the greatest. And when man has knowledge, he is motivated to *do*. Further, knowledge is a never-ending process. Each fragment of knowledge is a platform for added knowledge.

One of the great tragedies that is taking place in selling is the belief that the man trained in how to sell sells best. Too many sales managers do not understand that there is no one way to sell. And too many sales managers do not realize that the salesman who understands *why* certain principles, concepts, or ideas are used in selling can develop a creative approach to the sales problem.

The investment in time and money in the why approach to sales training is substantially greater than the investment required to train a man in

[1] This statement must be tempered by judgment. For instance, the company that hires door-to-door magazine salesmen does not, by the very nature of its work, get involved in manpower development programs.

how to sell. But if salesmen are to be trained to operate in the markets of the seventies and the eighties, there is only one approach that the firm can profitably follow, and that is developing each man to realize his full potential through the why concept. Human resources set the horizons for any company. Thus the successful executive of tomorrow will follow a strategy of excellence, not a strategy of numbers with respect to a sales force.

CHARACTERISTICS OF THE DEVELOPMENTAL APPROACH

Every true manpower development program is guided by the concept of total development. It is anticipated that any sales training program based on, for example, the behavioral sciences, will reach into all areas of a salesman's personal life and will assist him in becoming a more tolerant and understanding individual. Without the concept of total development, a program is not precisely aimed at knowledge but rather it is concerned about functions or sales techniques and how to use these techniques in selling the company's product.

Techniques are important, but such an approach by itself will not provide the basic materials and motivation for self-improvement. On the other hand, the problem-solving or the why approach is the basis for self-improvement. Thus the results of such a manpower development program will be a more productive sales force, not only in the short run but also and especially so in the long run.

It is recommended in any sales manpower development program that all learning situations and activities be bonded by recollection of experiences which relate to the particular situation or situations that are being discussed. Such an approach will induce salesmen to apply their mental abilities to the problems at hand. Further, this particular concept emphasizes the importance of an experienced salesman or sales manager leading the educational activities. The experienced man has the background needed to bond by recollection of experiences. He can combine theory and practical application.

The approach recommended in this book is essentially problem-oriented, since it is structured to use a case-dialogue approach. The learning experiences and activities revolve around problems to be solved by the salesman as a member of a group. The case-dialogue problems to be solved by the salesman must be realistic, everyday sales problems. They must duplicate situations which will be encountered in the actual performances of his everyday sales job.

In order to understand the entire task he is to do, the salesman must be engaged in learning activities and in learning experiences which will cause him to think, to understand relationships between the key situation presented and his experiences. The salesman who understands, who knows what he has to do, and how to do it will be most inclined to take these learning experiences to the field.

The educator should use a variety of techniques, methods, and aids. No one procedure is characteristic of the developmental approach. Just as it has been said that there is no one way to sell, it is stressed here that there is no one way to teach. The situational mix will constantly change, and the instructor's educational content mix will be adapted to changing learning situations. Any method, technique, or aid which would best accomplish the objectives of a particular lesson should be utilized; for instance, role playing may be preferred to the straight lecture method.

A major point suggested in the discussion above refers to an educational concept called readiness. This concept states that when an (individual) salesman has the ability to learn and a felt need or want to learn, he will learn. He is ready. His attitude, his values, his life, his intelligence, and his past experiences are all related to this concept. One of the basic reasons many students do not learn while in school is that the material is not meaningful to them. They are not involved. They do not participate. When a sales educator works with his salesmen, he is in the fortunate position of being able to make all the material meaningful to his salesmen.

An Inventory

Each sales instructor should remember that although the growth and development of each salesman will, in all probability, be continuous, the rate of development will vary considerably among the various salesmen. Each instructor must treat his salesmen as a group of individuals and use procedures which will best be applied to the various differences among them. A salesman develops from the point at which he is, not from some artificial starting at which the instructor would like him to be. It is suggested that each instructor complete an evaluation card for each of his salesmen and list the areas in which each salesman needs improvement. Compiling such information is not difficult. The instructor points out each salesman's strong points as well as his weaker ones, since this gives the instructor the opportunity to best capitalize on that man's abilities during the conference training sessions. It will also permit the salesman to express himself advantageously. When calling on a salesman who can readily expound on a particular point, the educator is giving that salesman an opportunity to satisfy one or more of his needs.

Each salesman is unique and a very special person. Each is very different in some ways from every other salesman. Each one wants to make good. Some are bright at one thing and confused about other things. All individuals are this way, so it is up to the instructor to be understanding and give each man the best opportunity to learn.

Bright salesmen catch on to some things so easily that the educator may think the others are just lazy. The bright salesman's easy answers and skillful classroom or meeting room demonstrations may tempt him to let down. However, he will have to work at the task of reaching the salesman at the bottom of the ability range. It isn't easy. The first impulse is to let the bright salesmen keep the session going, thinking the others will gain from listening and being with the people who appear to know.

However, the instructor must not concentrate on the slow salesmen to the extent that he slights the bright salesmen. The painfully slow and earnest struggles of lost souls at the bottom of the sales class may pull at his heart strings so strongly that he gives them some of the attention, understanding, and sympathy that should go to the more advanced salesmen who are, in all probability, destined to become the top producers.

In establishing a manpower development program, the individual directs management just as the student directs the educator. This is true insofar as only the policies, ideas, concepts, or educational programs (learning experiences) which are within the reach and attainment of the individuals can be put into effect. Educators must follow the same process. They must develop educational programs acceptable to and within the reach and attainment of the students. In brief, executives may establish policy and make decisions determining the firm's objectives and how those objectives may be attained, but the carrying out of the organization's objectives falls to employees or individuals at what is many times referred to as the performance levels within the organizational structure.

A decision concerning the cleanliness of a building falls to the janitor or custodian to perform the functions necessary to carry out the executive's objectives. In the same way, if a sales manager decides his salesmen should make more calls per day and have a greater sales volume per call or become market managers, the attainment of this policy rests squarely on the shoulders of the salesman. Therefore, before activating such a sales policy, it behooves management to determine whether or not the men could attain the goals desired. Then if it is beyond the interest, reach, or attainment of the salesmen, a program should be devised to prepare them or condition them to perform at the level desired.

Surely both management and educators have tools of authority within their reach. They can demand certain levels of performance. Yet it would seem that in the long run management, like education, obtains greatest success when it does not rely solely on authority to provide the major impetus needed to attain its goals. We have all heard statements like these: Management must be more leader than driver; management must give direction; management is both coach and quarterback. But what exactly is management?

What Is Management?

Management is that activity which makes things happen. Scientific management is a conscious, organized, human approach to management's responsibilities as contrasted to the day-in, day-out, hit-or-miss, rule-of-thumb approach. This is a direct way of saying management (someone in a position of authority by title) must set objectives or goals, and then devise activities through which these goals or objectives can be accomplished.

If the objective of sales management is to increase the sales effectiveness of its sales force, management must institute activities through which it can attain its objective. One of the activities put into effect by Pratt & Whitney (see Case 1 in Chapter 2) is a manpower development program. Management anticipates increased sales effectiveness as a result of this program. In the process of setting this objective (greater individual sales effectiveness) and establishing activities (a manpower development program) to accomplish this objective, management is automatically involved in the process of planning, organizing, and executing. And it is through this planning, organizing, and executing that management *makes things happen.*

It was stated above that the success or failure of the objectives of a firm or of an educator lies with the employee or with the student. It has been indicated also that both management and educators are in what may be referred to as positions of nonauthority. For instance, salesmen cannot be ordered to use principles of psychology, education, and communications in their sales effort. Salesmen must want to use these principles. The drive must come from within the individuals.

Many times, however, the instructor must motivate the salesman or at least provide the spark that starts the motivational process. These motivational factors may be intrinsic or extrinsic. Generally compensation motivates salesmen to call on customers. This form of motivation is more extrinsic than intrinsic. A skiing analogy will be used to illustrate the concept of intrinsic motivation. If an individual does not understand how to ski or has never had lessons in how to ski, there is a good possibility he would be little interested in taking up skiing. However, if an individual is persuaded to take a lesson and thus understands something about skiing, there is a good possibility he will become interested. He will be motivated to take more lessons and enjoy future skiing. This is intrinsic motivation. If the neophyte skier were paid for the ski trips, it might be an example of both intrinsic and extrinsic motivational factors. Obviously it is difficult to separate intrinsic and extrinsic motivational factors completely. It is certain, however, both play a role in whether or not an individual will do the job management wants done.

Continuing the skiing analogy, the real job of the sales educator is to encourage his salesmen to sample skiing (selling) in such a way that the experience or sampling is rewarding. To do this, the educator must have a desire to be a competent educator.

Desire to Be a Competent Educator

As mentioned, a management man has, to a certain degree, a moral obligation to help each of his men realize his full potential. Being a competent instructor goes a long way toward fulfilling this obligation, and this is not difficult. Perhaps the most important single ingredient is the desire to be. An instructor's attitude or desire toward teaching will not only determine the kind of a job he does, but it will set the limits to the kind and amount of satisfaction and enjoyment he will get out of his teaching effort.

The successful educator-instructor finds teaching both rewarding and fun. The reason it is rewarding to him is reflected in the words of a well-known educator who stated, "The most remarkable thing about man is his ability to learn. He benefits from his mistakes. He is constantly changing for the better. He always grows." A sales educator will have both the intangible and tangible satisfaction of implementing the growth pattern of his salesmen.

Two questions have often been debated: "Are salesmen made or born?" and "Which is the more important, product knowledge or sales ability?" These two questions can be put in perspective with respect to the manpower development program by rephrasing the questions to ask: "Are teachers made or born?" "Which is more important to the instructor, knowledge of the subject or the ability to teach?" Although these two questions are rather academic, they strike to the heart of the matter. A good salesman becomes a good salesman because he works at it. He acquires his sales skills through *time, experience, observations, discussion,* and *study.* He had certain abilities, intelligence, drives and other related traits, but his sales ability was augmented by time and experience. *It was made.*

In short, individuals are not born salesmen; sales ability is developed. But what about this question for the instructor, "Is knowledge of the subject or ability to teach more important?" It is the author's opinion that if an individual understands the sales process and can sell, he can teach. Generally speaking, there is relatively little difference between many of the basic techniques used in modern selling and those used in modern teaching. In both situations education is the primary goal. A salesman educates his customer; an instructor educates the student.

Again, the instructor must remember that in teaching and selling situations he is in positions of nonauthority. A salesman cannot order a customer to buy, and an instructor cannot order a salesman to learn. In both cases motivation is a key word. Experience in educating salesmen will parallel somewhat the salesman's experience with customers. Just as most customers are interested in a proposal, most salesmen want to learn. Some salesmen do not want to learn. The instructor must take the same attitude toward these salesmen that is taken toward difficult customers; they must be motivated to buy or learn.

Preparation

What kind of preparation is needed for instructional duties? Not much. The subject matter is at hand. The instructor has technical, product, and marketing knowledge in depth. What is more, he has a sales background. Perhaps though he lacks background in the principles of education. Much of the material needed to understand the general educational process has been discussed in the behavioral science chapters. The instructor will be surprised how quickly his experience will fit into the framework of a manpower development program which is constructed to utilize a conference, dialogue, case study approach. Moreover, as has been previously indicated, he is fortunate in that the sales material discussed in this program plus the specific adaptation of that material to company problems and to company sales situations will be especially meaningful to the salesmen. They will be interested. They will be involved. They will participate. When this is accomplished, about 90 percent of the educator's

A Manpower Development Program

battle is won. All of these activities will not happen by accident, however. Each instructor must prepare a lesson plan.

The Lesson Plan

A lesson plan merely states what the instructor plans to accomplish, that is, what his objectives are and what activities are needed to accomplish the objectives. It tells the instructor what educational aids (films, reading assignments, blackboard, visuals, etc.) are needed. Finally, a lesson plan contains a list of questions and points and materials that the instructor plans to cover.

The following sample preparation sheet is one used by the Pratt & Whitney salesmen as a discussion outline in their initial program with their distributor sales people. (For complete information on the Pratt & Whitney's sales roles, see Case 1, Chapter 2.) The Pratt & Whitney salesmen were instructed to change, adjust, and modify the proposed outline according to specific objectives, ideas, or concepts that they wished to discuss or accomplish. In addition to the preparation sheet, a dialogue analysis of the Franklin Machine Shop case is included as part of the lesson plan. One of the many reasons dialogues are interspersed throughout this book is that any instructor in any company can modify the dialogues to fit his company's situation.

Also included as part of this lesson plan is a brief dialogue of a hotel sales representative contacting a secretary and requesting an appointment with her employer. It is included to illustrate the many ways in which dialogues can be used to discuss a wide range of ideas and yet pinpoint specific ideas the sales trainer wants to emphasize.

Sample Preparation Sheet
for
Conference Discussion 1
Contact Stage

  I. Time: 1 hour, 2 hours, 3 hours, or 4 hours.

 II. Objective: To give industrial distributor salesmen selling P and W products an overall selling plan. Emphasis, however, in the first conference discussion will be on the contact stage.

III. General activities to accomplish objectives:

    A. Establish that there is no one way to sell. Emphasize the interaction between psychology, communication, and education.

    B. Explain why the conference method will be used, namely, to capitalize on each distributor salesman's ability and experiences.

    C. Explain the dialogue method and concept.

    D. Get considerable feedback. Remember the concept of catharsis.

IV. Visual tools and prereading assignments.

    A. Each man should have read chapters assigned and have completed preparatory examination prior to conference sessions.

    B. Have blackboard handy.

    C. See that each man has pad of paper, etc.

Selling: A Behavioral Science Approach

    D. You are in a group sales situation, so structure the visual tools you want to use so that you can sell your ideas effectively.

V. Specific activities for program 1.

    A. Discuss the interaction between the prospect's or customer's personal needs and business needs. Refer also to behavioral science section on needs.

    B. Discuss the overall sales task diagram in Chapter 12. Briefly cover discussion, doubts, and completion phases. Briefly mention "How and Why of Communication" and "Planning and Managing Sales Effort" material. Just give the salesman an overall plan for the sales training program.

    C. The contact stage—refer to contact diagram.

        1. Discuss what is meant by stimuli or inputs; outputs or responses.

        2. What is meant by the ten variables of any contact? Why do we use the word *variable?* How do you know when to use each variable?

        3. Very briefly, what is meant by problem solving (you will come back to that, so be brief on this discussion). Any examples of problem solving in this group? Get one or two.

        4. Maturity—what is it? Briefly refer to behavioral science material if you want to.

        5. What does prospect participation mean?

        6. What is meant by verification questions, permissive questions? How do we know when to use verification and permissive questions?

VI. The four quarters and ten variables of the contact stage. Use diagram in contact chapter as visual.

    A. Introduction quarter.

        1. Do you agree that the introduction phase is comparable to social amenities? What is meant by set?

        2. Is the middle-of-the-road strategy good advice? Does it tell us that the salesman must enact a number of roles? Does it suggest that the overenthusiastic salesman might kill a few sales?

    B. Director quarter.

        1. What determines direction?

        2. What specific plan should a salesman have before he contacts a prospect?

        3. How can a salesman change directions in a sale? What permits him to do this? Does the prospect give him any cues that suggest that he change direction?

    C. Future quarter.

    Once the future direction is determined, do we always stay on that track?

    D. Problem-solving quarter.

        1. What is problem solving? What kind of problems or needs are we talking about?

A Manpower Development Program

    2. Emphasize fact getting. The other steps in problem solving are not really important. There is no one way to do it.

    3. If executives or businessmen intuitively or by plan ask the four questions listed for the decision and problem-solving process, in what way is that knowledge important to the salesman?

  E. Empathy.

    1. What is empathy?

    2. How can the salesman establish empathy?

Dialogue Analysis as Part of the Lesson Plan

CASE 1 *Franklin Machine Shop* The Franklin Machine Company is a potential buyer of Pratt & Whitney machine tools, cutting tools, and gauges. This potential user operates a combined marine dry dock and machine shop. The machine shop does all the work required by the dry dock, but a fair amount of its work comes from general machine shop business. The company employs about fifteen machinists year round plus a number of helpers. Most of the equipment in the shop is in good condition; it is fairly stable and has been in operation quite a few years. Apparently the company bought a number of machines, drills, lathes, etc., between 1939 and 1945 and then again they bought additional machine tools through 1947 and 1952. The company until about ten or fifteen years ago was housed in a wooden building with a planked floor. The new brick exterior, concrete-floor building is not only much larger than the old building but also boasts of being fairly modernistic in structure. The company's balance sheet picture is only fair financially, and it is perhaps average or less than average in its profit structure. Recently the company has been obtaining a substantial number of subcontract work on government contracts supplying parts for manufacturer's finished products.

    Franklin, Sr., is president of the machine shop and Franklin, Jr., is the general manager, a position he has held for approximately ten or more years. Young Franklin appears to be more aggressive, and perhaps he is responsible for the increased flow of contract business.

SAMPLE DIALOGUE

    The salesman is Frank Hill of Pratt & Whitney and he is making a cold call on Mr. Franklin.

S Good morning, Mr. Franklin. I am Frank Hill of Pratt & Whitney, and I appreciate having this opportunity to see you. I know how busy you must be, but I can assure you that this call will be well worth your while. In fact, it won't take long, perhaps a minute or two to discuss my proposition with you.

I I see.

S Did you know that Pratt & Whitney has created a new line of Checkmate thread gauges?

I No, I didn't.

S Well, it's a great line and this is what I especially wanted to talk to you about, the new Checkmate gauges. It is an item which I think will work out well in your shop.

I   We are pretty well set on gauges.

S   Sure, but you don't know about these gauges. Tell you what, let me buy you a cup of coffee so I can have five or ten minutes of your time to tell you about the new Checkmate line.

This sample dialogue represents a salesman-oriented sales talk. It's a sales talk that is poorly done. It isn't customer-oriented but rather it represents an example of a one-sided communication process. Assuming, however, that the instructor were using this dialogue as discussion material, the following questions might be asked of the sales group.

1. How did the contact go up until salesman Hill said, "I know how busy you must be"?

2. What variables were included? (See Chapters 12 and 13 regarding variables of the contact stage.)

3. What do you think of the idea of mentioning, "I know how busy you must be"?

4. What do you think about the statement, "I assure you it will be well worth your while"?

5. What should salesmen usually try to accomplish in the first few minutes of the contact stage?

6. Do you attempt to give the prospect a chance to talk in the contact stage, or should the salesman control the interview by telling the prospect why he is there?

7. Should you make such a statement as, "Checkmate gauges will go well in your shop"? Why? Why not?

8. Should you ask the prospect to have a cup of coffee?

9. Was a climate of mutual compatibility achieved?

These questions seem fine, but can salesmen discuss them intelligently? The answer is a clear yes. Here is why. The dialogue used in Case 1 refers to the contact stage as discussed in this book as do all the questions posed. Prior to the conference meeting with salesmen, they would have read that chapter and the instructor have analyzed each dialogue and made notes concerning the dialogue. An illustration follows.

DIALOGUE 1

S   Good morning, Mr. Franklin. I am Frank Hill of Pratt & Whitney and I appreciate having this opportunity to see you. I know how busy you must be, but I can assure you that this call will be well worth your while. In fact, it won't take long, perhaps a minute or two to discuss my proposition with you. *(Variables are okay to where salesman states, "But I can assure you that this call will be well worth your while. In fact, . . ." What is the prospect's reaction to these statements? How can the salesman say, "I can assure . . ."? Why should a call take a minute or two? What about the word proposition? Why not proposal or purpose of this call. Discuss this dialogue from a prospect reaction standpoint. Obviously planning can be discussed.)*

I   I see.

A Manpower Development Program

S Did you know that Pratt & Whitney has created a new line of Checkmate gauges? (*This is a verification type question. It could be better, however. For example, "Pratt & Whitney has created a new line of Checkmate gauges. Have you heard about them?"*)
I No, I didn't.
S Well, it's a great line and this is what I especially wanted to talk to you about, the new Checkmate gauges. It is an item which I think will work out well in your shop. (*Again, how can the salesman say, "it will be well worth your while, . . ."?) Why not be specific and tie it in with Franklin's present work?*
I We are pretty well set on gauges.
S Sure, but you don't know about these gauges. Tell you what, let me buy you a cup of coffee so I can have five or ten minutes of your time to tell you about the new Checkmate line. (*"Sure, but you don't know about these gauges." This is a rather forceful statement. The prospect may resent this. Use the analogy of "coffee" [from simple stimulus-response selling] to show that the salesman did not get the prospect's thinking.*)

CASE 2 The hotel sales representative is calling on the trade association executive of an association with an annual convention attracting approximately 500 members and around 150 wives of the conferees. This is a cold call. The first stop is at the receptionist's desk.

S May I speak to Mr. Davis?
R Whom should I say is calling, please?
S Mr. Bill Smith of the Delta Hotel in Roxy. (*Receptionist calls Mr. Davis.*)
R Mr. Davis is busy now, but he can see you in about thirty minutes if you care to wait.
S I would be pleased to wait. I have a few telephone calls to make, so I will go down to the drugstore. I'll be back in about twenty minutes.
R You may use this telephone if you don't talk too long. (*It is more professional not to use the facilities in the office of the prospect. For instance, should the prospect come to the door and say, "I'll see Smith now," and Smith is using the phone, what is the prospect's reaction?*)
S Thank you very much, but I don't want to inconvenience you and I think one or two of my calls might be on the lengthy side. I'll be sure to be back in twenty to twenty-five minutes, however.
S (*Twenty minutes later the salesman walks to the receptionist's desk.*) By the way, you might want to give Mr. Davis my card if you have an opportunity to do so. (*This serves as a reminder that you have returned, and in some offices the receptionists do escort the salesman to the executive offices. If you have observed that the receptionist merely takes the message from Davis that he is free, you might just say, "By the way, you might want this card as a reminder of the callers Mr. Davis has had today."*)
R (*ten minutes later*) Mr. Smith, Mr. Davis will see you now.
S Thank you. (*Proceeds to Davis' office.*)
S Hello, Mr. Davis. I am Bill Smith of the Delta Hotel in Roxy. I want to thank you for giving me this opportunity of meeting you. (*You are using a*

Selling: A Behavioral Science Approach

direct approach; you have stated your name and your business and your firm's name. Be enthusiastic, friendly, poised and positive. But don't rattle off your opening statements. Give the cusomer a chance to talk; pause at times; let him tell you to sit down; shake hands if you wish. Manage the situation.)

D That's okay. Sit down, please.

S My call won't take long, Mr. Davis, but about two weeks ago I was talking to Mr. Blodgett of your association and he was telling me that possibly you are thinking of having a convention in or around Roxy in the next year or two. Is my information correct? (*Question technique. These few words give Davis a feeling that he doesn't have to worry about getting rid of the salesman. This statement helps remove or relieve sales tension. Don't use the worn phrase, "I would like five minutes of your time to explain a mutually profitable idea" or "I'm not here to high pressure or sell you." Don't mention that you aren't going to sell him, but, on the other hand, don't say you are. Your positive attitude indicates that you are there for a purpose—to satisfy the customer. With the question technique you get participation.*)

D Yes, we are thinking of the South for '62.

S That's good news, Mr. Davis. As you know, you'll receive real hospitality in most places in the South, but I'm especially interested in having you come to Roxy and more specifically in having you use the facilities of the Delta Hotel. Are you familiar with the Delta Hotel and, for that matter, with Roxy? (*Question technique. You question Mr. Davis to find out if the information you received from Blodget is correct and also give Davis a chance to talk. He might want to get rid of you, but on the other hand he might want to tell you, "Yes, we are thinking of Roxy. I sort of like the Delta Hotel, and you are just the man I want to talk to."*)

The Conference[2]

Conference is a round-table discussion of ideas, concepts, and problems. It may involve as few as three individuals or as many as twenty. For sales training, six to nine appears to be the most effective size. Obviously, if a firm has forty-six salesmen, the arrangement will involve four tables of seven each and three tables of six each. Utilizing certain rules, principles and skills, the conference leader can tap the abilities and knowledge of his salesmen for a profitable discussion of sales ideas, concepts, techniques, and sales problems. Whenever a number of tables are involved, someone will act as the overall conference leader or trainer and the salesmen will serve, on a rotational basis, as conference leaders. In general, most educators agree that the conference discussion approach is one of the finest educational methods available.

What Is Dialogue and Dialogue Training?

Referring to Webster, dialogue is "a written work in the form of a conversation; the passages of talk in a play, story, radio act, etc."

---

[2] The conference is discussed in length in chap. 20, "The Conference: A Case-dialogue Approach to Manpower Development."

A Manpower Development Program

Sales dialogue training refers to analyzing transcriptions of conversations between salesmen and prospects. It is a method by which reality and creativity, based upon educational learning principles, can be put into the training program. Utilizing dialogue creates realistic situations involving communications between people. These cases, dialogues, or conversations are analyzed for proper use or misuse of techniques, ideas, concepts, and strategies involved in selling.

Generally trainers experience difficulty in developing realistic situations for the skit and play-acting type of program and, of course, thus have the task of getting positive participation. However, both of these hurdles are readily cleared by taking the following four steps and building the sales training program around the case-dialogue approach.

Management educators or trainers should (1) use, if possible, verbatim transcripts and descriptions of situations; (2) act as sales grammarians and analyze the dialogue; (3) mimeograph or make slides of the sales situation dialogue (if slides are used, the dialogue is projected on the screen before the participating group of salesmen); and (4) have a group of trainees discuss the dialogue situation.

What is more realistic than the actual situation between the customer and the salesman? With dialogue the situation can move from the receptionist's or secretary's desk, from the executive, or from the group discussion, purchasing agent, engineer, or research man to the classroom.

The author has used a concealed miniature tape recorder in his travels with salesmen throughout the United States. The recorder also has a telephone adapter which enables the researcher to record two-way telephone conversations quickly and effectively. This midget tape recorder has its own built-in speaker system that allows the situation to be played back to an audience. It is readily adaptable to small and large audiences. Thus an actual recording can be used along with the verbatim transcription if the trainer so desires.

All too frequently training programs are developed almost exclusively around material that experienced salesmen or management contribute, and frequently this material involves unrealistic situations. For instance, salesmen tend to say they made the sale according to the procedures the company has trained them to use. This may or may not be the case. Further, many times what the salesman thinks he said or did during the sale may be far from what actually transpired.

Perhaps the most difficult part of the dialogue approach is analyzing the dialogue. But as the dialogues are developed or collected, it will become readily apparent that there is a multitude of situations ranging from the use of subtle sales techniques or principles to overt or brassy techniques which will be uncovered. Entirely new sales ideas crop up as well.

After a representative sample of actual situations has been collected, the dialogue is analyzed for realistic human relations or sales pointers. Dialogue should be selected that represents the psychological and educational principles, sales techniques, sales principles, concepts, or ideas that will reinforce what the instructor wants his salesmen to learn. Herein lies a wealth of material that can put new life into the training program for new salesmen or, perhaps what is even more important, for the reorientation of experienced salesmen.

The author has been using the dialogue concept as a training tool for over fifteen years and the best discussions have resulted when trainees are provided with mimeographed copies of the dialogue, in addition to having the dialogue projected on the screen before them. Apparently the big advantage of the mimeographed handouts is that some trainees appear to be more willing to discuss a particular dialogue after they have made a few comments in writing. Mimeographed copies of dialogues are extremely important whenever a number of conference tables have been established. In this way each table can effectively operate as a single unit.

Finally, dialogue sales training conferences can be a crucial step in preparing the salesman to role-play specific situations. The role play is just one step removed from one salesman reading the customer's lines and another salesman reading the prospect's lines. This is especially true if the salesman is instructed to role-play a specific type salesman as he reads the lines. For instance, Jim is told to role-play a tired salesman as he reads the lines. The other salesman may be taking the role of an enthusiastic prospect. The salesmen viewing this partial role play are then told to analyze what may be the prospect's reaction to this tired sales person. The sales trainer can, after the salesman has read a few lines, ask the salesman to restate the dialogue in his own words. This is the beginning of role playing.

Without some transition of this nature, role playing sometimes is reduced to horseplay, and frequently the trainees are embarrassed by play-acting. On the other hand, dialogue analysis trains the sales people to think, yet isolates and pinpoints the idea that the trainer wants to make. This gives the salesman a great deal of the knowledge needed to role-play a particular situation. Thus dialogue can provide a foundation for the knowledge needed for the role play as well as providing a transition from reading a dialogue—something any salesman can do easily—to role playing—something not all salesmen can do well.

Understanding Is Based on Relationships

The use of the problem-solving case-dialogue method and salesman-participation techniques help to develop understanding. The ability of a salesman to learn new knowledge is based on how well he has learned and understood old knowledge. Through understanding, the salesman is taken from where he is to where the educator wants him to go step by step. Each new bit of knowledge should be related to old knowledge, if possible.

It is well for the instructor to remember that a salesman does not need a clear understanding if someone else does the thinking. Therefore, a good instructor does not normally provide the answers to questions or problems without giving his salesmen every opportunity to think and to develop an understanding. Each salesman can develop a real understanding which he obtains from a variety of concrete experiences presented so that relationships are apparent. *Any* teaching technique which gets salesmen to do independent thinking will also help them gain understanding.

A Manpower Development Program

Develop the Ability to Think

Positive action by the educator helps each salesman develop his thinking ability. The salesman must learn that thinking is an ability which involves examining the problem, suggesting possible solutions, testing the suggested solutions, and evaluating the results. In addition to furnishing problems and questions which require thinking, the educator must guide each salesman so that he uses each of these factors in his thinking. It is important to examine the thinking methods the salesman uses in arriving at his answers. The question, "How did you arrive at that answer?" should be stressed and will be more beneficial than the question, "What is the answer?"

The Instruction Methods

As discussed in Chapter 14, the various methods used in teaching are often classified according to which of the four actions predominate. The *telling* or *explaining* method consists of the manpower development trainer telling or explaining the facts, principles, and theories he wants the salesman to understand. *Discussing* as a teaching method is recognized by the flow of information and ideas from the instructor to the salesman, from the salesman back to the instructor, and from salesman to salesman. The *showing* or *demonstrating* method portrays accurate procedures and operation of a particular technique or sales tool. Done under the supervision and guidance of the sales trainer, the *performing* method helps the salesman to learn by doing. Each of these methods, as previously explained, is *always* used in combination with one or more of the other methods. This is effective teaching.

Questions

In training, as in selling, questions must be asked at the right time. In the case of selling, questions must be used to guide and control the development of the sale, and in training they are used to guide and control the development of the topic, subject, technique, or strategy that is being discussed. From a sales standpoint, the main test of a good question is the extent to which it helps to attain the salesman's objective in a particular sales call. In training the main test is the same—how well it accomplishes the trainer's objective.

A question must be selected, worded, and used according to the purpose the trainer has in asking it. Questions are used for any of the following purposes:

To obtain salesman attention
To arouse interest
To open discussion
To provoke thinking
To accumulate data
To distribute discussion
To arrive at conclusions

Selling: A Behavioral Science Approach

To develop a subject
To direct observation
To discover a salesman's weaknesses
To check a salesman's understanding
To change discussion trends
To limit or end discussions
To obtain salesman participation

If questions are to be successful in stimulating and directing thinking during the manpower development program, they must be thought-provoking and asked in proper sequence. Therefore the instructor plans his questions beforehand. The questions should trace the thought he wishes the salesman to follow and emphasize the relationship he wishes them to see. The instructor therefore writes the key questions in the sequence which follows the desired pattern. To help plan his key questions, the sales trainer should:

1. Make his questions a challenge to the salesman. Questions should be difficult enough so that they will stimulate thinking. The characteristics of a good question are similar to those of a good problem.

On the other hand, the questions must not be too difficult or the salesman will flounder or be embarrassed. For instance, if the trainer asks a salesman, "Can you suggest two or three specific things we attempt to accomplish when we first contact a prospect?" there may be at least ten points that could be brought out. The instructor is wise to restrict the question. Others in the group will enlarge and add to the question as the instructor uses follow-up questions. If no salesman mentions the point of getting information as one of the things that is accomplished in the approach, the instructor asks another question about this specific concept. He might ask, "Have we fully explored the idea that perhaps during the contact stage we should attempt to get information from the prospect?" There is an obvious reply, of course, and he is then prepared to follow up with types and kinds of information he wants to get and how he elicits this information. This is a sequence of questions.

2. Take into consideration individual differences. A question which is challenging for one distributor salesman may be very easy for another and unanswerable for a third. The questions should be adapted to the level of ability of the salesman.

3. Make the questions answerable. The wording should be definite, clear, and concise. The salesmen must know exactly what is being asked. The question must be worded in terms which the salesman understands. He must have the same mental picture of what is wanted as the instructor.

The questions should never contain the exact wording of the assigned reading material except in cases where dialogue is being discussed.

4. Make each question center on only one idea; each question must emphasize one point. Two or three questions should not be combined into one question. The question, "Jim, would you explain the reasons why we contact prospects, and demonstrate several ways in which of these you think is best for us to use in general," quite obviously is a minimum of three broad questions. It has too many ideas.

A Manpower Development Program

A broad question like, "Jack, what are the four steps in the sale we are generally concerned with?" may be asked, however. This is different from four questions which might require a series of points as answers for each. The reply to the question above is contact, discussion, doubts, and completion of negotiation. It may also include the planning and preplanning steps. The purpose in the question might have been to enable the instructor to state, "Yes, this is the total sequence of activities which we want to follow in developing our sales approach. And today we are going to concentrate on the first step, the contact stage." From then on, most of the questions should be specifically related to the contact stage and contain one central idea.

5. Emphasize the understanding of relationships rather than the memorizing of facts. Questions that ask how or why require the salesmen to analyze the situation, see relationships, and arrive at conclusions. Generally such questions are preferred over those that ask who, what, where, or when—which are generally used for recalling facts. In the previous question asked, "What are the four steps to the sale?" a good memory will provide an answer. Compare this to the instructor asking the question, "How do we contact prospects?" This takes thought.

6. Phrase the question to indicate purpose and type of response desired. For instance, each of the following words indicates the type of answer wanted: *classify, compare, criticize, define, discuss, explain, illustrate, interpret, justify, outline, review, summarize, trace,* and *verify.* These words and others like them have definite value in framing questions.

Summary

Manpower development is a process initiated by management to establish a program and a climate in which each man can realize his full sales potential. This program carries a dual obligation which involves both management and salesman. Management must lead; it must initiate. But each salesman has an obligation in terms of a want to realize his full potential. Each salesman who lacks "a want to" is a serious detriment to other salesmen. There can be no place in the company organization for a salesman who does not advance intellectually in product knowledge and in sales skills. Company success, which is eventually the success of the sales force, requires total effort, not superb effort by a few and mediocrity by most.

To capitalize fully on a manpower development program, an inventory of each salesman is made by management. This determines where the group is. Management must then take the group from where it is to where it wants the group to go.

Education is a great motivational force. When man has knowledge, he is motivated to do. A manpower development program gives man knowledge. This program is based on product knowledge and sales skills with emphasis on the why, not the how. The why approach or, in other words, an analysis of the principles of psychology, education, communication, management, and social psychology as they relate to selling, provides a platform for each salesman to realize his full sales potential.

The developmental approach recommended in this book is structured around a problem-solving, case-dialogue approach. Emphasis, however, is on realistic sales material. The case-dialogue approach includes a brief introductory statement describing a sales situation. The sales situation is enacted. That enactment is described by dialogue. In essence dialogue is written record of the conversation between the salesman and prospect in a sales situation. The conference approach is used as a conceptual framework in which the conference leader can use the four methods of teaching to get the full participation of each salesman. Each trainer or conference leader must have the desire to be a competent educator; he must prepare lesson plans; he must establish a program and structure meaningful material.

Chapter 19   DISCUSSION QUESTIONS

1 To what extent do you believe that management has a moral responsibility to establish a climate within the company so that each salesman can realize his full potential? Would you change your opinion if the company was engaged in low-cost, door-to-door selling? Does the company that pays its salesmen a commission rather than a salary have an obligation to its sales force with respect to manpower development?

2 What are some of the major reasons why a company should develop an inventory that would permit the sales trainer to appraise what may be the individual's need for training?

3 Which is more important to the sales instructor, knowledge of the subject or the ability to teach? Why?

4 Do you agree with the author's statement that if the material is meaningful to the salesman and if they would participate that 90 percent of the sales educator's battle is won? Explain.

5 What is meant by dialogue analysis? What relationship do you see between dialogue analysis and the case approach? Why might dialogue analysis be more effective than a case study?

6 Why is the conference method considered an excellent training device?

7 Is it possible for an individual to develop the ability to think? How?

8 The statement is made in this chapter that understanding is based on relationships. Do you see any relationship between that concept and the salesman discussing his product in terms of a firm's problem? Explain.

9 What is the relationship between methods of instruction and how individuals learn? Why should the sales trainer plan key questions to facilitate the learning process?

the conference
a case-dialogue
approach
to manpower
development
20

THE CONFERENCE DEFINED

Much of the material in this book has been written about how to involve the prospect or customer in the sales situation. Most of that material applies equally well in involving the salesman in the sales training program. This chapter is specifically designed to explain how the instructor or conference leader involves the salesman in the sales training program.

Everybody is in a conference—at least it appears that way. We call on an executive and the secretary reports that he is in a conference. Invariably this means that he is not to be disturbed. We read a paper or listen to a telecast and learn that politicians are in conference. We may have a conference in our home. In getting ready to plan a vacation, the family may sit down to decide whether they should have a new car and a one-week vacation or keep the old car and have a three-week vacation.

Just what is this conference which plays such an important part in our daily lives? A conference is a meeting of individuals, preferably a small group, in a round-table situation. The purposes of this meeting are to find answers to questions or solutions to problems and to adjust differences of opinion. The conference is a pooling of the knowledge and experience of a group of individuals through consultation and discussion of a problem in which they have a common interest. It is democracy through discussion because all decisions reached in the conference are group decisions.

No matter how the conference is defined, discussion is an essential part of it. In any conference, each member of the group must be given an opportunity to talk, to express his opinion, to contribute his knowledge, or to tell how he has solved comparable problems to the one under dis-

Selling: A Behavioral Science Approach

cussion. He must be free to criticize or question the statements of others and to defend his own views. If the conference is to be completely successful, each member must take part in the discussion, contribute his knowledge, and aid in the solution of the problem. No one member must dictate the decision, nor should one member influence the decisions and conclusions because of position of authority. In fact, most of the value of the conference comes from this mutual interchange and pooling of knowledge, experience, and opinions.

The Case-dialogue-conference Method

The case-dialogue approach to manpower development is built around the conference meeting as a training tool.[1] Sales cases, sales dialogue, and an analysis of those cases are used as conference materials. With the case-dialogue philosophy of training, the preceding definitions of a conference are not strictly adhered to. There is no one solution or any one way to sell. Therefore the concept that the group must reach a decision which will be followed by the group must be modified. In general, the group will agree on most of the points in principle, but not all salesmen will, or perhaps should, actually utilize the group decision on how to handle a particular situation.

The instructor who utilizes the dialogue concept as material for the conference method will exercise more control than would his counterpart in a pure conference. The role of the conference leader utilizing dialogue can be compared to that of the leader conducting a conciliatory conference.[2] In a conciliatory conference there are conflicting interests which affect the decisions and conclusions of the conference. Normally the solution reached is one which is acceptable to all, but not completely satisfactory to any, of the parties involved. In other words, each side must make concessions in order that the group may reach agreement on the problem. In a sales conference, the leader may encounter individuals who have conflicting, perhaps even selfish, interests which will tend to influence their decisions and thinking. These individuals can even retard agreement within the group, In this instance, the leader will be a conciliatory conference leader.

Since a case-dialogue-conference method (with subtle instructor control) is being employed as the subject matter of an educational program, perhaps these sales training conferences could be called suggested conferences or directed solutions conferences. Regardless of the title given the conference, this method is vitally important in educating salesmen.

A dialogue-conference reaches for solutions that are based on a penetrating analysis of the problem or the topic under discussion. The dialogue-conference approach uniquely permits the use of each of the educational methods (telling, discussing, demonstrating, and doing) and appeals to each of the salesman's senses to the degree needed to best accomplish the goal of each conference session.

---

[1] The development of dialogues, how to use dialogues as training materials, and the educational value of dialogues is discussed in chap. 18.

[2] Labor and management conferences are the best known examples of this type of conference.

The Conference: A Case-dialogue Approach

The instructor is forced to rely on group discussion in order to involve the participants mentally. Each salesman who presents his views must organize his thoughts. Thus such an approach promotes thinking. With mental participation there is understanding, and with understanding there is motivation—the desire to do.

To be successful the dialogue-conference method requires a suitable group of salesmen and a leader who uses the chair judiciously.

THE CONFERENCE LEADER

The conference leader occupies the chair. He must be a leader. He must be able to communicate. He must enjoy working in a conference setup. He must know that there is a time to talk and a time to listen, a time to be enthusiastic, and a time to be restrained, and a time to occupy the center of the stage and a time to be in the wings.

One trait the conference leader must possess is that of sensitivity; he must be sensitive to people, situations, and events. The chair or conference leader is in a position of pivotal importance. He is the hinge and door to productive or fruitful discussion. With an accomplished leader in charge, discussions will open up and swing easily from point to point.

Although the dialogue-conference method by itself is an exciting experience and stimulates group discussion, the success or failure of the conference lies largely in the conference leader's hands. His own zest and enthusiasm must be apparent and contagious. He must have and show complete confidence in the dialogue conference method. At the very outset he must arouse interest in the conferees, make them aware that the dialogues are actual problems in the field—that a problem does exist—and he must show them by his own actions and thinking that the solution to the problem is important. Throughout the conference he must keep the discussion aimed at a solution, drawing out all pertinent information, taking full advantage of all group experience, and at the same time discouraging irrelevant discussion.

It is the responsibility of the conference leader to see that everyone contributes to the discussion and that no one person monopolizes it. He must protect the right of each salesman to be heard. He must organize these individual contributions into some sort of unit and point out the common elements in similar cases. After encouraging the salesmen to evaluate all the possible solutions, he must get his salesmen to work together with him in the solution of the common dialogue problem. He must exhibit his sincere interest in their opinions. Finally he must lead them to conclusions based on a complete analysis of the problem.

The chair, or conference leader, must do all this and still remain in the background. He must be master of the situation yet keep attention focused on the group and the problem. He must make his salesmen or group feel that this is their meeting and that its success depends on their participation and their solutions. In short, the chair's authority should be deemphasized.

The conference leader must not act as though only he knows the truth and he is present to pour that truth into empty heads. This is basic to a good discussion. He should steer the discussion but not give the answers. He is expected to guide the discussion along orderly and fruitful lines. But the group, with his help, is supposed to pool its knowledge and its thinking rather than receive the answers from an authority. He never says, "I'll explain this to you." Rather he says, "Let's see if we can get to the core of this problem and agree on a solution."

The conference leader cannot be an expert. According to *Webster's New World Dictionary,* the word *expert* as used in the United States Army is the "highest of three ratings of efficiency of a rifleman—a marksman." The point is that the chair must not zero in on the subject under discussion. He cannot set himself as a final authority on any subject. His job is to accomplish the objective of the sales conference, not to impress the salesmen with his own knowledge.

Pressure should never be brought on the group to agree with the conference leader's views. When he rephrases a conferee's contribution, the chair must be careful not to change the meaning of the statement. When he summarizes the group's conclusions, he should not insert conclusions he wishes the conferees to reach.

In wording questions, in rephrasing, and in summing up, the conference leader uses language which the group can understand. The questions and statements should be clear and concise. Such meaningless expressions as "in any way, shape, or form," "the worse for wear," "do justice for the occasion," "the things involved," should be avoided.

The chair must never depreciate itself. If the conference leader's performance or his preparation is not so good as it should be, he should never apologize for it; the conferees will discover this fact without his pointing it out. The training program, those in authority, the company, company policy, or the conferees should never be criticized. The conference leader must keep personalities out of any discussion. The conferees should not be permitted to criticize each other.

All this suggests that the chair or conference leader is confronted with a complex and difficult situation in conducting a conference. This is not the case. Through utilizing the proper educational strategy and tactics, the role of the conference leader can quickly be accomplished.

THE CONFERENCE IN ACTION

The Preliminary or Preparatory Examination

When it comes to the content of sales training programs, some of what is published today appears to underestimate the intelligence of the average salesman. For instance, management is told that salesmen do not like examinations. Some writers suggest that an examination makes the sales program a classroom situation. As one writer states, "Don't use examinations. Salesmen don't like going back to school. Treat them like adults."

In the author's opinion, the statement should be, "Treat your salesmen like the intelligent, mature individuals they are. Give them an opportunity to check their own understanding of the sales material. Mature salesmen like going back to school when classes are intellectual but practical and when the salesman has an opportunity to participate with his own ideas, concepts, and thinking. It may be compared to the classroom relationship that exists between the professor and the graduate student."

There are books written on how to develop and give examinations. It will be sufficient here to state the purpose of a preliminary or preparatory examination, to illustrate an actual examination, to explain how it can be used, and to explain some of the outputs from an examination.

The following represents five questions from a fifteen-question multiple-choice examination on the contact stage that the author has used with experienced salesmen. These specific questions are now being used by Pratt & Whitney salesmen in conducting their distributor sales training program throughout the United States.

PREPARATORY QUESTIONS

Contact Stage

1. One of the real purposes of this course is to:
   a. Give the salesman product knowledge
   b. Give the salesman a formula for selling, such as the attention, interest, desire, action sequence
   c. Give the salesman a canned sales talk
   d. Provide concepts, ideas, and principles with which the salesman can better determine the correctness or incorrectness of his sales effort
   e. None of the above
2. Feedback means, to the salesman:
   a. Having coffee early in the morning with a waitress, of course
   b. Listening to another salesman, especially after you talk to him
   c. Listening to a radio
   d. Prospect responses or cues, both verbal and nonverbal, as a result of inputs by the salesman in a given sales situation
   e. That he does not need moment by moment feedback to give a skilled sales performance because in most sales situations the salesman does not need feedback
3. Two-way communication means:
   a. None of the following
   b. A process devoid of feedback, but one in which salesman and prospect can reach a mutual understanding
   c. A process that relies on nonverbal feedback
   d. A process like the attention, interest, desire, action sequence of selling
   e. Using a canned sales talk
4. Problem solving is:
   a. Something the distributor salesman does not have to be concerned with since after all the prospect makes the decisions, not the salesman
   b. Something the salesman does not have to be concerned with because the mechanism of behavior persistence helps the salesman in solving the prospect's problem
   c. Something the salesman must be alert to because the salesman who

Selling: A Behavioral Science Approach

is not alert to problem solving in the contact stage may quite easily overlook obvious solutions

d. Easily utilized by the salesman who uses a canned one-way communication sales talk

e. None of the above

5. A permissive question is:

a. Always used in combination with the verification question

b. Always used permissively since it is difficult for a prospect to refuse information when the salesman courteously says, "If I may" or uses some similar term

c. Not only to be used permissively but should also identify the area the salesman wants to ask questions about

d. A question form that never gets participation

e. None of the above

What is the purpose of the examination? Note that its title is Preparatory Questions. It is just that. It is designed to prepare the salesman to discuss specific material in the conference classroom situation. Each question is structured to cover a specific point. This examination relates to the contact stage of the sale. Many of the four or five possible answers to each question have been designed to bring out a particular point that may be worthy of discussion.

Here is how the examination may be given. Prior to coming to the classroom situation, each salesman is given an assignment to read, for example, The Contact Stage. The class, say, thirty salesmen, is divided into five tables of six each. After the salesmen at one table complete the examination, a chairman at the table takes over and the salesmen discuss the best answer to each question. They arrive at one answer which represents the thinking of that particular conference table.

Now the general conference leader takes over. He instructs each chairman to report the answers his group has selected. After all tables have reported, the general conference leader reads the correct answer. Thus group is matched against group. If the general conference leader so desires or the sales trainer so desires, he can inject a little more fun in the total program by giving modest prizes to the table that wins.

This examination technique has been extremely successful for the author. Why? Because the examinations are meaningful, and the salesmen have an opportunity to participate. This examination procedure reinforces previous learning. The group discussions are exceptionally valuable. Salesmen discuss much of the material in terms of everyday sales situations. Even the most experienced salesman learns in the group situation.

A case in point Each salesman can become a conference leader. When the material in a chapter is assigned, a case or dialogue may also be given to the student or salesman on which he must lead a conference. A rating sheet can be developed to cover the various conference techniques and strategies used in a chapter. After the student or salesman has led his conference session, the other members of the group can complete the rating sheet. If the student's and salesmen's conference leadership role is to be discussed by the group, it should be discussed as a learning experience for obvious reasons.

The Conference: A Case-dialogue Approach

Conducting the Conference

The group members should be told what the conference leader expects them to do. Readiness must exist. This is one reason why the conference leader gives an examination and makes conference leadership assignments or role-playing assignments to the group prior to the discussion.

Planned introductory remarks start the conference. At all sessions except the first one, a brief summary of the previous session can be given.

The nature of the subject and how this ties in with the last session can be indicated. A succinct resume of what the day's session will entail is helpful.

A question must be asked which will start the entire group thinking on the dialogue situation, problem, or topic. Normally this is done with an overhead question. This type of question will be discussed under the topic that follows.

The initial question should be followed with follow-up questions in order to bring out all of the group knowledge of the topic and to take full advantage of all the salesman's experiences. All salesmen must participate.

Throughout the conference, the instructor must so choose and word his questions as to keep the discussion centered on the dialogue subject, problem, or situation to be discussed.

In order that all the suggestions can be accomplished, the conference leader must be thoroughly familiar with the various types of questions and the proper use of each type. The questions must be selected and worded according to the purpose in asking them. In Chapter 14 the purposes for asking questions in conferences were stated as follows: to open discussion, to provoke thinking, to distribute discussion, to develop a subject, to change discussion trends, to arrive at conclusions, to check salesmen's knowledge, to accumulate data or information, to stimulate interest and hold attention, and to limit or end discussions.

Specific Question Forms

Questions are classified according to the way they are asked or directed as overhead, direct, and reverse or relay.

Used to start a discussion, the overhead question is directed toward the entire group. No indication is made as to who is to reply. For instance, the question, "Are there any techniques that we should use in most contact situations?" is not addressed to any one salesman. The overhead question is designed to make the entire group think about the problem. In general, questions are first stated as overhead questions, and then, after a pause, the individual who is to reply is identified.

A direct question identifies a particular individual as the one to whom the question is directed. An example of this is, "Jim, what do you think about the relationship between the direction quarter of the sale and planning?" The direct question has many uses. It enables the instructor to draw the timid man into the discussion. Noting that this man has said nothing, the direct question gives the individual time to prepare an ansewer. The instructor can ask for his views. A direct question can be also used to give an inattentive individual a job—to think! Further, the instructor may want to direct a question to a certain conferee because he has special information he can present to the group, or because the question is strictly an individual one. It may refer to a situation the instructor knows has been handled by someone from time to time. The instructor may wish to direct a question to a particular individual because he is an enthusiastic individual and will give the group a pickup at a certain point, or in leading a wandering discussion back to the subject, the instructor may want to direct a question to a clear-thinking member of the group.

There are two major disadvantages of the direct question. If the instructor, for instance, states the individual's name and then asks the question, there is a possibility that other members of the group may not think about the question and will wait for the specific individual to reply. That's human nature. And a direct question must be worded so that it will not antagonize, create a feeling of inferiority in, or embarrass the individual of whom it is asked.

The reverse or relay question may be used when a salesman asks the instructor a question. The instructor refers the question directly back to the salesman who asked the question, or he relays the question to another salesman. For instance, Frank asks the instructor or conference leader, "Ted, what do you think is the real difference between the future and problem-solving quarters of the contact stage?" Ted, the conference leader replies, "That is a good question, but you probably have some idea on it. Could you tell us what you think?" or "Jack, will you comment on Frank's question?"

Questions are also classified according to the way they are used in controlling the discussion. These classifications are lead-off questions or follow-up questions.

A lead-off question is used to start a discussion on a new topic. The lead-off question is invariably an overhead question, but it should be more thought-provoking than the general overhead question. The instructor should prepare a lead-off question for each topic before the conference gets under way.

Follow-up questions keep the conference going. They may be overhead or direct questions. These questions should be planned prior to the beginning of the conference, but instructors often have to structure most of their follow-up questions on the spot. This is especially true when the discussion takes an unexpected turn. Nevertheless, preparing follow-up questions in advance prepares the instructor to develop follow-up questions on the spot.

Guide to Good Questions

The question technique is to the conference leader what words are to the orator. This may be an overstatement of the importance of the question technique, but it is the conference leader's most important tool. By and large the success of the dialogue conference will depend on asking the right question at the right time.

The Conference: A Case-dialogue Approach

The general strategy used in asking questions is as important as the framing of the questions. Good questions may serve little purpose if poor techniques are used in asking them. This is especially true in group conferences. The following general rules of questioning will be of value to the conference leader as he develops his philosophy of conducting the conference sales training program.

1. Questions should be distributed fairly among salesmen. This does not mean that the conference leader has to ask every salesman exactly the same number of questions. But he must avoid calling on the eager or attention-demanding salesman and slighting the quieter, timid one. Permitting the eager salesman to monopolize the answering can well destroy the sales training program. In fact, it is even a disservice to the eager salesman, since he may well lose the friendship of the group.

2. Salesmen should not be called upon in a fixed order. Frequently the conference leader has a tendency, either unconsciously or consciously, to develop an order in which he calls on individuals. It doesn't take long before the salesmen learn the sequence and pay attention only when they are about to be called on. This is human nature too.

3. Group answers should not be permitted. This practice should never be permitted. Those who answer loudly will cover up for those who do not.

4. Questions should not be too difficult nor too easy. If a question is too difficult, the instructor will get little or no response. If it is too simple and requires no thought, it has no value and will encourage slovenly thinking.

5. Questions should not cover too much ground nor be too narrow. "What did your author have to say in this book?" is a question that is much too broad. A better question would be "What were some of the major points that the author made in the contact chapter?" Better still is the question, "What were some of the variables of the contact referred to by the author?"

On the other extreme, questions so narrow in coverage make the discussion turn into a question and answer session and should be avoided. Some questions will merely get a yes or no answer. If the instructor asks, "Mr. Smith, do you agree with the answer just given?" Smith is apt to reply yes. Questions which ask how, what, and why are better suited for the dialogue-conference method. However, the instructor should be careful of the why question which puts a man on the defensive when he has to prove a statement he made.

6. Answers to questions should always be acknowledged. When a salesman replies to a direct question or states an opinion on an overhead question, the instructor should acknowledge the response. "Thank you, Jim," or "Okay, Jim," expresses the instructor's appreciation for the answer. In expressing appreciation for the response, the instructor must be careful not to show preference for that particular salesman's point of view.

7. Good answers should be commended. Terms such as *good, excellent,* are compliments which should be saved until a salesman answers a question well.

Real judgment has to be used here, for praise given to a group can be quite thin when it is repeated many times. Sometimes, if all the salesmen in the group expect the instructor to be complimenting them on their answers with a *good,* they are somewhat concerned when they do not hear the compliment. In brief, complimentary remarks are used judiciously.

8. Questions are used to keep salesmen alert. In the course of a discussion or explanation, the instructor may detect signs of inattention or daydreaming on the part of the salesman. A question addressed to the inattentive salesman will alert him. The question should be designed to get his attention and his thought rather than to embarrass the salesman.

9. Repetition of questions should be held to a minimum. Questions should be asked in normal conversation tones, loud enough to be heard by all salesmen the first time. Frequently, when there is no immediate response to a question, an instructor will say, "What I mean is . . ." and continue with the question as stated the first time. This may be a good strategy if the question is a difficult one and one for which the salesmen do not have an immediate answer.

The salesman's reply to the instructor's question should not be repeated. Doing so wastes conference time; it is discouraging to the salesman who gave the answer, and it dampens group discussion. In addition, it encourages lax or poor thinking and poorly expressed answers. Occasionally the instructor may want to condense or rephrase an answer, but this should not be done too often.

10. Adequate time should be allowed for answering the questions. If the question concerns information which the salesman should have at his fingertips, a few seconds may be ample time to allow for an answer. However, if the question is one which requires thought, the conference leader should actually discourage a reply which is so prompt that it indicates little thinking has taken place. The instructor should ask the salesman to explain how he arrived at his answer. In the case of dialogue, it is sometimes difficult for a salesman to explain how he arrived at an answer. Nevertheless, this concept the instructor should consistently have in mind. The class may well bog down, however, if a salesman has too much time to answer. A long silence can be devastating to class or group interest.

When a man is unable to answer a question, the instructor must not let him flounder indefinitely. He should come to his aid by thanking him and passing the question back to the group or on to some other conferee.

11. Salesmen must be taught to consider every question thoughtfully and evaluate every answer.

The conference leader accomplishes this by addressing the questions to the entire group before calling the name of the salesman who is to answer. Then, if the instructor has the salesman make his reply to the other salesmen in the class rather than to him, he can call on someone else in the group to evaluate the answer.

Controlling and Stimulating the Conference

The conference leader employs various techniques to control and stimulate the discussion. Some of these are described below.

The chair per se can serve the instructor as a device to aid in controlling the discussion. When seated, the instructor exhibits interest in the group's comments and shows a willingness to permit free discussion. When he rises, the group's attention shifts to him. The members then expect him to take over the discussion or to exert a closer influence on them.

A chair placed off to one side will be helpful when the instructor wishes to withdraw from the group. By moving over and sitting in this chair, he effaces himself as a target, and with the instructor out of range, the salesmen may start shooting questions at each other.

There are dozens of unobtrusive ways in which an instructor can gain and get the full attention of the group. When the discussion becomes rather heated between two individuals, he can rise and walk slowly around the table. He may even walk up and stand before the two heated participants. In any event, as he rises, the group members follow the instructor with their eyes, giving him the attention. There will be a lull in the conversation, and he can then get it under control. When the discussion drifts from a particular point under discussion, the instructor can rise and stand in thoughtful attitude suggesting, perhaps, that the group members stop and think, or he may get attention by merely saying, "There's a point to remember." Or he may drop an ash tray from the table or thump the blackboard.

If the conference leader deliberately misinterprets a salesman's statement, he is using a device to get the salesman to defend his point of view or to discuss the subject further. The salesman will want to clarify his statements or strengthen his arguments. At times it may be just the technique needed to stimulate discussion.

A similar, but more subtle, technique for stimulating discussion is when the instructor pretends he doesn't quite understand the salesman's statetment. He uses this device when he fears that a statement is not clear to all or when he feels that the salesman's thinking lacks organization. A pretended lack of understanding forces the salesman to clarify both his statement and his own thinking.

Summary

A conference is a meeting of individuals in a round-table situation with the purposes of finding answers to questions or solutions to problems and adjusting differences of opinion. Discussion is an essential part of the conference method. In this book the case-dialogue approach is used as a medium to facilitate the group interactive process within the structure of the conference method.

Dialogue enactment is only one step removed from role playing and thus can be used as an extremely effective introduction to role playing. Generally role playing as a form of manpower development is best carried out within the conference structure. In addition to role playing, a preliminary examination involves the salesman in the conference.

The conference leader occupies the chair. The chair is a symbol of authority, but the true conference leader will deemphasize it. His role is to initiate and to steer discussion but not to dominate it. He is a facilitator. He wants to get group participation. He wants to adjust a program to each of the individual participants within the conference session.

In general, the best method of conducting the discussion is by the use of several basic question forms. The overhead question is directed to the entire group, and it is used to initiate a discussion. With the overhead question no specific person is asked to answer, thus causing each member of the group to think about the question before it is discussed. The direct question, on the other hand, is aimed at one specific individual. It gives the conference leader considerable control. With the direct question the conference leader can direct a question to an individual who may have unique knowledge and thus can contribute to the group; he may bring a wandering mind back into the discussion; he may direct the question to the timid individual and thus get more participation. The reverse or relay question is used whenever a question is directed by a participant to the conference leader. The conference leader then reverses the question directly to the asker or relays it to another individual for a reply.

Several general rules of questioning follow: Questions should be distributed fairly among salesmen; the salesmen should not be called upon in fixed order; the conference leader should not permit group answers; the conference leader should command good answers; repetition of questions should be held to a minimum; adequate time should be allowed so that the participant can answer the question, and the conference leader should strive to make each salesman consider every question and evaluate every answer.

The conference leader employs various techniques to control and stimulate the discussion. These include such simple things as sitting or standing at strategic times, the placement of his chair in relation to the group, and his deliberately misinterpreting or his pretending to misunderstand a salesman's response.

Through using the strategy and techniques indicated in this chapter, the conference leader can direct a most successful manpower development conference.

Chapter 20 DISCUSSION QUESTIONS

1 Do you see any limitations to a conference method of sales training? Explain.
2 What characteristics do you think the conference leader should exhibit? What is the major role of the conference leader?
3 Is it possible that the conference leader may be doing a disservice to the salesman by directing questions to the salesman who has the ability to answer most questions?
4 Is there any particular reason why the conference leader shouldn't call on salesmen in a fixed order?

The Conference: A Case-dialogue Approach

5 How is it possible for a conference leader to command good answers when his role is merely one of facilitating the conference discussion?

6 What is the real difference between the direct question and the overhead question?

7 Do you think it is wise for the conference leader to use the reverse method, or would it be a better choice in most cases to use the reverse and relay method?

8 If the salesman apparently cannot answer a question, should the instructor probe to give that salesman an opportunity to find an appropriate answer to the question? Discuss.

9 Under what circumstances might the conference leader deliberately misinterpret a salesman's statement?

10 It is commonly stated that the salesman does not like to take examinations. Why might this be true?

group
selling
or communication
in the group

21

INTRODUCTION

Salesmen may be involved in group communication in three ways. From time to time, the salesman invariably communicates with his peers in groups of three or more. These discussions may be formal or informal.

In today's markets more and more salesmen are required to function as conference leaders. This dimension of group communication is especially important to manufacturer's salesmen who work with other manufacturers or with distributors, or to distributor salesmen who work with retailers. The importance of this type of group communication is underscored by the very fact that a number of companies engaged in systems selling—for example, International Business Machines, National Cash Register, and Burroughs are giving their salesmen training in various forms of conference leadership.

Finally, more and more salesmen are involved in pure group selling. By definition, group selling will refer to all sales situations in which the salesman gives an exposition for ten to fifteen minutes or more about his company's products or services in front of two or more individuals who represent the buying group. This last form of group communication is the subject matter of this chapter. But if the concept of exposition were changed to discussion, then much of the material presented in Chapter 20 in the section on The Conference Leader would be germane to the subject matter of this chapter. Since conference leadership is closely related to group selling and since each salesman who has read and practiced the strategies and tactics outlined in Chapter 20 is well-grounded on how to operate as a conference leader, this form of group communication will be used to establish the starting point of this discussion.

Skills, knowledge, tactics, and strategies learned as a conference leader are comparable to the skills, knowledge, and attitude needed in group selling. A conference leader acts as a cohesive force. He utilizes tactics and skills to obtain group interaction. The experienced conference leader can function in many roles. With equal skill he can dominate or be persuasive or involve the group in total or the individual as a member of a group. He can channel both the group and the individual's discussion as to quality, content, and time. A skilled conference leader knows how to use various question techniques and tactics of the chair to accomplish many purposes. To repeat, many of these attributes, skills, and tactics used in conference leadership are used in group selling. But the mix is different. In group selling, planning is different. The leader's role is different. The interaction of participation is especially different. Finally, the group-selling function from the salesman's perspective is action-oriented.

PLANNING FOR THE GROUP SALE

As a person-to-person salesman, each sales representative plans. He manages his time, his market opportunities, and his specific sales effort. He gets information. He is a facts researcher. As a conference leader, each salesman plans. He prepares lesson plans, establishes goals, and determines the activities needed to accomplish these goals. He establishes a sequence of activities that enable him to direct or lead the conference group to a predetermined and desired goal. He uses many tactics to do this, from planned questions to tactics of the chair. He prepares material such as films, mimeographed handouts, or visuals of various sorts to support his discussion material. Finally, he summarizes each conference. In addition, he understands the laws of learning and knows how and why people learn. He is especially aware of the fact that he must get participation and present meaningful material to obtain best results from the group.

In varying degrees the preceding discussion applies to group selling, but much of what the salesman will do as a planner will vary with the situation. The salesman's time, the problem involved, the money involved, the power structure of his company in contrast to the customer company, and perhaps a host of other factors will furnish guidelines as a basis for his procedures. In general, however, the salesman involved in group selling will spend a great deal of his time in planning. He plans so that every minute of his group selling time is invested productively.

There are, however, special problems associated with planning for the group sale. These special problems are (1) knowing each member of the group, (2) limiting the size of the group, (3) establishing the agenda, (4) handling product services or company limitations, (5) utilizing the barrier theory, and (6) achieving agreement.

Knowing Each Member of the Group

In some situations it is close to impossible for the salesman to determine who will comprise the buying group. Many times, however, the salesman is able to get this information beforehand. Salesmen for Superior Coach school buses can easily determine who will attend a meeting con-

Selling: A Behavioral Science Approach

cerning the purchase of school buses. School board members will be involved in the purchase and they are known, as is the composition of subgroups or committee within the school board organization. This same situation prevails for most salesmen engaged in group selling which involves public institutions or levels of government. American Cast Iron Pipe Company salesmen invest a considerable portion of their time in group selling. They can easily determine who the consulting engineer is. Their actual sales task is difficult but they can even get information about other forms of pipe that are being considered and can plan accordingly. In other forms of group selling, such information may be more difficult to obtain. Some companies do not want the salesman to know ahead of time who will attend a meeting regarding the purchase of equipment. This may be especially true when the decision makers are all at the executive level.

Dialogue illustrations In most sales situations the salesman has an excellent opportunity to learn the identity of the buying or decision-making group at the moment the group sales situation is established. This is demonstrated in the following two dialogue cases.

In case dialogue 1 the salesman has surveyed a company's needs and has presented a proposal to an executive. The transition from a survey sale to a group sale is the subject matter of this dialogue. In case dialogue 2 the sales situation is initiated by a purchasing agent. He tells the salesman that his company is interested in hearing a discussion about the salesman's XYZ machine.

CASE DIALOGUE 1

S . . . and with this idea in mind, Mr. Franklin, I would like to make a survey of your gauge needs, and we will then present a report to you. Would that be all right with you?
R Well, I suppose so, but what do you have in mind?
S In brief, it is this, Mr. Franklin. I would like to look over some of the jobs being done now and see if there are any gauges or, for that matter, other nonproductive items that I could recommend which would enable your men to do more productive work.
R Well, we're always willing to listen to advice. When would you want to do that?
S I could start tomorrow morning, Mr. Franklin, but I would like to start a little preliminary work right now if it would meet with your approval.
R Okay. Whom do you want to talk to? And, by the way, I want to make it very clear that I don't want any of our production work to be disrupted.
S You can be sure, Mr. Franklin, I will not in any way interfere with your work program.

One week later:

S Hello, Mr. Franklin. Beautiful day, isn't it?
R Yes, indeed, more sun than I've seen in a long time.
S Mr. Franklin, the complete report is here.
R (*smiling combined with a positive look of interest*) It looks impressive, but is it any good?

Group Selling

S   Yes, I think so, but you'll have to be the final judge, of course. The first page presents in outline form some of the facts contained in the report. I would like to go over the outline and present in capsule form some of the major ideas involved.
R   Yes, that sounds good. I'd like to take a general look at the survey you've done, first of all.
S   All right, with that idea in mind, Mr. Franklin, on page 1 the general outline is given. The first item pertains to gauges. According to your supervisor, you have six major jobs in operation now or to be put into operation before long. These jobs are listed on . . .

For the next thirty minutes, the salesman and Mr. Franklin discuss the survey. Franklin now states:

R   That's a nice piece of work that you've done here, and I'm certainly impressed with it. But before I make a final decision, I want to show this report to several of our people and discuss it with them.
S   All right, Mr Franklin, I can understand that. Is there any particular time that I should call back?

That is one way of handling the situation. It may be the correct way. It will depend on the situation. However, there are two other courses of action. The salesman may press for the sale if he thinks that is the correct thing to do, or he may decide to remain in as close contact with the sales situation as possible through the group-selling concept. Deciding to follow the latter strategy, the salesman continues·

S   I can understand the fact that you want to talk this over with some of your men. However, may I make a suggestion that from past experience has proved to be a time-saver.
R   What did you have in mind?
S   Having you as a customer is very important to us, Mr. Franklin. We want to do the best job we can for you now and in the future. So here is my suggestion. I will make copies of the report I just gave you so that you can give them to the men you have in mind. We're equipped to handle that.
R   Well, that's okay. Several more copies would be helpful.
S   May I have the names of the people involved, Mr. Franklin? I would like to personalize each particular folder—that is, if you don't mind.
R   No, that's okay. Sounds good to me. They would be Jacobs, Ferrer, and Brown.
S   Good, I have met these gentlemen. Another question I would like to ask is whether it would be possible to get Mr. Jacobs, Mr. Ferrer, Mr. Brown, and Mr. Winslow together so that we could have a group discussion of the project. I of course wrote the project and did the research work here in your plant to develop it. So I am very familiar with every detail involved. I would come to such a meeting prepared with larger visuals of the project so that whenever any questions come up, I can be ready to answer them.
R   You say you've done this before?
S   Yes, frequently. I think approximately ten times so far this year. (*Franklin*

appears to hesitate, so the salesman waits a moment.) Most of the executives I have worked with feel that when the reports are looked at individually, it takes a great deal more time and each man is less sure of the final decision than when they have a half hour devoted to a decision-making group conference. I wouldn't recommend it, Mr. Franklin, if I didn't think it would be very helpful to your organization.

R   Well, we haven't done that before, but it sounds like a good idea. Yes, I will set up a time for that meeting.

S   What are the best times for you?

R   Probably Thursday morning on the 20th around ten o'clock because we devote some of that time to other matters that involve all these people anyhow. Yes, we'll plan on you at ten o'clock.

CASE DIALOGUE 2

In this case dialogue the salesman has been called to a plant and told by the purchasing agent that his company is interested in X product produced by the salesman's company. He is asking the salesman to come to the plant at eleven o'clock on X date to explain the merits of his product before a group of people who will be involved in the purchase. The dialogue continues as follows:

R   Can you be here?

S   Indeed I can, Mr. P. A. But may I ask you a few questions about the meeting? It would be helpful to me in planning my presentation.

R   Sure, go ahead. That's no problem.

S   About how many people will be present?

R   Let's say about seven or eight, but some men will be coming and going. There may be as many as ten.

S   Evidently there will be some people, though, who will be closely involved in the purchase of equipment and who will probably remain for most of the session. In other words, is there a core group involved?

R   Yes, I would say there will be four or five people.

S   Could you give me their names and positions in the company, Mr. P. A.?

R   Well, why do you want to know that?

S   This is a major purchase for any company, and I know that when you and your people make a final decision, you want to make it on all the facts that you can possibly have at hand. And I know that you want these meetings to be as profitable as possible. With that idea in mind, I would like to meet briefly with each man involved and leave materials or whatever else I may do to give him information he may want prior to the meeting. Some of that material, of course, I can send in the mail, but it would be best if I first knew what each man wanted.

R   Sure, there is no reason why you can't. The people are Al Reken, the shop superintendent, . . .

S   Thank you. I probably will need only a few minutes with each of the men. By the way, would it be all right if I tell them that you have given me their names so that I could contact them regarding the purchase of the XYZ machines?

Group Selling

R It looks to me like you will have that machine sold before the meeting.
S Well, that would be nice if it could happen, but this will be just a process of getting and giving a little information. In any event, I will look forward to the opportunity of the group presentation.
R OK.
S Also, are there any particular recommendations you would have for me regarding that group presentation?
R Not really, but I might mention that we will hold you to twenty minutes. Every once in a while a salesman will get involved in a debate with a few of our more wordy people and never get his plan across, so be careful about that.
S Thank you, Mr. P. A. I appreciate your suggestions. Oh yes, one other question. Could you tell me the room the meeting will be in so that I can get a look at it and get some idea of the physical setup?
R Sure, that is L-7. In fact, I will walk down and show it to you. I am going that way for a cup of coffee.

In the first case dialogue, the survey, the salesman met the men involved in the final decision-making process while he was making the survey. This is ideal, provided of course that the salesman knows enough about the individuals to help him in the group presentation. In that situation, it was assumed that the salesman did get acquainted with the men or he would have asked Mr. Franklin if he could stop by and visit with each of the men prior to the meeting. In the second situation, the salesman has not met the men involved in the purchase. He wants to know each man and get his thinking for several reasons.

1. He wants to determine how important each man may be to the decision-making process.

2. He wants to determine, if possible, something about each man's personality traits.

3. He wants to determine, if possible, each man's knowledge concerning the equipment involved. This point is especially important since the salesman may find that at times he can develop certain people in the purchasing organization as resource people and supporters of his program or plan. If he has a knowledgeable, cooperative man in the group, he may stop his talk and draw on that resource man by stating, "Mr. Jennings, the shop superintendent, has unique knowledge of that particular application of this machine. Mr. Jennings, would you take a moment to comment on it?"

4. He wants to determine, if possible, each man's emotional involvement with the decision-making process.

5. He wants to determine, if possible, each man's feelings about the other people involved in the purchase of the equipment.

6. He wants to get some ideas of the overall climate that prevails in the purchasing firm.

If the salesman has not been able to obtain the names of each member of the group, he would do well to ask for an introduction of each group member and his function at the start of the first group meeting. For instance, is the individual there in place of his boss, or is he just getting information on various problems of the firm? Perhaps he is just what is called in college "a visitor"—that is, a noncredit student who apparently has an interest in a particular subject.

Many times these introductions will give the perceptive salesman some insights into who is the speaker of the group, who is the decision maker, or who is in a strong position to influence the decision. If the salesman knows the respective roles of the participants, he is in a better position to place all comments and attitudes into perspective. But above all, after it has been determined who the decision makers are, all members of the group must be treated equally.

When two or more salesmen are presenting a plan as a member of a team, it is recommended that one salesman be considered the quarterback. He calls the plays. He takes the initiative in introducing his team to the buying group. The selling team should be sure to get names and job positions clearly in mind before the group discussion begins. Five or ten minutes spent by the two groups in getting to know each other can be crucial to the success of the sales effort.

Limiting the Size of the Group

In most circumstances the salesman should try to keep the group small. Time is important, and normally the salesman is given a certain amount of time to present his proposal. If the group is too large, the salesman may have to ignore some members. These members may be offended and therefore may not be very receptive to the salesman's exposition.

At times the salesman is in a position to suggest that the number of participants be limited. He may say, for instance, "Mr. P. A., it has been my experience that in most situations, whenever the group gets beyond ten, it becomes more difficult to get the viewpoints of the participants. For this reason, it may be advisable to limit the number of participants. What do you think?

There is an exception, however, to the rule that the salesman should try to keep the group small. When the salesman knows of one or more men in the purchasing company organization who could be of assistance during the group, he may ask that these people be added to the group. The individual may have special knowledge the salesman can draw on, and the man may be a firm supporter of the salesman's product. Many times it is quite easy and natural for the salesman to suggest that a certain individual or several individuals be included in the discussion. This is true when the salesman has made a survey of a company's needs. He may remark, for instance, "Jim, while I was doing this survey, I was very much impressed with the knowledge of Smith and Haynes concerning the technical application of the XYZ machine to your needs. Would it be permissible for me to recommend that they be included in this meeting?"

In most cases, however, the size of the group is beyond the control of the salesman. Often it is easier to change situations than individuals. It is good business to establish the most favorable situation as to time, place, and the number of participants.

Establishing the Agenda

To establish a meaningful agenda, the salesman must be acutely aware of how his proposal can best meet the needs of the firm. He will have to get all the facts concerning the firm and its problems, and then he must fully understand how his proposal will best meet the needs of the company. In addition, he must fully understand the competitor situation.

The well-established agenda, supported by outlines, flip charts, short films, models, or other tools of dramatization, should not only involve the participants but should also help reduce group tension.

The salesman will be wise to plan time to give group participants an opportunity to express tensions or frustrations concerning his proposal. A timely discussion of problems frequently has therapeutic value. It reduces individual tensions and is known as catharsis. For instance, a question by the salesman such as, "Gentlemen, what are some of the problems or risks that you see in realigning your production flow?" may have great tension-reduction value. It is entirely possible that such a question will bring about a discussion of what one individual may regard as the problems, risks, or dangers involved. These problems may be the importance one department may lose in a realigned production flow; personnel not being trained to handle new types of machinery; how automation reduces the number of employees; the profit factors involved; costs on investment; competition or changing markets; or any one of 100 other points. If the problems or dangers, as seen by any one of the group members, are brought into the open, a head of steam building up in that one individual may be thwarted.

Handling Product Services or Company Limitations

The question here is this: Should the salesman point out only the strong features of the product or proposal and not mention any limitations of his product or proposal or gloss over any supposed limitations? What should he do?

In most cases it is best if the salesman points out any limitations in his proposal that he believes might, at the end of his exposition, be picked off by members of the listening group.

If his product line or proposal is perfect, there is no problem, but the underlying assumption of this discussion is that no product or proposal is completely free of limitations. Further, it is assumed that the salesman's product is as good as or superior to competing products. Thus limitations in any product or proposal in no way imply that a sale won't be made.

One of the basic reasons a salesman should refer to his product limitations in more than just a glossing-over manner is that he will be in a stronger position by voluntarily conceding limitations than if a group participant, especially one who leans toward another product, points out the limitations as a specific reason for not buying. It is akin to the logic behind the concept of forestalling, discussed in this book as a method of handling prospect doubts. Keep in mind that the salesman has limited time and cannot afford to get into diverse opinions or bickering among group participants.

Another factor to be considered in handling the problem is the number of meetings the buying group plans to have before it makes a decision. Obviously, if there are several meetings, the limitations of the salesman's proposal will be brought out in any event. Thus, taking the initiative and briefly discussing limitations in a positive, straightforward manner will give the salesman a solid footing with the group. He shouldn't act apologetic. Usually no one proposal or piece of equipment solves all problems.

Frequently what may appear to be limitations are not important to the real reason for the purchase. For instance, a piece of equipment the salesman is selling may perform ten machine operations. It may perform six with excellence, and it may have limitations in the other four areas. It may not have, for instance, machine tolerances in certain operations equal to some competitive machine. But if the machine is being purchased for 90 percent of its work in the area in which the salesman's machine does excellent work, it is entirely possible his proposal will receive serious consideration. It will depend upon competition, of course. In brief, the salesman should first differentiate his machine or proposal by concentrating on what his machine or proposal does best. Then he can tackle the limitations.

In addition to the preceding situation, several salesmen representing competing companies are often asked to present plans or proposals to a group, and the decision is made at the end of the session. In such a situation it is best to be last on the program. Failing this, the salesman, like the debater, should request an opportunity to return and present a rebuttal after other salesmen have been heard.

One final point. If the salesman accepts the philosophy that it is advantageous to discuss limitations or supposed limitations in his product or proposal, then he should review the chapter in this book dealing with prospect doubts.

Utilizing the Barrier Theory in Group Selling

The barrier theory of selling is best understood if the reader visualizes a series of hurdles like those used in high- and low-hurdle track meets. These hurdles are mentally established in the prospect's mind by the salesman. He does this by eliciting favorable responses or admissions from the prospect during the sales interview. The salesman's discussion topics are so phrased that the prospect indicates that he desires or wants certain specific things. The end result is such that should the prospect decide not to approve the salesman's proposal, he, in effect, must mentally deny all the admissions he made during the sales talk.

How this is accomplished by the life insurance salesman and other salesmen is clearly explained in Chapter 9. A review of that material will be helpful to the group salesman. However, at this point the question is this: How can the salesman in group selling establish mental barriers in the minds of the group participants? The following three monologue excerpts illustrate how this can be done.

The first monologue represents an industrial sales situation. The industrial salesman is giving an exposition before a group of ten individuals. The amenities have been omitted.

MONOLOGUE 1

"Is modernization important? Is staying ahead of competition important? Are lowering costs, developing greater precision work, and in fact planning for the years ahead important? Of course they are all important. These are some of the specific reasons that, as several of you gentlemen have indicated, were behind your decision to investigate recent developments in numeric controls. And with these ideas in mind, I would like to take approximately fifteen minutes to relate how Press and Press equipment can fit into your overall plan. But it would be very helpful if you would raise questions as I go along in the explanation."

The second sales situation finds a school bus salesman before a group of school board members. The amenities have been omitted.

MONOLOGUE 2

"Is safety important? There is no question about that. I am sure that every member of this school board is greatly concerned with school bus safety and how that relates to the well-being of the children in this school system. And I want to assure you that Superior Coach shares this concern with you. Last year 290 children were killed in school bus accidents. According to *Government Report Bulletin 48*, copies of which are in the brochure in front of you, many of these accidents could have been avoided. According to this report there are five major areas of school bus construction that can help avoid accidents. First, air movement . . . Superior Coach air movement systems provide not only ice-free windows during the cold blizzard winter days but vapor-free windows as well. Not even the breath of forty-six school children will vaporize the front or rear section of the bus. To the driver this means . . ."

In the third monologue, part of the school bus salesman's summary is illustrated.

MONOLOGUE 3

"In conclusion, ladies and gentlemen, as members of this school, you know the decision you make here today is crucial. Not crucial from the standpoint that the decision is being made now but rather what that decision means in the future. The facts that have been presented here today assure you, in my opinion, that as you look back on that decision you make today, say five years from now, you will know it was the right one because you will know that everything possible has been done concerning school bus safety for the children in this school system. And you will know as you look at the cost figures after considering depreciation, maintenance, and capacity of the buses that the lowest possible student trip cost has been obtained. Ladies and gentlemen, as you look out that window and see those school buses in front of this school system five years from now, you will see school buses that still have a bright yellow finish absolutely unmarred by rust. The body will be rust-free because of the zinc coating. . . ."

Achieving Agreement

In person-to-person sales situations the salesman uses numerous tactics which assist in achieving agreement. He plans his sales effort. He analyzes accounts or prospective account situations. He uses a number of tactics for getting information and giving information. He uses various question forms and acquires skills in evaluating and interpreting prospect reactions by observation. He has acquired skills that enable him to seek agreement from the initial contact with the prospect to the completion of negotiations.

In group selling the situation is different. It may be more difficult to obtain agreement. Why? Simply because whenever there are individuals involved, there may be differences of opinion. Much of what is known about man points to this conclusion. If each man in the group has a different position in the company and if each man has a different adjustment to life, then there are bound to be differences. Nevertheless, this should not retard the sale, since each salesman competitor is confronted with the same situation. And as has been pointed out in this book, the real difference in selling today is the salesman. He is the one that makes his presentation and differentiates his product and thus has a better opportunity than competing salesmen to achieve agreement among group participants.

The salesman who differentiates his product will do a number of things to get agreement in the group sales situation. He will:

1. Limit the agenda to pertinent points. He will not spend valuable time on side issues. There are reasons why the user company should buy the salesman's product. He will concentrate on these points.

2. Admit the limitations.

3. Make every point clear and concise. And every point, if possible, should be directed to fulfilling the needs of the user company.

4. Support each statement with fact or have a backlog of fact to support the statements if needed.

5. Use visuals and other aids that will reinforce the telling phase.

6. Draw conclusions frequently. This should be done for each section or major topic discussed. The concept of spatial and temporal summation is especially important here and should be used. When the salesman summarizes, he reinforces previous points made.

7. Limit the size of the group, if possible. The exception is when the salesman suggests that certain individuals be included in the group who can be of assistance to him.

8. Meet each individual who will be attending the group sales situation prior to the group sale. In this way the salesman has an opportunity to learn more about the individuals' needs and interests in the situation.

Group Selling

From the enumeration above, two points stand out clearly—the importance of planning and the importance of the individual in the group sale. If planning is important in person-to-person selling, then it is many times more important in group selling. This is clear by the very nature of the situation. Generally in the person-to-person situation, the salesman has a better opportunity to get information concerning his prospect prior to his call and to gain information during the call than has the salesman involved in group selling.

There is some evidence that the decision-making process may be easier in group situations than in the individual situations. It is frequently difficult for an individual to make a decision. Usually he has fragmentary knowledge on which to base his decision. Further, an affirmative decision infers that the individual has a knowledge of the consequences of the decision and approves of those consequences. This imperfect state of knowledge often causes doubt and makes the decision-making process more difficult for an individual.

In the group sales situation, however, the decision responsibility is shared. Thus it may be easier for individuals within the group to give their okay to a proposal. Unquestionably this is the situation when two or three individuals in the group with some authority and with good source credibility favor the proposal. For example, the engineer who comments on an engineering problem has more source credibility than the purchasing agent. In this instance, the decision is made more easily through a group situation than if the purchasing agent had to make the decision alone.

INTENT OR ROLE OF THE PARTICIPANT

In conference situations obtaining group cohesiveness is not difficult. The conference leader has many tactics he can use, and the group is basically oriented to solving basic sales situations and thus has a common root. Furthermore, the conference leader usually knows each individual's reaction to the sales training conference and can adjust to the needs of the individual.

Obtaining group cohesiveness in the group sales situation is more difficult. Not as many proved tactics are available in group selling. The group may not have a common root and obtaining premeeting knowledge of each individual may be beyond the realm of possibility for the salesman. These factors make the group sales situation much more difficult than the conference situation. These disadvantages may be partially offset, however, if the salesman knows the role or intent of the individual participant. This will help the salesman to get group cohesiveness.

As has been indicated, even more than in conference sessions, each person in every group sales situation must be regarded as a unique individual. He may represent a minor position in the group sales situation, but he is a unique individual and must be treated as such.

Time, tests, records, etc., assisted the conference leader in obtaining knowledge of individual participants in the conference sessions. In person-to-person selling an analysis of the individual personality is made through planning, observation, questions, tasks, and discussion. Obviously such forms of analysis are not feasible in most group sales situations. But the role participants play in the group situation can be conceptually recognized, and thus each salesman can more easily establish a coping behavior for various situations. Admittedly this is difficult. For instance, it may be impossible to know if a man has been sent by his department to "throw a wrench in the works," or to present obstacles in the form of intershop or interdepartmental difficulties, or if he has some special agreement with some other individuals involved, or even if he has received gifts to thwart the salesman's effort, or if he has been sent to the meeting to specifically enlighten the group on his departmental grievances, or if he wants to wash the department linen in public. Nevertheless, remedial tactics are available.

The situations as mentioned do take place, but evidence indicates that in most groups the expectation of the members is that the group should be doing something, getting somewhere, and making progress. Groups are expected to transfer from one given point or situation to some other projected point or situation. Stating it another way, groups are expected to make progress toward some sort of accomplishment.

If certain factors are present, the group will be cohesive and the members will function toward the group goal at a fairly high level. These factors are:

1. Knowledge that business needs can be fulfilled by functioning with the group.

2. Knowledge that personal needs can be attained through belonging to the group. These needs may range from need recognition or personal prestige to need succorance.

3. The feeling of cooperation among members rather than competition.

4. The feeling that members share a common fate or fortune.

In view of these factors, the best advice to the salesman is to establish a group goal and be aware of the factors of group cohesiveness and then be prepared to adjust to the individual's role in the group.

The intent of the individual in a group, according to Dr. King, professor of sociology at North Carolina College, may be a task function, group function, or individual function. Based on the intent of the participants the functions are listed as follows:

FUNCTIONS SHEET[1]
(*Based on Intent of Participant*)

A. Task functions
 1. Initiator-contributor
 2. Information giver
 3. Position stater
 4. Elaborator
 5. Coordinator

[1] Charles E. King, *The Sociology of Small Groups*, Pageant Press, New York, 1962, pp. 108–109.

6. Orientor
7. Evaluator-critic
8. Energizer
9. Information seeker
B. Group functions
1. Encourager-rewarder
2. Harmonizer-mediator
3. Good group member
4. Gate keeper
5. Standard setter
6. Follower
7. Group observer
C. Individual functions
1. Playboy
2. Sympathy seeker
3. Aggressor
4. Dominator
5. Blocker
6. Recognition seeker
7. Self-defender
8. Self-observer
9. Vacillator

In a limited research by the author, which covered eight group sales presentations (involving a total of forty-two participants) to school boards, municipal commissions, and industry, most of the group members appear to enact several roles. These roles, interpreted in terms of the individual's behavior activities as identified by the author, were information giver, information seeker, position stater, coordinator-harmonizer, evaluator-critic, blocker, recognition seeker, aggressor, and self-defender. Some individuals appeared to be rather dogmatic and perhaps recognition seekers but still functioned positively in the group by being information getters and givers.

In general there was considerably less personal interaction among these groups than among the conference groups identified on pages 96–101 of the behavioral science material. At no time in any of these group sales situations did the author identify behavior activities that could be considered hostile or belligerent toward the salesman. Some individuals were at times hostile toward each other. Surprisingly enough, of the forty-two participants, seven could be classified as noticeably indifferent or disinterested, yet no salesman used specific tactics to involve those individuals.

Summary

Much of conference leadership theory is applicable to group selling. The skills, knowledge, and attitude needed in conference leadership are also needed in group selling. The mix, however, is different. This is true of planning and of the leader's role and is especially true of the inter-action between participants. Also, the group sales situation is action-oriented, at least from the salesman's perspective.

In group selling the salesman will plan so that every minute of his time is invested productively. In contrast to person-to-person selling, there are a number of special areas of difficulty associated with planning for the group sale. These areas of difficulty are (1) knowing each member of the group, (2) limiting the size of the group, (3) establishing an agenda, (4) handling product services or company weaknesses, (5) utilizing the barrier theory of selling, and (6) achieving agreement.

Each salesman involved in group selling should make every effort possible to know each member of the buying group. He wants to learn each person's position in the company, each person's needs, each person's knowledge of the topic under consideration, and each individual's involve-ment in the decision-making process. This knowledge will guide the sales-man's activity in his total group-selling effort. How the salesman obtains knowledge of the individual has been illustrated with dialogue in this chapter.

A group that is too large to work with may seriously impede the sales-man's progress towards obtaining group agreement. The salesman has a number of tactics he can employ not only to structure the group size but also to affect the composition of the group.

In every group sales situation a meaningful agenda must be estab-lished. This can be done only if the salesman relates the material he presents about his product or proposal to the needs of the firm. A well-established agenda supported by various visuals will involve the partici-pants and may substantially reduce group tension.

How should the salesman handle what may be weaknesses in his prod-uct, company, or services? Should he mention only the strong points con-cerning his proposal and entirely skip or gloss over lightly any possible weaknesses? The recommended approach is that it is best if the salesman points out any weaknesses in his proposal rather than waits for a member of the group to comment on them. Psychological fact suggests that if the salesman follows a strategy of identifying weaknesses, he will be in a much stronger position in his group presentation.

The barrier theory can be employed in group selling probably more effectively than it can be employed in the individual man-to-man sales situation. In this chapter dialogue was presented to illustrate how the salesman can employ the barrier theory in group selling. In addition, the barrier theory was discussed in Chapter 9, "Six Approaches to Selling."

Normally it is more difficult to obtain agreement in the group sales situation than in the person-to-person sales effort. It is entirely possible, however, that in many cases the salesman's task in achieving agreement is easier in the group structure than in the person-to-person sales situa-tion. The central idea involved in this thinking is that in the group sales situation decision responsibility is shared. Achieving group agreement is especially enhanced when one or more individuals with some authority and with good source credibility favor the salesman's proposal.

Group Selling

Finally, the salesman who effectively differentiates his product will have an excellent opportunity of achieving group agreement. How the salesman differentiates his product in the group sale has been the subject matter of this chapter.

One of the unique ways in which a salesman can obtain group agreement is through establishing group cohesiveness. There are many ways in which the salesman can obtain group cohesiveness, but the salesman can best obtain this if he has some knowledge concerning the intent or role of the participants in the group discussion.

Chapter 21   DISCUSSION QUESTIONS

1   Assume that you are a salesman and you are required to perform two roles in your selling duties. The first role is that of the conference leader, and the second role is that of group selling. Discuss the relationship you see in the tactics used in these two forms of communication.

2   Why is it advisable that the salesman know each member who composes the buying group prior to his group sales situation?

3   In what way might the salesman affect who will comprise the buying group?

4   Are there any particular reasons why the salesman should attempt to limit the size of the purchasing group?

5   How is it possible for the salesman to develop certain people in the purchasing organization as resource people and supporters of his program or plan?

6   Why should the salesman determine, if possible, each man's decision-making power within the purchasing group?

7   Discuss why it is important that the salesman establish an agenda for the group sales situation. Should he mimeograph an agenda and pass it out to the participating members?

8   How is it possible for the salesman to reduce what may be tensions that have been built up prior to the purchase among the purchasing group's members?

9   Would you recommend to a salesman that he concede limitations in his product, company, or service during his group presentation, or should he not mention them until they might be mentioned by a member of the purchasing group?

10   In what way does the barrier theory operate in group selling?

11   What should the salesman do to facilitate achieving agreement during the group sales presentation?

BIBLIOGRAPHY

Anderson, John E.: *The Psychology of Development and Personal Adjustment* (New York: Holt, Rinehart and Winston, Inc., 1949).

Beckman, Theodore N., and William R. Davidson: *Marketing,* 7th ed. (New York: The Ronald Press Company, 1962).

———, **Harold H. Maynard, and William R. Davidson:** *Principles of Marketing,* 6th ed. (New York: The Ronald Press Company, 1957).

Berelson, Bernard, and Gary A. Steiner: *Human Behavior: An Inventory of Scientific Findings* (New York: Harcourt, Brace & World, Inc., 1964).

Berlo, David K.: *The Process of Communication* (New York: Holt, Rinehart and Winston, Inc., 1960).

Berne, Eric: *The Structure and Dynamics of Organizations and Groups* (Philadelphia: J. B. Lippincott Company, 1963).

Black, Max: *Critical Thinking* (Englewood Cliffs, N.J.: Prentice-Hall, Inc., 1946).

Blair, Glenn M., R. Stewart Jones, and Ray H. Simpson: *Educational Psychology* (New York: The Macmillan Company, 1962).

Boring, Edwin G., Herbert S. Langfeld, and Harry P. Weld: *Foundations of Psychology* (London: Chapman & Hall, Ltd.; New York: John Wiley & Sons, Inc., 1948).

Britt, Steuart Henderson, and Harper W. Boyd, Jr. (eds.): *Marketing Management and Administrative Action* (New York: McGraw-Hill Book Company, 1963).

Bross, Erwin D.: *Design for Decisions* (New York: The Macmillan Company, 1961).

Bruner, J. S., and L. J. Postman: "On the Perception of Incongruity: A Paradigm," *J. Personnel,* 18, 206–23 (New York: Personnel Development, Inc.).

Bursk, Edward C.: "Thinking Ahead," *Harvard Business Review* (Cambridge, Mass.: Harvard School of Business, September–October, 1956).

Burton, Philip W., and G. Bowman Kreer: *Advertising: Copyrighting* (Englewood Cliffs, N.J.: Prentice-Hall, Inc., 1962).

Campbell, Jr., and H. Hepler (eds.): *Dimension of Communication* (Belmont, California: Wadsworth Publishing Co., 1964).

370

Bibliography

Canfield, Bertrand R.: *Salesmanship Practices and Problems,* (New York: McGraw-Hill Book Company, 1958).

Carson, Gerald: *The Old Country Store* (Fair Lawn, N.J.: Oxford University Press, 1954).

Cartwright, Dorwin, and Alvin Zander: *Group Dynamics* (New York: Harper & Row, Publishers, Incorporated, 1953).

Cash, Harold C., and W. J. E. Crissy: *A Point of View for Salesmen* (New York: Personnel Development, Inc., 1957).

Cooper, Joseph D.: *The Art of Decision Making* (Garden City, N.Y.: Doubleday & Company, Inc., 1961).

Cruze, Wendell W.: *General Psychology for College Students* (Englewood Cliffs, N.J.: Prentice-Hall, Inc., 1951).

Dirksen, Charles J., Arthur Kroeger, and Lawrence C. Lockley: *Readings in Marketing* (Homewood, Ill.: Richard D. Irwin. Inc.. 1963).

Drucker, Peter F.: *The Practice of Management* (New York: Harper & Row, Publishers, Incorporated, 1954).

Ferguson, Grace B.: *Essentials in Interviewing* (New York: Harper & Row, Publishers, Incorporated, 1962).

Gagne, Robert Mills: *Psychology of Human Performance* (New York: Holt, Rinehart and Winston, Inc., 1959).

Gentry, Dwight L., and Donald L. Shawver: *Fundamentals of Managerial Marketing: A First Course* (New York: Simmons-Boardman Publishing Corporation, 1964).

Golver, John G.: *Business Operations: Operational Research and Reports* (New York: American Book Company, 1949).

Greif, Edwin C.: *Modern Salesmanship: Principles and Problems* (Englewood Cliffs, N.J.: Prentice-Hall, Inc., 1958).

Haas, Kenneth B.: *Case Problems in Salesmanship* (Englewood Cliffs, N.J.: Prentice-Hall, Inc., 1953).

Hackett, Herbert, Martin Andersen, Seth Fessenden, and Lessie L. Hagen: *Understanding and Being Understood* (New York: Longmans, Green & Co., Inc., 1957).

Hattwick, Melvin S.: *The New Psychology of Selling* (New York: McGraw-Hill Book Company, 1960).

Hodnet, Edward: *The Art of Problem Solving* (New York: Harper & Row, Publishers, Incorporated, 1955).

Hollander, Stanley C.: *Sales Devices Throughout the Ages* (New York: Joshua Meier Company, Inc., 1953).

Irwin, Richard D.: *Author's Manual* (Homewood, Ill.: The Dorsey Press and Richard D. Irwin, Inc., 1960).

Jones, John G.: *Salesmanship and Sales Management* (New York: Alexander Hamilton Institute, 1917).

Kelley, Eugene J., and William Lazer: *Managerial Marketing: Perspectives and Viewpoints* (Homewood, Ill.: Richard D. Irwin, Inc., 1958).

King, Charles E.: *The Sociology of Small Groups* (New York: Pageant Press, 1962).

Kirkpatrick, Charles A.: *Salesmanship: Helping Prospects Buy,* 3d ed. (Cincinnati: South-Western Publishing Company, 1956).

Krech, David, and Richard S. Crutchfield: Elements of Psychology (New York: Alfred A. Knopf, Inc., 1961).

Lapp, Charles L.: *Training and Supervising Salesmen* (Englewood Cliffs, N.J.: Prentice-Hall, Inc., 1960).

Selling: A Behavioral Science Approach

Levitt, Theodore: *Innovation in Marketing* (New York: McGraw-Hill Book Company, 1962).

————: "Marketing R & D for Marketing Innovation," *Chemical and Engineering News* (Washington, D.C.: American Chemical Society, vol. 39, no. 42, Oct. 16, 1961).

Lindzey, Gardner, (ed.): *Handbook of Social Psychology* (Reading, Mass.: Addison-Wesley Publishing Company, Inc., 1954).

Maier, Norman R. F.: *Problem-Solving, Discussions, and Conferences: Leadership Methods and Skills* (New York: McGraw-Hill Book Company, 1963).

McCann-Erickson, Inc.: *A Marketing Profile of "The Big Sixties"* (New York: McCann-Erickson, Inc., 1960).

McCloskey, Gordon: *Education and Public Understanding* (New York: Harper & Row, Publishers, Incorporated, 1959).

McDonald, John: "How Businessmen Make Decisions," *Fortune* (New York: Time, Inc., August, 1955).

McKinney, Fred: *Psychology of Personal Adjustment* (New York: John Wiley & Sons, Inc., 1960).

Mayer, David, and Herbert M. Greenberg: "What Makes A Good Salesman," *Harvard Business Review* (Cambridge, Mass.: Harvard School of Business, July–August, 1964).

Maynard, Harold H., and Theodore N. Beckman: *Principles of Marketing* (New York: The Ronald Press Company, 1952).

Meloan, Taylor W., and John M. Rathwell: *Selling: Its Broader Dimensions* (New York: The Macmillan Company, 1960).

Morell, Parker: *Diamond Jim* (New York: Garden City Books, 1935).

Morgan, Clifford T.: *Introduction to Psychology* (New York: McGraw-Hill Book Company, 1956).

Nichols, Ralph G. and Leonard A. Stevens: *Are You Listening?* (New York: McGraw-Hill Book Company, 1957).

Otteson, Schuyler F., William G. Panshchar, and James M. Patterson: *Marketing: The Firm's Viewpoint* (New York: The Macmillan Company, 1964).

Owens, Richard N.: *Introduction to Business Policy* (Homewood, Ill.: Richard D. Irwin, 1954).

Peterson, Carlton A., and Milburn D. Wright: *Salesmanship: Principles and Methods* (Homewood, Ill.: Richard D. Irwin, Inc., 1955).

Rieser, Carl: "The Salesman Isn't Dead—He's Different," *Fortune* (New York: Time, Inc., November, 1962).

Russell, Frederic A., and Frank H. Beach: *Textbook of Salesmanship* (New York: McGraw-Hill Book Company, 1955).

Samuelson, Paul A.: *Economics: An Introductory Analysis* (New York: McGraw-Hill Book Company, 1951).

Saxton, A. H.: "Jobbing 50 Years Ago," *Iron Age* (Philadelphia, Pa.: Chilton Company—Book Division, Jan. 4, 1906).

Schutte, William M., and Erwin R. Steinberg: *Communication in Business and Industry* (New York: Holt, Rinehart and Winston, Inc., 1960).

Shaffer, Laurance F.: *The Psychology of Adjustment* (Boston: Riverside Editions, Houghton Mifflin Company, 1936).

Shaw, Steven J., and Joseph W. Thompson: *Salesmanship: Modern Viewpoints on Personal Communication* (New York: Holt, Rinehart and Winston, Inc., 1960).

Simon, Herbert A.: *Administrative Behavior* (New York: The Macmillan Company, 1961).

Bibliography

Skinner, B. F.: *Science and Human Behavior* (New York: The Macmillan Company, 1953).

Smith, Henry P.: *Psychology in Teaching* (Englewood Cliffs, N.J.: Prentice-Hall, Inc., 1962).

Staats, Arthur W., and Carolyn K. Staats: *Complex Human Behavior* (New York: Holt, Rinehart and Winston, Inc., 1963).

Stanton, William J., and Richard H. Buskirk: *Management of the Sales Force* (Homewood, Ill.: Richard D. Irwin, Inc., 1962).

Staudt, Thomas A., and Donald A. Taylor: *A Managerial Introduction to Marketing* (Englewood Cliffs, N.J.: Prentice-Hall, Inc., 1965).

Stone, Calvin P. (ed.): *Comparative Psychology* (Englewood Cliffs, N.J.: Prentice-Hall, Inc., 1951).

Strong, Edward K.: *The Psychology of Selling and Advertising* (New York: McGraw-Hill Book Company, 1925).

Terry, George R.: *Principles of Management* (Homewood, Ill.: Richard D. Irwin, Inc., 1953).

Thompson, Joseph W.: *Blue Cross–Blue Shield Manpower Development Program Book* (Indianapolis, Ind.: Blue Cross–Blue Shield, 1962).

————: "Increasing Hotel Sales Effectiveness, *The Hotel Monthly* (Chicago, Ill.: Clissold Press, March, 1963).

————: *National Office Furniture Sales Manual* (Chicago, Ill.: National Office Furniture Association, 1962).

————: *Norge Dry Cleaning and Laundry Village Sales Manual* (Grand Rapids, Mich.: Rich Machinery Company, 1962).

————: *Pratt & Whitney Distributor Manpower Development Program* (West Hartford, Conn.: Pratt & Whitney Corp., Inc., 1965).

————: "What College Graduates Say About Employers' Sales Training," *University of Illinois Bulletin* (Urbana, Ill.: University of Illinois, vol. 47, no. 58, April, 1950).

————, **and William Lazer:** *Pratt & Whitney Manpower Development Program* (West Hartford, Conn.: Pratt & Whitney Corp., Inc., 1964).

Townsend, William W.: *Bond Salesmanship* (New York: Holt, Rinehart and Winston, Inc., 1924).

Vance, J. O.: "The New Salesman," *Sales Management* (New York: Sales Management, Inc., Dec. 15, 1963).

Vreeland, Richard C.: "Customers: A Neglected Sales Force?" *Small Marketeer's Aids* (Washington, D.C.: Small Business Administration, no. 83, September, 1962).

Weil, Sidney: "Good Old Fashioned Selling, What Is It?" *Sales Management* (New York: Sales Management, Inc., Dec. 15, 1963).

Weiss, E. B.: *Vanishing Salesman* (New York: McGraw-Hill Book Company, 1962).

Wilson, John M.: *Open the Mind and Close the Sale: The Key to Success in Selling!* (New York: McGraw-Hill Book Company, 1953).

INDEX

Abasement need, 78
Accounts, classification of, 49–50
Achievement need, 77
Acquisition need, 77
Acting, mechanical, 96
  (*See also* Role)
Action language, 168–169
Adjustment, 124–128
  (*See also* Coping behavior)
Administered price, 14–17
Affiliative need, 71–78, 86
Aggression need, 78
Agreement, in group selling, 362–363, 366
  in person-to-person selling, 362
AIDA theory, 142–145
Approach-approach conflict, 131–132
Approach-avoidance conflict, 132
Argumentative prospect, 305–306
Aristotle, 107, 158–159
Armour, Tommy, 38
"As if" dimension, 102
Attention, 143, 260–272
  direction of, 262–272
  faked, 188–190, 196
  involuntary, 262
  shift of, 192–193, 260–261
  voluntary, 260

Autocrat, 178–179
  (*See also* Behavior, activities, of executives)
Autonomy need, 78

Balance-sheet close (*see* T-account close)
Barrier theory, 149–151
  in group selling, 360–362, 366
Basic "why," 283–285
Behavior, activities, of executives, 178–179
  nonverbal, 250
  observation of, 249–254
  of prospect, 74, 80–82, 125–126
  of salesman, 75–76
  thwarting of, 70–71
  verbal, 252–254
  coping (*see* Coping behavior)
  patterns of, 63, 74, 104
    involuntary and voluntary, 250–254
    worksheet for respondent reactions, verbal and nonverbal, 256
  persistence, 227
  of role, 92–94
  (*See also* Role)

Behaviorists, 163
Benefitizing, 17, 75–76, 181
  by Blue Cross-Blue Shield, 176
  by Pratt & Whitney, 175
  (*See also* Product, knowledge of)
Blamavoidance need, 78
Blue Cross-Blue Shield, 50, 109, 140, 153, 206, 245–247, 265
  benefitizing by, 176
Boomerang method, 288–290, 297
Brady, Diamond Jim, 1, 9–10
Brinkmanship, art of, 276
Brochures, design of, 26–27
  (*See also* Visuals)
Buildup close, 312–315, 319
Burden concept, 248–249
Business need, 72
"Buying signal," 310

Calls (*see* Cold call; Personal call; Sales call; Telephone call; Two-call system)
Canned sales message (*see* Sales message, memorized)
Cards, evaluation, 323
  facts, 98
  personal, 207–208
Case-dialogue approach, 333–334, 340
  examples of, 23–37
Case-dialogue-conference method, 340–341
Channel of communication, 159
Channels-of-distribution policies, 28
Charged word, 194–195
Chemical communication, 157
Clarification process, 280–286, 297
Clincher close, 316–318
Closes, techniques of, 114–117, 253, 305, 309–319
"Clown" selling, 148–149
Coalition concept, 171–172
Cognizance need, 78
Cohesiveness, 363–364, 367
Cold call, 232–233
Communication, 156–196, 276, 301, 313

Communication, act of, 57–58
  through action, 157
  channel, 159
  device of, 264
  difficulty of, 82
  ideal, 57
  levels of, 157
  model of, 158–160
  nonverbal, 165–167
  of printed word, 157
  purpose of, 161–167
  receiver of, 159, 181
  score, 183–184
  source, 24, 159, 181
Communications-orientation, 156
Company controls of, 52–56
Compatibility (*see* Empathy)
Compensation, 125–126
  method of, 289–290, 297
Competence, 168, 172–173
Competition, foreign, 156
  motive of, 87–88
  pure, 14–15
  (*See also* Differentiated product)
Completion stage of selling, 308–320
  (*See also* Closes)
Compliment technique, 312, 318
Compromise (*see* Set, redirection of)
Concentration, 192–193
Conference, 26, 94–96, 239, 332–350
  in action, 342–350
  conducting, 345
  controlling, 348–349
  defined, 339–340
  discussion in, 339–350
  leader of, 24, 95–96, 341–342, 345–353
    role enactment of, 98–100, 105
    role variations of, 95
  participant in, 363
  roles in, 94–95
  (*See also* Examination)
Conflict, 131–134
Connectionism, 107–108
Conservance need, 77

Construction need, 77
Contact stage of selling, 82–84, 104,
    111–112, 164, 198–236
  decision-making in, 230–231
  diagram of framework of, 204
  four quarters of, 225–236
  information in, 198–206
  over-all view of, 204–205
  strategy of, 205–206
  variables of, 204–205, 213–220,
    231
  (*See also* Initial contact)
Continuous yes technique, 312–313,
    319
Contrariance need, 78
Contrast in directing attention, 263–
    264, 277
Cooperation, 87–88
Coping behavior, 72, 153, 196
  with argumentative prospect, 305–
    306
  with ego-involved prospect, 304
  with executives, 178–179
  with glad hander, 302
  with grouch, 304–305
  with impulsive prospect, 305
  with procrastinator, 301–302
  with silent prospect, 301
  with skeptic, 304
  with slow prospect, 302
  with timid prospect, 303
  (*See also* Adjustment)
Counteraction need, 77
Creative selling, 5, 52–53, 137–139,
    145, 267
Criticism, 20, 123–124
Cues, 75
  nonverbal, 94, 165, 168
  verbal, 165, 189
Curiosity approach, 206–207
Customer (*see* Prospect)
Customer-oriented salesman, 61, 84,
    145–148

Daily plan card, 53
Deaf spots, 194–196
Decentralization principle, 47–49

Decision-making process, 24, 123,
    308–309
  in contact stage, 230–231
  in depth selling, 153
  in formulized approach, 143–
    144
  in group selling, 363
  in needs-satisfaction approach,
    147
  of organization, 121
  in stimulus-response selling, 139
  (*See also* Completion stage of
    selling)
Decoder, 159
Defendance need, 77
Deference need, 78
Deficit conditions of needs, 70
Democratic leader, 179–181
Demonstration, 152–153
  customer-oriented, 241–242
  method of, 239–242, 257, 335
  one-sided, 240–241
Denial, direct, 287–288, 297
  indirect, 287–289, 297
Depth selling, 60, 143, 151–154, 162
  compared with formulized ap-
    proach, 152–154
  decision-making in, 153
  diagram, 152
  (*See also* Manpower development
    program)
Deselling, 137
Developmental question, 243–247,
    257
Dialogue training, 332–334, 349
  (*See also* Role playing)
Differentiated product, 11–17, 29–
    37, 104, 352–367
  in group selling, 367
  (*See also* Competition)
Direct denial, 287–288, 297
Direct question, 95, 254–255, 345
Direction, of attention, 262–272
  in contact stage, 225–226, 231
Discussion, 152–153
  in conference method, 339–350
  method of, 237–239, 278
  stage of selling, 237–278

Dominance need, 78
Door-to-door salesman, 5, 141, 147
Doubts (*see* Objections)
Dramatization stage of selling (*see* Showmanship)
Dynamism, 168, 173–174

Economic theory, 14–17
Educational psychology, 58, 107–114
  laws of, 108–112
  tools of, 238–243
Educator, in manpower development program, 322–337
  preparation for, 326–327, 336–338
  using case-dialogue approach, 333
  in role enactment, 99
  salesman as, 107–118
Ego, 103–104, 130–131
  bruised, 109–110
  need, 73
Ego-involved prospect, 303–304
Ego-oriented salesman, 121
Egocentrism, 128–131
Egoistic need (*see* Status need)
Emotional close, 314–315, 319
Emotions, 102
  control of, 122–123
  process of, 110–112
  (*See also* Behavior)
Empathy, 67, 102–105
  in contact stage, 213, 232
  description of, 203–204
Encoder, 159
Equilibrium, 80, 88
Evaluation, card of salesman, 323
  by observation, 249–254
Evaluative question, 243–244, 257
  examples of, 247–248
Examination, preparatory to conference, 342–344
Executive, background of, 10
  behavior activities of, 178–179
  characteristics of, 178–179
  communicating with, 177–180

Executive, and decision-making process, 230–231
  self-image of, 93–94
  (*See also* Leader)
Exhibition need, 77
Expectancy concept, 65–68
Expense budget, 51
Expertness, 172–173
Explaining method (*see* Lecturing method)
Exposition, 352
  need, 78
Eye-contact, 189

Face-to-face communication (*see* Person-to-person communication)
Facts, card, 98
  (*See also* Role playing)
Faked attention, 188–190
Fast-talking salesman, 2, 133, 190, 290
Fear motive, 85–86
Feedback, 25, 88–89, 111, 154, 181
  in barrier theory, 149–150
  in contact stage, 205
  defined, 78–79
  to firm, 177
  purpose of, 164–167
  in stimulus-response selling, 141
  (*See also* Communication)
Felt need, 70–72, 80, 131
Files, of present accounts, 49–50
  of prospect, 54
  of prospective accounts, 49–50
Flexibility of schedule, 47
Follow-up question, 346
Force, 70
Ford Mustang, 287
Forecasting, 44–45
Forestalling concept, 286–288, 359–360
Formulized selling, 142–145
  analysis of, 143–145
  compared with depth selling, 152–154
  decision-making in, 143–144

Formulized selling, limitations of, 142–143
Future, in contact stage, 226–227, 231
  of sale, 246

General Mills, 13–16
Gestalt, 117
Gestural communication, 157
  (*See also* Sign language)
Gestures, 168–169
Gimmick, 142, 266–268
  in contact stage, 222
  (*See also* Tension, reduction of)
Glad-hander, 302
Goals, 46–47, 70, 80
  specific, 122
Grouch, 304
Group, communication, 157
  functions of, 365
  participant in, 363, 365
  worksheet of, 364–365
Group selling, 24, 147, 352–367
  agenda for, 359, 366
  agreement in, 362–363, 366
  cohesiveness of, 363–364, 367
  decision-making in, 363
  differentiated product in, 367
  leader of, 352–363
    responsibilities of, 353–363, 366
    tactics of, 363, 366
  participants of, 363–365
  planning for, 353–363
  role playing in, 97–99
Grouping principles, 117–118

Habit, 137, 188–191, 196
  of work, 122
"Heated acting" concept, 96, 101
  (*See also* Role playing)
Hesitation-choice pattern, 63
High-level selling (*see* Creative selling)
High-pressure selling, 145, 319
Homeostasis, 84

Homeostasis, emotional, 150–151
Hotel salesman, in contact stage of selling, 216–218
  painting prospect into picture, 272
  in showmanship stage of selling, 242
  using, buildup close, 313–315
    moving visual, 266
Human relationists, 163

Implied consent clincher close, 316–317
  with summary technique, 316–318
Impulsive prospect, 305
Incentives, in conflict, 132
  as motivation, 84–88
Incongruity, in directing attention, 268–269
  in roles, 132–133
Indirect denial, 287–289, 297
Indirect questions, 254–259
Individual functions, 365
Infavoidance need, 75–77
Information, in contact stage, 198–206
  personal, 198, 254
  in planning stage of selling, 198–200
  by way of two-call system, 209
  (*See also* Feedback)
Initial contact, 206–213, 225
  example of, 233
  (*See also* Contact stage of selling)
Inputs, 204–205
Instructor (*see* Educator; Leader)
Insurance salesman, 6, 140, 147
  in discussion stage of selling, 245–246
  painting prospect into picture, 270–271
  training of, 99
  using, barrier theory, 149–151
    curiosity approach, 206–207
    emotional close, 314
    evaluative question, 248
    moving visual, 265–266

Intensity, of conference leader, 95
  to direct attention, 262–263, 277
  involvement, 96
  of motivation, 73
  of role enactment, 94–96, 99–101,
    300–306
Interruptions (*see* Interview, inter-
    rupted)
Interview, 112
  compared to psychological inter-
    view, 83–84
  in contact stage, 205–213, 227
  in formulized selling, 144
  interrupted, 272–276
  order of, 225–231
    example of, 231–236
  (*See also* Sales call)
Introduction, importance of, 225
  letter of, 207–208
Introspection, 120, 185–186, 251–
    252
Inviolacy need, 77
Involuntary attention, 262
Isolated point stimulation, 116
Isolation in directing attention, 266

Laissez-faire leader, 179–181
Language, action, 168–169
  object, 168–169
Law, of belonging, 112–114
  of effect, 108–114
  of exercise, 110–114
  of readiness, 110–114
Lead-off question, 346
Leader, characteristics of, 178–181
  of conference (*see* Conference,
    leader of)
  of group selling, 352–363, 366
Lecturing method, 238, 335
Lesson plan, 327–332
Letter, of introduction, 207–208
  of recommendation, 207
  of sales, 208–209
Listening, 183–196
  effectively, 183–187
  improving methods of, 186–191
  practicing, 187–196

Listening, roadblocks to, 185–191
  speeds of, 191–196
Lobby case, 235
Low-level selling, 5, 145
Low-pressure selling, 19, 145, 151,
    162

Management, 28, 324–325
  guidance, 52–55
  programming, 42–52
    development of, 45–46
    goals of, 46, 70, 80
    theory, 43–49
Manpower development program,
    23–25, 29, 321–338
  characteristics of, 322–338
  example of, 24–25
  training group, 98–101
  (*See also* Conference; Depth Sell-
    ing; Group selling)
Manufacturer's salesman, 5, 34–37,
    140
  cases of, 23–25
  in contact stage of selling, 219–
    220, 235–236
  in discussion stage of selling, 245
  expertness of, 172–173
  finding prospect's needs, 199
  in group selling, 361
  level of role playing, 97
  painting prospect into picture,
    271
  training of, 97–99
  using, action words, 269
    buildup close, 312–315
    clarification process, 284–285
    clincher close, 316–318
    curiosity approach, 207
    demonstrations, 240–241
    evaluative question, 247
    moving visual, 266
    survey method, 209–210
    trial closes, 309–310
Market manager, 1, 21, 25–29, 55
  responsibilities of, 27–28
  training of, 23–25
Market penetration, 51

Marketing concept, 20, 24, 31
    example of, 14
    twenty-eighth principle of, 4
Maturity, 74, 128
    characteristics of, 120–124
    in contact stage, 205
    in listening, 183–196
Mechanism of behavior-persistence, 227
Mental barriers, 146
Mental set, 60–61, 200–201
Mental state in formulized selling, 144, 153
Minor-point clincher close, 317–318
Monopoly, 12–15
Mood selling, 148–149
Moods, 102
Motivation, 70, 123, 158, 261
    cycle, 70–89, 147
    diagram, 71
    factors of, 325
    incentives as, 84–88
    intensity of, 73
    tools of, 85–88
Motives, identifying, 80–84, 88
    (*See also* Behavior, activities;
    Fear motive; Needs)
Motor set, 60
Motoric act, 96, 101
Movement, in directing attention, 265–266, 277
    in handling interrupted interview, 274, 277
    (*See also* Visuals)

National Cash Register Company, 52–53
Need awareness, 72
Needs, 70–90, 124, 147
    as basis for objections, 282
    deficit conditions of, 70
    of firm, 71–72, 89, 196
    identifying, 74–77, 82, 199
    perception of, 73–75, 88
    of prospect, 72, 89, 145–146, 196, 301–306
    types of, 67, 70–78, 80, 86, 88, 131

Needs-satisfaction approach, 145–148
    decision-making in, 147
Norge Company, 12, 41–48, 97, 156
Novelty, in directing attention, 266–268
    (*See also* Gimmick)
Nudging (*see* Clincher close)
Nurturance need, 78

Object language, 168–169
Objections, 279–307
    business reasons for, 281–282
    in depth selling, 153
    forestalling, 286–288, 359–360
    handling, 280–291, 297
        guideline for, 281–286
        tactics for, 286–291
    invalid, 287–289, 291
    meeting, 280–281
    personal reasons for, 282
    stage of selling, 279–307
    valid, 289–290, 297
Objectivity, 123
Office furniture salesman, 32–33, 115–116, 146
    in contact stage of selling, 218–219
    painting prospect into picture, 271–272
    selling two price lines, 295–296
    using, action words, 269
        buildup close, 313
        clincher close, 316–317
        compensation method, 289–290, 293–294
        demonstrations, 242
        survey method, 210–213
        trial close, 311
Offset technique, 289–290
Order need, 77
Order-taker salesman, 137
Organization, decision-making process in, 121
    in management programming, 47–49
    at territorial level, 56

Outputs, 204–205
Overcontrollers, 101
Overhead question, 95, 345

Painting prospect into picture concept, 270–272, 277
Participation, 86–87
of prospect, 111, 237
Pause, as communication device, 264
in continuous yes technique, 313
in handling silent prospect, 301
in interrupted interview, 276
Pavlov, 107, 140–141
Peddler, 7–12
Perception, 58–68, 117
in contact stage of selling, 200–201
of nonverbal behavior activities, 251
of role, 92–94, 106
Perceptual set, 60–61, 200
Performance method, 242–243, 257, 335
Permissive question, 213–215, 231, 245–246
Person-to-person communication, 57–58, 166–167
closeness in, 170–171
Person-to-person selling, 17, 95–98, 362
role playing in, 97–98
Personal selling, 1, 28
Persuaders, 175–177
Persuasion, 94, 174, 180
Physiological need, 70–72, 80, 88, 131
Planning, for group sale, 353–363
lessons (*see* Lesson plan)
management program, 43–44
stage of selling, 38–56, 198–200
and verification questions, 214
Play need, 78
Portfolio, 263
use of, 129–130
(*See also* Visuals)
Praise concept, 85, 114, 108

Pratt & Whitney, 45, 50, 97, 122, 198, 219, 232, 235, 324, 327–332, 343
benefitizing by, 175
Price, 291–297
administered, 14–17
breakdown of, 293–294
as investment, 294–295
as objection, 287–297
policies, 28
of two lines by salesman, 295–297
Problem-solving approach, 4, 17–21, 123, 130
in contact stage of selling, 205, 227–231
examples of, 23–27
process of, 24, 230
solutions of, 227–230
Procrastinator, 301
Product, benefits, list of, 74–75
relating, to firm's needs, 74, 154–155
to individual's needs, 74–75, 154–155
(*See also* Benefitizing)
knowledge of, 174–177
limitations of, 359–360
policies, 27
presold, 13
quality of, 293
(*See also* Differentiated product)
Production planning, 51
Projection, 127–128
Promotional policies, 28
Prospect, assets of, 48–49
behavior activities of, 74, 80–82, 125–126
characteristics of, 300–306
decisions (*see* Decision-making process)
files, 54
interest in, 184–187
knowledge of, 299–306
painted into picture, 270–272
participation of, 111, 237
peculiarities of, 187–188

Prospect, resistances of, 83–84
  roles of, 95
  satisfaction of, 72
  tactics to use with, 300–306
  (*See also* Needs, of prospect)
Psychology, 58, 67, 82–84
  (*See also* Educational psychology)
Punctuality, 168–170
Punishment, 85–86

Qualitative records, 54–55
Quantitative records, 53–54
Questions, in conference, 342–350
  forms of, 345–346
  guide to, 346–348
  in contact stage of selling, 204
  as contrast, 263
  in discussion stage of selling, 243–248, 257–258
  in handling interrupted interview, 273–275
  interaction of, 104
  in manpower development program, 335–337
  strategy of, 347–348
  technique of, 111–112
  types of, 95, 213–216, 231, 243–248, 254–259, 281–287, 345–346
  use of, 84, 126

Rationalization, 126–127
Readiness, 201–205, 323
  law of, 110–114
Rebate, 44
Recognition need, 77
Recommendation, letter of, 207
Records, qualitative, 54–55
  quantitative, 53–54
Refined "why," 283–287
Rejection need, 78
Relay question, 346
Repetition, of stimulus, 114–116, 264

Repetition, used, in completion stage of selling, 265
  in dealing with procrastinator, 302
  in directing attention, 264–265, 277
  in handling interrupted interview, 273–274
  in summary technique, 314
Reports, monthly, 53
  of sales calls, 53
"Respect" selling, 148–149
Response, 115
  (*See also* Stimulus-response selling)
Retail salesman, 177
  level of role playing of, 97
Retention need, 77
Reverse question, 346
Role, 91–106
  behavior of, 92–94
  enactment of, 24, 92–96, 99–101, 300–306
  expectation of, 92–93, 104
  incongruency of, 132–133
  of individuals in discussion group, 95
  levels of, 96–97
  perception of, 92–94, 106
  of prospect, 95
  of salesman, 94–95
  (*See also* Sales manager)
  situations, 188
  (*See also* Behavior, patterns of)
Role playing, 96–101, 105
  of conference leader, 99–100, 105
  effectiveness of, 100–101
  in group selling, 97–99
  levels of, 96–97
  in person-to-person selling, 95–98
  by sales managers, 99–100
  in training session, 24, 98–99
Route salesman, 5, 39–41, 63, 141
  level of role playing of, 97

Sales call, 80
  pattern of, 50–51
  on regular customer, 246
  reports of, 53
  (*See also* Cold call; Interview)
Sales letter, 208–209
Sales manager, 63
  training of, 99–100
Sales message, 63, 74–75, 161, 181
  memorized, 61–62, 75, 129, 140–141, 238, 280
  preparation of, 220
  purpose, 161–165
  salesman-oriented, 222
  standardized, 129
  structuring of, 309
Salesman, as conference leader, 344
  in contact stage of selling, 225–236
  critics of, 20
  evaluation of, 323, 337
  fast-talking, 2, 133, 190, 290
  guidelines for, 178–179
  image of, 162
  new, 11–21, 147–148
  personality of, 16
  as problem solver, 17–21, 25, 62, 72
  program of, 45–46
  roles of, 95
  status position of, 131, 151
  in training sessions, 100–101
  traveling, 7–12
  types, 5
  (*See also* Customer-oriented salesman; Door-to-door salesman; Ego-oriented salesman; Fast-talking salesman; Hotel salesman; Insurance salesman; Manufacturer's salesman; Office furniture salesman; Order-taker salesman; Retail salesman; Route salesman; Sales manager; Self-oriented salesman; Task-oriented salesman; Traveling salesman)
Salesman, of yesterday, 2–3
  (*See also* Behavior, activities, of salesman; Self-appraisal; Self-image, of salesman)
Satisfaction, 70
Scheduling, 46–47, 55
Selective question, 249
Self-appraisal, 76, 120, 185–186, 251–252
Self-image, of executives, 93–94
  of salesman, 91–92
Self-oriented salesman, 61–62, 121–122, 142
Selling, approaches to, 136–155
  broader dimensions of, 3–5, 57
  function of, 5
  history of, 6–9
  new world of, 1–21
  old image of, 2
  stages of (*see* Completion stage of selling; Contact stage of selling; Discussion, stage of selling; Objections, stage of selling; Planning, stage of selling; Showmanship, stage of selling)
  theories of, 18
  types of (*see* "Clown" selling; Depth selling; Group selling; Mood selling; Personal selling; Respect selling; Team selling)
Sense organs, 59–62
  stimulation of, 102
Sentence-stepping, 190–191, 196
Service selling, 5
Set, 60–62, 68
  redirection of, 64, 132
  rejection of, 65
  (*See also* Mental set; Perceptual set)
Set-answer approach, 280–284, 291
Shifting attention, 192–193, 260–261
Shotgun approach, 141, 147
Showing (*see* Demonstration)
Showmanship, 9

Showmanship in dealing with procrastinator, 302
stage of selling, 259–277
Sign language, 168–169
(*See also* Gestural communication)
Silent prospect, 301
Similance need, 78
Sincerity, 148
Situation management, 3–5, 17
Situation-management-oriented concept, 137–138
Size to direct attention, 262–263, 277
Skeptic, 304
Slow prospect, 302
Social need, 71–74, 88, 131
list of, 77–78
Sour grapes strategy, 127
Source credibility, 94, 167–174, 181
diagram of, 167
Space, 168–171
Spatial summation, 115–117
in dealing with impulsive prospect, 305
Speech rate–thought rate gap, 191–193, 196
with impulsive prospect, 305
with slow prospect, 302
Spoken communication, 157
SRO clincher close, 317
Staff position (*see* Organization, in management programming)
Standard Block and Supply Company, 31–32
Standing room only clincher close, 317
Status need, 67, 71–73, 76, 86, 131
Stimulus, 60–63, 68, 75
pattern of, 63–64, 277
repetition of, 114–116, 264
(*See also* Stimulus-response selling)
Stimulus-response selling, 62–63, 139–142
Succorance need, 78
Summary technique, 114–117, 313–314

Summary technique, with implied consent close, 316–318
Superiority need, 77
Survey, method of, in contact stage, 209–213
transferring to group selling, 354–358
Survey team, 98
Sympathy, 102–106

T-account close, 315, 319
in dealing with procrastinator, 302
Task functions, 364–365
Task-oriented salesman, 121–122, 128–130
(*See also* Maturity)
Team selling, 24, 358
to group, role of, 99–100
Techniques approach, 220–222
Telephone call, 208
and sales letter, 209
Telling method, 238, 335
Temporal summation, 115–117
Tension, binding, 94–101
in dealing with argumentative prospect, 306
threshold of, 101, 105, 122
in contact stage of selling, 220–222
reduction of, 70, 105, 124, 143, 220, 268
examples, 220–222
in group selling, 359
unconscious buildup of, 70
Territory, analysis of, 45, 49, 56
screening, 49–50
Thinking, ability of, 17, 335
creative, 138
guided by set, 61
real, 285
Thwarting, 71
Time, analysis of, 51–52
Time, management of, 41
(*See also* Punctuality)

Timid prospect, 303
Total development concept, 322
Touch communication, 157
Training, amount of, 143
  of market managers, 23–25
  sessions, 97–101
  (*See* *also* Conference; Group
    selling; Manpower develop-
    ment program)
Traveling salesman, 7–12
Trial close, 309–311, 319
  in dealing with impulsive pros-
    pect, 305
  use of, 253
Trustworthiness, 168–171
Two-call system, 209
  examples of, 234–235

Undercontrollers, 101
Use-need, awareness of, 72
Vacillation, 132

Ventilation concept, 255
Verbal skill (*see* Sales message)
Verification question, 213–216, 231,
    245–246
Visuals, 129–130, 260, 263
  communication by, 157
  in group selling, 359
  in handling, interrupted interview,
    273–275
    procrastinator, 301
    silent prospect, 301
    timid prospect, 303
  moving, 265–266, 277
  (*See* *also* Brochures; Portfolio)
Voluntary attention, 262

"Why" concept, 281–287
Wondra flour, 13–16
Word, action, 269–270
  charged, 194–195
  negative, 269–270